ZWARTE ZEE,
eertyts
PONTUS EUXINUS,
Door N. Sanſon de Zoon,
Geographe du Roy

ABACHE

Tob ou Damanyko
gorod
Alof
ou Tana
Lacaria
Bacmachi
Tarmagno
Azara
PETIGORI.
Cagia
Mapopa
Copa
Tzercos
Carolimiano
Mauro lac
Zicchia
Mauro
Zicchia
Alb. Zicchia
Zuaco
Costa Aiazo
Cacari
S. Sofhia
AVOGASI.
Pozonda
Sauatopoli
Coro
MIN
Tama ſi
GRE
Fazzo
LIE.
Lonaṭ
Archa
Santhia
Rifo

E ou MER MAIEVRE

VXINVS.

Chriſtonda
Lauora
Tripoli
Trebizonda
Tur
NI.
Simifo
Pormon
GENECH.
com
Libaton
Ciogalla
Pormon fl.
Maraſt
ani
AMASIA.
Chiorme
Arſingan
Amafie
olim
Giamich
e.
E
Tocato
Caifaria
Raſhà
TOCAT
Sunas
PEGIAN.
SVVAS.
Tifaria
Sogian
Chiangare
Charaifar
Sauaſhia
Mangoli
Antitaur
A MINOR.
Acfara
Arcalach
Arana
Nigdia
Abiach
ANADO
Kors
LE

The Black Sea

The Black Sea

A HISTORY

Charles King

OXFORD
UNIVERSITY PRESS

OXFORD

UNIVERSITY PRESS

Great Clarendon Street, Oxford OX2 6DP

Oxford University Press is a department of the University of Oxford.
It furthers the University's objective of excellence in research, scholarship,
and education by publishing worldwide in

Oxford New York

Auckland Bangkok Buenos Aires Cape Town Chennai
Dar es Salaam Delhi Hong Kong Istanbul Karachi Kolkata
Kuala Lumpur Madrid Melbourne Mexico City Mumbai Nairobi
São Paulo Shanghai Taipei Tokyo Toronto

Oxford is a registered trade mark of Oxford University Press
in the UK and in certain other countries

Published in the United States
by Oxford University Press Inc., New York

© Charles King 2004

The moral rights of the author have been asserted
Database right Oxford University Press (maker)

First published 2004

British Library Cataloguing in Publication Data

Data available

Library of Congress Cataloging in Publication Data

Data available

ISBN 0-19-924161-9

1 3 5 7 9 10 8 6 4 2

Typeset by Newgen Imaging Systems (P) Ltd., Chennai, India
Printed in the USA

For Lori

About the Author

Charles King is an Associate Professor in the School of Foreign Service and the Department of Government at Georgetown University, where he also holds the university's Ion Rațiu Chair in Romanian Studies.

Contents

Acknowledgments

The Armenian historian Agathangelos compared writing to a sea journey: Both writers and sailors willingly put themselves in peril and return home eager to tell stories about what they have encountered. I now understand what he meant.

More than once in this project, I stepped where I should not have gone. I loped into the gutted shell of a mosque in Nagorno-Karabakh, only later noticing the casing of a rocket-propelled grenade and wondering whether its unexploded colleagues might still be around. I jumped with equal abandon into the history of the Black Sea, knowing a lot about some of it, a little about more, and nothing about a great deal. The whole journey has been an instructive one, which is the point of writing anyway, and I am deeply grateful to all those who helped me along the way.

Dominic Byatt, my editor at Oxford University Press, got excited about the project when it was just an idea and, with Claire Croft, saw it through to the end. Susan Ferber in the New York office offered sage advice at a crucial point. Hakan and Ayşe Gül Altınay provided a wonderful retreat, the back room of their apartment on the Bosphorus, where I first thought about the book's broad outlines.

Most of the text was researched and written beneath the statue of Herodotus in the Main Reading Room of the Library of Congress—there is no place like it—and I am very grateful to the library's professional staff, including those in the Prints and Photographs Division, the Rare Book and Special Collections Reading Room, the Geography and Map Reading Room, the Africa and Middle East Reading Room, and the European Reading Room, in particular Grant Harris. The staff of the Hoover Institution archives, especially the director, Elena S. Danielson, were outstanding. Librarians and archivists at Georgetown University, the British Library, the Public Record Office (London), the Library of the Romanian Academy (Bucharest), the Central Historical Archive (Bucharest), and the Piłsudski Institute of America (New York) were generous with their time. Chris Robinson drew the maps.

I benefited from several seminars and conferences at which pieces of this book were presented, but I thank especially Nicholas Breyfogle, Abby Schrader, and Willard Sunderland, who allowed me to intrude on a conclave of Russian historians at Ohio State University in September 2001. The Fulbright fellowship program and Georgetown University made possible extended trips through the

Balkans, Ukraine, Turkey, and the south Caucasus in 1998 and 2000. My travels before and since are also owed to the Rațiu Family Charitable Foundation, via its endowment to Georgetown. Tony Greenwood and Lawrence and Amy Tal provided agreeable lodging and conversation on my trips to and from the sea.

I have benefited greatly from the knowledge of many professional colleagues and friends who indulged my naive questions or read parts of the manuscript, but none should be held responsible for my not heeding their advice. They include Alexandru Bologa, Anthony Bryer, Ian Colvin, Owen Doonan, Marc Morjé Howard, Christopher Joyner, Edward Keenan, John McNeill, Willard Sunderland, and four anonymous reviewers for Oxford University Press. I am not a genuine expert in most of the specialist fields on which this book touches, so I am very grateful to those who are. Their painstaking work is recognized in the notes and bibliography.

A special word of gratitude goes to my frighteningly talented research assistants, Felicia Roşu and Adam Tolnay. May they finish their doctorates and find the jobs they deserve. Another Georgetown graduate student, Mirjana Morosini-Dominick, helped with an important translation.

And then there is Lori Khatchadourian, the archaeologist in the family, who offered invaluable advice at every stage and made my life better for reasons far beyond that, and to whom this book is lovingly dedicated.

On Names

Around the Black Sea, spelling bees can be political events, so a word on my use of language is in order.

The chapter titles in this book are some of the many names by which the sea has been known. The earliest ancient Greek name, *Pontos Axeinos* (the dark or somber sea), may have been adopted from an older Iranian term. It may also have reflected sailors' apprehension about sailing its stormy waters, as well as the simple fact that the water itself, because of the sea's great depth, appears darker than in the shallower Mediterranean. How that name was transformed into the *Pontus Euxinus* (the welcoming sea) of later Greek and Latin writers is uncertain. Perhaps the irony was intentional; perhaps it was just wishful thinking.

The most common name in Byzantine sources was simply *Pontos* (the sea), a usage that made its way also into Arabic texts as *bahr Buntus*, which amounts to the intriguingly redundant Sea Sea. But many other names were in use in the Middle Ages, especially in Arabic and Ottoman writings, and were often associated with particularly prominent cities, whence Sea of Trabzon and Sea of Constantinople. The designation Great Sea also appears in the Middle Ages in various forms, including the Italian *Mare Maius* and *Mare Maggiore*. Still other names were derived from whichever group happened to be dominant around the coasts at any particular time—or whichever group an author wanted his reader to think was dominant. Hence, labels such as the Scythian Sea, the Sarmatian Sea, the Sea of the Khazars, of the Rhos, of the Bulgars, of the Georgians, and others. In Arabic sources, the Mediterranean was, by contrast, the Sea of the Romans (that is, of the Byzantines).

Compared to all these, *Black Sea* is rather young, at least as a widely accepted name. It appears in early Ottoman sources in various forms, and was perhaps in colloquial usage from very early in Ottoman history. Its first appearance in a west European language comes at the end of the fourteenth century, but it did not receive broad currency until three centuries later. Before then, European labels were mainly adaptations of those of the classical age, such as *Pontus* and *Euxine* in English, terms that still have poetic connotations which the pedestrian *Black Sea* lacks. "Like to the Pontic sea, whose icy current and compulsive course ne'er feels retiring ebb...," says Shakespeare's enraged Othello, "even so my bloody thoughts, with violent pace, shall ne'er look back. ..."

But why "black?" No one knows for sure, but there are at least three major speculations. One is that it was simply a throwback to the earliest Iranian/Greek designation, which had been preserved among the inhabitants of the Black Sea littoral long after writers in mainland Greece and Rome had come to use the more inviting *Euxinus*. That older name could have been carried to the west during the Turkic migrations into Anatolia, eventually becoming the Ottoman *Kara Deniz*, (the black or dark sea). A second view is that *kara*, which also has the connotation "great" or "terrible," was taken into Ottoman usage from the common Great Sea label used by medieval European, especially Italian, sailors and mapmakers. A third explanation is related to the color-coded geography of Eurasian steppe peoples. In this schema, which has its roots in China, the points of the compass are associated with particular colors: black for north, white for west, red for south, sometimes blue for east. Although how this system works obviously depends on one's vantage point, the Ottoman designation of the sea to their north as "black" may be rooted in this Eurasian tradition, either as an echo of the Ottomans' own distant past as Eurasian nomads or a convention that later Ottoman geographers adopted from the Mongols. In Ottoman and also in modern Turkish, the Mediterranean is, by contrast, known as the White Sea (*Ak Deniz*).

As Russians and west Europeans became more familiar with the sea in the seventeenth and eighteenth centuries, they probably translated into their own languages the term that the region's major power was using at the time. That borrowing was probably replicated in other languages of the region, which were undergoing the process of modernization and standardization at roughly the same time. The result of this convoluted history is that today the sea's many names are really, in translation, the same: *Karadeniz* in Turkish, *Maure Thalassa* in modern Greek, *Cherno More* in Bulgarian, *Marea Neagră* in Romanian, *Chorne More* in Ukrainian, *Chernoe More* in Russian, *shavi zghva* in Georgian—all of which mean literally "black sea."

For place names, I generally use the form appropriate to a particular historical period. Hence, *Trapezus* in antiquity becomes *Trebizond* in the Middle Ages and *Trabzon* today. Where there is more than one name in use in any period, I use the one that is more widely known; Greek names, for example, usually appear in their Latinized forms. I use *Constantinople* before 1453 and *Istanbul* after, even though the older name was common in various forms even during the Ottoman period. Older English spellings—such as "Sebastopol" or "Batoum"—have been replaced by their modern forms, except in direct quotations; the same goes for names of cultural groups ("Tartars," for example). By *Greeks* I usually mean people who probably spoke a variety of the Greek language, even if they had little conception of themselves as Greek in a modern national sense. I am careful to use *Ottoman* to mean associated with the Ottoman empire; it is not the same thing as *Turk* which, until the twentieth century, is problematic as a designation for people whom we would now call Turkish-speakers. I have retained the unfashionable word *Turkoman* (rather than *Türkmen*) to refer to Turkic nomads and their rulers in Anatolian history, in order to distinguish them from the people and culture of the modern country of Turkmenistan in central Asia.

Languages that use alphabets other than the Latin one are transliterated using a simplified version of the Library of Congress systems; no final soft-sign in most Russian words, for example. I have retained diacritical marks for languages that use them in the Latin script. Approximate pronunciations of the more troublesome letters are as follows:

â, î	"i" in cousin	Romanian
ă	"a" in about	Romanian
ı	"i" in cousin	Turkish
ö	"oeu" in French *oeuvre*	Turkish
ü	"u" in French *tu*	Turkish
c	"ch" in church before e or i; otherwise "k" in kit	Romanian
c	"j" in jam	Turkish
ç	"ch" in church	Turkish
ch	"k" in kit before e or i	Romanian
g	"j" in jam before e or i; otherwise "g" in goat	Romanian
ğ	silent, but lengthens preceding vowel	Turkish
gh	"g" in goat before e or i	Romanian
ş	"sh" in ship	Romanian and Turkish
ţ	"ts" in cats	Romanian

Unless otherwise noted, ancient sources in the footnotes refer to the translations in the Loeb Classical Library series published by Harvard University Press. References to ancient and Byzantine-era texts usually indicate sections rather than pages.

List of Plates

(between pages 138 and 139)

List of Maps

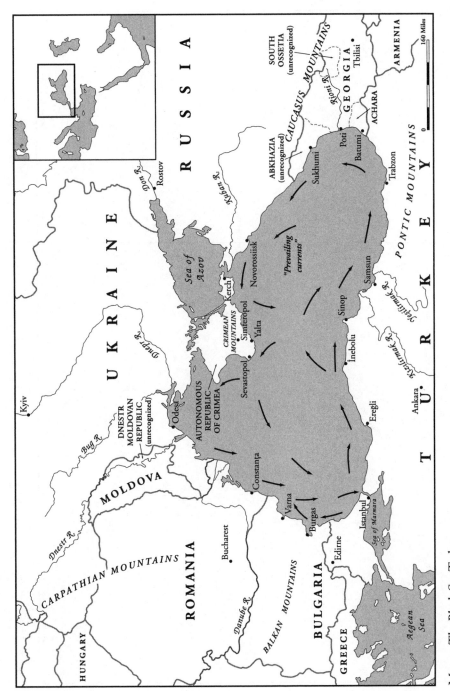

Map 1. The Black Sea Today

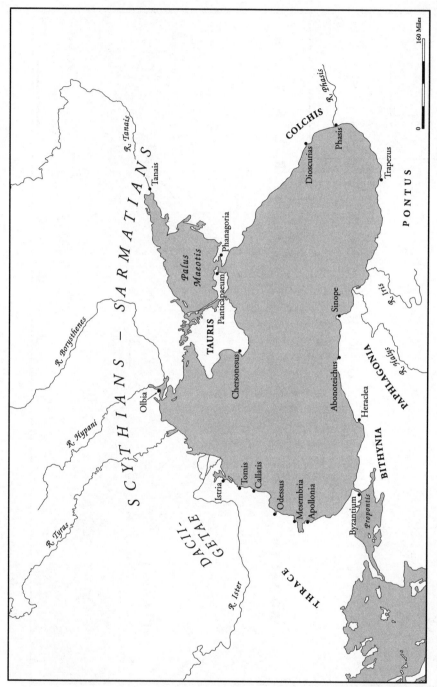

Map 2. The Black Sea in Late Antiquity

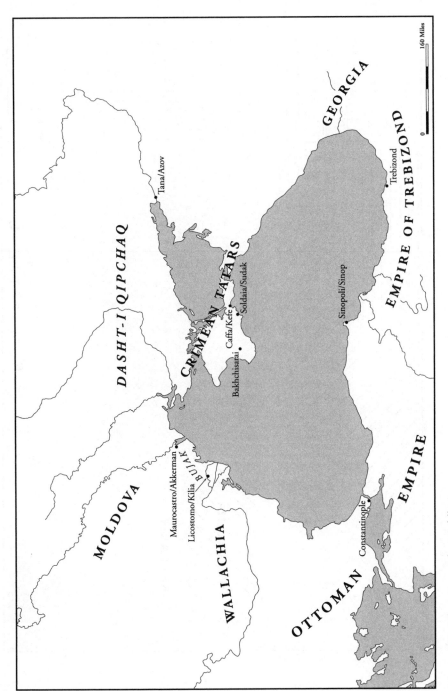

Map 3. The Black Sea in the Middle Ages

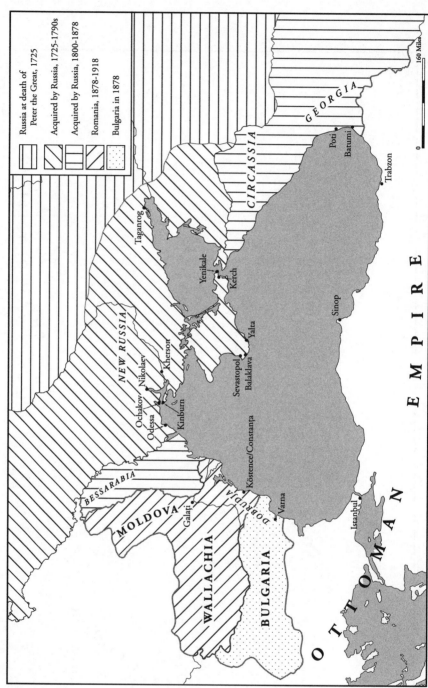

Map 4. The Black Sea in the Eighteenth and Nineteenth Centuries

Whatever the Antients have said, the Black Sea has nothing Black in it, as I may say, beside the name.

Joseph Pitton de Tournefort, royal botanist to Louis XIV, 1718

There's not a sea the passenger e'er pukes in,
Turns up more dangerous breakers than the Euxine.

Byron

The archaeologist's spade
delves into dwellings
vacancied long ago

unearthing evidence
of life-ways no one
would dream of leading now,...

W. H. Auden

1
An Archaeology of Place

People and Water

There is a deep landlubber bias in historical and social research. History and social life, we seem to think, happen on the ground. What happens on the water—during a sea voyage or a cruise down a river, say—is just the scene-setter for the real action when the actors get where they are going. But oceans, seas, and rivers have a history of their own, not merely as highways or boundaries but as central players in distinct stories of human interaction and exchange. As Mark Twain wrote about the Mississippi, waterways have a physical history—of sediments and currents and floods—but they also have a "historical history": of slumberous epochs and wide-awake ones, of the comings and goings of the characters who populate their shores.[1] Shifting our geographical gaze from real estate to bodies of water can be illuminating. It forces us to think critically about such labels as "region" and "nation," and the privileged role of these facile categories in how we carve up the world. It prompts a reexamination of the very meaning of place, how it changes over time, and how the intellectual lines that we draw around peoples and civilizations are far more capricious than might be imagined.

This book is about a sea and its role in the histories, cultures, and politics of the peoples and states around it. For some parts of the world, the idea of waterways as defining elements in human history is uncontroversial, even banal. We are accustomed to speaking about "the Mediterranean" as a meaningful place. As a modifier—Mediterranean cooking, a Mediterranean vacation—it conjures up an array of vivid images, of karst uplands and azure bays, of olives and wine and goats; as an object of research, it has been the focus of numerous scholarly studies, most famously Fernand Braudel's portrait of the

Mediterranean world at the dawn of modernity.[2] Other bodies of water, both greater and lesser, have their own unique associations. Mention the South Pacific or the Chesapeake Bay, the Amazon or the Mississippi, and a host of images comes instantly to mind, some of them tourist-brochure fictions, others drawn from the real-life experiences of the people along the water's edge. For these and other waterways, scholars have charted the common economic pursuits, styles of life, and political predicaments that have linked one coast with another, sometimes over great distances.[3]

Images and associations come less readily for the Black Sea. It is a body of water familiar to few people outside the region itself. For entire stretches of the Black Sea's history, from its possible formation some seven or eight millennia ago to the political revolutions and environmental crisis of the late twentieth century, there are no more than a few specialist monographs to tell its story. Major powers—from Byzantium to the Ottomans to Russia—at various times had the sea at the center of their strategic aims, but there has been little research on the sea in the history of these empires. It is also a body of water that is situated at the intersection of several different academic specializations, and thus central to none of them. Especially in the United States, the cold war produced certain geographical prejudices that have proved to be very durable. By and large, research on domestic politics and international relations, and even history and culture, are conducted within the same regional limits as during the cold war. Specialists in one domain only rarely cross into the other.

For the areas around the Black Sea, the result has been a tradition of history-writing and social analysis that has apportioned the coastline to different realms. The modern history of the Balkans is usually seen either as an adjunct to the history of central Europe or as a congeries of disconnected, ethnonational histories. The Ukrainian and south Russian lands are treated separately from the Balkans, either as a part of Russian imperial history or, in the Ukrainian tradition, as a tragic story of delayed national liberation. The same goes for the Caucasus, both north and south. The Ottomans lurk in the wings and occasionally come onto the stage, but after the formation of the modern Turkish Republic the Turks disappear almost entirely from Europe, becoming instead a part of the study of the Middle East. The policies of grant-making bodies and government-sponsored research programs reinforce these lines, in the social sciences as well as the humanities. In the United States, research on "Eastern Europe" is funded through one budget line, work on "the former Soviet Union," or something called the "New Independent States," through another; research on the Middle East, including Turkey, is financed through yet another.

This mental map, however, is of distinctly modern vintage. Not all that long ago, the idea of the Black Sea as a kind of geopolitical unit would have made a great deal of sense, not only to local populations and political leaders, but also to Western diplomats, strategists, and writers who spent their careers dealing with the sea and its discontents. In the nineteenth century, the Black Sea lay at the heart of the Eastern Question, the complex rivalries associated with the weakening of the Ottoman empire and the interests of Europe's great powers in how it would eventually be carved up. Between the two world wars, the area stood at the intersection of the turbulent Balkans, the Bolsheviks, and European protectorates in the Levant. Later, the countries of the region were on the front line in the global struggle between capitalism and communism, either as mavericks within the communist world, such as Albania, Yugoslavia, and Romania, or in the case of Greece and Turkey, as the vanguard of the West against the Soviet Union. Since the end of communism, southeastern Europe has become a region of troubled political transitions and relatively poor states, a worrying lacuna in Europe's project of creating a united and prosperous continent. The disruption caused by weak states and collapsing regional orders, the spillover of domestic squabbles into international conflicts, and the politics of trade and energy networks were some of the main issues around the Black Sea before the Second World War. They are on the international agenda once again.

This book is an effort to bring together the histories, cultures, and politics of the peoples around the Black Sea and to recall an older intellectual map of Europe's southeastern frontier. Apart from a relatively short time in the short twentieth century, Eastern Europe—at least the kind with two capital E's—was not the way most people thought about the eastern extremity of the continent. That stretch of territory, from the Baltic to the Black Sea, did for a time have a common ideology, similar domestic political structures, and generally congruous foreign policies. But the farther we get from 1989, the less cosmically important that thing called communism (if it ever was just one thing) is likely to appear, especially for those countries that were part of the communist world for only a single generation and for their neighbors, such as Greece and Turkey, whose tastes in authoritarianism were not of the Marxist variety. The history of Europe's east, in other words, is not the story of a place called Eastern Europe.[4]

In the 1990s, the idea of a homogeneous Eastern Europe was largely replaced by the notion of an equally heterogeneous southeastern Europe, a place at the timeless meeting place of mutually hostile religions and cultures, the transition zone between the real Europe and something else. Newspaper headlines seemed to provide ample proof: the bloody end of Yugoslavia; the wars of the Soviet succession, a series of small but vicious conflicts in Moldova, Georgia, Azerbaijan, and elsewhere; Turkey's decades-long war with Kurdish guerrillas. There was surely something about the strength of communal belief or allegiance to kith and kin that made this region perpetually at odds with itself.

As the eminent American scholar and diplomat George Kennan wrote about the Balkans, the violence of the 1990s could best be explained by the "deeper traits of character inherited...from a distant tribal past" of which the people of the region were the unwitting victims.[5]

But over the long sweep of history, it is difficult to argue that the lands around the Black Sea—an area that might be called the wider southeastern Europe or, to use an antiquated term, the Near East—have been more volatile, a sense of ethnic identity more deeply felt, or questions of land, custom, and religion more divisive than in any other part of Europe or Eurasia. In many periods, in fact, they were a good deal less so. If there is an overarching story to the history of this sea, it is not about conflict and violence, least of all the kind that is said to define the fracture zones between incompatible "civilizations." Rather, it is about the belated advent of the central organizing ideas of nineteenth- and twentieth-century Europe. It is a place to which the modern state came rather late, the culturally defined nation even later, and the nation-state even later still—not until the early twentieth century in some cases, not until the very end of that century in several others.

Much of the later parts of this book are about how the national idea came rushing into a world to which it had previously been alien, a world in which other poles of association such as occupation, religion or simple geography—being from the coast or the hinterland, from this village or that—normally held sway (and in which even these categories were rarely fixed). It is about how children came to define themselves in ways that would have seemed odd to their grandparents, and about how people whose identities were mixed and overlapping traded them in for homogeneous, national ones. This book also tells how a place that might once have existed as a meaningful geographic space was progressively unbuilt over the course of several centuries, how an array of human connections across a body of water rose and fell and rose again in tandem with changes in the political, economic, and strategic environment of Europe and Eurasia. It is an experiment in what might be called geographical archaeology. Its aim is to uncover a forgotten network of relationships, a filigree of human connections which, buried beneath the thin layers of communism and postcommunism, was in the latter half of the twentieth century hidden from view. At the center of this project lies the sea.

Region, Frontier, Nation

So far, I have been using some important terms rather cavalierly, so I should say something about what I mean by them and about their place in this book. One is "region." Region, like culture and race, is a concept notoriously difficult to define—and a word whose analytical uses usually mask a multitude of normative connotations. No regional label can stand too much interrogation. As soon as one tries to identify an essential set of characteristics that is meant to distinguish some broad geographical unit from some other, those characteristics begin to look frustratingly ephemeral. At base, however, regions are not about commonalities of language, culture, religion or other traits that the constituents of the region—whether individuals, peoples or states—might share. Rather, they are about connections: profound and durable linkages among people and communities that seem to mark off one space from another.

This book is concerned with a region whose dimensions are admittedly vague. Peoples, empires, and countries enter and exit at different points, sometimes accompanied by another character, Europe, and sometimes spurned by her. But the center of the stage is the sea and its littoral; the wings extend from the Balkans to the Caucasus mountains and from the steppeland of Ukraine and southern Russia to central Anatolia. Conveniently, almost all the countries in this area are today members of the Black Sea Economic Cooperation organization (BSEC), an international forum established in 1992 to strengthen commercial, political, and cultural ties in southeastern Europe.

But is this place really a region? The answer depends on what spectacles we wear. In the narrowest geographical sense, only six countries can claim membership: Bulgaria, Romania, Ukraine, Russia, Georgia, and Turkey. These states control the major port facilities and claim territorial waters off the coast. More broadly, however, a Black Sea region extends all the way from the Alps to the Urals, the entire swath of territory that constitutes the sea's drainage basin, which covers all or part of some twenty-two countries. What happens upstream on the Danube, the Dnepr, and the Don rivers has a major impact on the health of the sea and the livelihoods of the populations around it. In terms of history, parts of the sea have sometimes been controlled by a major imperial power, but the coastline has most often been divided among many local rulers and modern states. In terms of recent politics, in the early 1990s the littoral countries and several of their neighbors committed themselves to building a regional cooperation organization, BSEC; but those aspirations have largely been overtaken by competition for the real prize of the early twenty-first century— membership in the European Union—a prize that some members of BSEC are far closer to attaining than others.

What constitutes a Black Sea region depends not only on how one asks the question but also on when it is asked. In the ancient world, a string of Greek cities and trading emporia connected all the corners of the sea into a single commercial network. That network was shaken by the rise of powers from the hinterlands and by the advance of Persia and Rome; relations among Byzantines, nomadic peoples in the north, and Christian kings and princes in the Balkans and the Caucasus at first strengthened and then weakened it. In the Middle Ages, the Black Sea world was revived by the entrepreneurial spirit of the Genoese and Venetians and, for a time, came under the sway of a single empire, even of a single man, the Ottoman sultan. Later, the rise of Russia transformed the sea into the site of a centuries-long struggle between the powers that controlled its northern and southern shores. In turn, the national movements of the nineteenth and twentieth centuries, favoring smaller countries over empires, worked to bring bits of the sea and its littoral into the demesne of newly formed nation-states.

Today, it is difficult to argue that there is anything approaching a common Black Sea "regional identity" among all the inhabitants of the coasts or the states in which they live. Political trajectories and political realities across the wider southeastern Europe are varied: democratic and authoritarian, reformist and reactionary, real states and imagined ones. Political leaders are more likely to set themselves off from their neighbors—as more European, more deserving of membership in Euro-Atlantic institutions, or simply more civilized—than to engage in genuine regional cooperation. Still, the sea has long been a distinct place, a region defined by cross-sea relationships, both cooperative and conflictual, involving the movement of people, goods, and ideas. Over the long course of history, the communities around the coasts and in the hinterlands have touched one another in enduring ways. Religious practices, linguistic forms, musical and literary styles, folklore and foodways, among many other areas of social life, are joined together in a web of mutual influence that is readily apparent to even the most casual visitor—or at least to one who is able to look beyond the narratives of national uniqueness that, in the last century or so, have become dominant.

Another term that needs attention is "frontier." Owen Lattimore, the historian of inner Asia, once noted that a frontier is not the same thing as a boundary.[6] A boundary represents the intended limit of political power, the farthest extent to which a state or empire is able to exert its will on a geographical space. A frontier is the zone that exists on both sides of the boundary. It is a place inhabited by distinct communities of boundary-crossers, people whose lives and livelihoods depend on their being experts in transgressing both the physical boundaries between polities as well as the social ones between ethnic, religious, and linguistic groups. Frontier peoples—the Cossacks of Eurasia, the *coureurs des bois* of the Canadian forests, the mountain men of the American West, and many others like them—are not simply peripheral actors in human history but distinctive, highly adaptive cultures in their own right.

Attitudes toward these frontiers and their inhabitants can play a central role in the elaboration of imperial and national identities. The American historian

Frederick Jackson Turner argued that the rolling conquest of the West shaped a unique American identity, a blend of European and indigenous traits forged in the harsh crucible of the frontier. "As successive terminal moraines result from successive glaciations," Turner wrote in his famous essay on the frontier in American history, "so each frontier leaves its traces behind it, and when it becomes a settled area the region still partakes of frontier characteristics."[7] Turner was most concerned with the effect of natural challenges on social development, but he missed another crucial relationship. People shape themselves against the image of the frontier as much as, perhaps even more than, the frontier shapes them. As Lattimore's work revealed, encounters with Turkic-speaking populations in Eurasia were central to Chinese understandings of civilization and proper conduct. Likewise, in nineteenth-century Russia, expansion and settlement in Siberia and the Caucasus were crucial components of both Russian imperial identity and the vision of Russia as a continental, Eurasian power. One can find the same dynamics at work as much on watery frontiers as on terrestrial ones.

At various points in history, the lands around the Black Sea have been frontiers in both these senses: the locus of distinct communities defined by their position between empires or states, and a foil against which the cultural and political identities of outsiders have been built. However, to think of the sea as a timeless frontier at the meeting place of different civilizational zones—Greek and barbarian, Christian and Muslim—or perhaps as part of a periphery of the imagination—Oriental, Balkan, Eurasian—against which Europeans have perpetually defined themselves, is to read back onto the distant past the prejudices of the present.

Much of the sea was indeed a frontier in the former sense in the early modern period, when the steppeland along the northern shore was still a sparsely populated prairie—the "campi deserti et inhabitati" of early European cartographers—at the intersection of the Ottoman empire, Poland, and Russia. It was a frontier in the latter sense for much of the nineteenth century, when the Black Sea lay between Europe's rising and falling powers, the Russians and Ottomans. But the longer history of the sea and its littoral is not simply the story of a geographical periphery and its gradual absorption into empires and, later, modern states; nor is it only a story of the insidious construction of the region as backward and uncivilized. Rather, it is about the ebb and flow of the sea's peripheral status, a long sine wave oscillating between backwardness and isolation on the one hand, and substantial integration with the wider Mediterranean, European, and Eurasian worlds on the other. The frontiers that have run along the coastline or through the middle of the sea have been multiple—ecological, military, religious, economic, even epidemiological—but none has been perennial, and the outlines of one have rarely overlapped exactly with those of another.

When the ancient Greeks first encountered the Black Sea, it lay literally at the edge of the known world, a place inhabited by mythical beasts, half-men, and heroes. However, from the middle of the first millennium BC, the growth of Greek trading colonies not only stitched the coasts together but also brought them into a broader system of exchange with the Mediterranean. That integrated system lasted until the beginning of the first millennium AD, when the opening up of other sources of wealth, particularly grain from Egypt and the transportation route to the east through the Indian Ocean, reduced the significance of the Black Sea ports. These old connections were revived somewhat in the early Byzantine period, with the cross-sea commerce in furs and other products between Constantinople and the peoples of the forest–steppe zone in the north; but it was not until the thirteenth and fourteenth centuries that the sea was once again at the center of a global economic and social system, this time tied to the great commercial empires of the Italian city-states. That link continued until well after the Ottoman conquest of Constantinople. As the successors to the Genoese and Venetians, the Ottomans were for a time able to control most of the coasts through outright conquest or condominia with local rulers, and to use the region's resources to build their own empire. As Ottoman power declined in the Mediterranean, the Black Sea became a prize that the sultan guarded jealously, its coasts in large part sealed from foreign commercial and political influence. That situation would obtain until the opening of the sea to European merchants in the late eighteenth century. From that point on, the sea was never again the preserve of any single power, and the new race for access to the region's wealth, particularly the burgeoning grain trade from the southern ports of the Russian empire, restored the link with the Mediterranean and extended it to the Atlantic as well.

From the late nineteenth century through the twentieth, the coastline was carved up among a number of newly formed nation-states, with each asserting a right not only to a piece of the coast but also to a section of the coastal waters. The coming of the modern state, however, did not automatically ensure the easy integration of the littoral into broader economic and social structures. The coastal areas remained largely peripheral to the new states whose power centers lay farther inland—as they are, in fact, today. The provinces of Dobrudja and Bessarabia, bounded by the sea and the Danube and Dnestr rivers, were the most ethnically heterogeneous parts of Romania in the first half of the twentieth century and a hotbed of banditry and separatism; they are still culturally diverse areas inside Romania and the Republic of Moldova, where the stagnant economy and inadequate social services are major problems. In Ukraine the Crimean peninsula has been a persistent concern for the central government; its large

Russian-speaking population and substantial Russian naval presence, along with a Crimean Tatar minority that is jobless and discontented, have at times presented an obstacle to the consolidation of the new Ukrainian state. In Georgia a bloody civil war over the status of the coastal region of Abkhazia led to the effective loss of that area and the creation of a new, de facto Abkhaz state in the 1990s, with its capital in the port city of Sukhumi. Except in its Kurdish southeast, Turkey has not experienced the violence of some of its former Soviet neighbors, but its own Black Sea coast, populated by ethnic Turks, Turkomans, Laz, and Hemşin, among other groups, has been a serious development challenge; it has long been one of Turkey's poorest areas, and out-migration has been responsible in part for the influx of economic migrants to the slums that ring Istanbul. The modern history of the Black Sea is thus also the story of centers and peripheries within each of the states around its rim.

Finally, there is the term "nation." The ideology of the nation, as it has been understood in much of modern European history, contains at least three propositions. One is analytical: that the nation—defined in terms of a common language, a common culture, shared historical memories, and often a distinct homeland—is and always has been the fundamental unit in human societies, far more basic than class, religion or other forms of association. The second is normative: that the nation should command the exclusive allegiance of all its constituents, whose identities and destinies are bound to it. The third is prophetic: that in instances in which the demographic boundaries of nations and the political boundaries of states do not coincide, social movements that seek to rectify this disjuncture are both predictable and praiseworthy. The first proposition is normally called national identity, the second national self-determination, and the third nationalism. As any good undergraduate knows, these concepts have a history of their own. They emerged in the late eighteenth century, came to fruition in the nineteenth, and form so much a part of our normal way of thinking about human society and international politics that it is difficult to look back to an era before the national idea was dominant.

Today, in much of eastern Europe, history is usually viewed through a national lens. The main nodal points in the historical narrative are those in which previously unconscious nations come to perceive themselves as distinctive and then rise up to throw off foreign oppression. It is a story, in other words, about how peoples become nations and how those nations, in turn, become nation-states. That way of seeing things should not be surprising, of course. In some cases, east European intellectuals are still sorting through a range of topics officially forbidden during the communist period, including nationalism. In others, particularly in the new states that emerged out of Yugoslavia and the Soviet Union, many intellectuals see it as their duty to justify the states' new-found independence by reference to historical antecedents.

Yet writing the history of nations is always about silencing voices. It involves drawing lines around people, excising connections among human communities, and reading onto the messy past the lineaments of pure identities and immutable boundaries. The real life of peoples and cultures is usually cacophonous, perhaps occasionally choral, sometimes even gloriously so; but it is rarely solo. This book asks the reader to listen to some of those still voices from the past. It is about how, over the long course of history, the Black Sea has more often been a bridge than a barrier, linking religious communities, linguistic groups, empires, and, later, nations and states into a region as real as any other in Europe or Eurasia.

Beginnings

For millennia, people have known two things about the Black Sea. One was that sailing it demanded an iron will and an even stronger stomach. Stanley Washburn, a correspondent for the *Chicago Daily News*, covered the first Russian revolution from a steamer off the Crimean coast and offered a recipe for concocting something like the sea in the throes of a mid-winter storm. Take "one hole 900 miles long by 700 breadth," he wrote, rather exaggerating the actual size:

sow the bottom promiscuously with rocks, scatter a few submerged islands in the most unexpected places, and fill this in with the coldest water obtainable. Surround the shores with a coast like that of Maine, and wherever there seems, by any oversight, to be a chance of shelter, insert a line of reefs and ledges of sharp rocks....Now import a typhoon from the South seas, mix judiciously with a blizzard from North Dakota and turn it loose. Add a frosting of snow and sleet, garnish with white-caps, and serve the whole from a tugboat, and you have a fair conception of the ordinary December weather in the Black Sea.[8]

Ancient visitors would have agreed with Washburn's depiction. The Greeks perhaps adopted their earliest name for the sea, *Axeinos*, from an Iranian word meaning "dark" or "somber." Folk etymology may have transformed that name into *Axenos*, "unwelcoming," a label that would have fit with early sailors' own experience of its waters. Storms appeared out of nowhere. Impenetrable fogs obscured the headlands, making navigation impossible. From on board ship, the water appeared opaque, with a visibility of only a few meters, compared with the stunning clarity of the Mediterranean. Only sometime later did Greek and Roman seamen settle on the name that would eventually stick—*Pontus Euxinus*, the hospitable sea—which was perhaps meant to ward off the wrath of the gods.

Voyagers many centuries later would follow a similar logic in christening Africa's treacherous southern point the "Cape of Good Hope."⁹ Heaven, sailors seem to believe, appreciates irony.

The other thing that has long been known is that the Black Sea is a callow upstart as seas go, a relatively young body of water whose unpredictable behavior was perhaps the result of a violent birth. In the first century BC, the Greek traveler Diodorus Siculus encountered a strange legend among the natives of the Aegean island of Samothrace. The sea, old men said, had once swallowed their island. They claimed that in the murky past, the Black Sea to the east had been a great lake. At some point, it suddenly overflowed, destroying the villages around it and hewing out a narrow passage toward the Aegean, a channel that would become the straits of the Bosphorus and the Dardanelles. The deluge coming from the Black Sea was so great that the Mediterranean rose up and inundated entire islands. Now and then, Diodorus reported, Samothracian fishermen would find pieces of carved marble columns caught in their nets, the remnants of some lost civilization ravished by a flood.¹⁰

Diodorus was not alone in reporting such oddities. His contemporary, the geographer Strabo, argued that the sea had once been a lake and that the many rivers that disgorge into it had, in the recent past, filled it to overflowing. The water was so fresh, he said, that it could freeze over in harsh winters, when barbarians would blithely wheel their carts onto it and dig fish out of the slush.¹¹ Cattle were even known to wade into the shallows, eagerly drinking from the brackish waves that lapped around them.¹² Other peculiarities were reported in the straits that linked the sea to the Mediterranean. When fishermen cast their nets into the Bosphorus, the nets formed an S-shape; the top floated toward the Mediterranean while the bottom was drawn back on a deep countercurrent toward the Black Sea.¹³ Sailors even claimed that they could fight the top current by lowering tethered weights beneath their ships and allowing the hidden river below to pull them along.

These ancient accounts of the sea's origin and its characteristics were not quite as fantastic as they appear. Toward the end of the last ice age, some 18,000–20,000 years ago, the Black Sea was a small, shallow body of water, about two-thirds of its present size, a formation that geologists call the Neoeuxine lake. The lake was the last stage in a series of expansions and contractions over the space of several million years, when the Black Sea basin had at times been connected with the wider oceans, at other times linked with what would become the Caspian Sea, and at still other times isolated as a tiny, semi-saline lake. This new lake lay in a depression separated from the Mediterranean by a thin isthmus connecting Europe and Asia Minor. As the glaciers retreated, the melting ice water swelled the world's oceans. At some point, the lake was joined with the Mediterranean, with the waters hollowing out the narrow Bosphorus and Dardanelles and creating the intermediary Sea of Marmara.

Exactly how and when this happened, however, has remained a source of controversy. Natural philosophers in the Enlightenment adopted the view of the ancients—that the lake, filled up by the major rivers that empty into it, burst its banks and flooded the Aegean. Counting back through biblical genealogies, the French naturalist Joseph Pitton de Tournefort fixed the date of the deluge at some point before 1263 BC. "This Route [the Bosphorus] was certainly traced out by the Author of Nature," Tounefort wrote, "for according to the Laws of Motion by him establish'd, the Waters always throw themselves that way where they can find the least opposition."[14] For much of the nineteenth and twentieth centuries, scientists rejected these claims on two accounts. First, the available geological evidence seemed to point toward a gradual conjoining of the two seas, beginning about 9,000 years ago, as both the Mediterranean and the lake rose from glacial melting. Second, ancient geographers and their Enlightenment successors seemed to have the process reversed: The rate of increase in ocean levels after the last ice age would have far outstripped the rate of change in the Neoeuxine lake, which was fed only by river run-off. It was the Mediterranean that invaded the lake, not the other way around.

In the 1990s, oceanographers and geologists began to suggest a model of the Black Sea's evolution that combined both ancient and modern visions.[15] The creation of the Black Sea may have been both more recent and more rapid than had earlier been believed. Studies of the strata in the seabed's sediment have revealed something intriguing. The lower layers contain the remains of freshwater creatures, as one would expect in an ancient lake. The higher layers yield the remnants of marine life, deposited after the lake had become a sea. But between these layers, there is virtually no transition zone. The silt deposited between the time when freshwater animals dominated and the time when they were displaced by marine interlopers is miniscule, suggesting a mixing of freshwater and saltwater that, in geological time, was virtually overnight. Analysis of mollusk shells in the sediment points to a recent date for this change, perhaps only 7,500 years ago—*c.* 5500 BC—in the middle of the Neolithic period.

By then, along the Black Sea littoral, especially the southern coast, humans had established settled communities, perhaps building boats to sail across the ancient lake, trading and raiding on its distant shores. But the lives of these communities may have been suddenly transformed. At the time, the surface of the lake was far lower than that of the Mediterranean; the oceans, however, were beginning to rise. In time, the Mediterranean began to spill over into the lake. What began as a trickle soon became a torrent. Before long, the isthmus between

Europe and Asia was breached in a flood of water, pouring out from the higher Mediterranean and plunging down into the low-lying lake. The change in the lake's level seems to have been astonishingly rapid: perhaps as much as 6 in. a day, a speed that would have translated, in the flat steppelands on the northern shore, into an advance landward of up to a mile each day, until the Mediterranean and the new Black Sea reached equilibrium.[16] The former shoreline, lying about 150 m below the present sea level, is clearly detectable in underwater soundings.[17] In recent years marine researchers have reported tantalizing possibilities: the potential discovery of submerged human settlements sitting on the ancient shore. If the flood theory is correct—and it does have its detractors—the people who lived there would have witnessed the birth of a sea.

It does not take much to imagine the effect of these changes on the Neolithic communities that flanked the former lake, settlements that would have been uprooted as the waters advanced. They may have migrated from the lakeshore to other parts of Europe and the Near East. The making of the Black Sea would have been such a catastrophically memorable event that a folk version may have found its way into the oral traditions of the peoples of the Near East. As Diodorus Siculus discovered some five millennia after the sea's probable formation, people in the Greek-speaking world still told of a calamitous flood. Even older flood tales contained in the Sumerian epic of Gilgamesh and in the biblical Genesis may have had their origins in the rising waters of the Black Sea. Of course, deluge stories exist in many cultures, especially those that depend on seasonal river flooding to replenish the soil of low-lying agricultural lands; moreover, there is no reason to believe that such flood myths must necessarily have grown out of a single, real-world cataclysmic event. But if one is looking for an archetypal disaster inspired by the wrath of an angry god, the origin of the Black Sea is probably a good candidate.

Geography and Ecology

Today, the sea extends over some 423,000 sq. km, almost twice the size of the North American Great Lakes. It is a little larger than its neighbor, the Caspian, and about twice as deep, reaching depths below 2,000 m. From the Bulgarian port of Burgas in the west across to the Georgian port of Batumi in the east is 1,174 km; from the tip of Crimea in the north to the Turkish port of İnebolu in the south is only 260 km. For 2,000 years, sailors have claimed that from the middle of the sea on a clear day they could see headlands on both the northern and southern shores at the same time.[18] That is surely an old salt's tale, but it does reflect the degree to which people have thought of the two shores as natural partners and the sea itself as a compact unit. The journey across was relatively quick, and for a good part of the way one remained within sight of land.

In antiquity, writers compared the sea to a barbarian's compound bow, and that is not a bad analogy.[19] The western tip lies at the Bosphorus (or more properly, the "Thracian Bosphorus"), where the sea binds itself to the world's oceans; the eastern lies on the Rioni river, filled by water from the Caucasus mountains. In between, two arcs curve north. One passes the coasts of Bulgaria, Romania, and Ukraine, the other Georgia and Russia. The arcs bend sharply toward each other, forming two shallow gulfs. The western one sweeps around the mouths of the Danube and Dnepr rivers; the eastern one leads on to the strait of Kerch (also known as the "Cimmerian Bosphorus"), which connects the sea to its smaller sister, the shallow Sea of Azov. The two arcs meet at the archer's hand, the diamond-shaped peninsula of Crimea. The bowstring, although not nearly as straight as ancient geographers imagined, stretches across the length of modern Turkey.

The prevailing current runs along the coast in a counterclockwise motion, with two spurs moving across the middle of the sea to the north and the south. In 1823 a British navy captain claimed that he could travel from Odessa to Istanbul without hoisting a sail, simply by letting the current carry him along.[20] While ancient sailors generally preferred to hug the coastline, navigating by the headlands and taking advantage of the breezes coming off the shore, the Black Sea's currents would have made it easy to cross the narrow midriff—a journey of only a day and a night, according to Greek sources.[21]

The complementary currents are matched by the basic symmetry of the shoreline. The eastern and western extremities are fed by important rivers, the Danube and the Rioni, both of which produce strong currents that run counterclockwise at their mouths. In the northeast, the Don river flows into the Sea of Azov and, through the Kerch strait, into the Black Sea. That arrangement is copied in the southwest by another strait, the Bosphorus, where a top current carries the cooler Black Sea water out into the Sea of Marmara and then into the Mediterranean. (As the Greeks knew, a warmer, denser bottom current runs through the Bosphorus in the opposite direction.) In the north, the Crimean peninsula juts out like an arrow pointing south; on the southern shore, twin headlands, Kerempe and İnce, stretch up to meet it. The symmetry is so striking that some ancient geographers actually thought of the Black Sea as, in reality, two seas, a western and an eastern one, separated by the narrowest crossing point between Cape Sarych in Crimea and Cape Kerempe in Anatolia, a distance of only about 225 km.[22] Sailors were warned to beware of the sudden change when crossing this boundary line, where currents and winds could shift and spin a ship around.[23]

None of these features is exactly a mirror image of the other, however, for each serves as a channel of communication with different lands beyond. Follow the Danube upstream and you reach the heart of Europe, passing the great Hungarian plain and the Alps. Paddle up the Rioni and, after a brief tour of the flatlands, you discover the river's home in the raging streams of the Caucasus. Crimea gives way to the Eurasian steppe in the north, while the southern capes jut out from the Anatolian uplands.

The symmetry of geography thus masks an asymmetry of endowments. On the Asian side of the Bosphorus, the violent winds and waves have denuded the coastline. Above, the hills lead on to a plain that stretches south across Anatolia to the Taurus mountains. Farther along, the coast rises to steep hills and finally mountains, the first reaches of the Pontic Alps. The shoreline is narrow, at most a mile or so wide, at its narrowest no more than a beach of sand or gray pebbles and, today, a paved coastal highway. Lush forests of oak and pine cling to the mountains and press down to the sea. Then come the Caucasus mountains, angling from northwest to southeast across the land corridor separating the Black Sea from the Caspian. To the north, the Eurasian steppe comes right down to the sea, sometimes halting abruptly at a rocky cliff, at other times easing into the water along the shores of wide rivers and ending in a jumble of brackish estuaries, or *limans*. The wetlands of the north and west, fed by the wide Danube, Dnestr, Dnepr, and Don rivers, contrast with the minor deltas of the south and east, produced by the swift Kızılırmak, Yeşilırmak, and Rioni. The differences in climate are also striking. In the steppeland of the northwest, cold winters give way to hot, dry summers. In the uplands of the southeast, the subtropical climate produces mild winters and humid summers with considerable precipitation. It is the meeting of these two climatic zones—the cooler, drier continental with the warmer, wetter subtropical—that is responsible for the spectacular storms that sailors for millennia have dreaded.

The sea has a peculiar ecology and one perhaps linked to the sudden flooding of the Neoeuxine lake. When the Mediterranean intruded, the dense seawater sank to the bottom of the lake, leaving a far less salty upper layer, about half the salinity of the oceans. Water is now continuously exchanged between the Black Sea and the Mediterranean via the counterflowing top and bottom currents in the Bosphorus and Dardanelles straits. But in the sea, the stratification in salinity is constant; there is little circulation of water from bottom to top. This means that at depths below around 200 m the water remains without oxygen—anoxic—and, therefore, dead (save for some hardy bacteria). The bottom is a morass of black sludge, seething with hydrogen sulfide and giving off the odor of rotten eggs. A constant cascade of dead plant and animal life from the upper reaches falls to the sea floor, covering it like a blanket of snow. Low-oxygen strata can be found in many other bodies of water, but the Black Sea's is by far the largest. Nearly 90 percent of the sea's water volume lies in the anoxic zone, the biggest reservoir of hydrogen sulfide in the world.

The natural oxygen deficiency is enhanced by the decay of organic substances in the oxygenated zone. The sea's drainage basin covers roughly 2 million sq. km, including the catchment areas of the Danube, Dnepr, and Don, the second, third, and fourth largest rivers in Europe. This influx of freshwater brings with it vast amounts of organic matter, including the run-off from agricultural areas and waste produced by human communities. As the organic matter decays, it consumes yet more oxygen and further depletes the thin stratum of life-supporting surface water.

Marine life hangs on precariously in the thin top layer of an otherwise noxious sea. There are the ancient life-forms that have survived from the time of the Neoeuxine lake, such as the herring and sturgeon. Other species—the flounder, whiting, sprat, and Black Sea trout—migrated down the rivers from colder climes and adapted to life in the least saline areas along the coasts. The largest number of fish are the interlopers which swam into the newly formed sea from the Mediterranean several thousand years ago. These warm-water creatures now form some 80 percent of Black Sea animal life and include the species that have been the great prize of seafaring communities for millennia, many having similar names in otherwise unrelated languages around the coast: the Greek *pelamys* and the Romanian *pălămidă*, or bonito; the Russian *lufar'* and the Turkish *lüfer*, or bluefish; the Georgian *skumbria* and the Bulgarian *skumriia*, or mackerel; and the diminutive *hamsi*, or anchovy, so prized along the Turkish coast that songs are sung in its praise and even desserts made from its succulent flesh.

Fish have managed to adapt to the sea's ecological peculiarities and flourish in the upper strata. The barren depths, however, may hold their own treasures. In the early 1970s, the pioneering oceanographer Willard Bascom suggested that deep water, particularly the anoxic zone, might provide the perfect environment for marine archaeological research. With no oxygen, the water would be free of the wood-boring mollusks and other creatures that could destroy the hulls and frames of ancient ships.[24] Bascom was later proven right.

In the late 1990s, the explorer Robert Ballard, discoverer of the *Titanic*, led a team of researchers in a path-breaking study of the anoxic layer off the Turkish coast, around the ancient seaport of Sinope. With the aid of a small underwater robot, the team explored the depths, for the first time accomplishing what a lack of technology and the tensions of the cold war had previously hindered. One of the first finds was a Byzantine-era ship, dating to the fifth century AD, with some of the halyard still intact and the mast's knotted wood looking as if it had been shaped only days earlier.[25] Further research turned up a much older shipwreck, perhaps from the fourth century BC, off the coast of Bulgaria, which carried a cargo of amphoras and dried freshwater fish. As Ballard enthused, "the fuller picture is wonderfully bizarre: The possibility that every ship that sailed and perished on the Black Sea, from humankind's earliest wanderings to our own time—perhaps 50,000 separate wrecks—lies preserved" on the seabed.[26] These discoveries also had a tragic twist, however. Willard Bascom died only a few days before Ballard's team announced the first confirmation of his theories about the sea's depths.

There is little clear evidence to help us understand the cultures and customs of the earliest peoples of the Black Sea littoral or the precise ways in which they might have interacted. Inhabitants of the new, higher coastline raised permanent settlements, farmed, and worked precious metals; the world's oldest gold artifacts, from around 4500 BC, have been found along the Bulgarian coast. They probably knew of the existence of other peoples beyond the water and may have followed the coastline to meet, trade, marry, and fight. Ceramic and metal artifacts recovered from various sites reveal a consonance of design that suggests interaction and exchange.[27] Jade axes and spearpoints from the northwest, dating to the early second millennium BC, bear a striking resemblance to those found at Troy.[28]

Yet much of what we know of the groups that populated the littoral and perhaps even sailed across the sea comes from the Mediterranean culture whose representatives pushed through the Dardanelles and Bosphorus and began to establish permanent trading outposts in the region toward the middle of the first millennium BC. It was the ancient Greeks who ushered the sea into history and provided the first vision of it as a distinct place.

NOTES

1. Mark Twain, *Life on the Mississippi* (New York: Harper and Brothers, 1923), p. 4.
2. Fernand Braudel, *The Mediterranean and the Mediterranean World in the Age of Philip II*, trans. Siân Reynolds, 2 vols. (London: Collins, 1972).
3. For a general argument about the relevance of waterways, see Martin W. Lewis and Kären E. Wigen, *The Myth of Continents: A Critique of Metageography* (Berkeley: University of California Press, 1997). On various seas, see: Peregrine Horden and Nicholas Purcell, *The Corrupting Sea: A Study of Mediterranean History* (Oxford: Blackwell, 2000); K. N. Chaudhuri, *Trade and Civilisation in the Indian Ocean: An Economic History from the Rise of Islam to 1750* (Cambridge: Cambridge University Press, 1985); Kenneth McPherson, *The Indian Ocean: A History of the People and the Sea* (Oxford: Oxford University Press, 1993);

O. H. K. Spate, *The Pacific since Magellan*, 3 vols. (Minneapolis: University of Minnesota Press, 1979, 1983, 1988); Walter A. McDougal, *Let the Sea Make a Noise: A History of the North Pacific from Magellan to MacArthur* (New York: BasicBooks, 1993); Barry Cunliffe, *Facing the Ocean: The Atlantic and Its Peoples, 8000 BC–AD 1500* (Oxford: Oxford University Press, 2001).

4. Larry Wolff argues persuasively that the template of "Eastern Europe" as an underdeveloped and uncivilized borderland originated in the Enlightenment. But while Wolff is certainly right that Enlightenment thinkers came to think of Europe's eastern reaches in a particular way, it is doubtful that they conceived of "Eastern Europe" in the coherent political sense that the label acquired during the cold war. See Wolff, *Inventing Eastern Europe: The Map of Civilization on the Mind of the Enlightenment* (Stanford: Stanford University Press, 1994).

5. Carnegie Endowment for International Peace, *The Other Balkan Wars* (Washington: Carnegie Endowment, 1993), p. 11.

6. Owen Lattimore, *Inner Asian Frontiers of China* (New York: American Geographical Society, 1951), chapter 8.

7. Frederick Jackson Turner, *Rereading Frederick Jackson Turner: "The Significance of the Frontier in American History" and Other Essays* (New York: Henry Holt, 1994), p. 33.

8. Stanley Washburn, *The Cable Game: The Adventures of an American Press-Boat in Turkish Waters During the Russian Revolution* (Boston: Sherman, French, and Co., 1912), pp. 73–4.

9. W. S. Allen, "The Name of the Black Sea in Greek," *Classical Quarterly*, Vol. 41, Nos. 3–4 (July–October 1947):86–8.

10. Diodorus Siculus, *The Library of History*, 5.47.

11. Strabo, *Geography*, 1.3.6, 7.3.18.

12. Flavius Arrianus, *Arrian's Voyage Round the Euxine Sea* (Oxford: J. Cooke, 1805), p. 7.

13. Procopius, *History of the Wars*, 8.6.25–28.

14. Joseph Pitton de Tournefort, *A Voyage into the Levant*, trans. John Ozell, Vol. 2 (London: D. Browne, A. Bell, J. Darby et al., 1718), pp. 95–6. Besides Tournefort, the other important early geological study of the Black Sea is Peter Simon Pallas, *Travels Through the Southern Provinces of the Russian Empire, in the Years 1793 and 1794*, 2 vols. (London: T. N. Longman and O. Rees et al., 1802–3).

15. The paper that launched the debate over the sudden flooding of the Neoeuxine lake is W. B. F. Ryan et al., "An Abrupt Drowning of the Black Sea Shelf," *Marine Geology*, No. 138 (1997):119–26. For a counter-argument, see Naci Görür et al. "Is the Abrupt Drowning of the Black Sea Shelf at 7150 yr BP a Myth?" *Marine Geology*, No. 176 (2001):65–73.

16. William Ryan and Walter Pitman, *Noah's Flood: The New Scientific Discoveries about the Event that Changed History* (New York: Simon and Schuster, 1998), pp. 234–5.

17. Robert D. Ballard, D. F. Coleman, and G. D. Rosenberg, "Further Evidence of Abrupt Holocene Drowning of the Black Sea Shelf," *Marine Geology*, Vol. 170, Nos. 3–4 (November 2000):253–61.

18. Strabo, *Geography*, 7.4.3.

19. Strabo, *Geography*, 2.5.22; Ammianus Marcellinus, *Res Gestae*, 21.8.10.

20. George Matthew Jones, *Travels in Norway, Sweden, Finland, Russia, and Turkey; Also on the Coasts of the Sea of Azov and of the Black Sea*, Vol. 2 (London: John Murray, 1827), pp. 393–4.

21. Jamie Morton, *The Role of the Physical Environment in Ancient Greek Seafaring* (Leiden: Brill, 2001), p. 164, note 28.

22. Strabo, *Geography*, 2.5.22.

23. *Black Sea Pilot*, 2nd edn. (London: Hydrographic Office, Admiralty, 1871), p. 3.

24. Willard Bascom, "Deep-Water Archaeology," *Science*, Vol. 174 (October 15, 1971): 261–9. Bascom developed a ship, the *Alcoa Seaprobe*, with the capacity to lift wrecks from the seabed. It was his design that the CIA used to build the ship that clandestinely raised a sunken Soviet submarine in 1975. Bascom sued, unsuccessfully, for patent violation. Willard Bascom, *The Crest of the Wave: Adventures in Oceanography* (New York: Harper and Row, 1988), pp. 266–9.

25. Robert D. Ballard et al., "Deepwater Archaeology of the Black Sea: The 2000 Season at Sinop, Turkey," *American Journal of Archaeology*, Vol. 105, No. 4 (October 2001):607–23.

26. Robert D. Ballard, "Deep Black Sea," *National Geographic* (May 2001):68.

27. See Fredrik Hiebert et al., "From Mountaintop to Ocean Bottom: A Holistic Approach to Archaeological Survey along the Turkish Black Sea Coast," in J. Tancredi (ed.) *Ocean Pulse* (New York: Plenum, 1997), pp. 93–108; and Ballard et al., "Deepwater Archeology," p. 608.

28. Fredrik T. Hiebert, "Black Sea Coastal Cultures: Trade and Interaction," *Expedition*, Vol. 43, No. 1 (2001): 12.

Round the Black Sea ... are to be found, if we except Scythia, the most unlearned nations in the world.

Herodotus, fifth century BC

The sea! The sea!

Xenophon's troops on reaching the Black Sea coast, fourth century BC

How do you think
I feel, lying here in this godforsaken region...?
I can't stand the climate, I haven't got used to the water,
even the landscape somehow gets on my nerves.
There's no adequate housing here, no diet suited
to an invalid, no physician's healing skills,
no friend to console me, or with a flow of conversation
charm the slow hours away: weary, stretched out
amid frontier tribes, in the back of beyond, I'm haunted
in my illness by all that's not here.

Ovid, first century AD

2
Pontus Euxinus,
700 BC—AD 500

Our image of the Black Sea in antiquity is inevitably influenced by a limited set of literary sources, all with inescapable problems: the work of outside observers such as Herodotus, the historian of the fifth century BC, who may or may not have ever visited the region; self-serving memoirists such as Xenophon, who marched along the southern coast in the fourth century BC; geographers such as Strabo, from three centuries later, a more reliable guide since he was born not far from the coast (in modern Amasya, Turkey); and a bevy of political exiles and second-hand reporters, the former with a vested interest in playing up the insalubrious climate and hostile natives, the latter never beyond spicing up, or making up, a good story.

From a distance, Greek writers generally held a dim view of the peoples of the Black Sea, both the barbarians of the hinterland and the transplanted Greeks who founded the cities and settlements that eventually grew up along the coastline. Xenophon noted that the only truly "Greek" city he encountered all along the southern coast—from Trapezus to the Bosphorus—was Byzantium; the rest had been so influenced by contact with non-Greeks in the interior that they seemed barely recognizable.[1] What mattered most to many ancient writers was the contrast between the worlds they knew and the strange customs and beliefs of the peoples they encountered or heard about around the sea. Yet, as the work of generations of archaeologists and other scholars has shown, the Black Sea was not so much a place where the "civilized" and "barbarian" worlds met, but rather one where outsiders—Greeks and, later, Romans—became yet another part of the melange of lifestyles and customs that had long swirled around the shores. From the earliest Greek expeditions through the coming of Roman imperial legions, the blurring of lines between languages, peoples, and cultures was the hallmark of life along the water.

The Edge of the World

Greeks entered the Black Sea in the first half of the first millennium BC, maybe even earlier. At first perhaps searching for metals on the southern coast, they eventually extended their reach up the northern rivers into the Eurasian steppe zone. The attractions were clear. Wide rivers made navigation easy, and the abundance of fish and timber for shipbuilding were promising prospects for commerce. Burgeoning populations around the Aegean and the resulting pressure on food resources may also have propelled them to launch expeditions to the north.[2]

In sailing to the Black Sea, ancient visitors were moving into a world that was literally the frontier of human understanding. According to Plato, the world extended from the Pillars of Hercules to the Phasis (Rioni) river, from the western end of the Mediterranean to the eastern end of the Black Sea.[3] In ancient cosmology, the continents and islands existed on a plane encircled by Ocean, a boundless body of water that was the source of the world's great rivers—the Nile, the Danube, the Don. In theory, one could sail around the outer edge of the world and drop in via one of the river routes, or portage overland and get back to one's starting point by following Ocean's circular path.

Ancient writers dated the earliest Greek encounters with the Black Sea to the mythical Heroic age, and they imbued the sea with the same fantastic qualities that defined all the outer limits of the world. The sea was the locus of many of the myths that formed the warp and weft of Greek popular religion. A rocky island at the mouth of the Danube (or perhaps the Dnepr) was said to hold the grave of Achilles. On the south coast, Hercules descended to Hades in order to tame the guard dog Cerberus. The Amazons lived in the same neighborhood, at the mouth of the Thermodon (Terme) river in northern Turkey or, in an alternative version, on the Tanais (Don) river in southern Russia. The Crimean peninsula was the home of the Tauri, whose blood-thirsty priestess, Iphigeneia, sacrificed wayward travelers to Artemis. To the east, in the Caucasus mountains, the fire-stealer Prometheus lay chained to a rock with an eagle feasting on his liver, until he was rescued by Hercules.

When Mediterranean travelers encountered the real people who lived along the shores, they described them in terms not far removed from such fantastic stories. On the south coast, Xenophon reported that one warlike tribe, the Mossynoeci, could muster a raiding fleet of 300 dug-out canoes.[4] Along the western coast, marauding Thracians were said to hang out lanterns on the rockiest stretches of shoreline, hoping to attract sailors in search of a leeward bay; like moths, the sailors would make straight for their doom, leaving a treasure trove of debris strewn along the shore.[5] Stories about the fierce Tauri in Crimea may have been built on similar pursuits by local populations in Crimea. In the northeast, tales of coastal pirates who set out to attack wayward vessels gave rise to an entire mythical ancestry for the local populations. The Achaei of the Caucasus were said to descend from part of Agamemnon's host, lost on their way back home from the Trojan war. Their neighbors, the Heniochi ("charioteers"), were the putative descendants of the chauffeurs of the demi-gods Castor and Pollux, who accompanied Jason on his quest for the Golden Fleece. These two tribes reportedly prowled along the coasts in covered boats and bore down upon foreign vessels, hauling off their goods and rounding up the crew as hostages. They would then melt into the harborless coastline, hoisting their boats on their shoulders and disappearing like phantoms into the forest.[6]

There were still other groups who were only obscurely known, a carnival sideshow of human oddities catalogued by Herodotus, Strabo, Pliny, and other Greek and Roman writers. The region along the western coast, around the modern Bulgarian port of Varna, was said to have been occupied by a race of pygmies who were driven away by cranes.[7] The Hyperboreans—literally, the people beyond the north wind—were to be found in the extreme north, where they lived to an advanced age and performed miracles. Near them were races with even more outlandish quirks. There were the one-eyed Arimasps, who fought a perpetual war with the griffins for control of gold mines. Another tribe had double pupils in one eye and a likeness of a horse in the other. These lived next to a people with prodigiously long beards and another who ate lice, and others who turned into wolves and sported hooves like goats and slept for six months out of the year.[8]

Several ancient authors offered detailed lists of the tribes around the shore, but these are a mix of fancy and hearsay and, even well into the Byzantine period, only occasionally based on first-hand information. When the Greeks first arrived, the coast was probably already populated by a host of settled communities or nomadic confederations, but today we have only broad, mainly regional labels to distinguish them. In the west were the Thracians, known in later antiquity for their fighting skills and the use of the short sword. Farther north were the Scythians, some nomadic and some settled, who raised horses and cultivated the cereals that would attract Greek traders and settlers. To the east were a variety of warlike groups inhabiting the mountain vastness of the Caucasus and, in the lowlands, the Colchians, who may already have established a powerful kingdom in the Bronze Age, a collection of log-hut villages built on raised hillocks in the wetlands of the Rioni river.[9] Along the southern coast were the Bithynians and Paphlagonians, perhaps originally of Thracian origin, along with mountain tribes that had migrated westward from the Caucasus. Even peoples such as these, whom the Greeks acknowledged as wholly human, were sometimes endowed with a fabled past. The Colchians, Herodotus believed, were descended from the Egyptians, since both groups had curly hair, practiced circumcision, and wove linen.[10]

Any attempt to link the ancient inhabitants of the seaboard, whether fantastic or real, with one or another modern ethnic group is futile. No unbroken line runs between any ancient population—including the Greeks—and the modern peoples who now claim them as ancestors. Even some groups who were named by ancient authors as distinct peoples turn out to be frustratingly elusive in the historical record, appearing and then disappearing while leaving little evidence of their cultures and customs. That is the case with the one of the earliest recorded groups in the Black Sea basin, the Cimmerians. We know of them only because they were apparently forced to flee their homeland north and east of the sea and became mobile warriors; in their wanderings, they bumped up against older literate cultures in central Anatolia and Mesopotamia, who wrote of their arrival. The Cimmerians were said to have been chased from their own land by a group of invaders from the east, the Scythians. One group of Cimmerian migrants then pushed southwest into Thrace and another southeast into the Caucasus. The two wings converged in Asia Minor, disrupting the local kingdoms there before coming under Assyrian influence. It was perhaps history's earliest recorded foreign refugee crisis, a story that was already ancient history to Herodotus and other writers of the Classical period.[11]

The Cimmerians float like specters in the ancient texts of the Near East. The biblical Genesis links them to Gomer, one of the grandsons of Noah (10:2–3), while Jeremiah laments the invasion of cruel horsemen "from the north country," armed with bow and spear and with voices that "roar like the sea" (6:22–23). If such an invasion of northern nomads did in fact take place—whether as a single incursion or a series of nomadic migrations into Anatolia—textual evidence would date it to sometime in the eighth century BC. After that the Cimmerians quickly disappear from history; little other than occasional literary references remains. They did leave some footprints, however. They gave their name to the Black Sea's chief peninsula, Crimea, and the most famous of their number eventually ended up in America: Conan the Barbarian, prince of the fictional kingdom of "Cimmeria," was created by the pulp fiction writer Robert E. Howard in the 1930s, revived by Marvel comics, and immortalized in the cinematic oeuvre of Arnold Schwarzenegger.

The arrival of Greek sailors and traders in the Black Sea may even have been spurred on by the Cimmerian refugees, who carried with them news of the riches of the north,[12] for not long after the supposed Cimmerian invasion, Greek-speaking peoples on the Aegean began to take a keen interest in the region. Greek city-states in Ionia, along the coast of Asia Minor, sent out small-scale expeditions to the north and east. Enterprising captains rowed through the Bosphorus and hoisted sail beyond the rocky opening, perhaps following the current to the east along the coasts of Bithynia and Paphlagonia or using a favorable wind to turn to the west and skim the edge of Thrace.

"Frogs Around a Pond"

For all the epic elements that would later be injected into these expeditions, it was entrepreneurship, not conquest or adventure, that drove them. Stashed in the deep hulls of sailing ships or in the spaces beneath the benches of rowed vessels were cloth and amphoras filled with wine and olive oil. Returning ships were laden with wood for shipbuilding, cut from the forests of the Pontic Alps and the Caucasus, iron and precious metals extracted from the Caucasus and the Carpathians, millet from the delta of the Rioni, and wheat grown on plains watered by the rivers of the north. In time, Ionian mother-cities began to finance the construction of long-term settlements along the coasts. Permanent dependencies, housing expatriate Greeks who could serve as on-the-spot middlemen with local populations, began to emerge by the middle of the seventh century BC.

Several city-states sought to profit from the riches of the sea, but none excelled Miletus. The southernmost of the major cities along the Ionian coast, Miletus had long been a major commercial center in the Aegean, but in the mid-600s, it turned its full attention to the north. Over the next century and a half, before 500 BC, it was one of the most powerful cities in the Greek world, virtually controlling traffic through the Bosphorus and raking in the wealth from trade in cereals, metals, and preserved fish. Its colonies were among the jewels of the Black Sea coast: Sinope in the south; Dioscurias at the foot of the Caucasus; Panticapaeum, which guarded the entrance to the Sea of Azov; and Olbia, lying at the mouth of the Hypanis (Bug) river and providing an opening toward the grasslands of the northern steppe.

By the fifth century BC, the inhospitable sea had become far more welcoming to the Greeks than it had been in centuries past. Greek settlements speckled the littoral, a connect-the-dots of seaports that Socrates compared to "ants or frogs around a pond."[13] Seafaring vessels with their broad square sails arrived from ports on the Sea of Marmara and the Aegean. Smaller coasting vessels jumped from one colony to another, and dugout canoes carried goods up and down the widest rivers. Some of the cities remained entrepôts—*emporia*—serving the primary function of greasing the wheels of trade, or gained the title of city-state, or *polis*, with an autonomous government and publicly funded institutions. In time, the leaders of the most successful colonies improved the port facilities, adding docks or jetties to protect the harbors from the notorious storms and shoring up the coastline against erosion. Their dependence on the original mother-cities became distant memories, as new partners and patrons arrived on the scene.

Several of the cities were renowned across the Greek and, later, Roman worlds. Sinope (modern Sinop, Turkey) was "the most noteworthy of the cities in that part of the world," says Strabo in the first century BC.[14] It was situated along a narrow causeway, on the leeward side of a larger peninsula; its deep harbor was the best along the southern seaway from the Bosphorus to the Caucasus. The docking facilities included impressive roadsteads, and within the city were gymnasia, marketplaces, and colonnaded buildings. Walls encircled an imposing acropolis, while sheep and gazelles grazed nearby in the fertile plain of the Halys (Kızılırmak) river. Olives, unusual around the Black Sea, were also grown there. Trade in these and other products enriched the city. Sinope was the major stopping point before the crossing to Crimea, and its cross-sea connections were the lifeblood of the economy. Orange and black Sinopean amphoras, some with the distinctive imprint of an eagle holding a dolphin in its talons, are plentiful in archaeological sites on the northern shore.

Sinope grew so prosperous that it issued coinage and even set up its own dependencies; in fact, almost all the cities along the southeast coast were Sinopean foundations. The most prominent was Trapezus (modern Trabzon, Turkey) to the east. Although the natural harbor facilities were poor, Trapezus benefited from its geography. It was situated at the end point of an ancient land route that wound over the Pontic mountain range, through the Zigana pass, and across the Armenian plateau to the valleys of the Tigris and Euphrates rivers. The town's impressive citadel, built on a series of escarpments punctuated by deep ravines, provided a ready defense if the native highlanders who surrounded it turned hostile.

The cities along the Caucasus coast could not boast such accoutrements, but what they lacked in refinement they made up for in natural endowments and local color. At Phasis, the Milesian colony at the mouth of the Rioni river, timber was floated downstream and loaded onto coasting vessels, along with other items critical to shipbuilding: hemp for riggings, wax and pitch for sealants, and the famous Colchian linen for sails. In two or three days, the goods would arrive in

Sinope and be transferred to larger ships for the voyage to the Aegean.[15] Farther along the coast, at Dioscurias (near modern Sukhumi, Georgia), numerous non-Greek tribes would come down from the Caucasus mountains to meet foreign ships. Traders were said to require 130 interpreters to conduct their transactions there—surely an exaggeration, but probably not much of one.[16] In time, even the hinterland began to enjoy the fruits of commerce. By the first century BC, the area beyond Phasis boasted cities and farmsteads with tile roofs, marketplaces, and other public buildings, and a century later, the Roman historian Pliny reported that the many bridges that spanned the river were always laden with people on their way to market.[17]

Crimea had some of the finest natural harbors, and the abundance of fish in the nearby Sea of Azov would have been an attractive prospect. However, fear of native populations probably prevented large-scale Greek settlement there until relatively late. Colonists from Megara in mainland Greece established Chersonesus (near modern Sevastopol, Ukraine) in the fifth century BC, a foray by the Megarians that would later be eclipsed by their most important colony of all, Byzantium. But here, as in other parts of the sea, it was the Milesians who were the most energetic. Their colony at Panticapaeum (modern Kerch, Ukraine) controlled the entrance to the Azov; its acropolis held various public buildings, and its harbor was said to hold up to thirty ships. Farther down the coast to the west, the people of Theodosia (modern Feodosiia, Ukraine) built a harbor that could accommodate over three times that many, and the city was surrounded by a fertile hinterland that provided food for the urban population.[18]

Along the northwest coast, deep harbors were scarce, but the openings of major rivers and their coastal lakes were sources of fish and easy highways to the interior. According to Herodotus, the Borysthenes (Dnepr) river was the greatest among them:

The Borysthenes...is, in my opinion, the most valuable and productive not only of the rivers in this part of the world, but anywhere else, with the sole exception of the Nile.... It provides the finest and most abundant pasture, by far the richest supply of the best sorts of fish, and the most excellent water for drinking—clear and bright...; no better crops grow anywhere than along its banks, and where grain is not sown the grass is the most luxuriant in the world.[19]

Perhaps the earliest settlement on the entire northern coast, Berezan, was located on a peninsula (now an island) at the mouth of the Borysthenes. In time, this early colony was overshadowed by some of its younger and wealthier neighbors. Olbia lay on the Bug river, near the point where it unites with the estuary of the larger Dnepr. It may have had a population of some 10,000 at its height, with dedicated districts sacred to Zeus and Apollo and citizens buying and selling in a grand marketplace.[20] There, renowned goldsmiths manufactured intricate works of art that combined both Greek and barbarian elements of design, goldwork that is today among the most prized of the archaeological treasures of Ukrainian and Russian museums.

An even greater degree of exchange between Greeks and locals probably characterized the colonies that lay farther to the west: the Milesian cities of Istria and Tomis (modern Constanţa, Romania), near the Danube delta; Odessus (modern Varna, Bulgaria), a Milesian colony with a sheltered bay; and farther south, Mesembria and Apollonia (modern Nesebur and Sozopol, Bulgaria), Megarian and Milesian settlements with fisheries and good farmland. They were geographically closer to the centers of the Greek world and could, therefore, take advantage of both overland and seaborne trade; they were also nestled amid non-Greek Thracian peoples who, from the earliest days of colonization, already formed relatively settled and powerful political entities eager to profit from interaction with the newcomers.[21]

The growth of the Black Sea colonies was fueled by their place within the economy of the ancient world. A merchant ship with a fair wind could go from the Sea of Azov to the Aegean island of Rhodes in nine days,[22] and its fat-bellied hull held products whose value would have been appreciated across much of the known world. The wheat and barley cultivated in the interior were crucial to the food supplies of Ionia and mainland Greece. (In its war with Sparta, Athens came to depend on grain shipments from the region, and it was in part the Spartan blockade of the Dardanelles that forced Athens to capitulate.)[23] Hazelnuts, still abundant today along the entire southeastern coast, were shipped as far afield as Alexandria.[24] The poet Virgil offered panegyrics to the iron, strong-smelling oils, and pine timber that Roman ships brought from the area.[25]

Exotic animals and plants also made their way west. Traders on the eastern side of the sea discovered a peculiar, copper-colored bird with long tail feathers and succulent dark meat. It was caught in the low-lying fields near the colony of Phasis and exported to Greece and Italy. Eventually, Greeks and Romans would learn how to the rear the bird themselves, but its name gave away its origins—the "Phasian bird," or pheasant. A red tart fruit cultivated around the colony of Cerasus on the south coast became widely popular in the Roman period. According to tradition, the colony gave its name to the word that many peoples would adopt for the fruit—the Latin *cerasum*, the English cherry. In the exotic, though, there was always a whisper of peril. When Xenophon and his Greek mercenaries marched along the southern coast in the fourth century BC, they discovered that the region's delicious honey could cause madness.[26]

Fish were plentiful, and the ready supplies of salt available in various locales, especially in the shallows on either side of the isthmus connecting Crimea to the northern shore, meant that the catches could be preserved for the journey to the Aegean. Bonito and tunny were in great demand, either salted whole or cut into cubes and pickled. In Rome of the first century BC, a jar of pickled Pontic fish could cost as much as hiring a day laborer[27]—even if, as Pliny complained, such delicacies were known to cause prodigious flatulence.[28]

The great annual migrations of various fish species were times of intense work for fishermen and traders. In the winter, anchovies congregated in shoals in the warmest parts of the sea, in the shallows off Anatolia and Crimea. Toward the spring, they migrated to the north to spawn in the Sea of Azov. The anchovy's chief predator, the mackerel, wintered farther south, in the Sea of Marmara, and collected in schools in the spring for the journey toward feeding grounds in the Black Sea. The bonito followed its own pattern, migrating around the sea clockwise from the northwestern shelf to the Bosphorus over the summer and autumn. During these migrations, Strabo reported, the people of Trapezus enjoyed the first catch of bonito, the people of Sinope the second, and the people of Byzantium the last, as the schools hugged the shore seeking the outlet to warmer waters in the south. Even by the time the schools reached the Bosphorus, however, fish were still numerous enough to be caught by hand—or so fishermen claimed.[29] In the late eighteenth century, the naturalist Peter Simon Pallas still found peasants in southern Russia making a living in much the same way as their predecessors some two millennia before, catching fish in the Sea of Azov, cutting the bellies into slices, curing them, and exporting the product to the Aegean archipelago.[30]

"A Community of Race"

The vibrant commerce of the Black Sea depended not only on the energy of the Ionian mother-cities and their colonies, but also on the symbiotic relationship between Greek settlers and non-Greek natives. To Mediterranean settlers and travelers, the native peoples of the Black Sea were "barbarians"—non-Greek-speakers—to be sure, yet they were not necessarily considered barbaric, at least in the sense that the adjective now connotes. As in other frontier regions, the Pontic Greeks found their own way of adapting to and even adopting the cultures of the peoples they encountered—in part because of the fluidity of the very concept of "Greekness," in part because of the natural exchange of customs among cultural groups over long periods of sustained interaction. Over time, something of a hybrid civilization developed, a "community of race," as the Russian scholar Mikhail Rostovtzeff called it, that blended artistic forms, styles of life, and even languages of the coast and the hinterland.[31] As time went on, the clear cultural line between "Greek" and "barbarian" imagined by the poets and playwrights of Classical Athens became very fuzzy indeed.[32]

The precise characteristics of this symbiosis are unclear, but evidence of it is clearly visible in the archaeological record. Even writers such as Herodotus were impressed by how much it had resulted, already in his day, in a culture that owed a great deal to the mutual influences of settlers and natives. At Berezan the earliest Greek colonists copied the practices of locals by building dug-out houses to protect themselves from the winter cold.[33] Some cities integrated images of the barbarians into their coinage, and the so-called Thracian horseman—a rider with a flowing cloak—can be found on innumerable Greek funerary monuments along the western coast. Cultural influence worked in both directions. At Gelonus, a city in the land of a northern tribe known as the Budini, the barbarians erected statues and shrines in the Greek style, although carved in wood rather than stone, and celebrated the festival of Dionysus. Their language was a mixture of Greek and barbarian, says Herodotus, who even speculated that the natives were perhaps originally Greeks who had adopted barbarian ways.[34] (Herodotus may have been referring to a massive site, now excavated, on a tributary of the Dnepr river, which consisted of a wooden rampart over 30 km long.)[35] The ties between Greeks and non-Greeks sometimes extended all the way from the real world to the mythical one. Pausanias, as late as the second century AD, still contended that the mythical Hyperboreans paid tribute to the Athenians by delivering their first fruits via barbarian intermediaries living north of the Black Sea.[36]

Cultural mixing seems to have been especially pronounced in the north and northwest, for two main reasons. First, the region's landscape—flat coastal plains crossed by wide rivers—created an easy geographical link between the cities on the littoral and the interior. By contrast, on the southern and southeastern coasts, the colonies sat perched on the edge of the water, their backs against the uplands. Second, colonists in the north and northwest interacted with barbarian peoples whose civilizations and political structures seem to have been already well developed by the time the Greeks arrived. It was in this region that the Greeks encountered the Scythians, a broad spectrum of peoples who, in the imagination of writers in Athens and in other centers of Greek civilization in the Mediterranean, would come to represent the quintessential barbarians of the Pontic world.

For ancient writers, the label "Scythian" was primarily geographic. To be Scythian was to reside in a cold climate and probably live a nomadic life centered around horse-breeding. Our knowledge of the varied languages and cultures that existed beneath this umbrella comes mainly from Herodotus, whose evidence most likely came from the reports of other travelers or from simple hearsay. The Scythians, he says, thought of themselves as the youngest people. Their own myth of origin—associated with the union of a god and a river maiden—was only about a millennium distant.[37] They were divided into a number of tribes that spoke mutually unintelligible languages. Some grew grain for export; some lived in forests; some wandered about the treeless steppe. They fashioned their enemies' skulls into drinking cups and their scalps into cloaks. They milked mares by blowing into the animal's anus, and cleaned themselves by taking cannabis vapor baths, which made them "howl with pleasure."[38] They had a particular fondness for warrior gods, and would worship at an altar consisting of a brushwood pile surmounted by a sword. Some of their number were said to suffer from a disease that turned men into women (perhaps a reference to social androgyny or even to bleeding hemorrhoids associated with long periods on horseback).[39] Their greatest skill, Herodotus argued, was self-preservation, for when confronted with an invader, they could simply disappear into the steppe, fleeing like a herd of skittish deer.[40]

Herodotus's picture of the Scythians became the one that most ancient geographers accepted as a true depiction of all the barbarians of the north; it would eventually be adopted wholesale by Roman and Byzantine writers as well. Many Greek mainlanders would have had direct contact with real, live Scythians on whom these images, even the most fantastic ones, could be overlaid. In Athens, immigrant Scythian archers were employed as constables and featured in the comedies of Aristophanes, the ancient equivalent of the Keystone Kops. Archaeological evidence confirms part of what Herodotus had to say. A powerful nomadic culture did exist across the Pontic steppe, and the fondness for horses, cannabis, and war-making among these communities is well-documented from the excavations of numerous burial sites stretching all the way from modern Romania to the western borderlands of China.[41] Yet while the Scythians might have seemed the antithesis of civilization to writers in Ionia or mainland Greece, to Greeks on the Black Sea littoral they were both suppliers of food products for provisioning the colonies and for export, and a military power that could be either a threat or a source of security, depending on the political circumstances.

The real Scythians were a broad group of peoples, probably Iranian in origin, who originally lived as nomadic herders. They were among the earliest in a long line of peoples who migrated from central Asia to the west, driving before them vast herds of horses, sheep, and cows. By the 700s BC, they seem to have displaced the earlier Cimmerians, who themselves probably also migrated from the east.

The arrival of the Scythians in the Black Sea zone alarmed the kingdoms of the Near East. Records of conflicts with the Scythian host appear in several ancient texts, under names that prefigure later labels. They are perhaps the *Ashkenaz* of Hebrew sources (Genesis 10:3), and in the sixth century BC the Persians vanquished an eastern people they called the *Saka*. The famous rock relief at Behistun in western Iran depicts Darius and his subjugated enemies, with the shackled Skunkha, ruler of the Saka, shown with the long beard and pointed hat that were the standard visual representations of northern barbarians. (After conquering the Scythians of the east, Darius led another, unsuccessful campaign against their western cousins around 513 BC.)

When the Greeks came to the northern shore, Scythian tribes were already a major presence from the Danube to the Don river. By the 300s BC they exercised some degree of hegemony over the entire region, with perhaps only the Crimean highlands outside their realm. Some had given up the pastoral life and become settled agriculturalists, cultivating grains that would be particularly attractive to traders from the Mediterranean. The most spectacular archaeological finds in Ukraine and southern Russia date from this Scythian "golden age": housing complexes of wood and piled earth; elaborate burial mounds, or kurgans, which still punctuate the horizon across the steppe; and intricate gold artifacts, perhaps the handiwork of goldsmiths closer to the coast. Some of the goldwork originally reflected nomadic themes of sacred animals and the hunt, but in time the styles gave way to finely wrought depictions of domestic life—milking sheep, stringing a new bow, tanning a hide—and even gods and heroes borrowed from the Greek pantheon. Precious jewelry and impractically ornate weapons, including the typical *gorytos*, a combination bow-case and quiver, indicated that the mobile cultures of the steppe had gradually come to adopt many of the traits of their more settled Greek neighbors. This period may even have been associated with the reign of a particular king, one Ateas, the "Rex Scytharum" of later Roman sources, who is recorded as having died in a battle with Philip II of Macedon in the summer of 339 BC.[42]

The Scythians were skilled horsemen, and the horse formed the basis for the material culture and warrior ethos that so impressed outsiders. Various labels for Scythian tribes—such as "horse-milkers"—appear already in the *Iliad* and reflected the Greek fascination with their chief culinary peculiarity: the drinking of fermented mare's milk, a mild intoxicant still enjoyed today across central Asia. But while the horse was the animal of necessity, the deer was the animal of legend. Magnificent goldwork taken from Scythian tombs features endless deer motifs, the antlers spiraling across the animal's back in a style that would have pleased Art Nouveau enthusiasts many centuries later. Scythian warriors even fashioned elaborate antler headdresses for their horses, imbuing their domesticated animals with the mystical élan of the sacred deer.

Herodotus devoted more time to describing the Scythians than any other subject of his *Histories* except the Egyptians. In fact, the two peoples formed bookends to the Greek understanding of the fringes of the ancient world. The latter, says Herodotus, were the most cultured people on earth, and he took great pains to detail their customs, architecture, and agriculture. About the peoples around the Black Sea he was less enthusiastic. What struck Herodotus and other writers about the Scythians was the distance between their social mores and those of the Greeks—or, rather, the ways in which their customs seemed strangely parallel but different. They moved across the steppe in covered wagons, much as the Greeks plied the waves in ships. They commemorated their honored dead in grand festivals and built monuments to their heroes, but also ended up sacrificing humans in their frenzy. They drank wine but failed to cut it with water.

There was an important exception to this image of the uncouth foreigner, however. His name was Anacharsis, and he was one of the only men of Scythia whom Herodotus thought worth describing in any detail. In a roundabout way, he may also have invented Western civilization.

How a Scythian Saved Civilization

Greek writers generally portrayed the Scythians as antipathetic to outsiders, a parochial people who kept to themselves and regarded with suspicion ways of life foreign to their own—a claim that actually seems at odds with the clear evidence of cultural exchange in the archaeological record. But Anacharsis, Herodotus says, was unusual among his people for being a great traveler and a man of considerable learning. After living and teaching in many parts of the world, Anacharsis at last set out for home. He stopped to break his trek at a Greek colony on the Sea of Marmara before continuing up the Bosphorus and into the Black Sea. There he witnessed the rites of Cybele, a deity first worshipped in Asia Minor and whose cult eventually spread throughout Greece. Anacharsis was so impressed that he vowed to bring the rites to Scythia if the goddess were to grant him a safe onward journey.

She did, and so did he. Upon arriving home, he retired to a dense forest and, drum in hand, performed the rite just as he had seen it among the Greeks. But tragedy soon struck. As the poet Diogenes Laertius later described it:

> Returning to Scythia, the peripatetic Anacharsis
> Tried to win over his compatriots to the Greek way of life.
> But a winged arrow snatched him away to the Immortals
> Still holding an unfinished story in his mouth.[43]

In the middle of his reverie, Anacharsis was discovered by the Scythian king, who drew his bow and shot the prodigal tribesman dead. That is why, Herodotus reported, if anyone traveling in Scythia asks about Anacharsis, the locals will deny ever having heard of him, all because he ventured abroad and adopted the baleful customs of foreigners.[44]

By the time of Herodotus, in the fifth century BC, Anacharsis was already a widely quoted figure among the educated classes in Athens, a literary character known for his pithy observations on morality and his ability to take haughty philosophers down a peg—the Oscar Wilde of his day, perhaps. He remained a paragon of barbarian virtue for some time to come. Plato praised him as an ingenious inventor and a man of practical skill. Aristotle said he was an estimable rhetorician (but a bad logician). Strabo noted that he was a man of frugality and justice. Pliny said that he may have invented the potter's wheel and the modern anchor.[45]

Yet it is difficult to know whether Anacharsis ever really existed. There is no contemporary account of him, and little besides Herodotus's story to go on. Even that is suspect, since the story contains too many of the resonant images that Classical Greeks would have associated with Scythians in general—their supposed hatred of things foreign, the bow, the primeval forest—to be completely believable.[46] Still, the traditional story is that he was the scion of Scythian royalty, perhaps even the product of a union between a local king and a Greek woman. He may have come to Greece as an independent traveler or as part of a Scythian embassy, arriving around the beginning of the sixth century BC. He is reputed to have received two rare honors that would have identified him as wholly assimilated to Greek culture, Athenian citizenship and initiation into the sacred mysteries at Eleusis, but he was, nevertheless, always known to ancient writers as *Anacharsis ho Skythes*—Anacharsis the Scythian.

In Greek literature, Anacharsis was celebrated as the embodiment of practical wisdom despite his barbarian origins. In some ways, the simple fact of his foreignness provided a useful literary device. Putting words in the barbarian's mouth and letting him speak as a social critic was a favorite trope, and a common motif in several literary sources is the juxtaposition of Anarchasis and Solon, the down-to-earth barbarian moralist contrasted with the Athenian lawgiver. Plutarch even placed him among the Seven Sages, in imaginary conversation over sumptuous food and drink with the likes of Aesop, and with a young maiden combing his hair to tame his savage looks.[47] The distance between Greeks and barbarians, Plutarch seems to say, was never as great as one might think.

It was partly through Plutarch that Anacharsis passed from the Greek world to Rome and beyond, with his reputation as a gadfly and something of a sharp-tongued wag enhanced. He appears now and then on the margins of the great works of Western civilization from the Renaissance forward. Erasmus mentions his habit of sleeping with his hand covering his mouth, to show that words can be dangerous. Montaigne quotes him on the role of virtue in governance. He may even lurk in the background of Raphael's painting "The School of Athens," the disheveled man with the rugged looks and blonde hair peering over Aristotle's shoulder.

But the wise Scythian comes into his own in an unlikely time and place: in the late eighteenth century, as the subject of a French best-seller. The *Travels of Anacharsis the Younger in Greece*, published in 1788, is not really about Anacharsis at all, at least not the old one. It is an extended and entertaining overview of classical civilization, written by the Abbé Jean-Jacques Barthélemy, a Jesuit and keeper of medals in the cabinet of Louis XVI. Barthélemy was an authority on classical languages and numismatics who spent over three decades writing the seven volumes of the *Travels*. He imagined a journey by a younger Anacharsis, a descendant of his more illustrious forebear, from Scythia to Athens. During his travels, he meets all the sages of the day, engages them in conversation and debate, and in the process provides a detailed exposition of the ideas of the Greek philosophers and accounts of the major sites of the ancient world.

In its day, and for a century or more after, the *Travels* remained something of a publishing blockbuster. "Its success surpassed my hopes," Barthélemy later reflected. "The public received it in the most favourable manner; the French and foreign journals spoke of it with elogium." Schoolboys used it as their introduction to the classics. Any self-respecting bourgeois owned a copy, in French or one of its numerous translations. As the translator of an English edition noted,

The Work now offered to the English reader exhibits a complete view of the antiquities, manners, customs, religious ceremonies, laws, arts, and literature of ancient Greece, at the period of its greatest splendour. A knowledge of these has hitherto been only attainable by a laborious perusal of writers who have been little solicitous to join entertainment with instruction. The *Travels* of Anacharsis, on the contrary, are so written, that the reader may frequently be induced to imagine he is perusing a work of mere amusement, invention, and fancy; till his eye glances to the bottom of the page,.....[48]

There, in the footnotes, Barthélemy supported each quotation, argument, and conjecture with a reference to an original source. It became possible, at last, to acquire a sound knowledge of the classics without being able to read Greek or Latin—and to enjoy a good adventure story in the bargain.

The *Travels* had a major effect on the growth of French neoclassicism in literature and art and, in its many translations, on philhellenism across Europe. Travelers had Anacharsis, both the elder and the younger, in mind when they ventured onto the Black Sea. From the 1780s forward, a remarkable number of writers mention him in their own accounts of sailing across the sea and exploring its coasts. Some claimed to have found the very forest where the elder Anacharsis was killed by his comrades; others identified the site where the younger Anacharsis set off on his voyage to Greece—unaware, it seems, that Barthélemy's version was self-consciously fictional.[49]

The great popularity of Barthélemy's work points to the central irony of the Anarchasis story. The popular European vision of ancient Greece as ordered, rational, virtuous, and civilized—the vision that Europeans would eventually come to hold of themselves—was refracted through a Scythian lens. The form of Barthélemy's narrative, an account by a somewhat bemused traveler casting a fresh eye on familiar themes, was not unusual in the eighteenth century, but no single work in this genre had as great an impact on the average educated European's understanding of the art, architecture, and philosophy of the ancient world as the *Travels of Anacharsis the Younger*. It was a barbarian from the shores of the Black Sea who helped to introduce the ancient Greeks to the grammar schools and middle-class drawing rooms of modern Europe and, in a way, to introduce modern Europeans to themselves.

The Voyage of Argo

The reputation of Anacharsis the elder was in full bloom in the closing centuries of the first millennium BC. The critical virtues embodied by the wise Scythian proved to be a useful light that Greek philosophers could shine on their own societies. At about the same time, another story about the Black Sea was also widely popular. The legend of Jason and the Argonauts was known already to Homer and Hesiod, but the earliest full version of the story dates, like many of the Anacharsis proverbs and stories, from the Hellenistic period, the era stretching from the late fourth century BC to the rise of republican Rome three centuries later. Apollonius of Rhodes composed his *Argonautica*, the most important account of the Jason legend, in the third century BC, and it may have been due to the acclaim the work received that he was eventually named to a plum post, keeper of the famous library at Alexandria.

"It was King Pelias," Apollonius begins, "who sent them out." Pelias, usurper of the throne of Iolcus, had learned from an oracle that death would come to him in the form of a man walking with one bare foot. So when his nephew Jason limped into his court, having lost a sandal in the sticky mud of a river in its late winter swell, Pelias devised a plan to send Jason away on a dangerous expedition, and thus escape his fate. The task was to retrieve a golden ram's fleece from Aeetes, king of Colchis, which lay guarded by a serpent at the far edge of a tempestuous sea. A special ship, the finest that ever held oars, was built under the watchful eye of Athena, and in its hull lay a plank from Zeus's sacred Dodonian oak, which gave it the power of speech. The best and bravest, demi-gods and heroes, were assembled for the crew. The perilous voyage tested their skills. Hostile tribes lurked along the coasts, magical beasts rose up to bar the way, and once the treasure was in hand, a vengeful king and his family spared no effort to recover their stolen goods. In the end, the Argonauts returned to Greece, diminished in number but with the fleece and Medea, the Colchian king's daughter, in tow.

There have been many attempts to find the roots of the Jason legend in fact. As with the Anacharsis stories, travelers since antiquity have sought proof of places and practices described in Apollonius's epic. In the 1980s, the British adventurer Tim Severin even constructed a ship using Bronze Age techniques and took it from Greece to Soviet Georgia—modern Colchis—to show that such a journey would have been possible.[50] The earliest versions of the Jason story no doubt did reflect the experiences of ancient sailors, seen through the veil of popular mythology. The geographer Strabo knew how much the experience of the sea could lend itself to myth-making:

[T]he men of Homer's day, in general, regarded the Pontic Sea as a kind of second Oceanus, and they thought that those who voyaged there got beyond the limits of the inhabited world just as much as those who voyaged far beyond the pillars of Heracles; the Pontic Sea was thought to be the largest of the seas in our part of the world, and for that reason, they applied to this particular sea the term "The Pontus," just as they spoke of Homer as "The Poet."[51]

Even the Golden Fleece, Strabo said, perhaps had its origins in the use of sheepskins as a makeshift sluice for extracting gold from rivers, a technique known among the peoples of the Caucasus.[52]

However, searching for the real-life sources of the Jason legend misses the most important point about it. As a piece of literature, Apollonius's *Argonautica* was far more a product of the author's own time than a throwback to the earliest ages of Greek exploration of the Black Sea. Apollonius was writing at a time when the triumphs of Alexander the Great had given way to infighting among his generals and other rival claimants to his legacy. His conquests had made the language and culture of the Greeks dominant throughout much of the known world, but his death in 323 ushered in a period of perpetual warfare among his successors. During the Hellenistic age, it was left to writers such as Apollonius to reconstruct the glories of a mythical past, set against the harsh realities of the present. The tug of nostalgia, not the lust for adventure, is the real theme of his epic.

Even the route taken by Apollonius's Argonauts is revealingly anachronistic. Some of the world's earliest accounts of business travel come in the form of *periploi*, a combination of gazetteer and sailing guide, dating back perhaps as far as the sixth century BC. A remarkable change in the *periploi* occurs with time, however. The earliest ones instruct sailors to turn left as they enter the Black Sea—that is, to the west—and sail around to the north coast. It is only in much later accounts that sailors are told to turn to the right, toward the Caucasus. The reason for this early left turn is unclear, but it may have had to do with the more attractive prospects for trade in the north and west.[53] Cities such as Sinope, on the south coast, predated those in other parts of the sea, but it was the trade in fish and cereals, most plentiful along the Thracian and Scythian coasts, that would have attracted most visitors. Only later, with Sinope's creation of its own colonies farther to the east and the growth of eastern cities such as Phasis, did the long-distance route along the south coast become a regular one. In sailing straight for Colchis, then, the Argonauts were setting off in a direction that would have been far more likely in Apollonius's own day than in the misty past in which his narrative is set.

In the third century BC, and perhaps even before, any traveler to the Black Sea would have found many references to Jason and the Argonauts along the coast— headlands and bays named for incidents during the voyage and local myths associated with particular members of the crew. But these were probably relatively recent innovations, not remnants of an ancient voyage by heroic adventurers. What was a major event in the cultural memory of the Hellenistic age seems to have gone unremarked by the native peoples of the east. In the mythology and folklore of the peoples around the sea, there is a surprising dearth of information on the Argonauts and their alleged voyage. Only after trade with the Mediterranean world began to expand and cities began to flourish would Greek settlers and even Hellenized natives find it useful to link the histories of their towns with an imaginary past. Citizens invented foundation stories and alleged progenitors connected with the *Argo* and endued prominent geographical features with an ancient pedigree. The most significant headland on the southeastern coast is never mentioned in the *Argonautica*, yet it has been called Cape Jason (now Yasun Burnu in Turkish) for more than two millennia.[54] It is perhaps because of a similar logic that visitors can today enjoy "Argo" beer while dining at any number of "Medea" restaurants farther along the coast in post-Soviet Georgia. The art of marketing is not a modern invention.

"More Barbarous Than Ourselves"

For the first few centuries after the initial Greek expeditions, the colonies grew in fame and wealth. They exported grain and luxury goods to the Mediterranean and even produced their own share of philosophers and literati. Their success, however, depended on two things: a guaranteed export market, particularly in grain, to Ionia and mainland Greece and good relations with the non-Greeks of the interior. As time went on, neither of these factors was any longer assured. The conquests of Alexander the Great had little immediate impact on the Black Sea cities themselves, but the opening up of Egypt as a source of grain for the rest of the Mediterranean began to rob them of their privileged position as suppliers of essential foodstuffs. Patterns of trade began to shift to the south: down the Nile toward the Horn of Africa, down the Red Sea to the Indian Ocean and on to the east, overland from Antioch and Damascus to Persia and central Asia. Later, with the expansion and consolidation of Roman power in the eastern Mediterranean, these routes would become even more significant than the older one to the Black Sea.

Relations with inland barbarians also began to sour. The connections to the hinterland had long been delicate, and the cities were often compelled to pay off barbarian chieftains in exchange for peace. Thucydides reported that the cities along the western coast were obliged to deliver a huge quantity of gold, silver, and woolen fabrics to the Odrysians, a Thracian tribe which controlled much of modern Bulgaria.[55] But from the second century BC, even those older tributary relationships began to falter. Especially in the northern cities, the amount and frequency of tribute to barbarian rulers seem to have increased, with little left in local treasuries for public works. The *chora*, or agricultural outskirts, of many cities began to contract; public buildings were allowed to decay or were destroyed by attacks. Defensive walls were erected and then ruined, either from neglect or assault.[56] On the sea, piracy—uncommon in the age of Greek colonization— gradually began to appear, perhaps encouraged by local kings and barbarian rulers eager to profit from the activities of freebooters.[57]

Visitors were unimpressed with what they found in the old colonies. Many of the inhabitants had forgotten how to speak Greek, or pronounced it with such archaic accents that they seemed amusing shadows of their Ionian forebears. In the first century AD, the writer Dio Chrysostom claimed to have visited Olbia, the once flourishing city that Herodotus had described a few centuries earlier. The city was not quite what he expected.

The city of [Olbia], as to its size, does not correspond to its ancient fame, because of its ever-repeated seizure and its wars. For since the city has lain in the midst of barbarians now for so long a time—barbarians, too, who are virtually the most warlike of all—it is always in a state of war and has often been captured, the last and most disastrous capture occurring not more than one hundred and fifty years ago.[58]

The surrounding barbarian population, the Getae, had often been at war, attacking cities along the northern and western coasts, even raiding as far south as Byzantium. The Olbians, who had once maintained extensive environs of agricultural land, had retreated behind crumbling walls. The sanctuaries and funeral monuments were all desecrated. Ships from the Aegean came only infrequently. Even when ships did drop anchor, there were usually only pirates or petty shysters on board. As one Olbian complained, "As a usual thing those who come here are nominally Greeks but actually more barbarous than ourselves, traders and market-men, fellows who import cheap rags and vile wine and export in exchange products of no better quality."[59] The cultural mix in the colony could sometimes be confusing. Dio reported an encounter with a certain Callistratus, clad in trousers and a black cloak, like those worn by barbarian horsemen, and carrying a great cavalry saber on his belt. But for all these trappings, Dio suspected that he was really a Greek at heart. Callistratus, he implies, propositioned him.[60]

Rather than a source of enrichment or exoticism, the Black Sea was now looked upon as a place of exile, once again the inhospitable edge of the world imagined by the earliest Greek poets and geographers. Ovid, banished in AD 8 to Tomis on the west coast by the emperor Augustus, left the most poignant account of life on the sea during the period of the colonies' decline. It was a miserable place: cold, far colder, he claimed, than his native Abruzzi. In some winters the sea iced over, so that dolphins bumped their heads when they tried to jump. The snow lay on the ground for two years at a stretch, and wine came out as slush when you poured it from the bottle. Men walked about with icicles tinkling on their beards. All around were babbling barbarians, and marauders on swift ponies swept down from the north to carry off the few rudiments of civilization that the people had managed to acquire. "They call it the Euxine, 'hospitable,'" he wrote. "They lie."[61]

Ovid was, of course, a poet and one for whom embellishment was no vice, especially since he nurtured the vain hope that the more colorful his descriptions, the more likely a commutation of his sentence. But he was probably right about the profound changes that had taken place in the old Greek colonies. New sources of grain and trade routes to the east, now guarded by the growing power of Rome, made the treasures of the Black Sea pale in comparison, even if the odd jar of pickled fish was still enjoyed by Mediterranean connoisseurs as an exotic import from the far reaches of the earth. A shifting array of new actors crowded the coasts and the hinterlands: new nomadic peoples arriving from farther to the east, hybrid kingdoms of Greek-speaking elites ruling a mixture of Greek and barbarian subjects, and independent city-states with little connection to the Mediterranean world other than the memory of foundation by one or another Greek mother-city. The unity that might have existed during the period of Greek colonization gave way to a more variegated economic and cultural space, a frontier where the desire for political control came up against the challenge of disorder.

Pontus and Rome

In 62 BC a triumphal procession in Rome honored the general and consul Pompey. The spectacle lasted over two days and exceeded in magnificence any that had gone before. Inscriptions carried in the parade proclaimed the new conquests: Paphlagonia and Pontus; Armenia and Cappadocia; Media, Colchis, Iberia, and Albania; Syria, Cilicia, and Phoenicia; Palestine and Judea; Mesopotamia and Arabia. In all, 1,000 fortresses and 800 ships had been captured; 900 cities had fallen, and another thirty-nine had been founded. The spoils of war were immense. Hundreds of carriages and litters were required to bring the treasury of gold and jewels into the city.

Pompey himself entered in a gem-studded chariot, wearing a cloak that was said to have belonged to Alexander the Great. Behind him trailed a retinue of more than 300 subjugated dignitaries, all in native costume—the son and daughter-in-law of the king of Armenia, kings of the Jews and of Colchis, chieftains from the Caucasus mountains, miscellaneous pirates, and at the end, a gaggle of Scythian women, said to be Amazons.[62]

One important figure was absent, though. In his place came a likeness, nearly 12 ft high and made of solid gold. It was accompanied by some of his many sons and daughters, led to Rome as companions for the lifeless statue. The missing monarch was Mithridates, king of Pontus, whose fall was the focus of the celebration. A succession of Roman generals had battled him unsuccessfully for decades, until Pompey's leadership had at last revived the weary legions. But in the end, Mithridates denied the general his greatest glory, delivering the king in person to Rome. Two years earlier, sensing defeat, he had taken his own life and now lay in Sinope, in a stately sepulcher built by Pompey himself.

Both literally and figuratively, the conquests of the first century BC brought the Black Sea into the Roman world; the victory over Mithridates extended the frontiers of Rome east to the Euphrates river and north to the land of the Scythians. The new acquisitions more than doubled the republic's annual revenue in taxes and tribute and restored a degree of order to a zone that for two centuries had been plagued by warfare among local rulers. Ships could cross the sea without fear of pirates, and the local potentates that had controlled the coastline were now under the suzerainty of the Roman republic and, later, the empire.

The late Greek experience on the sea had been one of isolated urban islands, an unwelcoming hinterland on one side and an inhospitable sea on the other. The Romans, however, had grander ambitions. They sought to bring the Black Sea into an orderly empire and to benefit from the fish, grain, precious metals, and—especially important for an imperial power—fighting men that the sea and its littoral could provide. But as the experience with the elusive Mithridates illustrated, conquering the sea was never a simple task. The frontiers of the empire were never clearly delineated boundaries. They were literally a limit— *limes*, in Latin—a measure of the extent to which Rome could reasonably project its military might, and that measure was not always the same, even from month to month. Of course, the nature of Roman frontier policy changed over time, but by and large the process of Roman expansion around the sea rarely involved establishing state control, in a modern sense, over the outlying regions. Rather, conquest was mainly about altering the relationship between the empire and the indigenous populations[63]—striking deals, paying off potential adversaries, and where possible turning competitors into clients.

At its height, the Roman empire included more than half the Black Sea's coastline, from the Dnestr river in the northwest, across Thrace and Anatolia to the Caucasus in the east. Roman warships and merchantmen, with their banks of long oars and linen sails, visited ports all the way from modern Romania to Georgia. The sea was never at the center of Roman attentions, however. When the republic began its expansion in the eastern Mediterranean, in the 200s BC, most of the Black Sea region was divided among the independent kingdoms that had sprung up after Alexander the Great. Portions of the land south and east of the sea came under the control of one of his generals, Seleucus (the eponymous founder of the Seleucid empire), and areas to the west were at various times claimed by the kings of Macedonia. But for most of the Black Sea region, their power was rarely more than notional. In the Hellenistic period, the sea seems to have been in a parlous state. Most of the old Greek colonies were in disarray, taken and retaken by tribes from the interior, mere shadows of the robust marketplaces of a few centuries earlier. The coastline was dominated by peoples in whom outsiders had little immediate interest: the Getae and other Thracian peoples to the west, a bevy of Scythian and Sarmatian chieftains in the north, warlike Caucasus peoples to the east, and a few small kingdoms in Crimea and along the southern coast, some headed by Greek-speaking rulers who arrogated to themselves the title of monarch but who, more often than not, held their throne only until some more powerful neighbor decided to usurp it. There was, thus, good reason for the heroic nostalgia of Apollonius' *Argonautica*.

That might have been the way things had remained had it not been for the particular ambition of one set of rulers, the kings of Pontus. In the Hellenistic and Roman periods, the name "Pontus" referred both to the sea, as in the past, as well as to a specific region along the shore, the southeastern coastline running roughly from Sinope to Trapezus. Like their neighbors, the kings of Pontus had carved out control over their territory in the century or so of political turmoil that followed the death of Alexander. They governed a fertile region, the same area whose lush river valleys and dense forests had attracted Greek settlers centuries earlier. The grand mausoleums cut into the cliffs above their capital of Amaseia (modern Amasya, Turkey) testify to their strength.

Their real advantage, however, lay in their keen appreciation of the power of the sea itself—coupled with some strategic good sense. While other rulers in Asia Minor had contented themselves with the spoils of Anatolia, the Pontic kings looked around the coastline. They built a navy of sturdy galleys able to make the crossing to the north and strengthened ties with the old Greek colonies there. Across the sea, at Chersonesus, they concluded an agreement under which the kingdom would protect the city against Scythian incursions, and they secured the support of the cities on the western coast as well. Their friendly relations with the powerful Bosporan kingdom, centered in the old colony of Panticapaeum, guaranteed their access to fishing on the Sea of Azov. The kings also saw what the growing power of Rome meant for their own region. They aided Rome in the wars with Carthage and assisted the legions in defending Roman conquests in the east against local rivals.

Pontus reached its height in the first century BC, under a ruler of near mythical proportions, Mithridates VI Eupator. Mithridates came to power as a boy after the assassination of his father. The throne was not easily won. His mother sought to have him killed and to install a younger sibling in his place. Mithridates fled to the mountains, but in time he emerged from the wilderness with an army of supporters, imprisoned his mother, and put to death his usurping brother.

Ancient sources invested Mithridates with almost superhuman powers. He is said to have spoken nearly two dozen languages. He was a skilled hunter and warrior who could outrun and outride any opponent. In culture he was broadly Greek, speaking the *koine* language that had grown up from centuries of interaction among various Greek dialects and the influences of non-Greek peoples, but he drew much from the traditions of Persia and the east. Later dramatists and composers cast him as half Hellenic patriot, half Oriental despot. (Racine's version of his life was a favorite of Louis XIV, and both Mozart and Scarlatti composed operas with the king as the central character.)

Mithridates's ambitions were even greater than those of his predecessors. He used the old treaty with Chersonesus as a pretext for annexing the city. He took control of the Bosporan kingdom and installed a viceroy at Panticapaeum. Within a few years, he conquered Colchis, central Anatolia, and Bithynia, placing relatives and friends on the thrones. His lands extended along most of northern Turkey, southern Ukraine, and the western Caucasus. Tribute paid in wheat and silver enriched his coffers, and the lands of the north were active recruiting grounds for skilled cavalry and archers. He also concluded an alliance with Tigranes, king of Armenia, who had been pursuing the same expansionist aims in eastern Anatolia as Mithridates around the Black Sea.

His rapid conquests and powerful army worried the Romans. In the second century BC, Rome had acquired a toe-hold in Asia Minor, and the region along the old Ionian coast was soon transformed into the province of Asia, a province now separated from the powerful Pontic kingdom by only a thin array of pliant Roman allies. Mithridates, by contrast, was said to command 250,000 infantry and 40,000 cavalry, and a war fleet of hundreds of ships, with soldiers and seamen drawn from all the Black Sea's coasts. With only a token force in Asia, Roman commanders before Pompey could not face Mithridates directly, so they encouraged their local allies to act as proxies and stage a preemptive attack on Pontus. The plan proved disastrous. Mithridates easily overwhelmed the invading force and pushed across Asia Minor to the Aegean coast, renouncing his predecessors' alliance with Rome and promising a revival of Hellenic greatness against the new power in the west. In that campaign season, in 88 BC, he ordered the wholesale slaughter of all Roman men, women, and children whom his armies encountered, a total of perhaps 80,000 victims.[64]

His victories were spectacular. His warships ferried marines and foot soldiers across the Aegean to Greece, where he routed the Roman army and occupied Athens. Pushing forward, though, was difficult. His forces were constantly harassed by Roman troops, now reinforced from other regions, and the Greek cities had come to see the erstwhile liberator as little better than the Romans. Mithridates quickly concluded a peace agreement; he renounced his conquests and agreed to pay a fine to Roman authorities for disturbing the peace. That was hardly the end, however. What followed was a series of small but bloody wars, again pitting Mithridates against his neighbors and, in turn, against Rome.

Within a few years, Rome at last reached the end of its tether. The Senate invested ultimate military authority in Pompey and persuaded him to strike out to the eastern frontier. He had earlier achieved historic victories at the other extremities of Roman power, in Libya and Spain, which had allowed him to stage two triumphal processions in Rome before the age of forty. The Senate hoped he could earn yet a third.

The new campaign against Mithridates was swift. As in the past, the king staged a strategic retreat, attempting to entice the Roman legions into rugged territory and then wear them down. But Pompey refused to take the bait. When

Mithridates fled to the Caucasus, Pompey turned his attention to Armenia, quickly subjugating the king's ally, Tigranes. He then marched along the southern Black Sea coast, conquering cities that had earlier fallen to Mithridates and invading the Pontic kingdom itself.

In the meantime, the king made his escape, traveling north among the Caucasian tribes and avoiding the coast, which was patrolled by Roman ships. He finally arrived at Panticapaeum, where he had installed one of his sons as ruler of Crimea. With most of Pontus now in his hands, Pompey turned his attention to quelling rebellions elsewhere, leaving the exiled king to brood among the barbarians of the north.

In his Crimean redoubt, Mithridates was plotting his comeback. He drew up an elaborate plan to raise a new army among the Scythians and the Getae, march up the Danube, and with the assistance of the Gauls race down through Italy and attack Rome itself. This time, however, his aims overreached his abilities. Although he had initially been welcomed by some Hellenistic rulers in Asia Minor and the Black Sea, in time he had come to seem little more than a tyrant, extracting the same tribute for himself that he had warned local potentates they would be required to pay under Roman authority. Rebellions broke out among his own soldiers, and one of his sons, Pharnaces, persuaded the officers to crown him king in his father's place. Realizing that his throne was lost, Mithridates attempted suicide by drinking poison. When it failed to take effect, a merciful Gaul in his retinue dispatched him with his sword.

Pharnaces quickly sent Pompey a token of his good will and friendship, the body of his father. The embalmer had done a poor job, forgetting to remove the brain, and the decay of the soft tissue had distorted the face to such an extent that the king was barely recognizable.[65] But after confirming the body's identity, Pompey pronounced him the greatest adversary that Rome had encountered in the east and buried him in a specially built mausoleum in Sinope. After a few sweeping up operations, Pompey reorganized the newly acquired lands into the Roman province of Pontus and returned home to receive his triumph.

Mithridates, as it turned out, had foreseen his end. Before an early battle with Pompey, he dreamed that he was sailing the Black Sea in a fair wind, with the entrance to the Bosphorus just visible in the distance. He turned to his fellow passengers, congratulating them on their good fortune in coming safely to the passageway to the Mediterranean. But suddenly he found himself in the midst of a storm, his companions lost and the boat smashed, the great monarch tossed about on a small piece of wreckage.[66] His attempt to create a kingdom that would encircle the Black Sea suffered a similar fate. It was now Rome, not the old city-states or Hellenistic monarchs, that claimed much of the coastline.

Dacia Traiana

Even after the defeat of Mithridates, the Black Sea was still a restless place. Not long after Pompey's triumphant homecoming, Pharnaces, the king's treacherous son, reneged on his alliance with Rome and sailed across the Black Sea from Crimea, with the aim of reestablishing his father's empire. He was quickly dispatched by Caesar—a campaign that Caesar famously dismissed with the comment "Veni, vidi, vici."

That line belied the complicated nature of Rome's relationship with the peoples of the coasts and hinterlands. Both Mithridates and Pharnaces had very nearly assembled a strong coalition of barbarian peoples to challenge the power of Rome, and the ability of any group along the imperial frontiers to put together a credible military threat was a constant worry. One of the most important of these groups were the Getae of the western coast.

Long before Rome entered the Black Sea world, Herodotus had described the Getae as "the most manly and law-abiding" of the Thracian peoples, and he was fascinated by their bizarre religious beliefs, which included the idea that they could pass through death to a new life in communion with their god, Zalmoxis. Dying, they said, was merely changing residence, hence the epithet generally given to them by the Greeks, *athanatizontes*—the immortals. To the Romans, the Getae were generally known as the Daci, perhaps originally a separate tribe closely related to the Getae in language and culture. Over the centuries since Herodotus, they had grown powerful through trade, particularly in gold and silver which they dug from mines in Transylvania, the region beyond the Carpathian mountains northwest of the sea. They had long been feared warriors, but under their king Burebista, a contemporary of Julius Caesar, the Daci expanded their military and exerted control over the old Greek cities along the coast. They presented such a threat to Rome that Caesar planned an expedition against them, but the campaign was preempted when he and Burebista met the same fate, assassination by inconstant friends, at about the same time. Under Augustus, the Daci became nominally subject to Rome, but in winter, they marched across the frozen Danube to raid the imperial province of Moesia, in modern-day Bulgaria. "What's here is a Scythian rabble," complained Ovid from the seacoast during Augustus' reign, "a mob of trousered Getae."[67]

As with Mithridates in the east, the Romans fought a series of small wars with the Daci, yet each time the political outcome remained largely the same as before: a formal recognition of Roman suzerainty but little in the way of order. At the beginning of the second century AD, the emperor Trajan decided to destroy the power of the Daci and their king, Decebal, for good. In two separate campaigns from 101 to 106, he laid waste to Dacia. A massive bridge was built across the Danube, with twenty stone piers connected by arches and standing 150 ft high above the foundations. Supply lines stretched across the bridge and deep into Dacian territory. Roman troops eventually surrounded the capital, Sarmizegethusa, in the southern Carpathians, but like Mithridates, Decebal committed suicide before he could be captured and brought back alive to Rome. His head, along with a treasury of gold and silver found in the Dacian stronghold, made the journey instead. In celebration, Trajan staged 123 days of spectacles, involving 10,000 gladiators and the sacrifice of 11,000 animals.[68] To commemorate his victory, the emperor had a grand monument built, and on it a spiral relief giving a narrative of the conquest. It was dedicated by the emperor himself in 113 and still stands, as Trajan's Column, in Rome.

The Daci of the column would have been familiar to Herodotus. They are bearded, clad in trousers, with a fierceness in battle evident even on a piece of architecture intended to praise their subjugator. The distinctive Dacian scimitar, a weapon perhaps borrowed from other peoples to the east, made the legionaries' work especially bloody, and the cavalry tactics of the Daci, which owed much to the influence of the steppe Scythians, were formidable.

But what probably struck the conquering legionaries is how much they had in common with their barbarian enemies. For generations, the Daci had been in contact with the cities along the coast, and their walled fortresses of cut stones were as sophisticated as those found in the old Greek colonies. Moreover, the Romans themselves had earlier sent engineers to assist the Daci with their fortifications (the strategic problem of giving away too much technology that is also familiar to modern great powers). Their symbol, a wolf's head of metal attached to a windsock that flapped in the breeze, would eventually be adopted by the Roman legions as their own battle standard.

After the defeat of the Daci, their region became the province of Dacia—or Dacia Traiana, after its conquering hero—an area that covered much of modern Romania. Legionaries were stationed there and colonists imported from other parts of the empire to work the mountain mines and fertile lands of the Danube plain. The geographer Ptolemy reported some forty-four settlements in Dacia, and those, he said, were only the "most important towns."[69]

Dacia was always, however, a frontier province. Incursions of nomadic peoples from the northern steppe taxed the meager defenses, and it may have been only concern for the welfare of the settler population that prevented an early abandonment of the province. The area to the west was rather quickly brought under solid Roman control, but to the east, on the plains closer to the Black Sea, Roman influence was only one part of a complicated landscape. Plenty of Daci had remained in the new province, and nomadic peoples from the eastern steppe traveled the flatlands in the same wooden carts described centuries earlier by Herodotus. Many other peoples, both settled and pastoral, fished the Danube, farmed the floodplains, and hunted the Carpathian foothills. Roman power north of the Danube, such as it was, lasted only about a century and a half. By 275 the emperor Aurelian had taken the decision to quit Dacia and retreat with his legions south of the river, a natural boundary that could be more readily defended. Some Roman settlers no doubt remained, loath to leave their farmsteads and flocks; some may have moved farther north into the granite vastness of the Carpathians, in response to the influx of new peoples fanning out from the northern steppe.

The Expedition of Flavius Arrianus

Textual evidence about the nature of the Black Sea world in the Roman period, both before and after the abandonment of Dacia, is sketchy. Much of it is derivative of Herodotus, who wrote several centuries before the Romans even arrived in the region. One important source, however, is the account of one Flavius Arrianus, whose early encounter with the sea was as upsetting in reality as the old king Mithridates had found it in his prophetic dream:

[A] cloud suddenly arising burst nearly in an easterly direction from us, and brought on a violent storm of wind, which was entirely contrary to the course that we held, and from the fatal effects of which we had a narrow escape. For it almost instantly produced such a swell of the sea, as to make it appear hollow to the view, and caused a deluge of water to break [over us]. Our situation was then truly tragic, since as fast as we pumped out the water, so fast did it burst in upon us.[70]

The ships received a tossing, but Arrianus survived unscathed. That was a good thing for Rome, for he had just been appointed governor of much of the Black Sea's southern coast, including Mithridates' former kingdom, now subsumed within a province of the Roman empire.

His fortune at sea was in keeping with a charmed life. Arrianus—or Arrian, as he is usually known—was Greek by birth, a native of Bithynia, but served as a high-ranking military commander in the Roman army, the only Greek to hold such a position in his day. In his youth, he had nurtured a love of philosophy, and his notes on the lectures of Epictetus became a major document for students of Stoicism. He later turned to literary pursuits, compiling an important history of Alexander the Great, as well as respected treatises on military tactics, hunting, and India. In AD 131, at the age of thirty-five, he was named prefect of Cappadocia, the province into which the old kingdom of Pontus now fell, with responsibility for overseeing the Roman frontier along the eastern Black Sea and the Caucasus.

In Arrian's day, raiding parties from mountain peoples harassed the frontier, much as nomadic peoples were already beginning to do across the sea in Dacia. The Parthians, the major power to the east, were also actively building their empire and were always interested in profiting from Roman weakness. Piracy had been virtually eliminated on the Mediterranean, but it remained a serious problem on the Black Sea, sometimes encouraged by the very rulers who were supposed to be loyal to Rome. Security depended on striking deals with local potentates. One of Arrian's first duties as governor was to survey how these deals were working in practice and to provide a report to the emperor Hadrian, the successor to Trajan. A portion of that report has survived as his *Periplus Ponti Euxini*, or navigation around the Black Sea.

Arrian began recording his journey at Trapezus. The city was the last outpost of real Roman power in the eastern part of the sea; beyond it there were no more than occasional frontier garrisons. Even Trapezus, though, hardly counted as a civilized metropolis. The altars in the city were of rough stone, with shoddy engravings and misspelled inscriptions, "as is common among barbarous peoples." The emperor, he requested, should send new ones right away. The people of the old Greek city seemed loyal and good-hearted enough; they were proud of a recently erected statue which depicted the glorious Hadrian pointing out toward the water. But the resemblance was so poor, Arrian regretfully reported, that it did the emperor no honor at all.[71]

Leaving Trapezus, Arrian sailed along the coast to the east. Within a day his party had come to the port at Hyssus (near modern Sürmene, Turkey). There he found a company of Roman foot soldiers, whom he put through their paces. When they set off again, the early morning breezes that came off the river mouths filled the sails for a time, but the crew later had to set to the oars. Soon, the winds picked up again, this time with force. Great waves crashed up over the gunwales and flooded the deck. The hands set to bailing out the water, and only some skillful maneuvering by the captain prevented the ship's turning sideways to the waves. One of the other ships in the party lost control and smashed against the rocky shore. The ship was a loss, but Arrian ordered the crew to salvage the sails and tackle and to scrape the wax, a scarce sealant, off the hull.

The storm lasted for two days. When the party could once again take to sea, they sailed on to Apsarus (near modern Sarp, Turkey). Apsarus was said to have taken its name from Apsyrtos, heir to the throne of Colchis, who was supposedly murdered and buried there by his sister, Medea, as she fled with Jason and the Argonauts. The putative tomb had long been an attraction to travelers from the Roman west, a place of pilgrimage tended by the locals; but Arrian found something even more impressive in the town: a large, fortified Roman encampment, housing five cohorts in relatively good order. The prefect delivered their pay, which had been long in coming, and inspected the armaments and walled defenses. He also toured the sick ward, ministering to legionaries who had succumbed to the unhealthy air along the Acampsis (Çoruh) river.

Apsarus was an important garrison, for the nearby Acampsis was the eastern extremity of stable Roman power. When Arrian sailed past the river's mouth, he knew he was entering a place in which the Romans had only a meager foothold. He docked at the old Milesian colony of Dioscurias, where he found a small Roman outpost. The ruler of the hinterland was loyal to Hadrian, but there was little in the place to suggest Rome exercised any real power there. All along the eastern coast, hostile tribes made inland travel impossible. Rome was sometimes able to extort tribute and promises of loyalty from their leaders. The Laz people, governed by one King Malassas, were nominally subjects of Rome, as were the Apsilae under a King Julianus, who received his crown from Hadrian's father; the good graces of the Sanigae and the Abasci, whose king had been crowned by Hadrian, allowed Roman troops to be stationed in Dioscurias. But another group, the Sanni, had recently reneged on their promise to pay tribute and instead survived by plundering the cities of the coast. "We will oblige them to be more punctual," Arrian reported to Hadrian, "or exterminate them."[72]

That was braggadocio, however. As Arrian surely knew, there was little except skillful diplomacy and occasional cajoling to keep these peoples tied to Rome. That was why he was especially interested in finding out something of the political climate in areas beyond the real limits of the empire. He heard at Dioscurias that the ruler of the Bosporan kingdom, once controlled by Mithridates, had recently died, and that the political turmoil created by his death might open an opportunity for expanding Rome's interests on the northern coast. But other than that, information was sparse. People who might have had knowledge of happenings in the north were disinclined to share it with a nosy Roman official.

His report on other parts of the sea is crude, mixing legend and second-hand news of lands that were still imperfectly understood—and much of it reminiscent of the same fantasies reported by Herodotus some 500 years earlier. North of Dioscurias were "lice-eaters," Arrian told the emperor, and little was known about the Tanais (Don) river, except that it was believed to be the boundary between Europe and Asia. He reported that, according to his sources, the once flourishing port of Theodosia in Crimea was now deserted, and Achilles was said to come to inhabit the dreams of people who slept on the island at the mouth of the Danube.[73] Apart from giving a summary of sailing distances, that was all Arrian had to report. The rest he left to the imagination, just as the poets and playwrights of Herodotus' day had done.

The Prophet of Abonoteichus

There are no habitable offshore islands in the Black Sea, but to the Romans, the cities along much of the coastline might as well have been. They were oases of imperial power, some of them fortified and garrisoned, but often not much more. The earliest known map of the Black Sea, a drawing on a Roman-era soldier's shield, found along the Euphrates river, illustrates the point: The seacoast is shown as a succession of individual cities, nothing more. Even in those cities themselves, however, local society—a mixture of Roman soldiers, Greeks descended from the old colonists, barbarians from the interior, and the products of generations of intermarriage—little resembled that of urban centers closer to the Mediterranean. To westerners, the inhabitants of the Black Sea lands were at best credulous bumpkins, at worst semi-barbarians. A few decades after Arrian had retired from his frontier posting, the Roman satirist Lucian recorded a series of events that demonstrated just how bizarre the people of the Black Sea world could seem to observers from other parts of the empire.

Around AD 150 a magnificent prophecy was revealed in Abonoteichus, a town in the region of Paphlagonia on the southern coast (now the city of İnebolu, Turkey). Workers in a temple had discovered some mysterious bronze tablets which announced the advent of the healer Asclepius, son of Apollo. It turned out that, of all the magnificent cities on earth, the god had picked provincial Abonoteichus as the place to make himself incarnate. Divine ways, as always, were imponderable.

The local notables quickly made the city ready to receive the heavenly visitor. Construction on a new temple began, so that the god might have a place to rest and receive worshippers when he arrived. But when the foundation was nearly finished, yet another wonder appeared. A local man, one Alexander, discovered a perfectly formed egg amid the earthworks. When he cracked it open, out slithered a new-born snake. The animal, he announced, was in fact Asclepius. The god had at last come to Abonoteichus, prematurely and in an unexpected but not implausible form, inside his own incomplete temple.

Within days, the snake had miraculously grown to the size of a python, and Alexander was hailed as its chief intercessor. The god quickly set to work. Asclepius revealed oracles to his prophet, who in turn passed the tidings on to the faithful. To especially high-ranking citizens, the god would even speak directly, in Greek.

Over the next twenty years, Abonoteichus became the center of a major cult of Asclepius that rivaled any in the Roman world. Dignitaries journeyed all the way from Rome to have their fortunes told. Families competed to send their most beautiful sons to serve as choristers in the Asclepian temple and, perhaps, to catch a glimpse of the slithering god. Husbands gave up their wives, asking that they sleep with the prophet Alexander and bear his children as a sign of the god's favor.

It all worked brilliantly. The entire affair had, of course, been devised by Alexander himself. He was the one who had buried the original bronze tablets, and his laborious attempt to stuff a baby snake into a hollow goose egg had paid off even better than he could have hoped. The mature snake—the god incarnate—was his masterpiece. He had fashioned a head out of a kind of papier mâché and painted it with vaguely human features. Using a system of hinges and horsehair, he could open the snake's mouth and cause a forked tongue to dart out. He placed the head on a long snake's body and set it up in the temple to receive supplicants.

He also endowed the snake with the power of speech. By linking together the windpipes of several cranes, he formed a speaking tube which ran through the temple wall into another room. With a crowd gathered to hear the god, Alexander would excuse himself from the god's presence, retire to the back room, and like the Wizard of Oz, make his own words issue from the snake's mouth. When he happened to make a prediction that turned out to be false, the god would belatedly deliver an oracle to correct the mistake.

Business was good. The price of a prophetic utterance, especially one that came directly from the snake's mouth, was several times the price of a day laborer, and Alexander could manage well over a hundred prophecies per day. He took pleasure in his collection of comely chorus boys and the ready supply of women willing to service the prophet of Asclepius. He lived to a ripe age, almost seventy, but eventually came to a poetically fitting end. He died of a gangrenous wound to his groin, which became infested with maggots.

The enterprising prophet of Abonoteichus merely confirmed what many educated Romans probably thought about the peoples of the Black Sea. But Lucian asked his readers to overlook the gullibility of his victims. "To tell the truth," he wrote, "we must excuse those men of Paphlagonia and Pontus, thick-witted, uneducated fellows that they were."[74] If the inhabitants fell for a small-time charlatan with a talking snake, it was a forgivable vice. What could one expect, after all, for people who lived at the exotic extremity of the empire?

It is tempting to see the late Roman experience on the Black Sea as an effort to shore up weak borders against a growing barbarian threat—a clash of civilizations, the clean-shaven and skirted against the bearded and trousered. But as the local populations in places like Abonoteichus surely knew, those lines were never as clear as they might seem.

It could sometimes be difficult to tell the conqueror from the conquered. The soldiers whom Arrian inspected were probably a motley crew, assembled from the far reaches of the empire and from local populations: Alpine highlanders, recruits from Spain and Gaul, a few native soldiers from Trapezus and Colchis, maybe even some Daci as well.[75] Like soldiers before and since, those from far off learned how to survive in an unfamiliar environment by copying the habits of those who knew it best, their erstwhile enemies, now perhaps serving beside them as legionaries. As Arrian remarked in a treatise on military tactics,

[the emperor Hadrian] has obliged his soldiers to practice barbaric movements, both those of the mounted archers of Parthia and the rapid evolutions of Sarmatians and Celts. They have been obliged also to learn the native war cries proper to such movements—those of the Celts, and the Daci, and the Rhaeti. They have been trained also to leap their horses across trenches and over ramparts. In a word, in addition to their ancient exercises they have learned all that has been invented ... tending to grace or speed, or calculated to strike terror into the enemy, ...[76]

That meant, of course, that the cries on both sides of the battle lines often turned out to be the same. But Hadrian would have known all this from first-hand experience. Under his immediate predecessor, Trajan, he had served in the Dacian campaigns, hearing the whoops of barbarian warriors as they rushed out to meet his battle formations, and he had himself made a tour of the southern Black Sea coast, years before he sent his agent Arrian. He even named his favorite horse Borysthenes, after the river of Scythia.

In time, Romans would come to appreciate such reciprocal influences as never before. Pompey had introduced the Black Sea world to the Roman one; the conquest of the Pontic kingdom pushed the frontiers of the empire all the way to the Caucasus. In the centuries that followed, Roman engagement with the sea would be extended still farther—either to the directly administered provinces along the western and southern coasts or, via patron–client relationships, to the north and east. But soon the very distinction between the Roman and Black Sea worlds would fade away. Less than a century after the retreat from Dacia, the imperial capital picked itself up and alighted at the gateway to the sea—Byzantium.

NOTES

1. Xenophon, *Anabasis*, 7.1.29.
2. On the difficulty of dating the earliest Greek expeditions, see Thomas S. Noonan, "The Grain Trade of the Northern Black Sea in Antiquity," *American Journal of Philology*, Vol. 94, No. 3 (1973):231–42; and Stefan Hiller, "The Mycenaeans and the

Black Sea," in Robert Laffineur and Lucien Busch (eds.) *Thalassa: L'Egée préhistorique et la mer* (Liège: Université de Liège, 1991), pp. 207–16.

3. Plato, *Phaedo*, 109b.
4. Xenophon, *Anabasis*, 5.4.
5. Pierre Gilles, *The Antiquities of Constantinople*, ed. Ronald G. Musto, trans. John Bell, 2nd edn. (New York: Italica Press, 1988), p. xlv.
6. Strabo, *Geography*, 11.2.12.
7. Pliny the Elder, *Natural History*, 4.9.44.
8. Strabo, *Geography*, 11.2.1; Pliny the Elder, *Natural History*, 7.1.10, 7.2.17; Herodotus, *Histories*, 3.116, 4.24, 4.106.
9. David Braund, *Georgia in Antiquity: A History of Colchis and Transcaucasian Iberia, 550 BC– AD 562* (Oxford: Clarendon Press, 1994), pp. 50, 90.
10. Herodotus, *Histories*, 2.104–105.
11. The present state of knowledge about the Cimmerians is outlined in A. I. Ivanchik, *Kimmeriitsy: Drevnevostochnye tsivilizatsii i stepnye kochevniki v VIII-VII vekakh do n. e.* (Moscow: Russian Academy of Sciences, 1996).
12. Gocha R. Tsetskhladze, "Greek Colonisation of the Black Sea Area: Stages, Models, and Native Population," in Gocha R. Tsetskhladze (ed.) *The Greek Colonisation of the Black Sea Area: Historical Interpretation of Archaeology* (Stuttgart: Franz Steiner, 1998), pp. 8–68.
13. Plato, *Phaedo*, 109b.
14. Strabo, *Geography*, 12.3.11.
15. Strabo, *Geography*, 11.2.17.
16. Pliny the Elder, *Natural History*, 6.4.13. Cf. Strabo, *Geography*, 11.2.16, who says that this figure was overstated, but that there were still perhaps as many as seventy tribes.
17. Strabo, *Geography*, 11.3.1; Pliny the Elder, *Natural History*, 6.4.13.
18. Strabo, *Geography*, 7.4.4.
19. Herodotus, *Histories*, 4.53.
20. Michael Grant, *The Rise of the Greeks* (New York: Scribner's, 1988), p. 273.
21. The best source on the development of the western cities is Krzysztof Nawotka, *The Western Pontic Cities: History and Political Organization* (Amsterdam: Adolf M. Hakkert, 1997).
22. Chris Scarre, *The Penguin Historical Atlas of Ancient Rome* (London: Penguin, 1995), p. 81.
23. An expedition by Pericles brought many of the cities and entrepôts under effective Athenian control. By 425 BC some fifty Black Sea cities were payers of tribute to the Athenians. Braund, *Georgia in Antiquity*, p. 125.
24. Anthony Bryer and David Winfield, *The Byzantine Monuments and Topography of the Pontos*, Vol. 1 (Washington: Dumbarton Oaks Research Library and Collection, 1985), p. 128, note 35.
25. Virgil, *Georgics*, 1.58, 2.440–445.
26. Xenophon, *Anabasis*, 4.8. Cf. Pliny the Elder, *Natural History*, 21.45.77. Bees that pollenate the Pontic azalea are still known to produce hallucinogenic honey that the Turks call *deli bal*, crazy honey.

27. Diodorus Siculus, *Library of History*, 31.24.
28. Pliny, *Natural History*, 9.18.48.
29. Strabo, *Geography*, 7.6.2.
30. Peter Simon Pallas, *Travels Through the Southern Provinces of the Russian Empire, in the Years 1793 and 1794*, Vol. 2 (London: T. N. Longman and O. Rees et al., 1802–3), p. 289.
31. Mikhail Rostovtzeff, *Iranians and Greeks in South Russia* (1922; reprint New York: Russell and Russell, 1969), p. 11.
32. On the portrayal of barbarians in fifth-century literature, see Edith Hall, *Inventing the Barbarian: Greek Self-Definition Through Tragedy* (Oxford: Clarendon Press, 1989).
33. See S. L. Solovyov, *Ancient Berezan: The Architecture, History and Culture of the First Greek Colony in the Northern Black Sea* (Leiden: Brill, 1999).
34. Herodotus, *Histories*, 4.108.
35. Timothy Taylor, "Thracians, Scythians, and Dacians, 800 BC–AD 300," in Barry Cunliffe (ed.) *The Oxford Illustrated Prehistory of Europe* (Oxford: Oxford University Press, 1994), p. 389.
36. Pausanias, *Description of Greece*, 1.31.2.
37. Herodotus, *Histories*, 4.5.
38. Herodotus, *Histories*, 4.75.
39. Herodotus, *Histories*, 1.105.
40. Herotodus, *Histories*, 4.46.
41. See Sergei I. Rudenko, *Frozen Tombs of Siberia: The Pazyryk Burials of Iron Age Horsemen*, trans. M. W. Thompson (Berkeley: University of California Press, 1970); Rostovtzeff, *Iranians and Greeks*; Ellis H. Minns, *Scythians and Greeks: A Survey of Ancient History and Archaeology on the North Coast of the Euxine from the Danube to the Caucasus* (Cambridge: Cambridge University Press, 1913); Renate Rolle, *The World of the Scythians*, trans. F. G. Walls (Berkeley: University of California Press, 1989).
42. Rolle, *The World of the Scythians*, p. 128.
43. Diogenes Laertius, *Lives of the Eminent Philosophers*, 1.103.
44. Herodotus, *Histories*, 4.76–77.
45. Plato, *The Republic*, 10.600; Aristotle, *Posterior Analytics*, 1.13; Strabo, *Geography*, 7.3.8; Pliny the Elder, *Natural History*, 7.56.198. That is, an anchor with arms rather than a simple stone slab.
46. Jan Fredrik Kindstrand, *Anacharsis: The Legend and the Apophthegmata* (Uppsala: University of Uppsala, 1981), pp. 3–10.
47. Plutarch, *The Dinner of the Seven Wise Men*, 148c–e.
48. Jean-Jacques Barthélemy, *Travels of Anacharsis the Younger in Greece, During the Middle of the Fourth Century Before the Christian Aera*, trans. William Beaumont, Vol. 1 (London: J. Mawman, F. C. and J. Rivington et al., 1817), p. i.
49. See, for example, Marie Guthrie, *A Tour, Performed in the Years 1795–6, Through the Taurida, or Crimea, the Antient Kingdom of Bosphorus, the Once-Powerful Republic of Tauric Cherson, and All the Other Countries on the North Shore of the Euxine, Ceded to Russia by the Peace of Kainardgi and Jassy* (London: T. Cadell, Jr. and W. Davies, 1802), p. 29; Henry A. S. Dearborn, *A Memoir of the Commerce and Navigation of the Black Sea, and the Trade and Maritime*

Geography of Turkey and Egypt, Vol. 1 (Boston: Wells and Lilly, 1819), p. 313; Jean, Baron de Reuilly, *Travels in the Crimea, and Along the Shores of the Black Sea, Performed During the Year 1803* (London: Richard Phillips, 1807), bound in *A Collection of Modern and Contemporary Voyages and Travels*, Vol. 5 (London: Richard Phillips, 1807), p. 53; Edward Daniel Clarke, *Travels to Russia, Tartary, and Turkey* (New York: Arno Press, 1970) [reprint of Vol. 1 of his *Travels in Various Countries of Europe, Asia, and Africa*, London, 1811], p. 348.

50. Tim Severin, *The Jason Voyage* (New York: Simon and Schuster, 1985).

51. Strabo, *Geography*, 1.2.10.

52. Strabo, *Geography*, 1.2.10, 11.2.19. Modern travelers found the same practice among the Svans (Strabo's "Soanes"?), who live in the mountainous region of north-central Georgia, but there is no specific connection with ancient Colchis, lowland Georgia along the Phasis river. See, for example, Edmund Spencer, *Travels in the Western Caucasus*, Vol. 1 (London: Henry Colburn, 1838), p. 341. On a similar practice among Romanian Roma, or Gypsies, see James Henry Skene, *The Frontier Lands of the Christian and the Turk*, Vol. 1, 2nd edn. (London: Richard Bentley, 1853), p. 323.

53. Alexandre Baschmakoff, *La synthèse des périples pontiques: Méthode de précision en paléo-ethnologie* (Paris: Librairie Orientaliste Paul Geuthner, 1948), pp. 14–16. Braund argues that some of the earliest *periploi* are probably fourth century but perhaps relied on sixth-century sources. See Braund, *Georgia in Antiquity*, p. 17.

54. Bryer and Winfield, *The Byzantine Monuments*, Vol. 1, p. 119.

55. Thucydides, *History of the Peloponnesian War*, 2.97.

56. Sergei Saprykin, "Bosporus on the Verge of the Christian Era (Outlines of Economic Development)," *Talanta: Proceedings of the Dutch Archaeological and Historical Society*, Vols. 32–3 (2000–1):96. On the decline of the Caucasus cities, see Braund, *Georgia in Antiquity*, p. 63.

57. Gocha R. Tsetskhladze, "Black Sea Piracy," *Talanta: Proceedings of the Dutch Archaeological and Historical Society*, Vols. 32–3 (2000–1):13–14.

58. Dio Chrysostom, "Borysthenitic Discourse," 36.4. There is some controversy over whether Dio did, in fact, visit Olbia.

59. Dio Chrysostom, "Borysthenitic Discourse," 36.24.

60. Dio Chrysostom, "Borysthenitic Discourse," 36.7–8.

61. Ovid, *Tristia*, 3.13.28.

62. This description is based on Appian, "Mithridatic Wars," 116–17, and Plutarch, "Pompey," 45. The list of newly conquered areas is surely exaggerated: Pompey never set foot in most of them.

63. Peter S. Wells, *The Barbarians Speak: How the Conquered Peoples Shaped Roman Europe* (Princeton: Princeton University Press, 1999), p. 94.

64. David Magie, *Roman Rule in Asia Minor to the End of the Third Century after Christ* (New York: Arno Press, 1975), p. 217.

65. Plutarch, "Pompey," 42.

66. Plutarch, "Pompey," 32.

67. Ovid, *Tristia*, 4.6.47.

68. Cassius Dio, *Roman History*, 68.13–15.

69. Claudius Ptolemy, *The Geography*, trans. and ed. Edward Luther Stevenson (New York: Dover, 1991), p. 82.

70. Flavius Arrianus, *Arrian's Voyage Round the Euxine Sea, Translated; and Accompanied with a Geographical Dissertation, and Maps* (Oxford: J. Cooke, 1805), p. 3.

71. Arrianus, *Arrian's Voyage*, p. 1.

72. Arrianus, *Arrian's Voyage*, p. 9.

73. Arrianus, *Arrian's Voyage*, pp. 14–15.

74. Lucian, "Alexander the False Prophet," 16.

75. H. F. Pelham, "Arrian as Legate of Cappadocia," *English Historical Review*, Vol. 11, No. 44 (October 1896):637.

76. Quoted in Pelham, "Arrian as Legate," 640.

For as to the land about the Euxine Sea, which extends from Byzantium to the Lake [Sea of Azov], it would be impossible to tell everything with precision, since the barbarians beyond the Ister River, which they also call the Danube, make the shore of that sea quite impossible for the Romans to traverse.

Procopius, sixth century

They have in no place any settled city to live in, neither do they know where their next will be. They have divided all Scythia among themselves, which stretches from the river Danube to the rising of the sun. And every captain, according to the great or small number of his people, knows the bound of his pastures, and where he ought to feed his cattle, winter and summer, spring and autumn.

Friar William of Rubruck, French ambassador to the Tatars, 1253

It is in the countries around the Black Sea that one finds the residua of the peoples of Colchis and of Asiatic Scythia, the Huns, the Avars, the Alans, the Hungarian Turks, the Bulgars, the Pechenegs, and others, who came at different times to make incursions along the banks of the Danube, which had already been invaded by the Gauls, the Vandals, the Bastarnae, the Goths, the Gepids, the Slavs, the Croats, the Serbs, and all the peoples who came down from the north to the south.

Claude Charles de Peyssonnel,
French consul to the Crimean Tatars, 1765

3

Mare Maggiore, 500–1500

For Procopius, the historian of the early Byzantine empire, the Black Sea was a place to be avoided. Its coasts teemed with hostile tribesmen, and despite the best efforts of his patron, the emperor Justinian, to fortify several coastal settlements, the inland barbarians remained a constant concern. The most striking event he recorded about the sea was fittingly grotesque. A giant whale, dubbed Porphyrius, had been menacing shipping in the Bosphorus, so when the creature became stranded in shallow water, villagers rushed to the shore and hacked it to death with axes.[1] If only it were that easy with the barbarians.

Procopius wrote from Constantinople, a city whose gates opened on both the Pontic and the Mediterranean worlds. The city became the Roman capital in 330, when Constantine moved his throne there and cemented the division of the empire into western and eastern halves. It was an unlikely choice for an imperial center. It had been repeatedly destroyed and had never before served as the seat of a major kingdom or empire. But its physical setting in relation to the water was its chief advantage.

Byzantium was established as a Greek colony in the mid-seventh century BC. Tradition held that the oracle at Delphi had instructed one Byzas, a ruler of Megara, to found a city opposite the land of the blind men, and the site of the future city seemed to fit that description. It lay on a triangular promontory at the opening to the Bosphorus, easily defensible on two of the three sides, just across the strait from an older Megarian colony at Chalcedon. As Byzas must have reckoned, the Chalcedonians were blind, indeed. They had chosen to build on the hills and open lowlands to the east instead of the excellent headland just to their west.[2]

Byzantium was not the successor to Rome. In the minds of the Byzantines, it *was* Rome. The emperor's subjects called themselves, and for a time were called by others, *Romaioi* ("Romans"); their empire, in shorthand, was

"Romania." (A place called the "Byzantine empire" is the invention of later European historians.) There were two fundamental differences from the old Rome, of course. One was that the new empire was culturally Greek, built on the Hellenistic traditions that had been nurtured in the cities of the Aegean, the Black Sea, and the eastern Mediterranean. (Even today, Greek-speakers in Turkey are still known as *Rumlar*, an echo of this "Roman" past.) The other was that the imperial city now lay not at the empire's geographical center, on the banks of the Tiber, but near the imperial frontier.

Constantinople had the capacity to control access to the Black Sea, but the new Rome, unlike the old, turned out to be more a victim of its geographic destiny than a shaper of it. The great irony of the Byzantine centuries is that an empire whose capital sat at the entryway to a body of water that outsiders had long coveted for its riches demonstrated rather little desire to profit from it. For a time, the Byzantine army and navy successfully prevented any rival—Persians and Arabs, in particular—from gaining a foothold on the southern and eastern coasts; the city of Chersonesus in Crimea, fortified and refurbished by successive Byzantine dynasties, looked out for the empire's strategic interests in the north. But those achievements were primarily defensive. Beyond seeking to ensure access to grain, salt, and other supplies and to levy taxes on trade with the peoples of the northern steppe, the Byzantines were most concerned with warding off the ill effects of the sea, not prospering from its wealth. Once the sea's economic potential was again manifest, in the Middle Ages, the Byzantine emperors had by then given over virtually all their commercial interests to surrogates, the Italian city-states of Genoa and Venice. The Byzantine navy had dwindled to a small fleet charged with protecting the imperial city, and even then the citizens were often left to rely on a meager last line of defense: a massive chain, floating on pontoons, that blocked off the harbor of Constantinople from an attack by sea. They were still using it when the city fell to the Ottomans in 1453.

The cultural influence of Byzantium, however, was another matter. Orthodox Christian traders and seamen crisscrossed the sea, even at times when relations with inland powers were at their nadir. Greek-speaking communities continued to thrive along the coast, particularly in the southeast. Some areas remained largely within Constantinople's purview—such as Chersonesus and its hinterland and much of the Anatolian shore—but even when they could no longer be counted as part of the temporal empire, these and many other areas of eastern Europe were still part of the eternal one, the domain of eastern Christendom. While the former experienced periods of growth and decline, the latter expanded steadily, so that by the early Middle Ages other Christian kingdoms around the coastline, from the Bulgarians in the west to the Georgians in the east, felt ready to challenge the Byzantine emperor's claim to special status as universal sovereign. In the end, it was the coming of two groups that could be brought into neither the profane nor the sacred domain—the Catholic powers of the Mediterranean and the Muslim Ottomans—that changed the nature of life around the sea.

"The Scythian Nations are One"

Already by the time of Constantine, most of the hinterland was well beyond the empire's reach. The northern river courses, the mountain passes of the Caucasus, even the Danube plain, abandoned by Rome in the third century, were as foreign as they had been to Trajan and Hadrian. In the Byzantine imagination, the barbarian peoples, particularly those on the northern steppe, were the archetypal outsiders. They were everything that the "Romans" were not. Many were pastoral, with no settled cities; they did not speak Greek; they were not Christians; and they were not subjects of the one divinely ordained emperor.[3] In the Byzantines the cultural prejudices of Classical Athens thus met the political narcissism of late imperial Rome.

Yet, however great this cultural divide might have appeared to the empire's literate elites, in practice successive dynasties understood that the security of their empire and its capital depended on the willingness to compromise with the succession of peoples who moved out of the steppe and pressed up against the imperial frontiers. The interests of barbarian rulers had to be accommodated; otherwise, they could easily play off Constantinople against other eager patrons: the ever-present Persians and, later, the powerful medieval kingdoms of the Balkans and the principalities of central and eastern Europe. New peoples arrived from the Asian steppe, first settling on the northern and western shores and then, with the coming of the Turks, in the Byzantine heartland of Anatolia. Over each generation, these new immigrants also had to be brought into the imperial system—deals renegotiated, alliances reworked, and clients satisfied—or, at the very least, prevented from destroying it.

The steppe had long been an open highway between central Asia and Europe, and for almost the entire millennium of Byzantine civilization, traffic was heavy. Most of the immigrant groups—Sarmatians, Huns, Avars, Magyars, Pechenegs, Cumans—were the western edge of a series of population movements that began much farther to the east, in Mongolia and western China. Yet these migrations rarely involved hordes of whip-snapping horsemen thundering at full gallop across the treeless steppe. The metaphors of "waves" and "tides" of barbarian invaders obscure the fact that the movement of peoples toward the west was a gradual process that extended over many centuries.⁴ For some groups, it took generations to move the few hundred kilometers from the Volga to the Dnepr, still longer to make it to the Danube. Those who arrived from the east were by and large nomads, and with rare exceptions—such as the Huns in the fifth century and the Tatar–Mongols in the thirteenth—they moved slowly, always conscious of the need for adequate grazing lands and water for their herds.

Understanding each of these groups is difficult, for there is little to go on besides what sedentary, literate cultures said about them from afar; but one thing seems clear: Over the great sweep of Black Sea history from the end of the Roman empire to the coming of the Ottomans, a certain continuity of culture on the northern steppe, rather than the wholesale supplanting of one distinct group by another, was the norm. A local economy based on nomadic and semi-nomadic herding and long-distance trade, blending elements of Iranian and Turkic languages and cultural forms, and all influenced by long-term contact with Greek, Slavic, and Germanic populations, is perhaps as close as one can come to describing what that culture was like. "The Scythian nations are one, so to speak, in their mode of life and in their organization," wrote a sixth-century Byzantine author, using the same generic label for the northern peoples that Herodotus had used almost a thousand years earlier.⁵ Far more than older empires such as the Romans and Persians, the Byzantines were in sustained and intimate contact with these peoples beyond the sea. They could not avoid it, for from the earliest years of the empire, the threat that these groups could present, not only to Byzantine holdings in Crimea but also to the imperial city itself, was readily apparent.

Long before the establishment of the new Rome, the Scythians had given way to new arrivals, the Sarmatians, probably speakers of an Iranian language like the Scythians. They were already living east of the Don river in Herodotus's day and were, he claimed, the product of trysts between Scythians and Amazons.⁶ As they moved farther west, the region once known as "Scythia" gradually came to be called "Sarmatia," a "European" half lying west of the Don river and an "Asiatic" half to the east. (The cartographic convention that identified the Don as the boundary line between Europe and Asia would endure well into the nineteenth century.) The Sarmatians were followed by still other groups. Most, such as the Avars, followed the pathways from the east and made their way deep into the heart of Europe. Others, such as the Celts and Goths, filtered in from the north and west. Some groups were even able to reach across the sea to the south coast. Byzantine chronicles from the fourth century detail Gothic raids on Pitsunda and Trapezus along the eastern and southeastern coasts, and for a time the Goths even established a major base in Crimea, a small pocket in the southwest of the peninsula that would be known as "Gothia" well into the Middle Ages. (In the early 1400s, one traveler reported that his German manservant could easily converse with the locals, who retained some facility in their lost Teutonic language.[7]) Many groups adopted Christianity; some were given their own bishops and even awarded designated churches in Constantinople.

Procopius, who wrote during a period of Byzantine resurgence in the sixth century after a long period of territorial loss, was clear on the difficulties of securing Byzantine control of the sea and of protecting the few Greek-speaking communities that still speckled the coast. Garrisons had once been stationed all along the coastline, but most had by his day been abandoned. Procopius could not even hazard a guess as to the actual circumference of the sea; so numerous were the barbarians around it, especially in the north, that accurate information was now impossible to obtain. Apart from the occasional exchange of embassies, there was little interaction with these peoples, he said.[8] In some areas, however, Procopius's emperor, Justinian, did manage to reassert authority. Old ports that had fallen into disrepair were restored. At Trapezus he built an aqueduct to alleviate the persistent problems with fresh water. At Panticapaeum and Chersonesus in Crimea—which lay, said Procopius, "at the extremity of the Roman empire"—he found the walls in ruins and made provision for their restoration.[9]

The problem, of course, was that this "extremity" was not very far away. For the greater part of the Byzantine period, the main concern was not necessarily to capitalize on the advantages of the Black Sea, but rather to keep others from doing so. That was the chief worry of the emperor Constantine VII Porphyrogenitus. In the tenth century, Constantine assembled a manual of statecraft, *De administrando imperio*, for his son and heir, Romanus. The cast of characters around the sea had changed markedly over the centuries since Procopius, but the basic relationship between the empire and its neighbors was largely the same. The Slavs had appeared in the 600s, and by Constantine VII's time they had established a powerful empire in the south Balkans. In the north, the Sarmatians and Alans had given way to the Pechenegs, a Turkic people who had arrived from central Asia in the 800s. Farther to the north, a group the Byzantines called the Rhos—a Norse aristocracy governing a Slavic population—were already conducting lively trade with the coast or, when it suited them, making war on Constantinople. In the east and south were the Arabs, whose armies were fueled by the fervor of their new faith, Islam. Christian kings and princes in Georgia and Armenia were buffers against the Muslims, but their Christianity did not mean that they were beyond opposing the seat of Christendom itself when it was in their own interest to do so.

The Pechenegs were of particular concern to Constantine, for they were one of the linchpins of Byzantine security. Keeping peace with them meant that

Chersonesus would remain safe, and keeping Chersonesus safe meant that the Byzantines could retain some influence—economic and even military—on the northern shore. The Chersonites were intermediaries in the trade in hides and wax coming from the steppe, and they received in exchange such goods as purple cloth, ribbons, gold brocade, pepper, scarlet, and leather imported from Byzantine urban centers on the south coast.[10] The Pechenegs nominally provided protection for the city, but the relationship was usually closer to a protection racket. They knew that they could influence the Byzantines by applying pressure on their dependency in Crimea. In past centuries, Crimean ports had exported grain to the south, but the situation was now reversed. Chersonesus seems to have depended on the southern ports for grain supplies, while sending animal products taken from steppe nomads in return.[11] Moreover, since the Pechenegs also served as a useful check on the power of the Rhos and the Christian rulers in the Balkans and the Caucasus, good relations with them were critical.

Constantine advised that a yearly embassy be made to the Pechenegs. The embassy, he said, should try to secure a renewal of the longstanding treaty of friendship, and plenty of lavish gifts should be offered to sweeten the deal. The only problem with this scheme was that the history of good relations with Constantinople had actually sharpened the tribesmen's rapacity:

Now these Pechenegs, who are ravenous and keenly covetous of articles rare among them, are shameless in their demands for generous gifts, ... demanding this for themselves and that for their wives, and the escort something for their own trouble and some more for the wear and tear of their cattle. Then, when the imperial agent enters their country, they first ask for the emperor's gifts, and then again, when these have glutted the menfolk, they ask for the presents for their wives and parents.[12]

All the peoples of the north had grown used to this arrangement over the centuries; they continually increased the tribute they required in exchange for peace. A good emperor, therefore, needed to know how to rebuff their escalating demands diplomatically. If the Pechenegs asked for robes and diadems, he advised, tell them that those things are the emperor's alone and would be cursed if worn by anyone else. If they requested marriage to your daughter, say that your customs forbid it.[13] Most other demands could be accommodated.

There was one thing, however, that Constantine stressed should never, under any circumstances, be given to the Pechenegs. If they asked for it, he counseled, tell them coyly that it had been bestowed on the Romans by God and could not be shared. It was the Byzantines' most guarded state secret and one whose mystery died with the empire itself. It was a weapon they owed to the sea.

Sea-Fire

The earliest ships on the Black Sea—those known to Homer or the mythical Argonauts—were sleek and open-decked, and light enough to be pulled up onto beaches or portaged over river rapids. Their single square sail, masted amidships, could be used if the wind were favorable, but most of the propulsion was provided by oarsmen seated at narrow benches, one man to an oar. Gradually, open hulls evolved into covered decks, and successive decks were added on top of those. Ships with three banks of oars, the Greek trireme, became the main battle galley during the fifth century BC, seeing action during the wars with the Persians and between Athens and Sparta.

For the next several centuries, building better ships meant building bigger ones, with more banks of oars and multiple rowers straining to pull each massive blade. Gigantism in naval design reached its apogee among the Hellenistic kings, some of whom experimented with enormous rowed catamarans that featured multiple courses of oars on the four sides of the double hull. However, in the Roman period, the set-piece naval battles of the past gave way to new and varied forms of warfare, from chasing corsairs to quelling rebellious client kingdoms. The times demanded a ship adaptable to the varied needs of an imperial power, both full-scale warfighting and coastal policing. It was these smaller craft, fast two-banked galleys which the Romans had copied from pirate ships used in the Adriatic, that coasted along the Black Sea during the time of Trajan and Hadrian. They are depicted on Trajan's Column, docked at a Danube port during the Dacian campaigns.

By the middle of the fourth century AD, the trireme was largely extinct. Threatened with shortages of money and men, the late Roman empire returned to the smaller galleys of a thousand years earlier, and that basic design carried over into the Byzantine era. Most of the ships in the Byzantine fleet were single-banked galleys with each rower pulling his own oar. Twin masts, rigged with the maneuverable triangular sails favored by Arab seamen, could be used if winds were good, but in battle the captain would rely solely on the muscle power of his oarsmen, some of whom might also double as marines. A few larger ships, two-banked galleys with a crew of perhaps 200, were in service in the imperial fleet based at Constantinople, but in the provincial outposts—in Chersonesus or Trapezus, say—it was probably the smaller vessels that held sway.[14]

Greek and Roman naval commanders had two basic tactical options during a sea battle. One was to use their ships themselves as weapons, ramming the hull of the enemy vessel and perhaps forcing it to founder. That was the great innovation of the Greek trireme, with its sturdy hull construction and breakwater beak on the bow. The other was to slip close enough to the ship to board it or, if that proved impossible, to hurl projectiles at it. The Romans perfected this form of close-in fighting. Their oarsmen would steer alongside the enemy while marines waited to throw across a boarding plank and storm over the gunwales.

The Byzantines, however, effected a virtual revolution in naval warfare. At the center was the great secret that Constantine VII urged his son not to reveal to the Pechenegs. Sailors called it *thalassion pyr*—sea-fire. In the warship's bow, Byzantine sailors placed a long wooden tube, lined with bronze. One end was aimed at the enemy ship and the other connected to an air pump. A flammable substance was poured down the tube and set alight, while men at the other end worked the pump to send the flaming liquid arching toward the enemy. Large ships could be equipped with more than one tube, and the Byzantines even developed a handheld model for use by marines.[15] The substance was so destructive that it could burn even on the surface of the sea. The Arab chronicler Ibn al-Atir saw its devastating effects firsthand. "A flame-throwing tube could cover twelve men," he wrote, "and the flame was so violent and so sticky that no one could resist it. This was the weapon that the Muslims feared most."[16]

The earliest mention of sea-fire—which outsiders came to call "Greek fire"—dates from the sixth or perhaps seventh century. Its invention was attributed to one Callinicus, but the exact composition has remained a mystery. The raw material was probably crude oil, or naphtha, taken from above-ground deposits such as those on the Taman peninsula, near the old Greek colony at Panticapaeum on the northeast coast. Springs disgorged the sticky naphtha onto the surface, where it could be easily collected in pots. The region was known for its seismic activity, and later travelers to the area remarked on the smoke and heat created by underground fires.[17] Sea-fire became the centerpiece of Byzantine naval defense. It was largely responsible for the defeat of successive seaborne enemies, from the Arabs in the seventh and eighth centuries to the Rhos in the tenth, and for hundreds of years to come it would be a major bulwark against growing threats on all sides.

The naphtha wells of Taman were such a closely guarded element of the Byzantine arsenal because the advent of sea-fire actually accompanied the empire's decline as a naval power—a time when ships had need of precisely the defensive capacity that the weapon provided. For a time in the sixth century and perhaps again in the eleventh, the Byzantine navy experienced periods of greatness; it was able to win back lands around the Mediterranean that had been lost to invading barbarians and to check other powers on the Black Sea. The water was lauded as a symbol of Byzantium's universal empire and the chief advantage of Constantine's well-sited city. Poets in Constantinople waxed lyrical about the play of light on water and the thrum of waves against the shore, and imperial law codes even protected the right of property owners to a sea view.[18] But overall, the Byzantine romance with the sea was not matched by the empire's prowess as a maritime power. Inadequate state funds, the rise of other seafaring powers in the Mediterranean, endemic piracy, and simple imperial mismanagement all contributed to the empire's problems. And for successive imperial dynasties, engaging in long-distance maritime trade seemed to be of less interest than simply taxing it—a perverse consequence, perhaps, of the very location of the imperial capital at the intersection of major international commercial routes.

Khazars, Rhos, Bulgars, and Turks

At their height, the old Greek colonies on the northern coast had flourished because of two things: ready export markets in the south and relatively stable, but not overly powerful, political formations in the hinterlands with which trade could be conducted. In the late Roman empire, both those factors were interrupted. The rise of other trade routes to the east via the Indian Ocean undercut the importance of the Black Sea, and the long period of demographic change on the Eurasian steppe altered the relationship with inland powers.

It was not until several centuries after the foundation of Constantinople that relative stability returned to the north. That was the situation that both intrigued and worried Constantine VII. Good relations with the now powerful political entities that encircled the sea were critical not only because these groups had the ability to attack the imperial capital, as they had done on many occasions, but also because valuable supplies flowed along the cross-sea route: grains from the western and northwestern coasts, hides and other products from the steppe, furs from the northern forests, slaves from the Caucasus. The complex systems that linked the imperial capital and the various seacoasts can be seen in the Byzantines' relations with four political and economic powers from different periods: the Khazars, Rhos, Bulgars, and Turks.

For some three hundred years, from roughly the seventh until the tenth century, the Khazar state north and east of the sea was one of the most significant players in the international politics and economy of the Black Sea zone. The origins of the Khazars are uncertain, but their domain seems to have been centered on the plains north of the Caucasus mountains, touching both the Black and Caspian seas. They were the stuff of legend to Persian and Arab writers; ancient invasions were attributed to them, and like the Scythians and Sarmatians of antiquity, their name was sometimes used as an epithet for all the peoples north of the Caucasus.

The Khazar ruler, or khagan, once reported to a Spanish correspondent that his people were descended from Japheth, one of the sons of Noah, a mythical lineage also claimed by other peoples of the Caucasus and elsewhere. However, the Khazars were probably of Turkic origin—hence, one of the common names used by Byzantine writers: *Tourkoi*—and perhaps spoke a language akin to those of later Pecheneg, Cuman, and Tatar peoples of the steppe.

The Khazars grew powerful by serving as middlemen in the trade between central Asia and the west, a precursor of the commercial explosion along the same route in the Middle Ages. They held sway over the entire territory from the Volga river to Crimea and opened a trade link between the Caspian and the Black Sea. Their cities along the Volga and Don were major emporia where merchants from across Europe and Eurasia met to exchange salt, wax, fur, leather, honey, and slaves. The Arab traveler Ibn Fadlan, who visited the Khazar domains in the early tenth century, met bands of tattooed Norsemen who had rowed and portaged down river routes all the way from the Baltic Sea in order to trade there.[19]

Byzantines and Khazars had an inconstant relationship. They sometimes cooperated against Arabs, Persians, and Pechenegs, but Constantine VII advised his heir to forge strategic alliances with other powers as a hedge against Khazar ambition. Constantine had reason to be wary, for in the past the Khazars had sometimes interfered in Byzantine domestic politics, aiding one faction or another in the numerous succession struggles that plagued the empire. In 695 the emperor Justinian II was dispatched from his throne by a rival claimant, who also paid him the indignity of cutting off his nose and banishing him to Chersonesus, a city then under Khazar influence. Justinian made the most of his exile, however. He hatched a plan to attack Constantinople and looked to his Khazar hosts for support. He took the khagan's sister as a wife and received the city of Phanagoria as a dowry. With foreign help, he wrested the Byzantine throne from the usurper. His Khazar wife, baptized and christened Theodora, became the first foreign-born empress of Byzantium. Theodora's conversion was no great leap, though, for the Khazars were known for their supreme tolerance of other faiths. This pragmatism in spiritual affairs led them in an unlikely direction, toward the adoption of Judaism as the state religion.

The Khazars had a straightforward story about how they came to be Jews. In the distant past, the khagan Bulan, wishing to take on formal religious training, summoned learned men from among the Byzantines, Arabs, and Jews, and asked them to debate the relative merits of their faiths. Not surprisingly, the debate turned into a shouting match. Exasperated, Bulan asked the Christian and Muslim sages which of the two other religions was preferable. Both agreed that, forced to choose, they would prefer Judaism. That settled things as far as the khagan was concerned. Bulan announced that the Khazars, or at least their leaders, were now to become Jews, and he had himself circumcised to prove the point. The tale is surely apocryphal; medieval Slavic chroniclers would tell a similar story about how their forebears came to be Christians. But the Khazars do seem to have adopted Judaism at some point in the mid-700s. News of the conversion drew Jews from across the Byzantine and Arab lands, and scholars from Constantinople and Baghdad arrived to instruct the Khazar nobility in the faith.

This new Eurasian Jewish empire was widely known in the early Middle Ages, a real-world precursor of the fantastic kingdom of Prester John that would attract Christian adventurers to the east some time later. Most of what we know about the Khazars' conversion, in fact, comes from the correspondence of a Khazar khagan with a rabbi of Cordoba (itself perhaps apocryphal). Yet religious flourishing accompanied political decline. Within a few centuries, the empire had vanished altogether, leaving little physical evidence of its ever having existed. Its memory, however, lingered. The Caspian—the *bahr al-Khazar* to the Arabs and the *Hazer Denizi* to the Turks—preserved the Khazar name, and when Mediterranean seamen set sail for Crimea in the Middle Ages, they were heading for a peninsula they still called "Gazaria."[20]

The Khazar empire fell victim to new powers north of the sea. Periodic battles with the nomadic Pechenegs weakened their cities. More importantly, the expanding principalities of the Rhos in the forested north and along the river courses of the steppe zone looked jealously on Khazar control of the Volga and Caspian. By the late 900s, the Rhos had captured the major Khazar fortresses north of the Caucasus and rolled back Khazar power from around the Sea of Azov.

As with the Pechenegs and the Khazars, Constantine VII also warned his son about the Rhos. They lived north of the Pechenegs, sometimes raiding with them, sometimes being raided by them, but they generally strove to keep peace with the nomads, since the commerce in cattle, horses, and sheep was one of the mainstays of their economy. They also frequently traveled down the rivers toward the sea and sailed on to Constantinople. Laden with goods, their ships were always easy prey for Pecheneg raiders, especially when they had to portage over the rapids on the Dnepr or offload onto larger ships at the river mouths.[21] Sometimes large parties of Rhos launched their own raids across the sea. They attacked Constantinople in 860, an expedition reminiscent of the coming of the Goths several centuries earlier. According to one surely incredible account, the Rhos fixed wheels to their fleet of 2,000 ships and sailed across the open plains west of the city to frighten the Byzantine garrison on the walls.[22] They returned repeatedly, without the wheels and in smaller numbers, over the next two centuries.

The Rhos who made their way across the sea were perhaps a branch of the same Norse traders whom Ibn Fadlan had earlier found doing business with the Khazars on the lower Volga. Later Slavic chroniclers cast them as foreign princes invited to govern the fractious Slavs in the Dnepr river basin, but a gradual transformation is more likely. Norse traders originally floated down the northern river routes from the Baltic, and over time trading outposts sprang up to service these periodic visits. These, in turn, developed into permanent cities, either founded by the Norsemen themselves or taken over from the local Slavs. Eventually, these bands of armed Norse merchants came to adopt the language and customs of their Slavic subordinates. In the ninth century, Norse princes captured the city of Kiev, then a tributary of the Khazars. When Byzantine writers looked out on this growing power in the north, they used a variety of names for these new settlers—Scythians, Sarmatians, Varangians, even Hyperboreans—but the name that stuck was *Rhosoi*, the people from a land far beyond the northern seacoast that the Byzantines came to call *Rhosia*.

In the ninth and tenth centuries, the Rhos made major forays along both the northern and southern coasts, perhaps using the same Viking longboats that appeared at nearly the same time along the shores of Britain. As one Byzantine writer lamented, they

[spread] devastation from the Propontis [Sea of Marmara] and, overrunning the whole coastland, reached the native city of the Saint [modern Amasra, Turkey]; they pitilessly killed those of both sexes and all ages, giving no mercy to old men nor sparing children; but raising their blood-stained arms against all, they hastened to make ruin as far as they could.[23]

The relationship with the Byzantines was not always so conflictual, however, for the empire recognized early on that the princes of the north could be both an important partner as well as a useful ally against other enemies. For two centuries or more, river routes carried furs, amber, wax, and slaves between the Baltic Sea and Constantinople. Kiev, the greatest of the princely cities of Rhosia, or Rus' to the Slavs, flourished as an entrepôt on the Dnepr route. The relationship between Norsemen and Byzantines became so close that, in the tenth century, a corps of Norse mercenaries joined the Byzantine army, eventually forming the core of the emperor's household guard. The most famous of their number, one Harald Sigurdsson, would finish his life as King Harald III of Norway, the last Viking invader of Britain, felled by a Saxon arrow at the battle of Stamford Bridge in 1066.

The princes of the Rhos grew powerful from the trade with Byzantium and were so much a presence on the sea route linking the Dnepr estuary to the Bosphorus that some contemporary Arab geographers labeled the Black Sea the *bahr al-Rus*, as if the Rhos, not the Byzantines, were the real sovereigns of the sea. The Rhos could even at times dictate the terms of the relationship with their trading partner. In the late tenth century, Vladimir, prince of Kiev, demanded a sister of the emperor Basil II in marriage. He was initially promised Basil's sister Anna, but when the emperor seemed to go back on his word, Vladimir sacked Chersonesus. The emperor finally agreed to the marriage, on the condition that Vladimir convert to Christianity, so in 988 the prince had himself baptized and gained Anna in return. In one go, the Kievans were conjoined with the Byzantine royal house and also brought into the universal church. Christianity had already drifted up the northern rivers before Vladimir's conversion, but the baptism opened the way to numerous Byzantine influences—of alphabet, music, art, and architecture—that would shape the culture of the Kievan state and eventually of medieval Russia as well. Although now sealed by a dynastic marriage, the direct relationship between Byzantium and Kiev proved to be shortlived. In the eleventh and twelfth centuries, the coming of yet another nomadic people, the Cumans, cut off links between the northern cities and the coast, and trade diminished. For the Byzantines, the end of the profitable alliance meant that the northern coast slipped forever out of their grasp.

At the time, however, Basil II's link with the prince of Kiev was supremely fortunate, for the mercenaries whom the Kievans provided were crucial to a series of spectacular military victories during his reign. Those campaigns would also give the emperor his unusual epithet—*bulgaroktonos*, the Bulgar-Slayer.

The Bulgars had once been allies of the Byzantines, another of the many relationships forged on the edge of the empire, and at various times they had been critical in Byzantine domestic politics as well. In fact, when Justinian II returned to Constantinople with his Khazar wife in tow, he owed his resumption of power to the Bulgars. His father-in-law, the Khazar khagan, had been bought off by the reigning Byzantine emperor and had agreed to assassinate Justinian before he could attack Constantinople. Theodora warned Justinian of the plot, and the two escaped across the sea from Phanagoria to the Danube. There, Justinian found a far warmer welcome than he had experienced among his Khazar in-laws in the east. His new hosts, the Bulgars, provided the troops that allowed him to return in triumph to the imperial palace.

In Justinian II's day, the early eighth century, the Bulgars were a relatively recent appearance on the edge of the Byzantine empire, but like the Khazars, they were already of critical importance in the empire's foreign and domestic affairs, as their intervention in favor of Justinian showed. The original Bulgar homeland lay far to the east, up the Volga river, an area that cartographers were still showing as "Great Bulgaria" as late as the eighteenth century. The Khazars and Bulgars were probably closely related; their origin myths had them descended from the same son of Noah, and the Bulgar lands on the Volga were very early absorbed into the Khazar khaganate.

As part of the great westward steppe migrations, the Bulgars appeared in strength on the Danube in the late 600s. Under their chieftain, or khan, Asparukh, they crossed the river and subjugated the Slavic population to the south. Their arrival so troubled the Byzantines that Constantinople agreed to pay tribute to Asparukh and his successors and recognized their control of the lands between the Danube and the Balkan mountain range. When the Byzantines refused to pay up, war was often the result, usually with the Bulgars coming out on top. After one major victory, the khan Krum converted the skull of the Byzantine emperor Nicephorus into a chalice. What the Byzantines were unable to do by force of arms they hoped to achieve by the Gospel. The Bulgars were converted to Christianity in the ninth century and remained on the Byzantine side during the great schism that split eastern and western Christendom in 1054. By this stage, the Bulgars had lost most of the nomadic and Turkic traits of the past; they had gradually been assimilated to the Slavic language of the local population.

But a common religion failed to ease relations with Constantinople. Until nearly the end of the Byzantine empire, dealing with the Bulgar problem was a mainstay of Constantinople's foreign policy. In the tenth century, the Bulgar empire under Simeon—who now took the title of "Tsar of All the Bulgars and Greeks"—was perhaps the most powerful state in eastern Europe, and its capital, at Preslav, was said to rival Constantinople in its magnificence. The first empire fell to Basil the Bulgar-Slayer, whose Norse mercenaries helped rout the Bulgar troops. The chronicles recorded that Basil blinded ninety-nine of every hundred prisoners, leaving one sighted captain to lead the rest back to the Bulgar encampment. The Bulgar empire was then annexed by Byzantium, the first time in centuries that Constantinople had controlled most of the Balkan peninsula. But that arrangement, too, eventually broke down. A resurgent Bulgar empire emerged a century and a half later. This second empire, with its new capital at Turnovo, stretched at its height in the thirteenth century from modern Albania to the Black Sea. However, with the expansion of other Balkan kingdoms, such as medieval Serbia, it too would soon disappear.

Christianity had been a powerful tool of statecraft for Byzantine emperors in their relations with the Rhos and the Bulgars. Conversion did not always prevent conflict, of course, but from the Byzantine perspective it certainly meant that conflict was of a different type—something closer to a civil war within the bounds of Christendom than a battle across the lines between believer and infidel. If a neighboring people or state could not be brought into the empire or into a firm alliance, the next best thing was to bring them within the bounds of the church.

The situation was rather different in Anatolia, however. Although it formed the backyard of the empire itself, Anatolia had long been a place where languages, peoples, and religions were mixed: speakers of Greek, Armenian, Arabic, Caucasian, and Syriac languages, Christians and Muslims, heterodox and orthodox. But the arrival of a new group—Turkoman nomads—fundamentally altered political and social relations.

Although their original grazing lands lay on the central Asian steppe, the Turkomans began to press up against the eastern frontiers of the Byzantine empire in the eleventh century. They were nominally under the authority of the Great Seljuk empire centered in Baghdad, but as with all nomadic peoples, they were rarely under anyone's direct political control. Fearing for the safety of his own empire, the Seljuk sultan encouraged the Turkomans to push toward the west, goading them on with tales of grazing lands in central Anatolia and the prospect of plunder in the Byzantine towns and cities. In 1071 the Seljuks defeated the Byzantines at the battle of Manzikert in eastern Anatolia, a military victory that effectively opened the door to large-scale Turkoman migration all the way to the Aegean.

Over the next two centuries, Anatolia experienced the same slow migration of Turkic peoples that had earlier taken place on the steppeland to the north. Political control gradually passed from the Byzantines to a variety of local emirs drawn from the Turkoman hordes. Some had become settled or semi-nomadic and lived in an uneasy relationship with Byzantine peasants and urban centers. Warfare was frequent, yet it was usually sparked not by religious animosity between the Muslim emirs and the Christian emperor in Constantinople, but rather by local communities vying for grazing rights and by nomadic raiding on outlying farmsteads and larger settlements. Moreover, the two sides in these disputes were rarely the same from year to year. Local Byzantine aristocrats, even rival dynastic factions in Constantinople, frequently called on various emirs to assist them in the numerous civil conflicts that racked the empire.

The overlordship of the Great Seljuks ended with the coming of the Mongols in the thirteenth century. The Mongol invasion disrupted the Seljuk imperial system and sparked a new westward migration by still further groups of Turkoman nomads. The result was a new array of Turkoman emirates and confederations and the extension of their power to the coastal areas of the Black Sea. The Akkoyunlu ("white sheep") Turkomans held eastern Anatolia and western Persia. The Seljuks of Rum—an emirate that combined the names of two of its neighbors, the Great Seljuks of Baghdad and the "Romans" of Constantinople—claimed much of central and southern Anatolia. The coastal areas, including the major ports such as Sinope and Trebizond, were at various stages under the direct control of these and other groups or paid protective tribute to them.

These political changes were accompanied by the slow transformation of social life across the region. Some Christians, especially those disconnected from ecclesiastical authority in urban centers, converted to Islam. Some Greek- or Armenian-speakers came to speak a Turkic language. Some Turkoman nomads became sedentary and Christian. Some, no doubt, came to speak what we would now call Greek or Armenian or Kurdish or Georgian. Other nomads remained pastoralists, moving their herds from pasture to pasture and, when times were difficult, raiding settled villages and towns now occupied by people who, only a few generations before, had probably lived lives not very different from their own.

The Turkomans would remain in place even after some of their number—the Ottomans of northwest Anatolia—had transformed themselves from frontier emirate into Islamic empire. Although most Turkoman nomads became settled during the centuries of Ottoman power, pastoralists of various sorts survived. They are still to be found across the Near East, from the Turkomans of northern Iraq to the Çepni people of the southeastern Black Sea coast, shepherds who move their flocks of sheep and goats to upland pastures in the summer, much as coastal herders did in the waning days of Byzantine power.

Emperors had long worried about the princes of the Rhos, the Christian kings of the Balkans and the Caucasus, and the array of nomads who periodically poured out of the northern steppe or from eastern Anatolia. Yet, in the end, it was none of these groups that eventually separated the Byzantines from the Black Sea. Rather, it was the Latin powers of the west, divided from the emperors in Constantinople by both religious affiliation and political allegiance, that proved to be the empire's real undoing.

Since the eleventh century, the rise of central European powers had threatened Byzantine interests in the west. Much of Italy was lost to the Normans, the Italian maritime states commanded the Mediterranean, and French, German, and papal forces conspired to weaken the empire's remaining holdings. The Crusades repeatedly brought all these powers to the gates of Constantinople itself, and it was only deft diplomacy—and strategic marriages—that prevented them from sacking the city every time they made their way to the Holy Land.

By the time of the Fourth Crusade, diplomacy was not enough. In 1199 an expeditionary force assembled in Italy and persuaded the doge of Venice, Enrico Dandolo, to assist in an operation against Egypt. He agreed, but the price was a full share of any conquests made along the way. In the years that it took to outfit the Crusaders, the target shifted. It was no longer to be the Muslim infidels, but rather the schismatics in Constantinople. The Venetians had fought periodic wars with the Byzantines, particularly over trading rights in the eastern Mediterranean, and a crusade against the heretical emperor was the opportunity to secure their dominance in the economic affairs of the east. After much discussion of how to divide the future spoils, in the spring of 1204 the Crusaders finally launched an attack on the city. It fell quickly.

Contemporary chroniclers called it a "cosmic cataclysm." The destruction was immense. The great church of the Haghia Sophia was desecrated. Icons were thrown into the sea. Nuns were raped and young monks sold into slavery. One of the Crusader generals, Baldwin of Flanders, was elevated to the imperial throne, and a Venetian was made patriarch of the church, now formally in union with Rome. Some Byzantine nobles fled across the Sea of Marmara to Nicaea and set up an empire-in-exile that soon attracted many of the Greek-speaking aristocracy, as well as the displaced church hierarchy. In the great carve up of the empire—the *Partitio Romaniae*, as it was called—Byzantium was divided among its Latin conquerors. Outposts of Byzantine influence remained among the exiles in Nicaea, among a rival family line at Trebizond (Trapezus), and in a small kingdom in Greece; but the empire as a whole, whittled down over the centuries, was no more.

The history of the Byzantine empire on the Black Sea came to a close in 1204. The Byzantines managed to retake Constantinople in 1261, ending the brief period of Latin dominance in the east. But the restored Byzantium was no more than an empire of the Straits, a relatively minor power hemmed in by other Christian kingdoms in the Balkans and the Caucasus and the Turkoman emirates in Anatolia. Its economy and foreign trade remained largely in the hands of the Italians. The Black Sea, a short sail up the Bosphorus, was now effectively beyond the horizon of imperial control. Yet the end of the Byzantine era also ushered in a period of unparalleled economic activity around the coastline, a time when the sea was as close as it has ever been to the heart of Europe.

Business in Gazaria

In the late 1200s, Marco Polo sailed from Trebizond to Constantinople on his return journey from many years at the court of the Mongol emperor, Kublai Khan. He barely mentions the voyage:

[W]e have not spoken to you of the Black Sea or the provinces that lie around it, although we ourselves have explored it thoroughly. I refrain from telling you this, because it seems to me that it would be tedious to recount what is neither needful nor useful and what is daily recounted by others. For there are so many who explore these waters and sail upon them every day—Venetians, Genoese, Pisans and many others who are constantly making this voyage—that everybody knows what is to be found there.[24]

Travel along that route had become so commonplace that he felt it too boring to be included, a quotidian commute from one cosmopolitan trading center to another.

By the time Marco Polo arrived, the Black Sea was already at the center of an economic network that extended from the mulberry groves of China to the silk houses of Marseilles, from the fairs of Novgorod and Kiev to the bazaars of Tabriz. It lay at the crossroads of major international highways. "Silk routes" wound from China though central Asia, across the Caspian to the Volga, then overland to the Don river and from there into the Sea of Azov and the ports of Crimea; or along a southern road, across central Asia and Persia, then through Armenia to the port of Trebizond. The rivers of the north carried traffic through Poland and Russia to the Baltic Sea, an ancient route that had once brought amber to the Mediterranean but now bore silk, fur, and animal hides to the growing cities of northern Europe. Manufactured goods, especially textiles, arrived from central Europe and then spread out across the Eurasian steppe. Cereals and spices flowed in the opposite direction, into central Europe or out through the Bosphorus to the Aegean.

What people called the sea reflected these trading relationships. Some early Arab maps labeled it the *bahr al-Tarabazunda*, the Sea of Trebizond, after the port where caravans unloaded after the trek across Anatolia from Persia. Poles named it the *mare Leoninum*, the Sea of Lwów, even though that landlocked commercial city lay hundreds of kilometers to the northwest, in Polish Galicia.[25] To a new influx of sailors and traders coming from the city-states of medieval Italy, it was simply *il mare Maggiore*—the Great Sea. A merchant could start his journey in Genoa or Venice, sail half way across the Mediterranean, through the Straits and over the Black Sea, and at the end of it share a glass of wine with another Italian, probably even someone he knew. If a European importer could bring his Chinese silk or Indian spices as far as the Black Sea, they were almost home. If an exporter could deliver his wine or cotton cloth there, it was as good as sold. As the commercial houses of the Middle Ages discovered, get your merchandise to the Black Sea and you could get it anywhere in the world.

In the centuries when Byzantium grew from a provincial colony into an imperial capital, the Italian coastal cities were also developing as major maritime centers. Venice emerged from a jumble of island villages to become a mercantile empire whose interests extended all across the eastern Mediterranean. The city's early trade in cured fish with the Italian mainland was gradually transformed, by the early Middle Ages, into near absolute control of the sea routes from Asia Minor and the Levant to the ports of southern Europe. Across the peninsula, Genoa and Pisa lacked the geographical advantages of Venice; they looked out to the poorer western Mediterranean rather than to the richer east. But their powerful navies, built out of necessity during a series of wars with Arab raiders, emerged as rivals to that of the Venetian republic.

Venice was once part of the Byzantine empire, professing loyalty to Constantinople in exchange for protection against rapacious princes on the mainland, but in time that relationship was inverted. The Venetian navy grew strong, a byproduct of the need to protect shipping lanes against Mediterranean pirates, just as Byzantine seafaring decayed. Soon, the Byzantines came to depend on Venice as a surrogate navy. Already in the ninth century, the Venetians were given privileged commercial rights in the empire in exchange for naval protection, including the defense of Constantinople against its multiple besiegers. That early connection grew into a virtual monopoly on the eastern trade during the Crusades. Popes and princes had plenty of zeal, but the doge of Venice had the money. The Venetians provided financing for weapons and provisions and transported Christian troops to the Holy Land. By then, the Venetians had more interest in plundering the Byzantine empire than in continuing to protect it, and when the Crusaders ravaged Constantinople in 1204, it was Venice that profited most. In the partition of the empire that followed, three-eighths of the Byzantine lands went to the Venetians, including the Aegean archipelago, northern Greece, and the coasts of the Black Sea. Overnight, the republic acquired an empire.

Genoa and Pisa managed to eke out some concessions from the Byzantines, even during the period of Venetian dominance. In the 1100s they were granted business quarters along the Golden Horn. But the *Partitio Romaniae* presented a unique opportunity. While Venice enjoyed the fruits of its new acquisitions, Genoa forged an alliance with the exiled Byzantine dynasty that controlled the reduced "empire" of Nicaea in northwest Anatolia. The investment in that relationship soon bore dividends. When the exiles recaptured Constantinople and ousted the Crusaders in 1261, Genoa was given the privileged status that Venice had once enjoyed. The Genoese moved into prime quarters in the Pera section of Constantinople, on the hills across the Golden Horn from the emperor's palace. All the ports of the empire, including those on the Black Sea, were fully opened to Genoese merchants.

The Venetians and Pisans were loath to accept these new arrangements, however. More than a century of warfare among the three city-states followed, including spectacular naval engagements in the Bosphorus itself. The outcome was the destruction of Pisa as a major maritime power, the ascendancy of the Venetians in the eastern Mediterranean, and an uneasy condominium between

Venetian and Genoese merchants in the Black Sea. The old Greek colony of Tanais on the Don river, now called Tana by the Italians, became the Venetian doorway to the east and the terminus of the overland route from China and central Asia. Yet, in the race to profit from the Black Sea trade routes, Genoa was the real successor to the Miletus of antiquity. By the end of the 1200s, the Genoese had created a virtual empire of their own within that of the restored Byzantines. From the heights of Pera, the governor of the Genoese community, the *podestà*, could look out on a commercial dominion unrivalled in wealth and geographic extent. "The sea," wrote a Byzantine chronicler, "belongs to them alone."[26]

The entry of Italian commerce into the Black Sea revived the cities around the coast. Some had lain dormant throughout the period of the great movement of peoples across the northern steppe, while a few, such as Chersonesus, had weathered the period as a remote outpost of Byzantine influence on a tense frontier. By the late 1200s, however, the Black Sea was ringed with active port cities, many built on top of the former Greek colonies and now taking advantage of their position as entryways to the wealth of the east.

Most ships could go from Constantinople to Trebizond in a few weeks, including stops along the way to trade or take on supplies; with very favorable weather, the trip could be made in under a week if necessary.[27] From there, a ship could dart across to Crimea, anchoring at the old Greek port at Theodosia (renamed Caffa by the Italians), then continue into the Sea of Azov and on to Tana, the jumping off point for the overland portage to the Volga and then on to the Caspian Sea. All the way along the Black Sea coastline, the Genoese were dominant, both in commerce as well as in the local administration. Permanent Genoese consuls resided at Sinope and Trebizond, Sevastopolis (modern Sukhumi, Georgia) in the east, and Licostomo and Maurocastro at the mouths of the Danube and Dnestr, as well as in Caffa. The Venetians were present as well, especially at Tana and Soldaia (modern Sudak, Ukraine), but their supremacy in the eastern Mediterranean always meant that the Black Sea was of secondary interest to them.

Any visitor to these emporiums, especially those along the Crimean coast, would have encountered bustling workshops and markets filled with traders from across the known world. A dozen languages could be heard on the paved streets, with hawkers hashing out deals in a patois of Greek and Italian dialects. Bells from Franciscan and Dominican monasteries pealed the hours, competing with the Islamic call to prayer or the chants of Orthodox and Armenian priests. Townspeople and merchants crowded the audience hall of the consul's palace, seeking redress or hounding the notary to give his imprimatur to a contract. Caravans of camels and packhorses wound through the city gates and down to the harbor. Merchants from southern Europe—Italians, Catalans, and others—met growing numbers of Muslims and Jews, as well as a new rush of Orthodox Christians from the Peloponnese and the Aegean archipelago, some living permanently in the cities, others only wintering there before the return to the Mediterranean.

Several registers of Genoese notaries from this period are extant, and they give a remarkable picture of the diversity of trade among the seaports as well as the melange of people engaged in it. In April 1289, Guglielmo Vesano sold one-third interest in a transport ship, the *Mugetto*, to Vivaldino Laugerio. In May, Manuele Negrone sold to Mazzo di Campo and Obertino d'Albenga a thirty-year-old slave named Venali, originally taken into servitude on the Caucasus coast. In June, the Catholic Giacommo di Ghisulfo, acting as agent for Guglielmo di Saluzzo, received from the Muslim Kemal Takmadji a sum of money in payment for a shipment of cattle hides traded to him by Hassan, a Muslim from Syria then resident in Caffa. In April 1290, the Armenians Perra, Vassili, and Priche, along with the Orthodox Christians Theodore and Costas, acknowledged that Vivaldo Lavaggio, commander of a galley fitted out by Argun, the Mongol khan of Tabriz, recovered and returned to them all the property taken by a pirate named Iurzuchi.[28] With such remarkable exchange among many different communities and all over considerable distances, it is no wonder that Marco Polo felt little need to describe the Black Sea in any detail.

Evidence of Europeans' knowledge of the sea is also easily seen in the colorful sailing charts, or *portolans*, produced mainly by Italians and Catalans. The charts, now prized by museums and private collectors, were drawn on vellum and rolled up into scrolls to be taken on sea voyages. They showed direction by reference to prevailing winds and gave an outline of the coast, with all the major and minor ports labeled. The geographical detail in these charts, most of which date from the thirteenth to the fifteenth centuries, is extraordinary. Sharp headlands project out into the sea, interspersed with semicircular indentations representing inlets and bays. The shape of the entire sea, the position of the headlands, the outlines of Crimea and the Sea of Azov are all broadly correct—geographical features that maps for centuries after the end of Italian dominance would get imaginatively wrong.

Administration of the seaports and the Genoese communities along the coastline was formally directed by the *Officium Gazariae* in Genoa—one of the places where the name of the mysterious Khazars survived—but the epicenter was at Caffa in Crimea. Caffa had an elected senate and a civil bureaucracy. The chief consul, appointed directly by Genoa, was even better paid than the *podestà* in Pera and was charged with collecting taxes, drawing up a communal budget, and provisioning militias and appointing consuls in most other Black Sea ports.[29] The consul's administration oversaw the construction of imposing defenses, a wall of brick and stone interrupted by defensive towers and surrounded by a ditch.[30] The city's sweeping crescent-shaped bay held a herd of fat-bottomed long-distance ships, as well as feluccas and other small coasting craft imported from the Mediterranean. The great Arab traveler Ibn Battuta recorded that it held about 200 "ships of war and trading vessels, small and large." He saw many seaports in his life, but as far as he was concerned it was "one of the most notable harbors in the world."[31]

Another traveler, Pero Tafur of Cordoba, sailed into the harbor at Caffa on a clear day in the late 1430s. He had crossed over from Trebizond, a city that he had been happy to see melt into the haze. Trebizond, the ancient Trapezus, was governed by its own emperor, he said, who was a rival to the Byzantines, and Genoese and Venetian merchants were active there. But what had soured him on the southern port was his discovery that the emperor had married off his daughter to a local Muslim chieftain. What the men of Cordoba had died to keep from the Moor, Tafur must have felt, the men of Trebizond now freely offered to the Turkoman. Caffa, or at least a part of it, seemed closer to civilization. The city's governor greeted him warmly and personally saw to his needs. The inn where he was housed was satisfactory and the friars in the Franciscan monastery he visited pleasant. "The city is very large, as large as Seville, or larger, with twice as many inhabitants, Christians and Catholics as well as Greeks [Orthodox Christians], and all the nations of the world." Ships arrived daily from distant ports, he said, and the passengers' comings and goings filled the streets with a cacophony of languages. Spices, gold, pearls, precious stones, rich Russian furs, and slaves were bought and sold, and at prices that were often unbelievably low. He even bought several slaves himself, a form of charity, he reckoned, to prevent their falling into the hands of impious Muslims.[32]

For all the vitality of Caffa and the other cities that he visited, Tafur's final judgment was not positive. They were livable enough, for Oriental towns anyway, but none quite came up to the standard he had expected after hearing stories about the opulence of the east that circulated in Spain. It was so cold in winter that ships froze fast in the harbors, he said, and the hinterland was as inaccessible as India. The food was generally inedible, and most of the people in the marketplaces were bestial. The Franciscans and a few refined merchants struggled to provide a modicum of order, but it was not an easy project. "Certainly, if it were not for the Genoese who are there, it would not appear that the people have any lot with us"—Catholic Europeans, that is—"since there are so many different nationalities, so many ways of dressing and eating, and such diversity in the usage of women." A virgin, it was said, could be had for a measure of wine, a shameful exchange that he confirmed by having one himself.[33]

Tafur theorized that the inhabitants of the Crimean ports were probably civilized enough when they arrived from Italy—scions of the best families could be found residing there—but they had been gradually deformed by their association with the tribes of the interior, especially the Asiatic Tatars. Most of the inland areas in the north were controlled by Tatar chieftains, who had swept into the region as part of the Mongol invasion of the thirteenth century. The Italians at first negotiated the right to set up quarters in the coastal cities but then gradually expanded their control over the suburbs as well. Some Tatars lived among the Italians inside the city walls, but that did not prevent others from periodically holding the cities under siege. Whenever one or another khan became dissatisfied with his tribute, a swarm of armed Tatars would appear at the gates. It was only thanks to the superior weapons of the city militias—crossbows, cannon, and muskets—that the ports escaped the Tatars' depredations. Sometimes even that was not enough. More than once, the Italians had to rebuild their homes and businesses almost from scratch.

Tafur shared the anti-Muslim prejudice common to many Catholic European visitors to the Black Sea ports, at least those whose main concern was exotic travel, not living and conducting business there. He had been scandalized by the close associations between the Christian authorities in Trebizond and the Muslim emirs of Anatolia, and he was equally disconcerted by the way in which the Tatars mingled with Christians in the Crimean cities. But as with so many outsiders who visited the Black Sea coast, Tafur missed a crucial dimension of social relations there: It was to these Tatars—or rather to the vast Mongol empire of which they were originally a part—that the Italians owed much of their commercial success.

Pax Mongolica

The Mongols were the last of the great westward migrations from central Asia. Their move into the Black Sea region was fueled in part by the desire for conquest, in part by the natural peregrinations of a nomadic population that, like Eurasian pastoralists from centuries before, trailed along behind endless herds of horses, cattle, and sheep. The mass of these nomads were actually Turkic in origin, hence the name usually applied to them by contemporary observers— Tatars or, in an older spelling, "Tartars," a label that would come to apply to all the Mongol successors north of the sea—but their warrior class was perhaps dominated by men with roots in Mongolia. Like the Scythians of antiquity, however, they shared a single, broad pan-Eurasian culture and style of life common to speakers of a variety of different languages.

Under Chingis Khan, the Tatar–Mongol dominions expanded rapidly, stretching at the great khan's death in 1227 from the coasts of China to the

Black Sea. His successors moved even farther afield, ending the dominance of the Cumans on the Black Sea steppe, striking into Poland and Hungary, and subduing Persia and the Caucasus. The appearance of the Tatar–Mongol horsemen on the plains north of the sea worried the statesmen of Europe. News of the plunder of cities and the murder of their inhabitants swept before their cavalry, who seemed able to overcome even the best-fortified cities far into central Europe. Popes and princes called for new crusades against the infidels who had sacked Kiev, Cracow, and Budapest and now exacted heavy tribute from their new clients.

Chroniclers and later historians would look back on the period of Tatar–Mongol dominance as a dark night of Oriental despotism; the consonance between "Tatar" and "Tartarus," the Hell of classical mythology, was not lost on medieval commentators. But for a good part of the Middle Ages, the so-called Tatar yoke was, in fact, as much about enrichment as servitude. The two centuries or so of relative stability that followed the initial westward migration provided the political backdrop against which the commerce of the Near East, including that of the Italians in the Black Sea, flourished. Before, the Black Sea steppe and the cities along the northern littoral had been subject to a shifting set of overlords. Slavic princes competed with one another and with a variety of Turkic chieftains. Stability, when it was achieved, was more often the result of a careful balancing of interests and, as the Byzantine emperors had long understood, that balance could be upset as soon as a new group of nomads from the east arrived on the scene.

In the thirteenth and fourteenth centuries, however, the sea lay at the meeting point of two stable powers born of the Tatar–Mongol conquests: in the north the Golden Horde and in the south the Ilkhans, Mongol rulers who controlled Persia from their capital at Tabriz. A Catholic, Orthodox, or Armenian merchant could travel from one great Near Eastern trading city to the next—from Tabriz in northwestern Persia to Trebizond on the Black Sea to Tana on the Don river—and never venture beyond the realm of one of the descendants of Chingis Khan. Friar William of Rubruck, sent on a diplomatic mission to the Tatars by Louis IX of France, looked out across the sea from Soldaia and understood the extent of their power:

Towards the south stands the city of Trebizond, which has its own governor..., who is of the lineage of the emperors of Constantinople, and is subject to the Tartars. Next is Synopolis [Sinope], the city of the Sultan of Turkey, who likewise is in subjection unto them. All the land from the mouth of the Tanais [Don] westward as far as the Danube is under their subjection.[34]

For a merchant, trying to include the Black Sea as part of any eastward itinerary also made economic sense. A roundabout journey by sea from Constantinople to

Trebizond and then by caravan to Persia took a third of the time of a direct overland trip across Anatolia,[35] and the possibility of a storm at sea was always preferable to the certainty of impassable roads and highwaymen.

The leaders of the Tatar–Mongol empire were skilled warriors, to be sure, but they welcomed commercial or political relationships that might be to their advantage. Travelers such as Friar William and Marco Polo marveled at the sophistication of the Tatar–Mongol administration. Even subordinate khans, scattered across Eurasia, maintained a staff of interpreters who could translate the letters of friendship that came from western kings. In the Middle Ages, there were few places more cosmopolitan than the mobile tent city of a Tatar lord. When Friar William crossed the Don river and came upon the tents of Sartak, one of the great-grandsons of Chingis, he was surprised to find a Nestorian Christian serving as chief of protocol and a member of the Knights Templar regaling the crowd with his recent adventures in Cyprus. Farther east, at the seat of Sartak's grandfather, the Great Khan Mangu, he found a Parisian goldsmith; a Christian from Damascus; a French woman from Lorraine who had married a Russian carpenter in the service of the court; ambassadors from Baghdad, India, and the Seljuk Turks; and a hair-shirted Armenian monk intent on converting Mangu to Christianity.[36]

Before the era of Tatar–Mongol supremacy, it was rare to find Europeans on the northern steppe. The hinterland was dangerous, and the few intrepid travelers who attempted a journey had to resort to ingenious methods of ensuring their safety. In 1235 an ambitious company of four Dominican friars set out from Budapest to discover the ancient homeland of the Hungarians—thought to lie along the Volga river—and to convert their pagan cousins to Christianity. They floated down the Danube, then across the Black Sea and up the Don. All was well so long as they were on water, but the land journey to the Volga was fraught with peril. Cuman chieftains waged war on one another. Marauders roamed the steppe. Caravans and traveling partners were few.

As their stock of food dwindled and their purses grew light, they hit upon a novel idea. Two would voluntarily sell themselves into slavery so that the remaining two could have enough money to buy provisions, pay off robbers, and continue their proselytizing mission. The plan failed. After a few solicitations, the friars found that none had sufficient skills to attract a buyer; the most they could muster was a facility for carving wooden spoons. In the end, three turned back, leaving one valiant brother, Julian, to continue eastward. He never found his proto-Hungarian brethren, but he did find civilization. Somewhere along the Volga he came across a detachment of cavalry, a scouting party of the Great Khan, and was astounded to find that the party's interpreter spoke six languages, including German and Hungarian.[37]

Within a few decades, the sense of order represented by that cavalry unit spread all across the Black Sea. The commercial route that linked the sea to the plains of central Asia was so well-traveled that medieval Italians could read about it in guidebooks. Francesco Pegolotti, a Florentine banker, set down his advice for businessmen making their way east in a book, *The Practice of Commerce*, written in the early 1300s. The journey was not for the fainthearted, of course—it could take more than nine months to go from Tana to China, and Pegolotti advised that traders should allow their beards to grow long, in order not to broadcast their foreignness to shysters—but the travails of Brother Julian and his associates were now uncommon. "The route leading from Tana to Cathay is very secure both day and night," he wrote, and the detachments of armed cavalry that one could expect to meet along the way were a sign of the safe passage guaranteed across the Tatar–Mongol domains.[38]

For all their cosmopolitan connections, the Tatar–Mongols were at base a mobile society, composed mainly of shepherds and herders who migrated with their animals down toward the sea in the winter and north in the summer. They glided over the steppe with their yurts set on top of wheeled carts, the driver standing in the door and steering the oxen teams that labored before it.[39] Some time after Pegolotti, another merchant, Josafa Barbaro, climbed onto the walls of Tana and recorded his impressions of nomads on the move:

First, herds of horses by the [hundreds]. After them followed herds of camels and oxen, and after them herds of small beasts, which endured for the space of six days, that as far as we might see with our eyes, the plain every way was full of people and beasts following on their way.... We stood on the walls (for we kept the gates shut), and in the evening we were weary of looking.[40]

The sight and, even more, the sound—the squeal of solid wood wheels turning on axletrees, audible even over the horizon—would have been familiar to a traveler a millennium earlier.

The *pax mongolica* allowed commerce and contacts to flourish for a time during the Middle Ages. It set the stage for Europe's commercial take-off and piqued the interest of European explorers in finding a sea route to China. However, the rivalries among the successors of Chingis meant that the *pax* was often less than entirely pacific. Already by the mid-1300s, the Tatar–Mongol empire was little more than a loose system of often hostile appanages, each seeking to profit by raiding the flocks of the other. The Golden Horde fell victim to internal intrigues. Rival khans from the east, including the ambitious Tamerlane, briefly exerted their control and then left behind even more disorganization than before. A Chinese dynasty, the Ming, sloughed off Mongol control in 1368 and soon invaded Mongolia itself. The route to China was closed.

The height of long-distance commerce via the Black Sea port cities was thus relatively brief, probably peaking in the first half of the fourteenth century. Political disruptions among the neighboring Tatars and the growth of oceanic routes to the east diminished the importance of Tana and Caffa as international entrepôts. Yet even this limited period produced a free movement of peoples back and forth across the steppe and from one end of the sea to the other that had not been seen since the days of Greek colonization and the Roman imperium. Movement, however, had a price, for it opened the door to an unappealing newcomer, one that any European visitor to the Black Sea ports would have known only too well.

The Ship from Caffa

The populations of the Genoese and Venetian colonies were never primarily Italian. Caffa, for example, was perhaps only one-fifth Italian at its height.[41] Greeks—a general label that westerners used for all Orthodox Christians, including Greek-speakers from the Aegean and Anatolia, as well as people whom we would now call Romanians, Serbs, Ukrainians, and others—were represented in sizeable numbers, as were other Christians such as Armenians. There were also growing communities of Muslims, another general social category that included Tatars from the north shore, various peoples from the north Caucasus, Turks from Anatolia, and Arabs from the Levant.

For all the cooperation that must have existed in business transactions and transport, relations among these groups were not always congenial. There is a rough-and-tumble quality to any port city, and those on the Black Sea were no exception. Disputes over a slight, a transaction, or a woman, fueled by sweet Georgian or Crimean wine, sometimes turned violent. So it happened in Tana in the sultry summer of 1343.

A Venetian merchant, Andreolo Civrano, is said to have scuffled with a local Muslim, Omar. The subject of their dispute went unrecorded, but Omar ended up dead.[42] As news of his murder spread, Tatars within the town lashed out at Venetians, Florentines, Genoese, and Catalans—all the Franks, as Catholic Europeans were called—burning businesses and lodgings and threatening the stores near the port. The local Tatar khan, hearing of the merchant's death, blocked river traffic at the mouth of the Don and ordered revenge on Italian settlements as far away as Crimea.

Word of the crisis eventually reached Venice, and the republic moved to repair the damage and reopen the route up the Don. The Senate voted to banish

Civrano and to send a diplomatic mission overland to Tana to try to mend fences. The Genoese, however, were less enthusiastic about appeasement. They had dealt with the mercurial Tatars before—the Tatars had razed Caffa at the beginning of the century—and they were convinced that a show of force, not accommodation, would put the matter to rest. The Genoese consul in Caffa bucked up his Venetian counterpart, and in a rare moment of cooperation the two Italian communities pooled their resources, steeled themselves behind the walls of Caffa, and prepared to hold out against the inevitable Tatar assault.

It came the next year. As usual the Genoese were able to deploy an impressive array of weaponry against the khan's forces, and their control of the sea meant that the city could be easily provisioned. Shipping went on steadily throughout the summers of 1344 and 1345, despite the Tatar control of the overland routes to the center of the peninsula and along the coast. The Tatars, more accustomed to quick raids than to multi-year sieges, grew weary. A strange disease had also been working its way through the ranks of the khan's troops, a dispensation from God, the Genoese reckoned. But as his soldiers faltered, the khan decided that they could be of better use to him dead than alive.

He ordered his commanders to load the bodies of the deceased men onto catapults and to fling them over the walls into the city. The tactic worked for a while. A few residents of Caffa became ill, sprouting the same painful carbuncles that had appeared earlier on the Tatar soldiers, and expired in agonized throes. But the Geneose organized a brigade to toss the bodies into the sea as soon as they plopped from the sky. That seemed to stem the disease's spread. In time, the khan tired of the siege, just as the Genoese consul had predicted. A peace was hammered out, and the Venetians were able to return to Tana.

That was not the end, however. The very seaway that brought provisions from Constantinople during the siege now carried a darker cargo on the return voyages. Gabriele de' Mussi, an Italian notary, claimed to have been on board one of the ships that sailed from Caffa in the summer of 1347. That is doubtful, but his story of the journey from Caffa to the Mediterranean is probably based on the accounts of those who were. He reported that sailors fell mysteriously ill during the journey, and wherever they docked along the way—in Constantinople later in the summer, in Sicily in the early autumn, in Genoa by January 1348—the disease quickly jumped from the port into the heart of the city. The same deadly ailment that had afflicted the Tatar troops was now working its way along sea lanes back to Italy itself. Little more than a skeleton crew struggled ashore when de' Mussi's ship reached Genoa. "Confess, O Genoa, what you have done," he wrote. "We reach our homes; our kindred and our neighbors come from all parts to visit us. Woe to us, for we cast at them the darts of death! While we spoke to them, while they embraced us and kissed us, we scattered the poison from our lips."[43]

By the end of the century, the Black Death claimed as many as twenty-five million people, perhaps a quarter or more of Europe's population. The plague had been seen long before, of course. Diseases with similar symptoms—suppurated lesions, swollen glands or buboes (whence "bubonic"), followed by an excruciating and inevitable death in a matter of days—were known to the Romans. But it was the great openness of trade and maritime contacts that eased the disease's leap from Eurasia to the west, an expansion from the urban centers around the Black Sea to the growing towns and cities of medieval Europe. "The epidemic which then raged in northern Scythia," lamented the Byzantine emperor John VI Cantacuzenus, "invaded not only Pontus...but almost the entire universe."[44] Globalization, even the kind built on camel caravans and wood-hulled ships, has its victims.

Empire of the Comneni

When the Byzantine empire was torn apart at the hands of the participants in the Fourth Crusade, there were at least four major claimants to the title of successor to the new Rome. There was the Crusader empire itself, which commanded Constantinople but had little in common with the imperial traditions and practices of the Greek emperors whom it had deposed. A new empire was proclaimed in northern Greece, but it was rather quickly snuffed out. In Nicaea rival families of former Byzantine emperors bided their time, awaiting the opportunity to return to the city and reclaim the throne. And far to the east, another deposed dynasty, the Comneni, proclaimed their own empire centered in the ancient port of Trebizond. In 1261 the Nicene emperors returned to Constantinople and ousted the Latins; an alliance with the Genoese provided security for the restored emperor in exchange for trading privileges in the new empire. That dynasty, the Paleologi, would hold the city until the coming of the Ottomans. But even after the triumph of the Paleologi, the Comneni of Trebizond maintained their own separate state in the eastern Black Sea, a state that would keep the heritage of Byzantium alive even after the fall of Constantinople itself to the Ottomans. In fact, for the last two and a half centuries of the existence of the Byzantine empire, it was Trebizond—not Constantinople—that was the real imperial capital of the Black Sea.

The Comneni had originally reigned as emperors in Constantinople, beginning in 1057, and while on the throne they were one of the wealthiest and most illustrious of Byzantine dynasties. But in the two decades preceding the Fourth Crusade, they had fallen on hard times. A palace coup pushed them from power in 1185 and installed a rival family; many of the leading lights of the Comneni dynasty were brutally murdered. The two infant sons of the last Comnenus emperor, Alexius and David, were spirited away to the Caucasus, where they were taken in by the Georgian queen Tamar. There had long been a close relationship between the Byzantine and Georgian royal houses, with military pacts sealed by marriage, and the Comneni and the Bagrationi, the Georgian dynasty to which Tamar belonged, had enjoyed especially intimate ties. The queen, in fact, was probably the aunt of the two Comneni infants.[45]

The relationship with Georgian royalty was fortunate for the Comneni, not only because it almost certainly saved the family from total extinction but also because, at the time, Georgia was perhaps the most powerful state in the region. Some time earlier, King David II (the Restorer, reigned 1089–1125) had united the territories of inland Georgia and the coastal areas of Abkhazia under a single, Christian crown. As one of David's descendants, Tamar (reigned 1184–1213) built on that success and ruled during a period celebrated as the golden age of the medieval Georgian kingdom. She further extended the boundaries of the state, forged alliances with neighboring princes, and built a kingdom that was arguably the strongest economic and military power from the Balkans to the Caspian— far more significant, in fact, than any of the mini-empires created after the Byzantine partition of 1204. It was under her tutelage that the two exiled Comneni sons grew to maturity, perhaps speaking Georgian as well as Greek, reared in the sumptuous surroundings of Tamar's palace.

Little is known about why the two brothers, in their twenties at the time of the fall of Constantinople to the Latins, came to possess the city of Trebizond; but it may well have been that their aunt simply handed it to them. Tamar had been in a feud with the reigning Byzantine emperor, Alexius III Angelus, over his seizure of a sizeable donation she had made to the monks on Mount Athos. In the turmoil of the Latin invasion, she may have found it an opportune time to seize Trebizond, the emperor's easternmost port, as recompense.[46] In any case, in the spring of 1204, an army under the command of Alexius and David marched overland from Georgia and claimed the city as their own. There was probably not much of a fight; the city had long enjoyed a certain autonomy from Constantinople, and even Byzantine holdings across the sea—the port of Chersonesus and other parts of Crimea— were probably by this stage more dependent on Trebizond, particularly as a trading partner, than on the weak imperial administration in Constantinople. When the Comneni marched into the city, they thus laid hold not only to the city itself but to its cross-sea dependencies in Crimea as well.

The younger brother, David, continued along the coast, taking ports as far west as Heraclea Pontica and threatening the territory of the empire of Nicaea, even perhaps dreaming of a march on the Crusaders in Constantinople. David's adventure to the west, however, led to his own death in battle and the end of the expansion of his dynasty's domains. Thus, by around 1214 the borders of the new empire of Trebizond, now ruled by Alexius alone, ran from west of Sinope all the way to Georgia. Over this stretch of coastline and the Crimean dependencies— roughly the old Pontic kingdom of Mithridates—Alexius's successors took the title of "Emperor and Autocrat of All the East, the Iberians [i.e., the southwest Caucasus], and the Overseas Lands [in Crimea]." So central was the dynasty itself to the identity of this new state that the emperor was often called simply *Megas Komnenos*—the Grand Comnenus.

As with most imperial titles, that of the Grand Comneni was exaggerated. For a time, Trebizond may have paid tribute to the Georgians, and already by the end of Alexius's reign, the Crimean lands in the north had begun to slip out of Trebizond's control; Tatars and Italians would soon dominate there. But within their restricted parameters, both political and geographic, the Grand Comneni created a state that represented to many outsiders the apex of grandeur, an intriguing and almost mythical mixture of the decadent splendor of the Orient and the otherworldly piety of the Christian churches of the east. At its height, from the 1220s to the 1330s, the empire of Trebizond maintained diplomatic relations with all the major powers of the Near East and many in Europe; the emperor even received an embassy from the English king Edward I.[47] The city was well-placed to take advantage of the overland trade with Persia, and although the natural harbor was less than ideal, the emperors allowed Italian merchants to construct port facilities in the eastern suburbs.

As the historian Anthony Bryer has noted, most travelers who visited Trebizond arrived first by sea, and the sight that awaited them would have been magnificent.[48] The city would have been obscured by headlands until the ship was almost upon it. First, the bell tower of one of the city's major churches, dedicated to the Holy Wisdom, could be seen on the western outskirts, sitting on a plateau above the sea. Farther along, the city itself would come into view, a cluster of buildings placed on top of a series of dark gray escarpments, cut by deep ravines running toward the water, with the wall of the Pontic Alps behind. Gardens, vineyards, and orchards covered the city's slopes. Wooden bridges carried people across the ravines and inside the city walls, where a cluster of wooden houses pushed up against the citadel and the gold-hued imperial palace of the Comneni. The emperors had built a mole for ships where the lower city met the sea, but a commercial traveler would continue on around to the eastern suburbs. There, the Genoese and Venetians had built docks and warehouses around a small bay. In this lively commercial center, the traveler would find workshops and shipping companies, a crowded bazaar, inns for overland caravans, and a collection of churches and shrines kept by Armenians, Catholics, and others.

For travelers who set out to explore the city and its environs, even more wonders awaited. There was the church of the Holy Wisdom, the Haghia Sophia, far smaller than its sister in Constantinople but impressive nonetheless, with its separate bell tower and radiant frescoes.[49] The palace of the Comneni, situated in the upper part of the city, had floors of white marble and colonnaded halls covered by lofty golden domes painted with stars; the walls were decorated with portraits of former emperors and interpretations of their exploits.[50] Farther inland were a series of famous monasteries, enriched by the endowments of land and tax privileges granted by the Comneni. One in particular, the monastery of Soumela, was a favorite site of pilgrimage. A religious aerie carved into the side of a mountain and often shrouded in mist from the dense alpine forest below, it was by tradition founded in the tenth century and housed the famous icon of the Panaghia Atheniotissa, one of only a few icons said to have been painted by St. Luke.[51]

The Comneni enjoyed the longest uninterrupted reign of any dynasty of the Byzantine era. The splendor of their court impressed countless envoys from Europe, who came to establish trade links and diplomatic relations with the emperor, or simply to meet this curious potentate ruling at the edge of Christendom. Ruy González de Clavijo, an ambassador of the Spanish king, visited Trebizond in the spring of 1404 and met the Grand Comnenus Manuel III, who received him dressed in beautiful imperial robes, wearing a tall hat trimmed with marten fur and topped with a great plume of crane feathers.[52] Both the opulence of the court and the longevity of the dynasty, however, rested on two particular characteristics of the Trapezuntine state that, from a modern perspective, seem strangely at odds.

First, Trebizond was, far more than the multilingual and multi-religious population ruled by the emperors in Constantinople, a largely Greek state, that is, a state whose culture was built on the Greek-speaking imperial traditions of the old Byzantium, even though it was a culture which the Comneni knew as "Roman." (Neither the Comnenus emperors nor their subjects would ever have used the term "Hellenic" to describe themselves or their language and culture.) The heartland of the empire lay not in the city itself but inland, in the lush valleys that run up from the seacoast toward the mountains beyond. This region, known as the Matzouka (Maçka in modern Turkish), was situated directly on the caravan route between Trebizond and Tabriz. Its peasant population was dispersed in an array of small hamlets and farming communities, raising livestock and growing wheat for export to the coast. The great landowning monasteries of the region, such as Soumela, provided not only a stable administrative order, but also helped preserve a sense of cultural identity among the peasant population, an identity rooted in the traditions of the old Hellenistic east but transformed by the introduction of Christianity and sustained contact with the other peoples and cultures of Anatolia. The Matzouka was the only major area around the Black Sea where something approaching a continuous line of Greek-speaking settlement can be traced from antiquity to the twentieth century. In the late Middle Ages, Greek-speaking Christians formed nearly 90 percent of the population in the inland valleys south of Trebizond; by 1920 they were still around three-quarters.[53] It was only in the deportations that followed the Greek–Turkish war of the 1920s that this population would be virtually eliminated.

The other feature—and the one which accounted more than anything else for the political and economic success of the Comneni—was the empire's close relationship with the Muslim emirs of Anatolia. The land that lay on the other side of the Pontic mountains had been inhabited since the eleventh century by an array of Turkic peoples, some nomadic and some settled in the major cities. It was perhaps ironic, at least from a modern point of view, that the most "Greek" of the Byzantine regional powers was at the same time the closest to the people of the interior, people whom we would today call Turks; but for the Comneni, and indeed for most other political leaders, the gulf between Christian and Muslim was one that could be easily bridged. If there was some advantage, political, military, or economic, to be gained from a dynastic marriage, the Comneni were ready to oblige. That, in fact, was what the strict Catholic Pero Tafur had found so disconcerting when he visited the city on his way to Crimea in the early fifteenth century.

The interconnections with the Turkomans of Anatolia, and by extension with other Muslims such as the Ilkhanids and the Golden Horde, were so great as to make many of the dynastic lines indistinguishable. For example, under the longest-reigning Comnenus emperor, Alexius III (1349–90), the empire of Trebizond was locked into a system of political marriages that reached all across the Near East. One of the emperor's sisters was married to Kutlubeg, chief of the Akkoyunlu Turkomans. Another sister was married to a different Turkoman emir, Haci-Omar, and Alexius's daughter was given to Haci-Omar's son, Süleyman. Two other daughters were married to the emir of Erzurum and the emir of Limnia; after the latter's death, that daughter was in turn given to John V Paleologus, emperor of Byzantium. Still further daughters were wed to Kara Yuluk, the son of Kutlubeg (now Alexius's brother-in-law), and to Bagrat IV, the king of Georgia. Through those marriages, Alexius III became brother-in-law to two Turkoman emirs and father-in-law of four others, plus father-in-law of the emperor of Byzantium and the king of Georgia. Trebizond's most valuable export was undoubtedly its women.[54]

The reign of Alexius III marked the high point of Trebizond's fortunes. The complex system of dynastic marriages provided peace with the empire's neighbors and a stable of powerful in-laws on whom the emperor could call in the event of civil strife, such as an attempted coup or an uprising by Italian merchants (both reasonable worries). There was, however, another threat that Alexius had probably not foreseen, else he would no doubt have found another daughter to give away. It was the growing strength of another Muslim power, this one in the west, that would most concern the Trebizond emperors in the half century or so after Alexius's death.

Turchia

In the Middle Ages, where sailors went depended on when they went there. When the Italians first began their commerce in the Black Sea, they spoke of voyages to a land called "Romania"—that is, the empire of the new "Romans," with its seat at Constantinople. In the middle of the 1300s, however, "Romania" disappears from the records of Genoese and Venetian notaries. The Byzantine empire, of course, remained in existence for another century, but when sailors weighed anchor in the Adriatic, they were now heading for a place they knew as "Turchia."⁵⁵ Turkic peoples had long been a feature of the Black Sea littoral, from the Pechenegs of the middle Byzantine period to the Turkoman emirs of Anatolia and the Tatar–Mongols of the late empire. But by "Turchi" Italian sailors meant one group in particular, the people of the House of Osman, the Ottomans.

The traditional interpretation of the origins of the Ottoman empire stresses religion as the chief motivation for the remarkable growth of imperial power: Ottoman warriors were pushed forward by the strength of their Islamic faith, conquering lands not only for the glory of their sultan, but also to enlarge the domain of the faithful. The picture was far more complicated than that, however. The Ottomans were originally an unremarkable frontier dynasty, a combination of Turkoman nomads and Byzantine farmers, some perhaps converted to Islam, others still Christian, along with itinerant traders of various stripes, Muslim scholars and Greek, Armenian, and other townsmen—little different, in fact, from the mixed cultures of the other Turkoman frontier emirates across Anatolia. They spent as much time battling fellow Muslims as they did engaging in war with Christians, and in any case, the brand of Islam practiced by even the most observant was hardly the orthodox sort found in the great centers of medieval Islamic thought such as Damascus or Baghdad. Most importantly, no early Byzantine account ever mentions the Ottomans' alleged desire to conquer for their faith, even though the Byzantines themselves were the supposed targets of this religious fervor. The idea of warriors for Allah fighting the infidel is, in fact, a product of later Ottoman historians. Once the Ottomans acquired a real empire in the late 1300s and 1400s—with the conquest of the Balkans and finally of Constantinople—they had to manufacture a vision of their past that recast their heterodox nomadic ancestors as pious Muslims.[56] Later European historians simply accepted whole cloth the Ottomans' own propaganda.

The early Ottomans were different from other Turkoman emirates in one important respect, however, and that was geography. Their lands touched on the edge of the Byzantine empire, whittled down by the 1300s into little more than the area around Constantinople and the Straits. The Ottoman domains were situated just to the east, in the ancient region of Bithynia. That location gave them access to productive farmland and relatively wealthy towns, which could be raided when food and other resources provided by the pastoralists ran low. But it also meant that the Ottomans were, over the course of several generations, in intimate contact with Greek-speaking Christian communities nominally under the suzerainty of the Byzantines. In time, that relationship became one of cooperation. The Ottoman sultans provided some degree of order in a region that had long been plagued by political instability, and even for the emperors in Constantinople, the Ottomans were preferable to the western powers—Crusaders and Balkan kings— who constantly threatened to snuff out completely the remnants of Rome. In the early 1300s, twin processes were thus at work in the eastern borderlands of Byzantium: the slow transformation of the followers of the eponymous founder of the emirate, Osman, from nomadic raiders into settled landlords governing the outlying reaches of the weak Byzantine state; and the absorption of Byzantine peasants and townsmen into the emerging Ottoman cultural and political system—nominally Islamic but tolerant of other faiths, a mix of settled agriculture and pastoralism, constantly on guard against threats to its power.

Throughout the fourteenth century, the Ottomans rapidly expanded their realm. They took over the old frontier regions of the Seljuks of Rum and began to launch summer expeditions against the principalities and kingdoms across the Sea of Marmara in Thrace and the southern Balkans, often in alliance with the emperors in Constantinople, who were eager to fend off the troublesome rulers of Serbia and Bulgaria. Where the Ottomans succeeded, they did so not because of their ruthlessness or religious fanaticism—the two traits that would come to define the "Ottoman yoke" in the minds of many Europeans—but because of their consummate political skill. In fact, none of the great battles of the fourteenth century, including the famous encounter at Kosovo field in June 1389, involved only Muslims on one side and only Christians on the other— much less, anachronistic ethnonational categories such as "Turks," "Greeks," and "Serbs," words that simply did not mean the same thing in the Middle Ages that they mean today. Rather, they were contests between rival political alliances that cut across lines of language, ethnicity, religion, and even kinship. The royal houses of virtually every regional power from central Europe to central Asia were, at some level, commingled. In fact, the eventual conqueror of Constantinople, Sultan Mehmet II, actually had a reasonable claim to the Byzantine throne: He was the product of multiple marriages between Byzantine princesses and Ottoman sultans that stretched back more than a century.[57]

In the early fifteenth century, the emergence of another powerful but short-lived conqueror, the Mongol khan Tamerlane, reversed the Ottoman conquests in Anatolia and returned the region to the system of small emirates that had existed before the expansion of Ottoman power. But that setback also shifted the sultanate's center of gravity to the west. The Ottomans moved their capital from Bursa to Adrianople in Thrace (modern Edirne, Turkey), and in the very architecture of the city it is possible to see the rapid transformation of the Ottomans from imitators of the Seljuks to a modern empire in their own right. In the three spectacular mosques in the city center are arrayed three different architectural styles, each one defining different stages in the emergence of Ottoman imperial consciousness. The square proportions and low domes of the Eski Cami, built in 1414, are typical of the styles that the Ottomans inherited from the Seljuks of Rum. Just across the square, the Üçşerefeli Cami (1447), with the three balconies on one of its minarets (from which the mosque takes its name), is evidence of the Ottomans' having incorporated the building techniques and architectural tastes of the Byzantines. No longer are the multiple domes set low on top of supporting walls; now, a single massive dome reaches skyward, supported by a tall drum, as in the Haghia Sophia in Constantinople. And on the northeast side of the central square stands the magnificent complex of the Selimiye Camii (1575), the finest achievement of the master Ottoman architect Sinan, completed almost a century after Adrianople had yielded the title of imperial capital to Constantinople. Its soaring minarets, symmetrical design, spacious interior, and beautifully placed outbuildings mark the golden age of the Ottomans as empire-builders.

It was only a few decades from the time the Ottomans marched into Adrianople to their final assault on Constantinople. It was not that relations between the Byzantines and the Ottomans had necessarily turned sour. Rather, the Byzantines had simply become irrelevant as Ottoman allies. Not only could the Ottomans field an army far larger than that of the Byzantines, an army drawn from all the peoples of the Balkans and Anatolia, but they had begun to develop a significant naval capacity as well. After Tamerlane's death in 1405, the Ottomans reasserted their control over Anatolia, including the littoral areas of the Aegean and the Sea of Marmara. In these areas, the Ottomans took on the seafaring traditions of the coastal communities who now came under their suzerainty, a mixture of people whom we would now label Greeks and Italians, Christians and Muslims, perhaps some former Turkoman nomads who had taken to the sea, or Greek-speakers who had adopted Islam, or any combination of the above.

By the early 1400s, the Ottomans were able to put their own navy to sea. They set up an arsenal at Gallipoli and made use of the experience of the seaboard communities in the Aegean to construct ships. Soon, the Ottoman navy exerted control over Italian possessions in the Aegean, including strategic islands from which it could launch further assaults. That growing naval capacity turned out to be critical in the conquest of Constantinople, a long-standing goal of Ottoman strategists. From their arsenal at Gallipoli, the Ottomans commanded the Dardanelles, and already in the 1390s they had constructed a fortress up the Bosphorus from Constantinople to restrict access to the Black Sea. A second fortress across the strait, built in 1452, ensured complete control, so that Ottoman ships could sail through both straits unmolested by the weak Byzantines.

In the spring of 1453, the noose tightened. Sultan Mehmet II ordered his army to march out of Thrace and toward Constantinople. His ships, now sitting in the Bosphorus, made an attempt to occupy the harbor, but the Byzantines relied on the old technique of the floating chain and repelled them. The sultan then ordered the ships lifted onto carts, wheeled up over the highlands north of the city, and slipped into the Golden Horn, well inside the chain. With the harbor filled with Ottoman vessels and enemy soldiers pouring through a breach in the city walls, the Byzantines were soon overcome. Mehmet II entered the city in triumph on May 29. He gave the city over to his soldiers for looting, but a special decree mandated that no shipwrights were to be harmed. They were now to be employed in the service of the sultan's own navy, one that would soon make its first major foray into the Black Sea.[58]

An Ambassador from the East

Even after the fall of Constantinople, the emperors of Trebizond remained in place, now the last Byzantine dynasty still occupying a throne. For political leaders in Europe, that fact was of some interest. Not only did the Comneni have the legitimacy of a respected imperial dynasty, but their geographical location—behind the backs of the Ottomans—placed them in an important strategic position. Not long after Mehmet II's conquest, European powers devised plans for a new crusade to retake the city with the help of the Comneni. The fate of that plan and one of its chief proponents, a certain Ludovico da Bologna, are ample testimony of how little the Western world knew of the peoples around the sea— or, more accurately, how much had been forgotten since the apogee of Mediterranean commercial contact a century or so earlier. For a brief moment in the 1460s, Ludovico held European leaders enthralled by a grand scheme for wresting Constantinople from its Muslim conquerors.[59]

Little is known about Ludovico's early career, but he seems to have made a name for himself as an expert on the Christian kingdoms of the east. He may have traveled as far as India and Ethiopia as an ambassador of Florence, and in any case, he seems to have been knowledgeable enough to have been appointed papal legate to all the eastern Christians—Orthodox, Armenians, Maronites, Georgians, and the Comneni of Trebizond—in the 1450s. Whether he actually made a trip to these far-flung regions is uncertain, but he claimed to have done so, for in 1460 he returned to Europe and presented himself as spokesman for Oriental Christendom. He even brought along a collection of eastern ambassadors to plead with the pope and European kings for making a crusade against the Ottomans.

Ludovico's troupe met first with the Holy Roman Emperor, Frederick III, whom they convinced to raise a crusader army. They then moved on to Venice, Florence, Rome, and Paris. At each stop, the ambassadors would regale the court with tales of the Christians' antipathy to the Ottomans and their desire to join forces with the kings of the west to rid Constantinople of the Muslims.

As the embassy wended its way across Europe, Ludovico's hosts grew more and more dubious about the strange array of representatives whom he placed before them. Ludovico had a tendency to overplay his hand. In his earliest audiences, he presented six ambassadors from the east, including representatives of the king and princes of Georgia. Contemporary accounts of these meetings recorded one of the ambassadors variously as Custopa, Costopa, Custoda, Chastodines, and Cossodan—a result perhaps of the chroniclers' idiosyncratic spellings or of Ludovico's own imaginative renderings of his real name. By the time they reached Italy, another person had joined the group, one Michele degli Alighieri, who claimed to be not only a descendant of Dante but also the ambassador of the Grand Comnenus himself, David of Trebizond. When the group arrived in Rome, they had added two more envoys: an ambassador of Cilician Armenia, who wore a huge cloak and pointed hat and carried a remarkable assortment of musical instruments, and another ambassador from the Akkoyunlu Turkomans—both of whom looked strangely similar to the people who had previously been introduced as ambassadors of the Georgians.

Crowds flocked to see this strange assemblage, and at each stop the royal courts were obliged to provide food, lodging, and gifts from public funds.

Ludovico himself received praise and endowments from the European rulers. Pope Pius II named him patriarch of Antioch. Encouraged by these successes, Ludovico added still more ambassadors to his retinue, and by the time they arrived in France, the group had become practiced in the art of wowing the crowds. The ambassadors would begin by revealing their unusual haircuts— which bore some resemblance to the distinctive tonsures of Franciscan friars— while the Armenian ambassador played lively tunes on his musical instruments. When they came to Paris in May 1461, the group had even added an ambassador of Prester John, the fanciful Christian monarch whose kingdom was said to lie, in various versions, beyond the Caspian or in central Asia or India or China. After securing commitments of troops and support, Ludovico's group returned to Rome for a final meeting with the pope.

By this stage, Pius II had become suspicious. The "ambassadors" seemed to be having far too good a time at public expense, satisfying their voracious appetites and offering fawning praise to European monarchs, with little real concern for the military cause that they had earlier espoused. When the group finally arrived in Italy in August 1461, Pius II moved to stop the charade. He refused to grant Ludovico his credentials as patriarch of Antioch and arranged to have him and his associates arrested as imposters. Ludovico affirmed his good faith but quickly escaped Rome before Pius II could act. The embassy was dissolved. Ludovico's name pops up in various texts until the late fifteenth century, when nothing is heard of him again.

"In matters carried on from a distance," wrote Pius II after his last meeting with Ludovico, "there is abundant opportunity for deception and the truth can seldom be discovered."[60] What was the real purpose of Ludovico's mission? Probably business. He might have reckoned that helping to remove the Ottomans would lead to trade privileges for the Florentines, with whom he had connections, much as Genoese assistance to the Byzantines in 1261 had allowed them to take over from the Venetians. Ludovico would then have been in a favorable position to profit from the new power relationships in the region. That was perhaps also the reason for his contact with Michele degli Alighieri, probably a Florentine merchant who was seeking to establish trade ties with the Comneni of Trebizond.[61] The assortment of "ambassadors" may actually have been Franciscan missionaries in the Christian east, lured into Ludovico's scheme by the prospect of claiming Constantinople for the Catholics. When he began his journey, Ludovico had every reason to believe that the plan would work; his personal interests seemed to match perfectly with the interests of European powers in allying with Trebizond and the Turkoman emirs against the Ottoman threat. But as his journey across Europe continued, his chances of either making money or sparking a new crusade were quickly diminishing.

In the spring of 1461, Sultan Mehmet II began assembling his fleet, perhaps as many as 300 ships, some newly constructed, some requisitioned Italian vessels, and organizing his army for a new campaign. In March he left his palace in Adrianople and headed east, crossing over into Anatolia and meeting up with the main army column there. The army first marched on Sinope, which it easily took from the Turkoman overlord who controlled it. The fleet then hugged the coast and sailed farther east while the army marched across Anatolia and then turned north toward the sea.

In the late summer, with the fleet sitting off the headland, Mehmet ordered his infantry down out of the mountains and toward Trebizond. In a pouring rain on August 15—two centuries to the day after the Byzantines had removed the Crusaders from Constantinople—the emperor of Trebizond surrendered to the sultan without a shot's being fired. Although he could not have known it at the time, when Ludovico traipsed into Rome in the late summer of 1461, attempting to rally the pope's support for an alliance with the Grand Comnenus, the last remnant of Byzantium was already in Ottoman hands.

NOTES

1. Procopius, *Wars*, 7.29.16.
2. Herodotus, *Histories*, 4.144.
3. See Hélène Ahrweiler, "Byzantine Concepts of the Foreigner: The Case of the Nomads," in Hélène Ahrweiler and Angeliki E. Laiou (eds.) *Studies on the Internal Diaspora of the Byzantine Empire* (Washington: Dumbarton Oaks Research Library and Collection, 1998), pp. 1–15.
4. Walter Goffart, "Rome, Constantinople, and the Barbarians," *American Historical Review*, Vol. 86, No. 2 (April 1981):284.
5. Maurice, *Treatise on Strategy*, 11.2, quoted in Michael Maas (ed.) *Readings in Late Antiquity* (London: Routledge, 2000), p. 328.
6. Herodotus, *Histories*, 4.110–117.
7. Josafa Barbaro, *Travels of Barbaro*, in Josafa Barbaro and Ambrogio Contarini, *Travels to Tana and Persia*, trans. William Thomas and S. A. Roy (London: Hakluyt Society, 1873), p. 30.
8. Procopius, *Wars*, 8.5.31–33.
9. Procopius, *Buildings*, 3.7.1–10.
10. Constantine VII Porphyrogenitus, *De administrando imperio*, trans. R. J. H. Jenkins, new rev. edn. (Washington: Dumbarton Oaks Center for Byzantine Studies, 1967), pp. 6, 53.

11. Speros Vryonis, Jr., *The Decline of Medieval Hellenism in Asia Minor and the Process of Islamization from the Eleventh Through the Fifteenth Century* (Berkeley: University of California Press, 1971), p. 17.

12. Constantine VII Porphyrogenitus, *De administrando imperio*, 7.

13. Constantine VII Porphyrogenitus, *De administrando imperio*, 13.

14. Lionel Casson, *Ships and Seamanship in the Ancient World*, rev. edn. (Baltimore: Johns Hopkins University Press, 1995), pp. 148–51.

15. J. R. Partington, *A History of Greek Fire and Gunpowder* (Baltimore: Johns Hopkins University Press, 1999), p. 15.

16. Alexander Alexandrovich Vasiliev, *Byzance et les Arabes*, eds. Henri Grégoire and Marius Canard, Vol. 2, Part 2 (Brussels: Editions de l'Institut de philologie et d'histoire orientales et slaves, 1950), p. 150.

17. Peter Simon Pallas, *Travels Through the Southern Provinces of the Russian Empire, in the Years 1793 and 1794*, Vol. 2 (London: T. N. Longman and O. Rees et al., 1802–3), pp. 290, 297.

18. Robert Browning, "The City and the Sea," in Speros Vryonis, Jr. (ed.) *The Greeks and the Sea* (New Rochelle, NY: Aristide D. Caratzas, 1993), pp. 98–9.

19. Ahmad Ibn Fadlan, *Puteshestvie Akhmeda Ibn-Fadlana na reku Itil' i priniatie v Bulgarii Islama*, ed. Sultan Shamsi (Mocow: Mifi-Servis, 1992).

20. Links between the Khazars and later Turkic-speaking communities of Jewish "Karaites" in Crimea are almost certainly spurious. For a view sympathetic to the Khazar–Karaite kinship theory, see Arthur Koestler, *The Thirteenth Tribe: The Khazar Empire and Its Heritage* (New York: Random House, 1976). For a scholarly refutation, see Zvi Ankori, *Karaites in Byzantium: The Formative Years, 970–1100* (New York: AMS Press, 1968).

21. Constantine VII Porphyrogenitus, *De administrando imperio*, 4.

22. *Povest' vremennykh let*, quoted in Basil Dmytryshyn (ed.) *Medieval Russia: A Source Book, 850–1700* (Gulf Breeze, FL: Academic International Press, 2000), p. 10.

23. Quoted in Alexander Alexandrovich Vasiliev, *The Goths in the Crimea* (Cambridge, MA: Mediaeval Academy of America, 1936), pp. 111–12.

24. Marco Polo, *The Travels of Marco Polo*, trans. Ronald Latham (Harmondsworth: Penguin, 1958), p. 344.

25. Gheorghe Ioan Brătianu, *La mer Noire: Des origines à la conquête ottomane* (Munich: Romanian Academic Society, 1969), pp. 44–5.

26. Quoted in Michel Balard, *La Romanie génoise (XIIe–début du XVe siècle)*, Vol. 2 (Rome: Ecole Française de Rome, 1978), p. 501.

27. G. I. Brătianu, *Recherches sur le commerce génois dan la Mer Noire au XIIIe siècle* (Paris: Librairie Orientaliste Paul Geuthner, 1929), p. 157.

28. See G. I. Brătianu, *Actes des notaires génois de Péra et de Caffa de la fin du treizième siècle (1281–1290)* (Bucharest: Cultura Naţională, 1927).

29. Balard, *La Romanie génoise*, Vol. 1, pp. 142, 373.

30. Pero Tafur, *Travels and Adventures, 1435–1439*, trans. Malcolm Letts (New York: Harper and Brothers, 1926), p. 133.

31. Ibn Battuta, *Travels in Asia and Africa, 1325–1354*, trans. H. A. R. Gibb (New York: Robert M. McBride and Co., 1929), p. 143.

32. Tafur, *Travels and Adventures*, pp. 132, 134–5.

33. Tafur, *Travels and Adventures*, pp. 134, 137.

34. *The Journal of Friar William of Rubruck*, in Manuel Komroff (ed.) *Contemporaries of Marco Polo* (New York: Dorset Press, 1989), p. 55.

35. Anthony Bryer and David Winfield, *The Byzantine Monuments and Topography of the Pontos*, Vol. 1 (Washington: Dumbarton Oaks Research Library and Collection, 1985), p. 18.

36. *The Journal of Friar William of Rubruck*, pp. 88, 134–6.

37. Brătianu, *La mer Noire*, p. 230.

38. Francesco Balducci Pegolotti, *La pratica della mercatura*, Allen Evans (ed.) (Cambridge, MA: Mediaeval Academy of America, 1936), pp. 21–2.

39. *The Journal of Friar William of Rubruck*, p. 59.

40. Josafa Barbaro, *Travels of Barbaro*, in *Travels to Tana and Persia*, trans. William Thomas and S. A. Roy (London: Hakluyt Society, 1873), pp. 11–12.

41. Gilles Veinstein, "From the Italians to the Ottomans: The Case of the Northern Black Sea Coast in the Sixteenth Century," *Mediterranean Historical Review*, Vol. 1, No. 2 (December 1986):223.

42. Brătianu, *La mer Noire*, pp. 243–4.

43. Gabriele de' Mussi, *Ystoria de morbo seu mortalitate qui fuit a. 1348*, quoted in Francis Aidan Gasquet, *The Black Death of 1348 and 1349*, 2nd edn. (London: George Bell and Sons, 1908), p. 20.

44. Quoted in Gasquet, *The Black Death*, p. 12.

45. Alexander Alexandrovich Vasiliev, "The Foundation of the Empire of Trebizond (1204–1222)," *Speculum*, Vol. 11, No. 1 (January 1936):7–8.

46. Vasiliev, "The Foundation," p. 19.

47. William Miller, *Trebizond: The Last Greek Empire of the Byzantine Era, 1204–1461*, new enlarged edn. (Chicago: Argonaut, 1969), p. 31.

48. This description is based on the vivid picture painted in Bryer and Winfield, *The Byzantine Monuments*, Vol. 1, pp. 178–9.

49. The church was transformed into a mosque in the 1880s and the frescoes plastered over. Although the images were damaged when the walls were hacked to allow the plaster to stick, they nevertheless represent one of the greatest treasures of Byzantine-era frescoes anywhere. A full-scale restoration effort began in the late 1950s. See David Talbot Rice (ed.) *The Church of Haghia Sophia of Trebizond* (Edinburgh: Edinburgh University Press, 1968).

50. Bryer and Winfield, *The Byzantine Monuments*, Vol. 1, pp. 185–6.

51. The monastery has unfortunately long been allowed to decay, but an ambitious restoration program, supported by the Turkish government, began in 2000.

52. Ruy González de Clavijo, *Embassy to Tamerlane, 1403–1406*, trans. Guy Le Strange (London: George Routledge and Sons, 1928), pp. 111–13.

53. Bryer and Winfield, *The Byzantine Monuments*, Vol. 1, p. 251.

54. Miller, *Trebizond*, p. 69.

55. Balard, *La Romanie génoise*, Vol. 1, p. 6.

56. On this point, see Rudi Paul Lindner, *Nomads and Ottomans in Medieval Anatolia* (Bloomington: Research Institute for Inner Asian Studies, Indiana University, 1983).

57. Anthony Bryer, "Greek Historians on the Turks: The Case of the First Byzantine–Ottoman Marriage," in his *Peoples and Settlement in Anatolia and the Caucasus, 800–1900* (London: Variorum Reprints, 1988), p. 481.

58. George Makris, "Ships," in Angeliki E. Laiou (ed.) *The Economic History of Byzantium: From the Seventh Through the Fifteenth Century*, Vol. 1 (Washington: Dumbarton Oaks, 2002), p. 99.

59. This account of Ludovico is based on Anthony Bryer, "Ludovico da Bologna and the Georgian and Anatolian Embassy of 1460–1461," in his *The Empire of Trebizond and the Pontos* (London: Variorum Reprints, 1980), chapter 10.

60. Quoted in Bryer, "Ludovico da Bologna," p. 195.

61. Bryer, "Ludovico da Bologna," p. 186.

Faithful friend, if you have understanding,
Know that the mariner's art is a difficult one.
For these seas resemble an enemy's muteness;
Their storms remind one of his bitterness.

Pirî Reis, Ottoman admiral and cartographer, 1525

[Istanbul] holds an absolute dominion over the Black Sea. By one door only, namely by the Bosporus, it shuts up its communication with any other part of the world; for no ship can pass this sea, if the port thinks it fit to dispute its passage.... For this reason all foreign nations, if they want to entitle themselves to any prosperity in the immense wealth of the Black Sea, and all seaport and island towns, are obliged to court the friendship of this city.

Pierre Gilles, French ambassador to the Ottoman sultan, 1561

[T]he storm began to buffet us most unmercifully, nothing but thunder and lightning, hail and torrents of rain pouring down on us for three days and nights.... Of the passengers, some were vomiting, some praying, some vowing victims and sacrifices, some alms and pilgrimages....[T]he ship now touched the highest heavens, and now descended into the deepest of hells....I swore never to try the navigation of the Black Sea any more.

Evliya Çelebi, Ottoman traveler, 1684

4
Kara Deniz, 1500–1700

In rather short order after the conquest of Constantinople and Trebizond, the Ottomans took control of the major ports and fortresses around the sea: Caffa, the other Crimean ports, and Tana on the Don river in 1475; Anapa on the Caucasus coast in 1479; Maurocastro on the Dnestr and Licostomo on the Danube in 1484. It took longer to subdue the inland powers—the Christian rulers of the south Caucasus and the principality of Moldova, as well as the Muslim khan of Crimea—but by the early sixteenth century, they had all come to recognize the suzerainty of the Ottoman sultan. Within less than a century after the fall of Constantinople, the Ottomans could claim the sea as theirs.

Never before had an imperial power been able to dominate the entire littoral and much of the lands beyond. The navies and commercial vessels of most foreign powers were prevented from entering the Straits, and regional trade, previously dominated by the Italian city-states, now came under the hand of the sultan. Commercial routes were redirected so that merchandise passed through "Constantine's city" (as the former Byzantine capital was still called, even under Muslim rule) where it could be taxed or used to feed the burgeoning urban population. The sea and its products became the possession of the Ottoman state, a source of revenue that successive sultans guarded jealously. As a French ambassador reported, given a choice between admitting foreign ships and throwing open the doors of his harem, the sultan would probably have chosen the latter.[1]

Ottoman hegemony on the Black Sea lasted for three hundred years, from the rolling conquests of the late fifteenth century until the opening of the sea to European commerce in the late eighteenth century. Because of the strictures on the entry of foreign vessels, European diplomats in this period, as well as later historians, often termed the sea a "Turkish lake." The picture was far more complicated than that, however. The Ottoman empire strongly regulated exports from the Black Sea region, particularly grain, a strategic food source; but restrictions on foreign ships were put in place only gradually and enforced haphazardly, and even then only once the Ottomans began to feel threatened by the growing naval might of major European powers.[2]

Moreover, even though the Ottomans had been able to extend their power much farther around the sea than had their Byzantine predecessors, that power usually rested on striking deals with local potentates. Vassalage, not outright conquest, was the preferred method of dealing with the hinterlands. The Ottomans depended on stable commercial relationships with the northern coast, and force was usually too blunt an instrument of foreign policy if the goal was to encourage business. Of course, the sultans resorted to sword and cannon when necessary. Summer was the season of war, and most years saw Ottoman armies embark on long marches to correct one or another contumacious client or counter a threat from the preeminent powers of central and eastern Europe: Poland, Hungary, and later Russia. But until relatively late in the period of Ottoman control, the arts of diplomacy—enticing, tricking, persuading, and cajoling—were far more productive than outright war.

In terms of the political economy of the region, the great shift in the Ottoman centuries was the transformation of trade from primarily the enterprise of individual profit-seeking merchants to an activity taxed and regulated by the Ottoman state. The Byzantines had certainly attempted to control traffic through the Straits; there was no shortage of complaints from foreign shippers about the venality of Byzantine tax officials. But from the beginning of the thirteenth century, they had ceded their foreign commerce, and a good deal of their internal trade as well, to the Italians. The Ottoman innovation was to place the imperial city—Istanbul—at the center of the Black Sea regional economy, an effective spigot that could be turned on and off according to the wishes of the sultan. Given the need to provision the Ottoman capital and, later, the desire to prevent rival powers from getting their hands on the riches that the sea provided, the Ottomans well understood the relationships among geography, commerce, and state-building, far better, in fact, than had the Byzantines. "My Sultan, you dwell in a city whose benefactor is the sea," wrote the sixteenth-century scholar Kemal Paşazade. "If the sea is not safe, no ships will come, and if no ship comes, Istanbul perishes."[3]

As with any prized possession, the Black Sea was also the object of an obsessive concern. The Ottomans considered the sea theirs by right, a watery extension of the Balkan and Anatolian lands that constituted the heartland of the empire. But it was also a possession that could be easily pried away. Benefiting from trade with the northern coast meant first squelching the pirate activity that had plagued the Byzantines and then making sure that it did not reappear. Client states around the sea had to be corrected when their loyalty to the sultan waned. The aspirations of rising powers farther afield—Poland in the northwest, Russia in the northeast—had to be curbed before they impinged on Ottoman interests. As time passed, holding the sea became more and more a drain on state coffers, diminished already by the exigencies of maintaining other imperial possessions stretching from central Europe to Arabia. By the middle of the seventeenth century, what had once been a source of wealth and security, the empire's greatest geopolitical asset, came to look more and more like a strategic burden. The dark, forbidding Black Sea of early antiquity—literally, the *kara deniz* to the Ottomans—began to reappear.

"The Source of All the Seas"

The sultan often styled himself the "ruler of the two seas"—the Black Sea and the Aegean—and it is not difficult to understand the Ottoman fixation on commanding the passage between them. Holding the Straits had been one of the keys to the seizure of Constantinople. It remained the quintessential element in the security of the new Ottoman capital after the conquest. It also ensured easy travel between the two major components of the Ottoman state; western and central Anatolia on the one hand, the southern Balkans and the Aegean littoral on the other. Most importantly, the sea was critical to the Ottoman economy. Products from the north fed the growing metropolis. When Mehmet II entered Constantinople in 1453, he found a city virtually deserted. By the sixteenth century, the population had grown to perhaps 700,000, making Istanbul the largest city in all of Europe at the time.[4] That spectacular increase owed much to the deliveries of foodstuffs, especially wheat and salt, from the northern shore.

For all these reasons, the Black Sea held a particular place in the Ottoman imagination. It was considered a distinct region of the sultan's domain, bounded on the south by the Anatolian heartland and on the north by the *Dasht-i Qipchaq*, the open "Kipchak Steppe,"[5] which served as a buffer between the sea and the Poles and Muscovites to the north. In 1538 the Ottomans formally annexed the last piece of the littoral, the Bujak district lying between the Prut, Danube, and Dnestr rivers, and from that point the entire coastline was integrated into the well-guarded dominions of the House of Osman.

The western coast from the Bosphorus around to the Dnestr river, the Crimean ports and the coastal areas that connected them, and the straits of Kerch became *sancaks*, or sub-provinces, governed by appointed administrators. The southern coast was likewise divided into provincial administrations. The Caucasus coast, although never a directly administered district, was commanded by garrisons inside fortified ports. Areas farther inland were either directly administered or paid tribute to the sultan. Piracy, which remained a perplexing problem in the Mediterranean, seems to have been wiped out by the late 1400s, allowing cross-sea commerce to flourish.[6] Evliya Çelebi, the greatest of Ottoman travelers, spent time in nearly every corner of the Ottoman world, but he was convinced that the real center of the empire's strength lay in its command of the Black Sea. "But if the truth of the matter is looked at," he wrote in his *Seyahatname*, or *Record of Travels*, "the source of all the seas is the Black Sea."[7]

The wealth that the Ottoman state extracted from the coasts enhanced this image of the sea as the heart of the empire's maritime power. The Byzantine trade routes that had been controlled by the Italians remained in place even under the Ottomans, although with some important changes. Local merchants— Orthodox Christians, Armenians, Jews—who had flocked to the port cities under the Byzantines had long resented the Italian monopoly on commerce. The Ottomans, mindful of the lessons of Byzantine decline, were likewise eager to break the stranglehold of the "Franks," as Catholic Europeans were generally known. These twin interests came together in the late fifteenth century. Native merchants, of whatever religion, probably welcomed the arrival of the Ottomans as restorers of the system that had flourished under the Byzantines before the arrival of the interloping Italians. Many Byzantine citizens had no doubt bene-fited from the Italian domination of commerce; as in any system, political and economic elites found ways to accommodate themselves to the new realities and ensure that they made money. But with the coming of the Ottomans, perspica-cious merchants saw an opportunity to undo a system that had been in place for two centuries and to make their own preferential deals with the new sovereign power.[8] That logic went even further for inland powers, such as the Tatar khans of Crimea or the princes of Moldova, who had often attempted, unsuccessfully, to exert their own control over the port cities. They, too, saw in the Ottomans a useful counterweight to the dominance of the Italians and, moreover, a helpful ally against northern powers such as Poland, Hungary, and Muscovy.

Soon after the conquest, the fortifications around port cities were dismantled and the Italian consuls thrown out of office. The autonomy of the old Genoese and Venetian communities, including the administrative center at Pera, was ended. Ottoman tax inspectors were put in place and trade redirected; the free-wheeling commerce of individual merchants gave way to the demands of provi-sioning and enriching the imperial city. Individual Italians remained on the scene, and some in time even converted to Islam. Such conversions, along with immigration from Anatolia and the Balkans, led to a growth in the Muslim component of the populations. Almost half of Caffa's population was Muslim in the census of 1542, up from less than a quarter a few decades earlier.[9]

Many of the old trade connections that had prospered under the Italians now became dominated by other classes of merchants, but business remained vigorous. Cotton cloth from looms in Anatolia was transported from Sinop across the sea to Caffa and from there north to Russia and Poland; merchants returned with woolen cloth from western Europe or precious furs from the Russian north. Animal hides from the vast cattle herds and sheep flocks along the northwest coat, in the fertile pasturelands between the Danube and Dnepr rivers, came south to Anatolia, while pepper and other spices followed these routes to Hungary and Poland and on to the rest of Europe. The famous butter of Caffa, much prized in Istanbul, was packed for transport across the sea.

Ottoman tax authorities compiled registers of commercial transactions in the Black Sea ports, and those that have survived provide a vivid snapshot of the diversity of commerce in the early Ottoman period. In Caffa of the 1480s, for example, the fact that a new political elite was now in control seems to have done little to dampen the vibrancy of trade or the diversity of traders. Lorenc, a "Frankish" captain from Tana, was recorded as carrying a cargo of dried fish and cups. A captain Haracci-oglu, probably a Turkic Muslim, sailed from Trabzon to Caffa with a company of Orthodox merchants on board; their wares included cotton goods, wine, and arak, the anise liqueur favored throughout the Near and Middle East. Ali Rayis, a Turkoman from Samsun, transported furs. Other ships carried a remarkable array of goods: cotton, flax, and hemp; wheat, millet, and rice; olives, hazelnuts, walnuts; skins and hides of fox, marten, sheep, and cows; opium and beeswax; and, of course, silk.[10]

As under the Byzantines, Caffa occupied a central place in the Ottoman administration of the northern coast and in the integrated commerce of the entire Black Sea. Its superb harbor and port facilities made it an easy outlet for goods from the north and the natural partner of Sinop and Trabzon across the water. By the middle of the sixteenth century, it was home to perhaps 16,000 people, placing it just below such major imperial centers as Aleppo, Damascus, and Salonika.[11] Its important status earned the city the popular epithet of *küçük İstanbul*, little Istanbul.

But the bundles of cotton cloth and stacks of cattle hides piled along the quay were insignificant compared to the most profitable good trafficked there. As any traveler to Caffa during the Ottoman centuries would have discovered, the real source of that city's wealth, and of the Black Sea ports in general, was the trade in people.

"To Constantinople—to be Sold!"

The northern and eastern coasts had long been important suppliers of slave labor, even in antiquity.[12] Many ancient authors mention the trade in slaves in the Greek cities and emporia, and Athenian comedies included slave characters whose names gave away their Black Sea origins: "Thratta," a feminine form of the word for Thracian; "Getas" and "Davos," clearly of Geto-Dacian provenance.[13] Under the Byzantines, much of the wealth of Italian merchants came from their serving as middlemen in the movement of slaves from the northern and eastern coasts to Byzantium and then on to western Europe. The Black Death had caused a severe labor shortage in Europe, and merchants were eager to meet the demand for household servants and agricultural laborers. Although the enslavement of Christians was frowned upon by the pope, Catholic merchants were given license to buy their fellow Christians as a way of preventing their falling into the hands of infidel Muslims. Visiting in the early 1400s, several decades before the fall of Constantinople, the Spanish traveler Pero Tafur found the slave trade in Caffa to be the city's biggest business and one with a global reach. "In this city they sell more slaves, both male and female, than anywhere else in the world," he wrote. "The Sultan of Egypt has his agents here, and they buy the slaves and send them to Cairo." Tafur even took away clear evidence of the booming commerce in people: a man, two women, and their children, whom he brought back with him to Cordoba.[14]

The slave trade accelerated under the Ottomans, who instituted a system of taxation to regulate it. Slaves were by far the most significant single source of revenue on the Black Sea littoral. In the sixteenth century, the tax on slave sales accounted for 29 percent of total revenues coming to the Ottoman treasury from Crimean ports.[15] The average sale price was between twenty and forty gold pieces, enough for the living expenses of an adult for two or three years. From 1500 to 1650, the annual slave population trafficked via the Black Sea from Poland, the Russian lands, and the Caucasus probably reached over 10,000 people per year[16]—a small figure compared to the forced movement of people from west Africa to the Americas, but still the greatest volume of "white" slavery in the world.

As with any form of commerce, the slave trade was driven by both supply and demand—a supply of humans taken in war and in raids on sedentary populations in the forest zone north of the Black Sea steppe and in the Caucasus mountains, and a demand for servants and laborers in the Ottoman empire and Europe. Islamic law recognized only transmission of slave status from an enslaved parent to a child and capture in battle as legitimate routes to servitude.[17] Hereditary slavery was actually rare under the Ottomans, but war provided a steady supply of prisoners, who were either sent to slave markets or enrolled in the imperial corps of elite soldiers, the Janissaries. When the Ottoman army conquered the fortress of Maurocastro in 1484, some 2,000 prisoners were sent as gifts to the khan of Crimea, 3,000 boys were made Janissaries, and another 2,000 girls were delivered to the slave markets and harems of the imperial capital.[18] An equally important supply of slaves came from raids on villages lying north of the Eurasian steppe, along the edges of Poland and Muscovy, as well as in the uplands of the Caucasus. The Crimean khan and the nomadic Nogay Tatars, both vassals of the sultan, derived considerable revenue from the kidnapping and sale of Christian peasants. It is no exaggeration to say that, until the eighteenth century, the entire economy of Crimea, much of the northern steppe, and the Caucasus uplands rested on the commerce in people.[19] When Evliya Çelebi visited the northeast coast, he noted down several useful phrases in the local language that any future traveler might need to know. "Bring a girl" was one. "I found no girl, but I found a boy" was another.[20]

The supply of slaves from these sources fulfilled a lively demand. Owning slaves was a mark of social prestige, and households measured their wealth and status in part by how many slaves they were able to maintain. Most slaves were used as domestic servants; female slaves also served as wives or in the harems of the wealthy. Some engaged in a variety of other work, as agricultural laborers, craftsmen, and even mercantile assistants. Slaves who were taken or purchased by agents of the Ottoman state often wound up in military service, as infantry in the Janissary corps or as rowers on galleys. (The latter might, in turn, find themselves serving in the same capacity on French or Italian ships in the Mediterranean if they were captured in war.)

There was sometimes also a double demand equation at work in the Black Sea slave trade. Not only was there a desire for slave labor on the part of potential buyers, but there also seems to have been a willingness by some potential slaves to be bought. As late as the eighteenth and nineteenth centuries, numerous western travelers were impressed by the degree to which slaves and their families seemed, incongruously, to embrace servitude as a route to wealth and success. Individuals in economic straits might offer themselves to a Tatar slaver or an Ottoman ship captain for transport to a market in Caffa or Trabzon. Families might sell a son or daughter for similar reasons and, thus, if the child were placed with the proper wealthy master, forge a connection with a potentially helpful patron. Marie Guthrie, visiting Caffa in the 1790s, found these calculations among women who had been shipped there from Circassia in the north Caucasus:

I was more surprised, probably, than I ought to have been…at the perfect indifference with which the inhabitants of Caffa behold this traffic in beauty that had shocked me so much, and at their assuring me, when I seemed affected at the practice, that it was the only method which parents had of bettering the state of their handsome daughters, destined at all events to the haram;…in short, that, by being disposed of to rich mussulmen [Muslims], they were sure to live in affluence and ease the rest of their days, and in a state by no means degrading in Mahometan countries, where their Prophet has permitted the seraglio. But that, on the contrary, if they fell into the hands of their feudal lords, the barbarous inhabitants of their own native mountains…their lot was comparatively wretched, as those rude chieftains have very little of either respect or generosity toward the fair sex.[21]

Even observers who condemned most other elements of Ottoman society admitted that there was a certain logic to such seemingly perverse preferences. In the nineteenth century, the Prussian noble August von Haxthausen recounted his own experience with a group of six female slaves from Circassia, who were found on board an Ottoman transport vessel and "liberated" by a Russian warship:

In announcing to the girls their liberation, the [Russian] General ordered them to be informed that the choice was open to them, to be sent back to their homes with the Prince of their own race, or to marry Russians and Cossacks of their free choice, to return with me to Germany, where all the women are free, or lastly to accompany the Turkish Captain, who would sell them in the slave-market at Constantinople. The reader will hardly credit that, unanimously and without a moment's consideration, they exclaimed, "To Constantinople—to be sold!"[22]

In many, perhaps most, instances the experience of entering into servitude was obviously traumatic, especially for those taken in the most violent circumstances: captured on the battlefield or at sea, abducted from a frontier settlement on the Eurasian steppe, or pulled from a village in the Balkans. And since the quality of life as a slave depended very much on the social status of the master, generalizations about Ottoman slave-holding are difficult to make. But as observers such as Guthrie and Haxthausen recognized, the nature of slavery in the Ottoman empire sometimes made servitude a viable choice. The Ottomans had no conception of a "slave race." Slave status was not coupled with the idea of biological inferiority, it was rarely for life, and it was hardly ever transmitted from parents to children. There were social prohibitions on who could buy and be bought; Muslims were generally not to be sold to Christians and Jews, for example. Some distinction was made between "white" slaves from the Black Sea region and "black" slaves from North Africa, the Red Sea, and the Persian Gulf; but being in a position of servitude was not the province of any particular cultural group, and therefore held no connotation of inherent racial inferiority, as did black African slavery in the Americas.

There were also numerous routes to manumission, such as marriage to a free person or simply outliving one's master. Islamic law also encouraged good

Muslims to free their slaves, and Ottoman practice allowed slaves to be paid wages and to purchase their freedom over time.[23] Slaves were not a self-perpetuating social category—the idea of "breeding" slaves was abhorrent in Islamic societies—and the frontier lands of the empire were the only source of new inputs into the system. For young men and women from the Balkans, the Eurasian steppe, and the Caucasus, servitude could thus represent a route to privileged status in the Ottoman state. Many took that road all the way to the top of the imperial administration and society, serving as grand vezirs, military commanders, and wives of the sultan. In eastern Europe, romantic nationalists would later decry the rapacity of Ottoman slavers, who sold the youthful flowers of the nation into Muslim bondage. But for most of the Ottoman period, a sizeable number of the trafficked no doubt saw the voyage across the sea to Istanbul as something of an opportunity—for wealth, social advancement, and a new life at the center of the imperial system.

Domn, Khan, and Derebey

For later historians, the slave trade was one of the most loathsome aspects of the "Ottoman yoke," which delayed economic progress and alienated people from their proper homelands. Especially in the history-writing traditions of the Balkans, the Ottoman experience in general is still seen as a regrettable impediment to the social, cultural, and economic flourishing of the subject peoples. But the political and military relationships among the Ottoman state and the various vassal regimes in the region were far more complex than such an interpretation allows.

In the two centuries before the Ottoman conquest, the geopolitics of the sea was defined by the sorting out of new political arrangements and military competition among the remnants of two Eurasian empires, the Byzantines and the Tatar–Mongols. The Latin subjugation of Constantinople in 1204 had effectively ended the Byzantines as a major military and political force. Even after the reestablishment of Byzantine control over the city in 1261, the empire found itself overshadowed by other regional powers. In the south Balkans, the Serbian empire of the Nemanjid dynasty stretched all the way from the Adriatic to the Black Sea. North of the Danube, two Christian principalities, Wallachia and Moldova, were beginning to consolidate themselves after the decline of Byzantine power and the multiple migrations of eastern peoples. Similar processes were at work in the south Caucasus. The contraction of the Byzantine borderlands in the face of the Tatar–Mongol incursion of the thirteenth century left a region of many principalities and a few small Christian kingdoms—Kartli, Kakheti, Imereti—which battled one another more often than they stood united against a common invader. To the north, the demise of the Golden Horde had produced a political void in the steppe, which was now traversed by the nomadic Nogays, a Turkic people who were the successors to the Pechenegs and Cumans of centuries past. In Crimea, the last remnant of the Golden Horde held on in the person of the khan of Crimea, a member of the Giray dynasty that traced its heritage back to Chingis Khan.

Even before Mehmet II entered Constantinople, the Ottomans had extended their reach through much of the Balkans, destroying the Serbian empire and annexing Thrace. Much of the Black Sea coast, however, remained as it had been before, a congeries of small states that bordered on larger regional powers beyond—Poland, Lithuania, Hungary, the various principalities of Russia, and Persia. In this complicated milieu, the Ottomans chose a relatively low-cost strategy: to conquer outright the strategic fortresses and ports that would allow them unfettered control of the sea and then to forge agreements with the most powerful political entities inland. These agreements provided for some degree of autonomy over local affairs in exchange for tribute and professed loyalty to the sultan. That strategy entailed a certain amount of risk, however. The pinpoints of direct Ottoman power—fortified garrisons on river- and seaports—were targets of assault when the vassals decided to revolt, and patron–client relationships with powerful native rulers were stable only so long as the client did not receive a better offer from another potential patron. The advantages and hazards of empire by condominium were clear in the Ottomans' relations with three groups around the sea from the fifteenth to the seventeenth centuries: the princes of Wallachia and Moldova, the khans of Crimea, and the kings of Georgia.

Wallachia and Moldova, the so-called Danubian principalities, emerged in the region between the Carpathian mountains and the Danube and Dnestr rivers, an area that forms much of modern Romania and the Republic of Moldova. The area was populated by a mixture of cultural groups—Slavs, Romance- and Turkic-speaking peoples, and others—since it lay squarely on the path of the various cycles of westward migration from the Eurasian steppe. In the 1300s, local rulers consolidated their power, creating two distinct principalities that were originally subordinate to the kingdom of Hungary—Wallachia south of the Carpathians and Moldova to the east. The power of the Wallachian and Moldovan princes rested on two factors: the natural endowments of the territories they controlled, including wood products from the dense forests and animal skins from cattle herds on the river plains, and their geographical position astride important trade routes from the old Genoese ports at the mouth of the Dnestr (Maurocastro, later Akkerman) and on the northern arm of the Danube delta (Licostomo, later Kilia).[24]

By the fifteenth century, both principalities had established durable dynasties. Each experienced periods of greatness, as military powers and as centers of art and culture, under the princes Vlad the Impaler of Wallachia (reigned 1443–76, with interruptions)—the historical "Dracula"—and Ştefan the Great of Moldova (reigned 1457–1504). The Danubian princes, like many of their neighbors in the Balkans, were Orthodox Christians and looked to Constantinople as their spiritual center. Other than that, however, the Byzantines, by now only a weak regional power, played little role in Wallachian and Moldovan affairs. The real influence came from kingdoms farther to the north, Hungary and Poland, which saw in the two principalities a strategic highway to the Danube and the Black Sea as well as a useful shield between themselves and the Ottoman armies that had begun to make inroads into the Balkans. For much of the 1400s, the two principalities played off one potential patron against another—when they were not battling each other.

Modern Romanian historians speak of the period of Ottoman "conquest" in the fifteenth and sixteenth centuries, but that term would probably have made little sense at the time. The Danubian princes often sought accommodation with the Ottomans, even if that accommodation meant crossing over the line between Christian and Muslim. Wallachia paid tribute to the sultan already from the 1390s, Moldova from the 1450s. Rebellions were frequent thereafter, but there was rarely any concerted effort by the Danubian princes to present a united front against the Ottomans. So long as the sultan was able to provide a show of force against the client princes and to deliver protection in the event of invasion by another regional power, they were usually content with the autonomy that they were allowed in their own affairs. Unlike in the Ottoman lands south of the Danube, Muslim landlords were not settled in the Danubian principalities, and local princes (*domni* or *domnitori*), elected by noble assemblies or ruling as dynasts, continued on their thrones (an arrangement that would last until the early eighteenth century). The Orthodox church retained its place at the center of the Wallachian and Moldovan states, and there was no significant conversion to Islam, either voluntary or otherwise. Except for an agreement to provide troops against the enemies of the sultan and to pay an annual tribute and periodic fines for rebellious activity, the costs of recognizing Ottoman suzerainty were not particularly onerous. And since the Ottomans represented a friend in times of need, when the ambitions of the Poles or Hungarians fell on the principalities there were certain benefits to subjugation.

The relationship with Crimea was rather different. In the first place, the Crimean Tatars were speakers of a Turkic language and, as Muslims, part of the same cultural universe as the Ottomans. Even more important, they represented an unbroken link between the great empire of Chingis Khan and the newer empire of the Ottoman sultan. The dynasty of the Tatar khan, the Giray family, traced its lineage back through the Golden Horde to Chingis. Crimea thus represented not only a strategic asset to the sultan but an ideological one as well. The Ottomans' claim to the northern shore and to other parts of Eurasia rested in part on their connection to the Chingisid dynasty represented by the Tatar khans.

The relationship between Istanbul and the khan's palace at Bakhchisarai was therefore even looser than that with the capitals of Wallachia and Moldova. The khan controlled his own affairs and conducted a foreign policy that was at times wholly independent of that of the Ottoman court. Tatar raids on Polish, Russian, and even Wallachian and Moldovan cities and caravans provided a useful instrument for the Ottomans north of the sea, a way of fending off potential aggressors and of correcting rebellious Christian clients. The chief booty carried away from these raids—slaves—kept a supply of humans flowing from the Crimean ports to Istanbul. However, the independence of the Giray khans also meant that they could, at times, pursue policies that were contrary to the strategic interests of the Ottomans. Tatar incursions often threatened to provoke full-scale wars with Poland and Muscovy. In fact, from the late seventeenth century forward, Ottoman policy toward the Tatars more often involved attempts to control their reckless raiding than to use them as a lever against northern powers.

The situation in the Caucasus was even more intricate. Of all the areas around the sea, the Caucasus was the most difficult to control. The Circassian highlanders, the Abkhaz along the coast, and the various Georgian kings and princes in the south were so divided that there was no single political figure who could claim to speak on behalf of any sizeable part of the region. The inhospitable interior also meant that projecting military force beyond the thin coastline was often impossible. As under the Romans, the Ottomans therefore settled on generally leaving the highland tribes to their own devices, placing directly appointed administrators in the fortified ports, and striking political bargains with the lowland kings farther inland.

There was an important strategic reason to rely on pacts rather than outright conquest, especially in the Georgian lands. As a borderland between the Ottoman empire and Persia, the south Caucasus would have demanded significant resources to police, and successive sultans settled for relying on local feudal powers to raise their own armies and secure Ottoman interests against the Persians and their allies. (The same point could be made about Wallachia and Moldova, which were also buffer states between the Ottomans and

Hungary, Poland, and Russia.) That often meant, of course, that Georgian armies found themselves on opposite sides of the battle lines—the Ottoman-influenced kings of western Georgia, or Imereti, against the Persian-influenced kings of eastern Georgia, or Kartli–Kakheti, plus dozens of lesser rulers on either side. But as in many other parts of the Ottoman imperial system, it was strategic good sense, not religion or language, that usually determined the lines of allegiance.

The combination of centralized control of trade, complex systems of tribute and taxation, and loose political–military bargains with local leaders worked well for the first two centuries after the closing of the sea. The Ottomans were able to benefit from the resources of the littoral—both directly and in the form of taxes on trade—while the client states used their connections with the region's major imperial power for their own ends. However, by the seventeenth century, the system began to undergo two changes that would have a serious impact on the political and economic relationships around the sea.

First, within the lands directly controlled by the empire, the highly centralized administrative system created during the reign of Mehmet II (1451–81) gave way to a far looser one. Rather than relying on governors directly appointed by Istanbul and dispatched to the provinces, the state came to rely on local land-owning notables. The power of these local elites was recognized by the sultan, and in turn they provided for the collection of taxes and the raising of military forces during the campaign season. In some areas, these landlords developed quasi-dynastic, even partially feudal, systems within the lands that they adminis-tered. At the time when parts of western Europe were undergoing the transition from feudalism to centralized monarchies, the Ottomans were moving in the opposite direction, from central administration to tax-farming to the virtual devolution of power out to regionally based noble families.

The impetus for decentralization was the need to divest an overburdened central apparatus from the demands of directly administering a vast empire. However, the result, over time, was the weakening of the center against the power and interests of the periphery. This shift of power was especially evident across Anatolia, including along the Black Sea coast. There, the leaders of powerful regional families came to be known as *derebeys*, literally "lords of the valleys." Important owners of large estates, some of them associated with the old Turkoman families that had commanded parts of the coast even before the Ottoman conquest, came to dominate the regional economy and, therefore, politics. Major ports such as Sinop and Trabzon were run as the fiefdoms of leading families, with the center generally unable to change the status quo. The apogee of *derebey* power came in the reign of Sultan Selim III (1789–1807), who officially recognized their position and codified their privileges.

A second major change was the rise of stronger powers north of the sea, powers that began to have an influence on the client states around the coasts. When the Ottomans conquered the major port cities at the end of the fifteenth century, potential rivals in the region were few. The chief candidates—the kingdom of Poland, the kingdom of Hungary, and the grand principality of Muscovy—were geographically far enough away to cause little concern. In the sixteenth century, however, Poland and Muscovy began to grow in strength. Poland, united with Lithuania in 1569 to form the Polish–Lithuanian Commonwealth, extended its reach all the way from the Baltic Sea south into the Black Sea steppe. A persistent worry of the Ottomans was to prevent further encroachments by the Poles toward the south. The armies of the Tatar khan and the raiding parties of the Nogays were employed to harass Polish troops and prevent Slavic settlement in the steppelands.

Muscovy had likewise become an important regional power by the late 1500s. At the time of the Tatar–Mongol conquest in the thirteenth century, Muscovy had been only one of a number of Russian city-states forced to pay tribute; but the "Tatar yoke," mourned by generations of later Russian historians, was in many ways the engine of Muscovite ascendancy. The Muscovite princes served as facilitators in the Tatar–Mongol system of tribute collection, promising to deliver wealth from the several other Russian principalities in exchange for a cut of the take. In time, this system paved the way for political centralization. Under Ivan IV (the Terrible), in the sixteenth century, the grand prince took the title "tsar of all Russia," marking a change in both the geographical extent of Muscovite, now "Russian," power as well as the ideology that justified Muscovy's ascendancy. The Russians came to see themselves as inheritors of the traditions of the Byzantine empire and, thus, of the Roman empire as well (tsar, of course, derives from the Latin *caesar*). But they also looked back to the Tatar–Mongol period to justify their dominant role in Eurasia, a role sealed by Ivan's conquest of Tatar khanates along the Volga and in Siberia. These two sources, Roman/Byzantine and Chingisid, gave the tsar his chief claim to power across the Eurasian lands—and logically placed him at odds with the other claimant to these twin legacies, the Ottoman sultan.

The weakening of central power within the Ottoman lands and the rise of rival regional powers altered the strategic relationships around the sea. Client states now had new potential protectors—Poland and Russia—against whom they could play off the Ottomans or, in the case of the Crimean khans, against whom they could make war. The *derebeys* along the southern coast looked to their own affairs with little regard for what happened in the capital. In the end, however, these changes were only the background to the most pressing challenge that faced the Ottomans in the late 1500s and early 1600s. That challenge came from the sea.

Sailors' Graffiti

For much of the sixteenth and seventeenth centuries, the grand sea battles and smaller naval engagements that the Ottomans faced in the Mediterranean were unknown on the Black Sea. At the famous set-piece battle at Lepanto in 1571, the Ottoman fleet was largely destroyed by the combined forces of Catholic Europe; but there was to be no equivalent on the Black Sea until some two centuries later.

Ottoman naval supremacy rested on three pillars. The first, and clearly the most significant, was control of the Straits and the mouth of the Danube, the only two routes via which European ships could enter the sea. Even after Lepanto, the fortresses along the Dardanelles and Bosphorus and at the mouth of the Danube, as well as the strategic location of the imperial capital, helped maintain a choke-hold on travel to and from the Black Sea. Second, none of the states in the region could muster a naval force that might threaten the Ottomans. The absence of a Moldovan, Crimean or Georgian navy was, in part, the result of the political traditions of these entities themselves; after all, they had grown up in the plains and mountains of the hinterlands with little affinity for the sea. Even more important was the Ottomans' hold on the seacoast itself, which effectively kept the client states away from the water. It is only in these two strategic respects—control of the Straits and the effective isolation of the client states from the littoral—that the sea might be said to have been a "Turkish lake."

The third pillar, in some ways derivative of the first two, was the virtual absence of piracy on Black Sea for at least the first two centuries of Ottoman dominance. The sea "became fully controlled and...evil people of sedition no longer inhabited these parts," wrote the fifteenth-century chronicler Ibn Kemal.[25] That is a remarkable fact. Piracy was endemic in the Mediterranean in the early modern age, and much of the naval history of that period is the story of the effort by various regional powers either to combat or to encourage it. Pirates were both burdens and blessings, of course: the former when they attacked one's own ships, the latter when they could be induced to attack an enemy's. The growth of Ottoman naval power in the Mediterranean in the 1400s and early 1500s can to a certain degree be traced to the empire's desire to secure its shipping lanes against attacks by Italian and Levantine corsairs. Most of the armed ships in the eastern Mediterranean were freebooters of one type or another, with only

Venice, the Ottomans, and the Knights of Rhodes able to claim anything resembling a regulated, professional navy.[26]

Pirates, like any businessmen, need both bases and markets: a secure harbor from which to direct their operations and a place where they can offload their acquisitions. The great achievement of the Ottomans on the Black Sea was to deny them both. Major fortified ports were located on each of the coasts: Sinop and Trabzon in the south, Azov (the old Venetian Tana) on the Don river, Caffa in Crimea, Akkerman (the old Maurocastro) on the Dnestr, and Kilia (the former Licostomo) on the Danube. The sea's small size made patrol operations from these centers relatively easy. Since these ports were also the major commercial hubs, any potential pirates would have had a difficult time fencing their goods—which is why piracy, when it did surface, tended to be associated with the parts of the sea least easily controlled, the rugged southern and eastern coastline from Trabzon to the Caucasus. These were not only significant differences between the Black Sea and the Mediterranean; they also marked a change from the situation under the Romans and Byzantines. Seaborne brigandage had been a problem for the previous thousand years or more. Roman and Byzantine sources are replete with complaints about the ravages of pirates, from the Goths of the fourth century to the "Laz" (a general term for inhabitants of the southeast coast, people who today might be called Georgians or, in Turkey, still Laz) mentioned in later periods. After the late Middle Ages, however, references to corsairs virtually disappear from the sources.

It was in this relatively secure environment that business was able to flourish, and by all accounts the sea in the early Ottoman centuries was a hive of activity, for both local and international commerce. Cabotage—short-run coastal shipping—continued much as it had done since antiquity. Other forms of shipping included a combination of sea and river routes, with Ottoman vessels offloading goods at ports on the Danube, Dnestr, and Don and transferring them to foreign vessels or caravans; and sea-to-sea routes, with Ottoman subjects piloting ships to the Mediterranean and then offloading to foreign vessels in the Aegean archipelago or the Levant. A small number of foreign ships was permitted to enter the Black Sea in various periods. In the late sixteenth century, Ragusa (modern Dubrovnik, Croatia) maintained a lively commerce with ports along the western Black Sea coast, a result of the city-state's maintaining diplomatic ties with the Ottomans at a time when most other European powers were united against them.[27] The Ragusan trade probably declined in the seventeenth century, as Orthodox merchants from the Aegean archipelago came to dominate the business of transshipment from the Black Sea to the Mediterranean.

We know rather little about the nature of ships and seafaring communities, both military and commercial, during the early Ottoman centuries. The study of Ottoman seapower in general has long been ignored by scholars, a victim of the persistent prejudice that the history of the Ottomans on the water is mainly one of inferior seamanship buttressed by state-supported brigandage. From the early modern period to the present, the standard European perception of Muslim sailors in the Mediterranean—pirates who appeared from hidden harbors, bore down on Christian seafarers, and then hauled off their innocent captives to the depravities of the seraglio—has reinforced that view. However, it was Black Sea sailors themselves, both Muslim and Christian, who provided some of the most important evidence concerning the variety of ships and the evolution of seafaring under the Ottomans.

Like travelers before and since, visitors to the Ottoman seaports felt an uncontrollable urge to leave some graphic record of their presence, and many did so by drawing graffiti in the easiest places they could find: the soft frescoes and limestone facings of churches, some of which would later become mosques. The Haghia Sophia in Trabzon, the Byzantine-era church which shares the name of its imposing sister in Istanbul, is dotted with such graffiti; but some of the most spectacular examples are located in the city of Nesebur, the ancient Greek port of Mesembria, on the Bulgarian coast. The city's churches contain a rich collection of drawings, nearly 180 in all, some crude and schematic, others remarkably detailed, of sea vessels from the fourteenth through the nineteenth centuries. Together, they form a graphic history of seafaring through the entire Ottoman period, from the perspective of the sailors themselves.[28]

The evolution of ship design is easily seen in the Nesebur graffiti. The earliest ships are melon-hulled cogs, low amidships and with high platforms in the stern. The cog was introduced to the Black Sea in the 1300s by the mercantile republics of the Mediterranean, which had earlier taken the design from the merchants of the Hanseatic League. The cog was a short-run ship, uniquely suited to trade around the Baltic and the minor seas of the Mediterranean, and it proved equally suited to the Black Sea. Its fat bottom held bulk goods that could also be used for ballast, such as grain, but its single square sail meant that it was not built for speed or maneuverability. Journeys were short, from one port to another, or, at a maximum, from one end of the sea to Istanbul. Once through the Bosphorus, goods could then be loaded onto sturdier vessels for the journey across the Mediterranean. In stormy weather or in winter, cogs were unlikely to be found on the open sea; without a complex rigging system to allow a quick change of tack, an easy, favorable wind was essential.

The mercantile cog remained the dominant ship on the Black Sea in the early Ottoman period; but two other ship types also appear frequently in graffiti at

Nesebur and elsewhere. One is the caravel. The caravel was, like the cog, still broad of beam, but its rigging represented a huge improvement over the square sail. The experience of the Crusades had introduced western sailors to the triangular, or "lateen," sail and rigging of the Arabs. (The felucca boats of the Nile are premier examples of lateen rigging, with the sail hung from a long yard that shoots up at a severe angle to the mast.) In the caravel, merchants found a ship that provided both the cargo capacity of the old cog and the improved maneuverability allowed by the lateen sail; such ships could be turned into the wind rather than being forced to travel in the direction that the wind happened to be blowing.

Another type is the carrack. Carracks were, like the caravel, descendants of cogs, but their more complex rigging, including the addition of three or more masts rigged with both square and lateen sails, allowed them to move over greater distances and, especially in the growing state-controlled navies of west European powers, to carry a small crew of marines that could be disembarked aboard ships that were stopped at sea or boarded in port. They mark the beginning of the development of the idea that large sailing ships could be used both as vehicles for long-distance exploration and as maneuverable instruments of battle. It was carrack-type ships that formed the germ of the expanding navies of sixteenth-century Portugal, Spain, and England.

The cog, caravel, and carrack predominate in Black Sea graffiti, for they were the primary merchant ships that visited ports such as Nesebur. But scattered among them is another ship type—and one that reveals something important about the nature of life on the sea, particularly in the seventeenth century. The ship is the large galley (or, technically, a galeasse), a combination of sailing ship and large oared vessel, usually armed with cannon and outfitted with a company of marines. The odd sailor who happened to draw such a vessel in Nesebur may have been a member of the crew or, more likely, saw the ships from the shore. Similar galleys, with one or more banks of oars and a sail, either square or lateen, which could provide extra power in a favorable wind, would have been familiar to Roman and Byzantine sailors from centuries earlier.

Too much can be made of the supposed backwardness of the Ottomans as seafarers, but it is fair to say that the empire was a late modernizer as far as ship design was concerned. The battle of Lepanto in 1571 was the last great encounter in the Mediterranean between navies composed mainly of oared galleys, the Venetians and their allies on one side, the Ottomans on the other. But the Ottomans were still relying largely on oared ships as their primary naval vessel a century later, at a time when, in western Europe, armed sailing ships with multiple masts had long been in the ascendant. In Atlantic Europe, the coming of the age of sail depended on certain technological innovations—new rigging designs that allowed combinations of different sail types, plus elongated hulls that increased ship speed—but these design changes would never have caught on without the strategic end that they served: the need for more efficient and lower-cost navies that could be funded from state budgets. With the consolidation of monarchical states, building navies became the sine qua non of military superiority, even a source of national pride. Especially for states that also had overseas ambitions, large sailing ships were critical to long-range exploration and empire maintenance. Putting ships to sea, however, depended on having men to staff them, and the costs of outfitting a galley, with its large complement of oarsmen, was astronomical compared to the costs of the much smaller crew required on a sailing ship.

The Ottomans certainly had the capacity to innovate technologically. What they lacked were the strategic and economic imperatives that drove the changes in Europe. No outside power could place ships on the Black Sea, and with a ready supply of slave labor from the north, outfitting galleys with crews was not a pressing concern. There was, in fact, very little need even to launch any warships at all on the Black Sea, so long as it remained the peaceful preserve of the Ottomans alone.

In the late sixteenth and early seventeenth centuries, however, a new naval force irrupted from an unexpected source. It was a force that was able to use light, oared ships to conduct raids on coastal cities and fortresses, to attack merchant ships at sea, and to challenge the galleys of the Ottoman imperial fleet. That group—the Cossacks—proved what an anachronism the large galleys of the Nesebur graffiti had now become, even on the once pacific Black Sea.

A Navy of Seagulls

The popular image of Cossacks is one of knout-wielding horsemen racing across the Eurasian steppe, but in the century from roughly 1550 to 1650, the Cossacks were a significant naval power as well. They were first reported in the 1530s, floating down to the mouth of the Dnepr river and attacking the Ottoman fortress of Özi (Ochakov). In time, they extended their reach to the mouth of the Danube and all along the western coast; in 1614 they launched their first attack on the south coast, at Sinop.[29] Similar seaborne assaults continued until the middle of the seventeenth century. Ottoman and European sources mention their frequent raids, and the descriptions of the destruction they wrought are reminiscent of similar stories about the seafaring Goths and their attacks on Byzantium some 1,200 years earlier:

Going over the top of [Sinop's] ramparts and walls they entered inside and descended upon the center of the city and destroyed its circumference and edifices and shed the blood of several thousand men and women and struck [this] city with the broom of plunder and the fire of devastation and they left neither name nor sign of its buildings, turning it into a wilderness and a desert.[30]

According to Evliya Çelebi, the villagers around Sinop had given up planting gardens since they were certain their vegetables would be trampled in the frequent Cossack raids.[31]

Even if one allows for a certain amount of hyperbole in such accounts, it is clear that the Cossack attacks stunned the Ottomans. Before, the Black Sea had been largely free of piracy, and the arrival of Cossack raiders was treated by Ottoman officials and chroniclers as an unexpected outbreak of the same kind of troublesome seaborne banditry with which they were intimately familiar in the Mediterranean. Yet the Cossacks were far more than freebooters. Their appearance marked the growing assertiveness of a distinct society that drew its strength from the multiple cultures of the Black Sea's northern coast.

The Cossacks were precisely the kind of society that empires most worry about: people who take advantage of living on the uncontrollable frontier— geographical, cultural, and political—at the intersection of different established powers. The word "Cossack" probably derives from *qazaq*, a Turkic word meaning "free man." The Cossacks arose from the mix of Slavic peasants, Tatar nomads, former slaves, religious dissenters, mercenaries, and others who filtered into the ungoverned steppe region north of the sea, some coming from the Ottoman domains, others from Poland and Russia. Over time, they coalesced into a number of sub-groups, or hosts, distinguished by region and to a certain extent by language. The Zaporozhian Cossacks emerged along the lower Dnepr river, in the land below the dozen or so major cataracts that marked a natural barrier between the upper river and its lower course nearer the sea (a region literally *za porohamy* in Ukrainian, that is, beyond the rapids). Similar groups formed on other river courses, such as the Don. Cossack hosts in the east spoke a variety of Russian infused with Turkic words, especially in the military sphere; those in the west were more heavily influenced by what today would be called Polish and Ukrainian. In the sixteenth century, the various hosts crystallized around powerful chieftains and formed something like inchoate states. Their sources of livelihood were connected with life on the steppe and the coastal lowlands: raising (and raiding) cattle, sheep, and horses; serving as intermediaries in trade between the seacoast and the north; fishing; and, along with the Crimean and Nogay Tatars, providing slaves for export to Ottoman markets.

The Cossacks' venture into raiding on the open sea was a natural extension of their economic activities in the steppe region. As inhabitants of river banks and wetlands, they had developed a water culture that was a complement to their activities on the open plains. Their light, keelless rowing boats, called *chaikas* (seagulls), were particularly suited to river traffic, especially if a journey necessitated portage over rapids. (That form of travel had also characterized the Rhos of the ninth and tenth centuries; in fact, Cossack vessels bore a striking resemblance to those of the Rhos and their Norse forebears.) Made slightly larger to accommodate up to seventy men and outfitted with small cannon, the boats made formidable sea vessels. They sat low in the water and therefore out of sight from the coast or from a large galley until they were already upon their prey; with buoyant bundles of marsh reeds lashed to the gunwales, they were extremely difficult to sink. In the first part of the seventeenth century, the Cossacks were able to assemble fleets of up to 300 such boats and send them to every corner of the sea.[32] And with rudders at both bow and stern, they were far more maneuverable than the Ottoman war galleys that were normally sent after them.

Guillaume de Beauplan, a French military engineer in the employ of the Polish king in the 1630s and 1640s, provided a first-hand account of Cossack craft as they sailed down the Dnepr:

The boats are so close together that their oars are almost touching. The Turks are usually aware of the expedition, and they hold several galleys in readiness at the mouth of the Borysthenes to prevent the Cossacks from coming out to sea. However, the Cossacks, who have greater cunning, sneak out on a dark night close to the new moon, keeping themselves hidden in the reeds that are found for three or four leagues up the Borysthenes, where the galleys dare not venture, having suffered great damage there in the past. The Turks are content to wait at the mouth of the river, where they are always surprised [by the raiders].

However, the Cossacks cannot pass so quickly that they cannot be seen, and the alarm is then sounded throughout the whole country, even as far as Constantinople. The Great Lord [sultan] sends messengers all along the coasts…warning that the Cossacks have put to sea, so that everyone may be on his guard. All is in vain, however, since the Cossacks choose their time and season so advantageously that in 36 or 40 hours they have reached Anatolia. They land, each man carrying his firearm, leaving only two men and two boys on guard in each boat. They surprise the towns, capture them, loot and burn them, venturing sometimes as far as a league inland. Then they return immediately [to their boats] and embark with their booty, to try their luck elsewhere.

Beauplan also remarked on the ingenious military tactics of the Cossacks, who proved to be far stealthier sailors than the Ottomans:

Since Cossack boats rise only about two and one-half feet above the water, the Cossacks can always spot a ship or galley before they [themselves] can be seen [by their opponents]. They then lower the masts of their boats, and taking note of the direction in which their enemy is sailing, they try to get the evening sun behind them. Then, an hour before sunset, they row with [all their] strength toward the ship or galley, until they are about a league distant, fearing lest the prize may be lost to view. They keep this distance, and then, at about midnight (the signal being given), they row hard toward the vessels. Half of the crew is ready for combat, and waits for the moment of contact, in order to leap aboard. Those on the [enemy] vessels are greatly surprised to see themselves attacked by eighty or a hundred boats, their ships being suddenly filled with men and instantly captured. Thereupon, the Cossacks loot the ships of what they can find in the way of money, and goods that are small of bulk, and that water will not damage. As well, they remove the cast iron cannon, and everything else they may judge to be of use, before scuttling the vessel and her crew.... If they had the ingenuity to handle a ship or galley, they would take it with them as well, but they do not possess such skill.[33]

With expeditions such as these a frequent occurrence after the 1550s, the Black Sea was anything but a "Turkish lake."

The high point of Cossack attacks came in 1637. In that year, a large party of Don Cossacks laid siege to the fortress of Azov, which housed a garrison of a few thousand Ottoman soldiers and Tatar recruits. There were several Ottoman attempts to retake the fortress, but each illustrated just how powerful the Cossacks had become as an organized military, not just as raiders. Evliya Çelebi was present at a major counterassault on the fortress. He reported that the Cossacks numbered 80,000 men with a flotilla of 150 boats protecting the river side of the walls. The Ottomans assembled an army from across the Black Sea region. Land forces included men supplied by the governor of Rumelia in Thrace, 40,000 Tatars from the Bujak province, 40,000 Christian soldiers from Wallachia and Moldova, and 20,000 Christians from Transylvania. On the sea, the Ottoman imperial fleet consisted of 150 galleys and more frigates and boats, in all 400 vessels with 40,000 men on board. (Evliya's figures may be exaggerated, but the army and flotilla were clearly impressive.)

Despite this formidable array, the Ottomans had a difficult time. The Cossacks managed to hold out by digging defensive lines and to send in reinforcements by having men swim underwater through the river blockade, breathing through reed tubes and carrying their weapons in leather sacks. After two months, with winter fast approaching, the Ottomans finally gave up, leaving the fortress to the Cossacks but taking their revenge by plundering the countryside. The troops produced so much booty, Evliya reported, that prices sank to unbelievably low levels. A horse could be had for a piaster, a girl for five, a boy for six.[34]

The repeated debacles at Azov notwithstanding, the Ottoman fleet did have some success against the Cossacks. Beefed up patrols at the mouth of the Dnepr kept the largest flotillas from getting to the sea, even though smaller raiding parties, such as those described by Beauplan, were almost impossible to stop. Major Ottoman expeditions, involving hundreds of galleys and smaller craft, were launched up the Don. Over time, the Cossacks also no doubt suffered from a loss of capable men, since encounters with Ottoman galleys, however infrequent, usually ended with only a portion of the Cossack crews making it back home.[35] Even Azov eventually reverted to Ottoman control. The Cossacks first offered the fortress as a gift to the Russian tsar, who refused it for fear that it would lead to a full-scale war with the sultan; they then abandoned it in 1642 when they realized they had little use for a fortress, especially one that repeated sieges had nearly destroyed.

For the Ottomans, the cost of even partial success was considerable. The need to counter the Cossack threat pulled scarce naval resources away from the Mediterranean. The brisk trading relationship between the northern and southern coasts was also inevitably affected, since ship captains were keenly aware of the new danger presented by Cossack raiders. Over the longer term, the successes of a naval power with swift ships able to out-maneuver the slower galleys showed that the Ottoman military machine that had conquered all of southeastern Europe a few centuries earlier was not invincible. And with the Cossacks learning to take advantage of their position at the meeting place of rival powers—Polish, Russian, and Ottoman—they also demonstrated that the old Ottoman strategies of imperial accommodation were coming to an end.

The appearance of an informal Cossack navy marked a major change in the relationship between the Ottomans and the Black Sea. Until the mid-sixteenth century, their strategic control of the sea and its littoral could be taken for granted. Client states were sometimes restive, and along the Caucasus in particular, command of the coastline, much less the uplands, was sometimes no more than notional; but the Ottomans could for a time describe the sea as theirs. They held the only major approaches, via the Danube and the Straits. The entire southern and western coasts were provinces of the empire. The north was protected by an allied Muslim state and the barrier of the unfriendly steppe. The Ottoman strategic view of the sea was thus primarily defensive.[36] Imperial policy centered around keeping the approaches closed, the coastal fortresses strong, and the flat expanses of the *Dasht*, as far as possible, wild. Despite the Ottoman commitment to extending the boundaries of the sultan's domain and the abode of Islam—the way the Ottomans came to explain to themselves in retrospect their remarkable successes of the 1300s and 1400s—the ideology of expansion was notably absent in the north. The reason was simple: In the Black Sea, the Ottomans had a very good deal.

With the coming of the Cossacks, however, all that began to change. The sea and the northern steppe now became sources of insecurity, a vast expanse of land and water that the Ottomans found demanded more energy than ever before to pacify. The Black Sea was no longer an inland sea, a waterway bounded on all sides by lands that could be counted as part of the empire. It had now become a frontier. By the late 1600s, the growing power to the north, Russia, had begun to discover that this changed situation could be to its own advantage.

NOTES

1. "Kara Deniz," *Encyclopedia of Islam*, Vol. 4, pp. 575–7.
2. Halil İnalcık, "The Question of the Closing of the Black Sea Under the Ottomans," *Archeion Pontou*, Vol. 35 (1979):108.
3. Quoted in Elizabeth Zachariadou, "The Ottoman World," in Chistopher Allmand (ed.) *The New Cambridge Medieval History of Europe*, Vol. 7 (Cambridge: Cambridge University Press, 1998), p. 829.
4. "Istanbul," *Encyclopedia of Islam*, Vol. 4, p. 244.
5. "Kipchak" refers to the nomadic inhabitants of the steppe, whose languages were part of a distinct Kipchak branch of Turkic languages. Turkish is a member of the Oghuz branch.
6. Victor Ostapchuk, "The Human Landscape of the Ottoman Black Sea in the Face of the Cossack Naval Raids," *Oriente Moderno*, Vol. 20, No. 1 (2001):28–9.
7. Quoted in Ostapchuk, "The Human Landscape," p. 33.
8. Halil İnalcık, with Donald Quataert (eds.) *An Economic and Social History of the Ottoman Empire*, Vol. I (Cambridge: Cambridge University Press, 1997), p. 271. See also Gilles Veinstein, "From the Italians to the Ottomans: The Case of the Northern Black Sea Coast in the Sixteenth Century," *Mediterranean Historical Review*, Vol. 1, No. 2 (December 1986):221–37.
9. Orthodox Christians remained the majority in most other small cities on the northern coast. Veinstein, "From the Italians to the Ottomans," p. 224.
10. Halil İnalcık, *Sources and Studies on the Ottoman Black Sea. Vol. 1: The Customs Register of Caffa, 1487–1490* (Cambridge, MA: Ukrainian Research Institute, Harvard University Press, 1996).
11. Veinstein, "From the Italians to the Ottomans," p. 223.
12. I am grateful to Felicia Roşu for her assistance in the research and writing of this section. In antiquity, the volume of slaves from the Black Sea was probably less than that

coming from other centers in the Mediterranean. See David C. Braund and Gocha R. Tsetskhladze, "The Export of Slaves from Colchis," *Classical Quarterly*, Vol. 39, No. 1 (1989):114–25. The classic article on the Black Sea slave trade under the Ottomans is Alan Fisher, "Muscovy and the Black Sea Slave Trade," *Canadian–American Slavic Studies*, Vol. 6 (1972):575–94.

13. M. I. Finley, "The Black Sea and Danubian Regions and the Slave Trade in Antiquity," *Klio*, No. 40 (1962):53.

14. Pero Tafur, *Travels and Adventures, 1435–1439,* trans. Malcolm Letts (New York: Harper and Brothers, 1926), p. 133.

15. İnalcık and Quataert, *An Economic and Social History*, Vol. 1, p. 283.

16. İnalcık and Quataert, *An Economic and Social History*, Vol. 1, p. 285. Khodarkovsky estimates that 150,000–200,000 people were captured in Tatar raids on Muscovite lands in the first half of the seventeenth century alone. Michael Khodarkovsky, *Russia's Steppe Frontier: The Making of a Colonial Empire, 1500–1800* (Bloomington: Indiana University Press, 2002), p. 22.

17. Halil İnalcık, "Servile Labor in the Ottoman Empire," in Abraham Ascher, Tibor Halasi-Kun, and Béla K. Király (eds.) *The Mutual Effects of the Islamic and Judeo-Christian Worlds: The East European Pattern* (New York: Brooklyn College Press, 1979), p. 34.

18. Nicolae Iorga, *Studii istorice asupra Chiliei şi Cetăţii Albe* (Bucharest: Institutul de Arte Grafice Carol Göbl, 1899), p. 161.

19. A supplementary source of state-held slaves was the *devşirme*, or child tax, system, under which children were taken to Istanbul, converted to Islam, and employed in the Ottoman state apparatus and military. *Devşirme* was practiced from the fourteenth to the seventeenth centuries and applied mainly to Slavic Orthodox populations in the south Balkans.

20. Evliya Çelebi, *Narrative of Travels in Europe, Asia, and Africa, in the Seventeenth Century*, trans. Joseph von Hammer, Vol. 2 (London: Oriental Translation Fund of Great Britain and Ireland, 1834), p. 58.

21. Marie Guthrie, *A Tour, Performed in the Years 1795–6, Through the Taurida, or Crimea, the Antient Kingdom of Bosphorus, the Once-Powerful Republic of Tauric Cherson, and All the Other Countries on the North Shore of the Euxine, Ceded to Russia by the Peace of Kainardgi and Jassy* (London: T. Cadell, Jr., and W. Davies, 1802), p. 154.

22. August von Haxthausen, *Transcaucasia: Sketches of the Nations and Races Between the Black Sea and the Caspian* (London: Chapman and Hall, 1854), p. 8.

23. İnalcık and Quataert, *An Economic and Social History*, Vol. 1, p. 284.

24. See Şerban Papacostea, "La pénétration du commerce génois en Europe Centrale: Maurocastrum (Moncastro) et la route moldave," *Il Mar Nero*, Vol. 3 (1997–8): 149–58.

25. Quoted in Ostapchuk, "The Human Landscape," p. 28.

26. Palmira Brummett, *Ottoman Sea Power and Levantine Diplomacy in the Age of Discovery* (Albany: State University of New York Press, 1994), pp. 95–8.

27. Nikolai Ovcharov, *Ships and Shipping in the Black Sea: XIV–XIX Centuries*, trans. Elena Vatashka (Sofia: St. Kliment Ohridski University Press, 1993), pp. 19–23.

28. The major study of these drawings is Ovcharov, *Ships and Shipping in the Black Sea*, on which my discussion is based.

29. Ostapchuk, "The Human Landscape," p. 39.

30. Ahmed Hasanbegzade, *Tarih-i al-i 'Osman*, quoted in Ostapchuk, "The Human Landscape," p. 46.

31. Evliya Çelebi, *Narrative of Travels*, Vol. 2, p. 39.

32. Ostapchuk, "The Human Landscape," pp. 41–3.

33. Guillaume Le Vasseur, sieur de Beauplan, *A Description of Ukraine*, trans. Andrew B. Pernal and Dennis F. Essar (Cambridge, MA: Harvard Ukrainian Research Institute, 1993), pp. 67–8.

34. Evliya Çelebi, *Narrative of Travels*, Vol. 2, pp. 59–64.

35. Beauplan, *Description of Ukraine*, p. 69.

36. Ostapchuk, "The Human Landscape," p. 35.

The prince desired a little kingdom, in which he might administer justice in his own person, and see all the parts of government with his own eyes; but he could never fix the limits of his dominion, and was always adding to the number of his subjects.

Samuel Johnson, 1759

She wishes, at one and the same time, to form a middle class, to admit foreign commerce, to introduce manufactures, to establish credit, to increase paper-money, to raise the exchanges, to lower the interest of money, to build cities, to create academies, to people deserts, to cover the Black Sea with numerous squadrons, to annihilate the Tartars, to invade Persia, to continue aggressively her conquests from the Turks, to fetter Poland and to extend her influence over the whole of Europe.

Louis-Philippe, comte de Ségur, French ambassador to Russia,
about Catherine the Great, 1787

Ships anchor at the foot of ravines, deep among green basins,... A gallery of ports & harbors, formed by the interchange of promontory & bay. Many parts like the Highlands of the Hudson, magnified. Porpoises sport in the blue; & large flights of pigeons overhead go through evolutions like those of armies.... No wonder the Czars have always coveted the capital of the Sultans. No wonder the Russian among his firs sighs for these myrtles.

Herman Melville, on a steamer traveling up the Bosphorus, 1856

Pag. 64.

ANACHARSIS

Ex gemma antiqua.

1, 2. Travelers to and from the Black Sea world: Anacharsis the Scythian was a widely known literary figure among educated Greeks of the Classical period—the rough barbarian from the Pontus, civilized by the influence of Hellenic culture. The Roman poet Ovid was exiled to the seacoast in the first century AD, and his contacts with the peoples of the region inspired his famous lamentations on the plight of the exiled intellectual. A statue in his honor now stands in the main square of the Romanian port of Constanţa, the ancient Tomis.

3. The Dacian king Decebal commits suicide just as Roman troops descend upon him. Part of the sequence celebrating the Dacian wars on Trajan's Column in Rome.

4. Byzantine sailors employing "sea-fire" against an enemy ship, from a fourteenth-century manuscript. In this early version of a flamethrower, the Byzantines most likely used petroleum products from the Black Sea region as combustible fuel.

5 *(above)*. The striking Soumela monastery, inland from the port city of Trabzon. Soumela was one of the major church institutions to benefit from the patronage of the emperors of Trebizond. Until the virtual disappearance of Greek-speaking Christians in the region in the 1920s, Soumela remained a center of Greek cultural life in the Pontic hinterland.

6 *(left)*. A Circassian woman in traditional costume, the essence of exotic beauty to both Ottomans and Europeans in the nineteenth century. The movement of slaves, both women and men, from the northern and northeastern coasts to Anatolia (and often then to Europe) was one of the mainstays of the early Ottoman Black Sea economy.

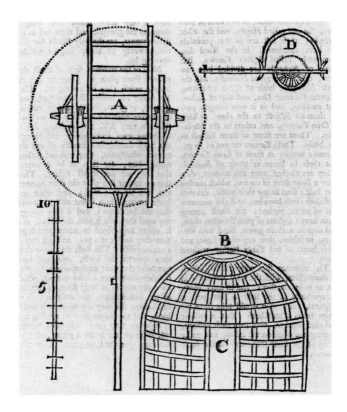

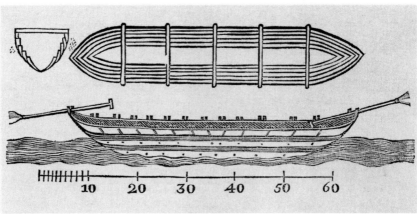

7. Transport by land and sea: Seventeenth-century diagrams of the cart used by Nogay nomads on the Black Sea steppe and of the *chaika*, or small boat, used by Cossack raiders in their encounters with Ottoman warships.

8 *(left)*. The bust of John Paul Jones by Houdon. Jones, the famous naval hero of the American War of Independence, ended his career in the service of Catherine the Great on the Black Sea. But conflicts with Prince Potemkin and others close to Catherine led to his leaving Russia in disgrace.

9 *(below)*. Heinrich Buchholtz, *Allegory of the Victory of the Russian Fleet over the Turks in the Turkish War of 1768– 1774* (1777). Peter the Great looks on as Catherine the Great completes his strategic vision: the acquisition of unfettered Russian access to the Black Sea and the Mediterranean. The victory of 1774 opened the Black Sea to Russian-flagged commercial vessels and paved the way for the rapid expansion of the economy of the Russian south.

10. Rough traveling: A "nocturnal battle with wolves" in Moldova, from a travelogue by Edmund Spencer, 1855. Although a sail on the Black Sea became a regular part of the Grand Tour in the nineteenth century, travelers still needed a sense of adventure to journey to the more remote inland regions of the Balkans, Carpathians, and Caucasus.

11. Cossack Bay at Balaklava during the Crimean War. Crowded conditions in ports and encampments meant that disease was rampant among both Allied and Russian troops.

12 (above). Divers with apparatus and support team at the Ottoman Imperial Naval Arsenal, circa 1890, from the photo albums of Sultan Abdülhamit II. The Ottomans embarked on a major naval modernization program in the late nineteenth century, but as in the Crimean War, the empire remained largely reliant on the naval power of its west European allies.

13 (left). A hand-dug oil pit in Romania, 1923. Petroleum became the twentieth century's equivalent of the nineteenth-century grain exports from the Russian and Balkan ports.

14. A ship filled with refugees and White Army soldiers fleeing Sevastopol during the Russian Civil War, 1919.

15. Fortunes of war: Refugee children from the Russian empire arriving at London's Waterloo Station, en route to South Africa for adoption, circa 1920. From the 1860s to the 1920s and beyond, forced population movements brought monumental change to the demography of the Black Sea region.

5

Chernoe More, 1700–1860

Diderot's *Encyclopédie*, the Enlightenment's great compendium of human know-ledge, contains a brief entry on the Black Sea. The "Pont-Euxin" is described as lying "between Little Tartary and Circassia to the north, Georgia to the east, Anatolia to the south, and European Turkey to the west." The author of the entry adds helpfully that it is not a *pont* in the sense that an empty-headed French courtier might understand it—that is, not a "bridge"—but rather "an Asian sea."[1]

That was in the 1750s. Over the next hundred years, Diderot's geography became obsolete. From the second half of the eighteenth century, the Russian empire extended its reach to the warm ports of Crimea, pushing back the Ottomans and unseating their client, the Tatar khan. In the west and east, the empire also began to influence the kings and princes of the Balkans and the Caucasus, casting Russia first as the protector of eastern Christendom and later as the liberator of oppressed nations from the Turkish yoke. By the mid-nineteenth century, the Black Sea could no longer be described as "Asian" at all. It was now divided between the waxing and waning powers of eastern Europe, the Russians and the Ottomans, a waterway on which two sets of imperial ambitions came into intimate contact—something closer, in fact, to the *pont* in the courtier's sense, not Diderot's.

The sea's sideways slide into Europe began with the changing strategic rela-tionship between the sea and the steppe. For the Ottomans, keeping the sea peaceful and the northern steppe wild had been the twin imperatives of security since the fall of Constantinople. So long as most foreign vessels were barred from entering the Black Sea and a stable relationship could be maintained with client states along the littoral, the Ottomans held a virtual monopoly on the sea's wealth; and the Eurasian steppe, traversed by nomads and Tatar raiding parties, represented a natural check on the ambitions of northern powers. For the

Russians, the imperatives were exactly the reverse. As the Cossack sea raids had shown, the Ottomans were vulnerable to concerted attacks from the northern shore, but to reach the sea, Russia first had to move across the inhospitable grass-lands on its own southern frontier. Inhabited by a shifting array of Cossacks, peasants, and Nogay nomads—and much of it inhabited by no one at all—the steppe had long been a source of irritation. It was from this "wild field," as both Russian and Polish writers called it, that Tatar bands descended on Christian vil-lages and made off with plunder and people, a land of brigands and outlaws, a refuge to which dissatisfied peasants could repair when they tired of working for one or another landlord farther north.

A central feature of Russian state policy from the reigns of Ivan the Terrible (1533–84) to Peter the Great (1689–1725) was the effort to make the steppe into something definite and controllable, to make the frontier, in other words, into a boundary. That plan, however, placed the Russians in direct competition with the Tatar khans and, by extension, with the Ottoman empire. What began as a more or less defensive policy of state security developed, over the course of the eighteenth century, into an ideology of expansion. First under Peter and then under Catherine the Great (1762–96), Russia embraced the imperial idea, wrapped up in the civilizing rationalism of the Enlightenment and the desire for conquest that had long preoccupied older imperial powers in western Europe. The drive to control the steppe became a push to conquer the sea and then, in the culmi-nation of Russian visions of itself as the successor to Rome, as a project to take the Straits and place a Russian prince on the throne of a revived Byzantium. The new empire was to be the bearer of civilization to the benighted south, reaching out across the Black Sea to the Mediterranean and laying hold of the legacy of Constantine. In various permutations, that strategic aim would set the course of Russian foreign policy until the very end of both the Russian and the Ottoman empires in the tumult of the First World War.

The clash of imperial aims provided the context for developments around the sea in the eighteenth and nineteenth centuries. The nodal points in the sea's development are the treaties that ended each in a long progression of wars, first between the Ottomans and central European powers and later between the Ottomans and Russia. In 1699 and 1700, the treaties of Karlowitz and Istanbul represented the beginning of Ottoman imperial retreat, with the loss of territo-ries in central Europe to Austria, areas northwest of the Black Sea to Poland, and parts of the north–central and northeast littoral to Russia. The treaty of Belgrade in 1739 granted Russia control of the important fortress at Azov and allowed limited Russian trading rights on the sea. In 1774, under the treaty of Küçük Kaynarca, the Ottomans at last agreed to allow Russian merchant vessels to sail the sea unimpeded, a concession that would be extended over the next several decades to include other foreign merchantmen as well. Russia's expanding influence was codified in 1829 and 1839. In the treaties of Adrianople and Hünkâr İskelesi, the Ottomans recognized full Russian naval rights on the sea and guaranteed free passage through the Straits; the sultan also ceded further territories along the northern coast, made effective Russian protectorates out of Wallachia and Moldova, and established a clear border in the south Caucasus.

Under Hünkâr İskelesi, the sultan agreed to close the Dardanelles to foreign vessels at Russia's request, a worrying sign to western powers of the tsar's designs in the Near East. Russian aspirations, however, were curbed during the Crimean war, when Britain and France came to the aid of the embattled sultan and forced Russia to agree to a treaty that made the sea a neutral international space, barred to all warships. Russia would eventually repudiate the terms of the peace treaty and in the last major Russo-Turkish conflict, in 1877–8, rush through the Balkans, and threaten to march on Constantinople itself, an outcome averted only because of the muscular diplomacy of Britain and France. The Ottoman empire, a regional power that had once been a threat because of its strength, had now become a problem because of its relative weakness in the face of Russian encroachments. How to manage that strategic shift would form the basic conundrum of European diplomats and strategists in the Near East for the rest of the nineteenth and early twentieth centuries.

Sea and Steppe

It is difficult to overestimate the place of the insecure steppe in Russian state policy in the two centuries bracketed by the reigns of Ivan the Terrible and Peter the Great. Dealing with it was a central component of the transition from principality to empire, from Muscovy to modern Russia. The steppe was a region where two different visions of power and society came into contact: in the north, the urban, military–bureaucratic Muscovite state, built on the legacy of the tax-farming role it had been accorded by the Tatar–Mongol khans, and with a developing sense of itself as a Christian state with a claim to the legacy of Byzantium; and in the south, a fluid array of hordes and khanates, with a social system based on the kinship relations of traditional societies, mainly nomadic, notionally Islamic.[2]

The real source of conflict between these two systems lay not in any of these traits, however, but in the complex relationship between violence and property. For the Muscovites, organized violence was the preserve of the state, and the use of the army, assembled by the nobility for campaigns against rival powers such as

Poland and Lithuania, was to protect the domains of the grand prince and the property of his subjects. By contrast, the nomads of the steppe, as well as their patrons, the Crimean khans, gained considerable wealth from armed entrepreneurship: pillaging cities and villages to the north, enforcing tributary relations, even persuading a potential trading partner to offer privileged terms. In the seventeenth century, the Crimean khan could field an army of up to 80,000 horsemen, and even small-scale raids by nomads could include as many as 3,000 cavalrymen armed with sabers and bows.[3] However, the job of the army was not to secure a state—there was, after all, nothing like a modern state to speak of—but to provide the means of enrichment for individual soldiers and their leaders and, in the case of slave raiding, to secure a fungible commodity that could be traded with the preeminent power across the sea, the Ottomans.

The economic and social effects of Muscovy's security problem were far-reaching. Trade was interrupted. Tribute paid to the khans sapped the state treasury. The loss of labor was also substantial. Perhaps as many as 200,000 Slavic Christians were captured in the first half of the seventeenth century alone, and even when the captors allowed the slaves to be redeemed—which Muscovy financed by special public levies—the ransom represented a further drain on state coffers.[4] The historian Michael Khodarkovsky has calculated that the amount the tsar paid to the Crimean khan in the first half of the seventeenth century in tribute, ransom, and taxes on trade was as much as six million rubles, the equivalent of the funds necessary to build some 1,200 small towns.[5] If Muscovy's rise to dominance had been built on its privileged relations with the khans of the Golden Horde, Russia's retarded urbanization and economic backwardness in the early modern period was in no small measure a result of the depredations of the Horde's successors in Crimea and on the steppe (even if many individual captives no doubt learned to accommodate themselves to life in Tatar or Ottoman hands).

Throughout the sixteenth and seventeenth centuries, the tsars worked first to mitigate and then to eliminate the ill effects of the insecure periphery, or *krai* (from which the name Ukraine derives). State funding mechanisms were put in place to buy back captives. Multiple lines of defense—earthworks, felled trees, ditches—were constructed on the northern edge of the steppe zone. Diplomatic overtures were made to the Crimean Tatars in an attempt to halt excursions by freelance raiders. Under Ivan the Terrible, Russian policies became more assertive. Ivan took the title of tsar of all Russia—no longer simply grand prince of Muscovy—and moved against the successors of the Golden Horde. The khanate of Kazan on the Volga fell in 1552, the khanate of Astrakhan on the Caspian in 1556, and the khanate of Siberia in 1581. Payment of tribute eventually ceased. Russian colonists were sent into the newly conquered lands, and relations were forged between the state and the Cossacks, with the tsar recognizing the authority of the Cossack leadership in exchange for protection of the expanding frontier.

If there was an ideology of conquest at this stage, it was not one of empire. There was no civilizing mission on the part of the Russian state, nor was there a clear sense that the move against the remnants of the Golden Horde crossed some basic line between civilization and savagery or even between Christianity and Islam. Rather, the more aggressive move toward the south and east began as a solution to a basic security problem, wed to a growing sense on the part of the Russians that they—not the khans—were the real heirs to the legacy of the Tatar–Mongols.

By the middle of the seventeenth century, the steppe was hardly tame, but it had changed from an insecure frontier into something closer to a boundary. New defensive lines, pushed farther and farther south, checked large-scale assaults; and various Cossack hosts, now in league with Russia, launched their own punitive raids on the Tatars. In the middle of the century, Russia's alliance with the Zaporozhian Cossacks enabled the acquisition of further territory in the west; in 1654, after supporting an uprising by the Cossacks and then winning a war against the Poles, the tsar claimed the Ukrainian steppeland, including the city of Kiev. With the acquisition of eastern Ukraine, the tsar's influence extended over much of the old territory of the Golden Horde, from the shores of the Caspian across the steppe to the Dnepr. The Russian state still did not border on the Black Sea, but it controlled the two major access routes from the north, the Don and Dnepr rivers. This was the setting for the greatest change on the sea since the fall of Constantinople: the appearance of an organized, state-funded navy that could challenge the hegemony of the Ottomans.

A Flotilla on Azov

When Peter the Great ascended to the throne in 1689, his domains touched the oceans at only one port, at Arkhangel'sk on the White Sea, frozen for much of the year. The Baltic was the purview of Sweden; the Black Sea belonged to the Ottomans. Within about a century and a half, though, Russia had extended its reach across the Baltic and had developed a warm-water navy that could enter the Mediterranean, by way of Gibraltar, and saw action as far afield as Egypt. It had constructed ports and naval bases all across the northern littoral of the Black Sea, from Odessa in the west, to Sevastopol in Crimea, to Novorossiisk in the east. Russia had become, in short, a European naval power, and one that could begin to wrest full command of the sea away from Istanbul.

Peter was convinced that the greatness of the Russian state depended on securing access to the Black Sea, a major step toward weakening the ability of the Ottomans and the Tatar khans to threaten Russia's new possessions in the south. The origins of the Russian naval presence on the sea were less than auspicious, however. Peter's initial attempts to gain a foothold on the coast were abject failures. A campaign against the Ottoman fortress of Azov in 1695 ended in the rout of Russian and Cossack forces. The Ottomans and their allies had the strategic advantage of being able to support their army and provision their garrisons with naval forces, and the lesson for Peter was that Russia's fortunes in the south depended fundamentally on the ability to meet the Ottomans on the water.

Azov was a critical military target. The fortress commanded the lower reaches of the Don river, blocking Russian passage to the Sea of Azov, and thus to the wider Black Sea. If Russian ships were ever to sail beyond the river's mouth, taking the fortress was the first step. Shortly after his first failed attack on Azov, Peter launched a program to outfit a naval force of galleys and gunboats that could assist in a new campaign. A prototype galley was delivered from Holland, and on that model, other ships were assembled near Moscow and transported overland in sections to Voronezh on the upper Don. By the summer of 1696, Peter had created a flotilla of some two dozen warships and smaller craft. In early May, the ships left Voronezh and floated down the Don, accompanied by a small detachment of Cossack boats, toward another encounter with the Ottoman garrison. A Swiss, François Lefort, served as admiral of the entire fleet, while Peter himself took the lower-level position of commanding a division of galleys.[6]

Even before the Russian forces arrived, Cossack boats had already been harassing Ottoman ships that were attempting to resupply the garrison. By late June, the entire Russian armada had arrived off Azov, and the appearance in force of the Russians, along with continual Cossack sea raids, dissuaded the Ottoman ships at the mouth of the river from attempting to break through to the fortress. Land forces laid siege, and in about a month the Ottoman garrison surrendered. Azov had been taken before—by the Cossacks alone in 1637—but the contrast with the earlier conquest was extraordinary. When the Cossacks overran the fortress and offered it up to Tsar Mikhail Romanov, the tsar refused the gift for fear that it would spark off a wider conflict with the Ottomans, a war that would surely have ended in a Russian defeat. Mikhail grandson, however, took Azov himself, in no small measure because of his newly constructed navy.

The success of the Azov campaign encouraged Russia's shipbuilding efforts, and after the conclusion of a truce with the Ottomans in 1698, the Russians now had the ability to put their ships to trial on open water, on the Sea of Azov. Shipyards at Voronezh and other points nearer the mouth of the Don produced warships at incredible speed. Most of the old galleys used in Peter's campaign were replaced by sailing ships of up to fifty-eight guns. In 1699 the newly outfitted Russian fleet consisted of ten ships and two galleys; by 1702 fifteen more gunships had been added. In all, between 1695 and 1711, fifty-eight battleships were laid down on the Don and its tributaries.[7] An ambitious project to dig a canal between the Volga and Don rivers—a plan to connect the Black and Caspian seas that the Ottomans themselves had once entertained—was begun under the direction of a British engineer.[8] Peter was now putting to use the skills that he had acquired on his celebrated embassy to the shipbuilding centers of western Europe in the late 1690s.

Throughout the first two decades of the eighteenth century, Peter's attentions were often pulled in different directions. In a long-running war with Sweden, the theater of battle was dangerously close to the new capital of St. Petersburg. Significant resources were devoted to bolstering naval strength in the Baltic, which would eventually become the centerpiece of Russia's naval power. The project to build a southern navy soon fell by the wayside. Ships rotted at anchor, and the canal plan, fraught with financial problems, was abandoned. Russian ships never managed to move beyond the shallow Sea of Azov; the approach to the Black Sea guarded by Ottoman fortresses on the Kerch strait.

The taking of Azov had been a resounding victory, but Peter's attempts to repeat that success elsewhere were disastrous. In 1710 Peter formed an alliance with Dimitrie Cantemir, prince of Moldova and technically a vassal of the Ottomans, to launch a new war against the sultan. Victory would mean an effectively independent Moldovan principality, allied with Russia, and unfettered access to the Danube river. The war was a short-lived adventure. The combined Russian and Moldovan forces were annihilated in short order by the Ottoman army, and the Peace of the Prut, signed in 1711, had major consequences for both allies. The historical right of Moldovan princes to control their own affairs was ended, and directly appointed administrators were sent from Istanbul. (A similar arrangement, known as the Phanariot system, was put in place in Wallachia in 1716.) For Russia, the price of defeat was the loss of all the possessions along the sea as well as the scuppering of the Azov fleet. Some of the ships were handed over to the Ottomans, the rest destroyed. The Azov fortress was ceded back to the sultan. The Russian naval presence in the south was now effectively back to where it had been fifteen years before.

Peter's early experiment on the Don and the Sea of Azov was not for naught, however. The Azov fleet demonstrated once and for all that the Ottomans could be defeated with the right combination of land and naval forces, targeted against key fortresses on the northern shore. In fact, the disaster of the 1710–11 campaign was due in part to the fact that Peter and Cantemir attempted to meet the Ottomans on the open field, rather than engage in a coordinated land and sea attack on a critical outpost, as had happened at Azov. The vulnerability of the Ottomans on the sea had been clear from the Cossack campaigns of the seventeenth century, but after the building of the Azov fleet, it was evident that the Russian state could also achieve strategically what Cossack raiders had managed to do haphazardly much earlier. It also convinced any skeptical Russian nobles and administrators that European naval technology, and even European captains and sailors, were vital to the modernization of Russia's fighting forces.

The reigns of Peter's immediate successors were taken up with the frequent back-and-forth conquest and surrender of fortresses and territory. Russia launched a new attack on the Ottomans and the Crimean Tatars in 1736 and managed to secure control once again of Azov, as well as the fortress of Ochakov at the mouth of the Dnepr river. In the peace treaty that ended the war, however, Russia was forced to relinquish its territorial conquests and, while retaining Azov, agreed to dismantle the defenses and keep no warships on the sea.

It was not until the reign of Catherine the Great that the results of Peter's early ventures to the south would be fully realized. The great change in Catherine's policy was that, far more than among any of her predecessors, Russian actions were driven by a clear ideology of imperial conquest. The security problems of the "wild field" had been reduced, if not eliminated, during the late seventeenth and early eighteenth centuries. Ukraine east of the Dnepr river had been taken into the Russian state—now properly an empire—and Peter's successors had also added a small bit of steppeland north of Crimea, almost to the Dnestr river. Tatar raiding had diminished, and the Cossacks had become an effective, if inconstant, frontier ally. For Catherine and her advisers, however, particularly the resourceful and colorful Prince Grigorii Potemkin, the culmination of Russia's modernization was to be not simply the taming of the steppe but the elimination of the Ottoman threat once and for all through the restoration of Christian sovereignty over Contantinople.

The first step in this plan was to win control of the sea, and in 1768 Catherine launched the first of two wars against the Ottomans during her reign. Russian land forces pushed around the northwest coast, occupying Wallachia and Moldova; another detachment moved south into Crimea and, in short order, defeated the army of the Crimean khan. In the most spectacular move of the war, Catherine dispatched her Baltic fleet, the pride of Russian seafaring since Peter, around Europe into the Mediterranean and, in a surprise attack, sank much of the Ottoman navy in the Aegean in the summer of 1770.

The treaty of Küçük Kaynarca ended the war in July 1774. Russia received several major fortresses around the sea, including Azov and Taganrog on the Sea of Azov (which gave Russia effective command of that body of water), Kerch and Yenikale on the Straits of Kerch (which opened up a secure route to the Black Sea), and Kinburn at the mouth of the Dnepr (which guarded the route between the Dnepr estuary and the wider sea). In times of peace, Russian ships could now sail down either the Don or the Dnepr, the two most important northern waterways, and enter the sea. Russian merchant ships were given the right to sail "free and unmolested" all the way across the sea and through the Straits into the Mediterranean. Russia now held a secure footing all along the north shore. The influence of the sultan was whittled down to command of only a few fortresses and the title of religious leader, or caliph, of the Muslim Tatars.

Cleopatra Processes South

After the military victories of Catherine's first major war with the sultan and the diplomatic victories of the Küçük Kaynarca treaty, the expansion of Russian interest in the newly acquired lands was rapid. The Zaporozhian Cossacks, formerly treated as an ally of the tsar in the south, were now subordinated to Russian imperial control; the Cossack headquarters on an island in the Dnepr river was destroyed in 1775, a move that brought the entire river under the control of the Russian state. Crimea, long a dependency of the Ottomans, had been made independent in the peace treaty, but this nominal status was in the main a mask for Russian influence; in 1783 Catherine formally annexed the region by simply posting an announcement that the khan and his people were now subjects of the Russian emperor. The pretext had been the inability of the Tatars to govern themselves—even though the khans had never actually asked for the independence thrust upon them a decade earlier—but the result was the further expansion of Russian territory toward the sea and weakening of the remnants of Ottoman power on the northern shore. The degree to which the frontier had now become part of an expanding European empire was to become abundantly clear only a few years later.

Catherine desired to survey the lineaments of her new possessions, and in the first half of 1787 she journeyed from St. Petersburg to Crimea in a procession that deserves to be counted among the grandest displays of sovereign majesty in the age of enlightened despotism. Louis-Philippe, comte de Ségur, the French ambassador to the Russian court, accompanied the empress on her journey and left a famous account in his memoirs.[9]

Ségur was acquainted with all the personages of note in his day. He had known Washington, Kosciuszko, and Lafayette (his nephew) when he served as an officer with the Continental Army; he had corresponded with Frederick the Great and Joseph II; he had been attached to the courts of Louis XV and XVI. But his time with the "Cleopatra of the North," as he called her, was quite unlike anything he had witnessed before. "Nothing less resembles ordinary travelling, than the journeys of a court," Ségur wrote. "Travelling alone, one sees men, countries, customs, establishments such as they really are; but in accompanying a monarch, the traveller finds every thing prepared, disguised, coloured for the purposes of display; and in the words and actions of men under such circumstances he scarcely discovers more sincerity than in manifestoes of politicians."[10]

The party that set off from St. Petersburg in January 1787 was a mobile court. Fourteen carriages and nearly 200 sleds carried Catherine, her many guests, and their belongings. At each stop along the route, hundreds of fresh horses were waiting to be harnessed for the next leg of the journey. Because of the bitter cold, everyone was wrapped in bearskin blankets and fur pelisses, with sable hats bobbing as the company rushed along the icy roadways. Catherine's habit was to rise each morning at six o'clock, confer with her ministers, breakfast, then set off at nine for a full day of traveling, leaving plenty of time to acknowledge her subjects, who assembled at the entrances to the cities to witness the spectacle.

As Ségur observed, this entire display was designed not only to celebrate the triumphs over the barbarous Turks, but also to convince Catherine's new subjects as well as her foreign guests that Russia—or at least its empress—could no longer be counted among the savage nations of the world. "She knew at that time many people, especially in France and at Paris, still looked upon Russia as an Asiatic country, poor, plunged in ignorance, darkness and barbarity; that they affected to confound the new and European Russia with the Asiatic and savage Muscovy." The pomp of the procession was calculated to convince all concerned that the empress's "little household," as she called it—her empire—was on the road to improvement and that a portion of the Black Sea now lay squarely within her enlightened domain.[11]

Catherine's route took her down the Dnepr river to Kiev and from there on to Crimea. At each stop, a magnificent palace was hastily erected for the empress by her chief minister and paramour, Prince Potemkin, where she could entertain the visiting dignitaries who came to join her procession, including the king of Poland and Joseph II of Austria. Trees were uprooted and put in a more appealing arrangement. Villages were spruced up and peasants dragooned into expressing their spontaneous joy at the sight of the sovereign. A flotilla of river boats, including seven massive galleys, with perhaps 3,000 crew, oarsmen, and guards, was assembled to ferry the party down the Dnepr, while special music was performed by ensembles on the decks.[12]

"It was like a magic theatre," Ségur wrote, "where ancient and modern times seemed to be mingled and confounded with one another, where civilization went hand in hand with barbarism, and the contrast was rendered the more extraordinary by the marked difference and great variety of the manners, figures and costume of the persons who composed the whole."[13] There were princes and merchants, army officers in full-dress uniforms, mounted Cossack lancers, Tatar nobles now bowing before their new sovereign, princes of Georgia bringing tribute to the Christian empress, and envoys from the nomads of the steppe. In addition to the parades, military displays, and courtly entertainments, the grand diversions arranged by Potemkin could be truly impressive. At one point, a hill at the edge of the Dnepr was cut with a long ditch, which was then filled with flammable material. At night, a mass of fireworks was set off on the summit, so that the fire spread down the ditch to the bottom of the hill, a manmade volcano that thrilled the assembled dignitaries.[14]

The survey of the southern lands ended in Crimea. Catherine briefly visited the khan's former palace at Bakhchisarai and made provision for its renovation. (It was because of Catherine's decision to preserve the palace rather than raze it, as had often happened in conquered lands, that it remains a tourist attraction even today.) Some of the procession's dignity was lost in negotiating the narrow streets around the palace, where confused Tatar residents and shopkeepers looked on in amazement. A visit to the newly constructed naval base at Sevastapol followed, where Catherine received a salute from the small Russian fleet assembled in the harbor—all the while under the watchful eye of Ottoman vessels anchored just off the coast. By the middle of the summer, Catherine had tired of life on the road and gave orders to return to St. Petersburg, where she arrived to a momentous reception in July.

Ségur eventually returned to France and found himself caught up in the pandemonium of the French revolution. The barbarism of the streets of Paris, he later recalled, contrasted sharply with the grandeur of Catherine's procession to the south. Russia was now in the middle of a transformation from backwardness to civilization precisely at a time when the center of enlightened thought and culture seemed to be moving in the opposite direction.

Having quitted the magic circle, I was not longer to see, at each moment, as in our triumphant and romantic journey, new objects of surprise; fleets suddenly created, squadrons of Cossacks and Tartars, coming from the remote parts of Asia, illuminated roads, mountains on fire, enchanted palaces, gardens raised in a night, savage caverns, temples of Diana, delightful harems, wandering tribes, dromedaries and camels wandering through deserts, hospodars [princes] of Wallachia, and dethroned princes of Caucasus and persecuted Georgia, paying homage, and addressing their prayers to the Queen of the North.[15]

The action and romance of life along the Black Sea had been traded for the plodding march of history.

Ségur was right about the major changes at work along the northern shore, but one of the most significant developments in the social life of the newly conquered steppelands had taken place already more than a decade before Catherine's procession. Large-scale steppe nomadism, a way of life that had remained little changed since the Scythians of antiquity, was giving way to settled agriculture and state-sponsored colonization. That shift was exemplified by a massive movement of people far more tragic but no less grand than the empress's own journey of 1787.

The Flight of the Kalmoucks

One evening during their trip with Catherine, Count Ségur and the Austrian emperor Joseph II took a stroll to see the steppe in the moonlight. Watching camels and shepherds lazily drift across the landscape, the count remarked to the emperor that "it appears to me rather like a page from the *Arabian Nights Entertainments*, and that I am walking with the Caliph Haroun-al-Raschild."

A bizarre sight soon shook them from their reverie. The emperor rubbed his eyes and strained to see in the dim light. "In truth, I do not know whether I am awake, or whether your allusion to the Arabian Nights has enchanted me," he said, "but look on this side." Ségur turned to where the emperor had pointed to find a large tent gliding across the grassy plain, apparently propelling itself. As they rushed forward to investigate, out popped thirty men, who had been moving the tent to a new location by holding onto the wooden staves from the inside. Everyone had a good laugh.

The men were "savage Kalmoucks," as Ségur called them, "who bear a true resemblance to the Huns, whose ugliness in days of yore inspired as much terror in Europe as did the renowned sword of their ferocious monarch Attila."[16] Although Ségur could not have known it, they were also among the last of their kind, the remnant of a people that had once dominated the lands to the north-east of the Black Sea, all the way to the Caspian. Less than two decades before Ségur encountered them, most had left the region behind in the last dramatic wave of nomadic movement across the Eurasian steppe.

The Kalmoucks—or Kalmyks in modern spelling—were a nomadic Mongol population, Tibetan Buddhist by religion, who had migrated from western China in the middle of the 1600s.[17] The traditional grazing lands for their immense herds of horses, sheep, and cattle had become threatened by neighboring Muslim peoples, and like the many migrants before them, from the Scythians to the Mongols of the Middle Ages, they moved en masse toward the west, to the lands between the Volga and Don rivers and beyond. More than a quarter of a million people may have been included in this search for new pastures.

In the seventeenth century, there was little to stand in their way. Much of the Black Sea steppe, especially to the east, was under no strong central control. Russian power was limited to concluding alliances with local Turkic rulers and with the Cossacks. The advance of the Kalmyks had important consequences. By displacing local nomadic allies of the Russian state, the Kalmyks left the southern borderlands open to raids from a host of groups westward as far as Crimea. In the winter of 1636–7, another group of Turkic pastoralists, the Nogays, fled across the Don and took refuge in Crimea after news of an impending strike by the Kalmyks. The movement of the Nogays to the west may actually have opened up a route for the Cossack advance on the Azov fortress in 1637.

As in the past, the tsars learned to make peace with their new southern neighbors. With the annexation of eastern Ukraine in 1654, Russia was in need of strong friends to counter the threats posed by the Tatars of Crimea, the Poles to the west, and, farther afield, the Ottomans. Written agreements were drafted under which the Kalmyks pledged support for the Russian tsar in return for payments to Kalmyk nobles and protection against local raiding parties. The goal was to reduce the Kalmyks to the status of loyal subjects by identifying and privileging one of the many Kalmyk tribal rulers—in effect, creating a centralized Kalmyk authority which had not existed in the traditionally diffuse pastoral society. Things never worked that smoothly, however. The Kalmyks often played both sides of the table, trading horses with the Crimean Tatars while professing loyalty to the Russians. When Moscow objected, the Kalmyks countered that the alliance was an arrangement between two equal and sovereign powers, not between a suzerain and a subordinate.

The relationship changed significantly over the next century. As the power of the Russian state grew and the steppe ceased to be the danger that it had been to Muscovy, the need for mobile border guards decreased. Peter's seizure of Azov and advances in Russian military technology, especially the use of heavy artillery, reduced the threat posed by both Ottomans and small-scale raiders in the south. The pacification of the frontier attracted settlers, who were encouraged to move to the Don–Volga region by the government. Along the two rivers, Slavic-speaking Orthodox populations grew as traders and business people flocked to take advantage of new opportunities. State-run enterprises such as vineyards, silk factories, and salt mines attracted Russian workers and their families.[18] Farmers turned the soil of the steppe, making hayfields of the grasslands that had once fed Kalmyk herds.

As in the American West, the relationship between settlers and nomads was tense. Kalmyk raiding parties, continuing the tradition of stealing from local rivals, now targeted the newly arrived Russian settlers, who saw in the practice little more than common thievery. Some Kalmyks, grown dependent on handouts from the Russian state, gave up the nomadic life and settled in the burgeoning frontier towns, where they eked out a living as fishermen and occupied the lowest stratum in the new society. Even then, as a later traveler remarked, "their uncontrolled and vagrant habits" put them at odds with life in agricultural settlements.[19] Horsemen could be seen "galloping their horses through the streets of the town, or lounging in public places.... Like all nomad tribes, they are so much accustomed to an uncontrolled and erratic life, that nothing but extreme indigence can compel them to cultivate land and reside in any fixed habitation."[20]

The ties between Russians and Kalmyks had once been of mutual benefit. The Russian state provided some degree of military protection and even monetary gifts to Kalmyk leaders; the Kalmyks in turn provided a mobile military force to protect the southern frontier and a ready supply of horses for the Russian cavalry. By the late eighteenth century, all this had changed. Grazing lands were quickly disappearing beneath the plow. Hostile settlers derided nomadic traditions. Representatives of the Russian government fueled internecine rivalries that decimated the Kalmyk population and destroyed communal institutions. Missionaries, sent out by the state-supported Orthodox church and by German Protestant colonies in southern Russia, worked to convert the Kalmyks and, as a later missionary wondered, perhaps even "make them into Russians or Germans."[21] The loss of grazing space decreased the size of the remaining herds, which in turn impoverished those who chose to maintain their nomadic way of life.

Among Kalmyks dissatisfied with the fruits of civilization, there had long been rumblings about returning to western China, a far-away idyll of endless grasslands, crystal-clear rivers, and no settlers. Whenever the issue had arisen, gifts and cajoling from Russia, as well as the threat posed by hostile nomads to the east, usually deterred them. In late 1770, however, the Kalmyk leader Ubashi Khan came before his people with a daring proposal: that the entire Kalmyk people would pick up their tents and drive the herds eastward, back to the lands of their ancestors.

What followed was an exodus of epic scale. In January 1771, exactly sixteen years before Catherine's triumphal procession to Crimea, as many as 300,000 people carrying tens of thousands of tents and driving ten million head of sheep, cattle, horses, and camels set out on a 3,000-km journey to China.[22] The spectacle must have been breathtaking. The horde was headed by the chief lama and other religious leaders, followed by the khan and his retinue. Women and men alike were dressed in their finest clothes and displayed their wealth in the adornment of their horses, which were decorated with red ribbons and tinkling silver bells. Loping pack camels, draped with bright carpets that skimmed the feather grass, carried bundles of folded tents and household goods. Children clung tightly to the top of the swaying pile. Poorer families hauled their goods on wooden carts or on oxen. The immense, cacophonous herds brought up the rear, goaded forward by swift outriders. On the margins of the troupe, young men hunted with dogs or intentionally fell behind, racing at full gallop to catch up to the main column. The whole multitude stretched out for many kilometers in every direction, tied together only by the long, thin strings of the camel trains.[23] The English writer Thomas De Quincey was so taken by the story of their flight that he composed a fictionalized account of the journey, which he saw as an event both majestic and primordial: "In the unity of purpose connecting this myriad of wills, and in the blind but unerring aim at a mark so remote, there is something which recalls to mind those almighty instincts that propel the migrations of the swallow and the lemming, or the life-withering marches of the locust."[24] (De Quincey's prejudices were not much different from those held by Greeks about the Scythians or Russians about their nomadic neighbors.)

By mid-January news of the mass emigration reached St. Petersburg. Catherine, worried about the loss of her subjects to a foreign power, ordered her governors to put a halt to it, and a detachment of dragoons and Cossacks was assembled for the task. Yet, by the time they set out in pursuit in early spring, the Kalmyks were too far ahead to catch, and the poorly provisioned Russian troops were no match for a people whose food supply—the herd—was itself always mobile. The Russians were the least of the Kalmyks' worries, though. Along the way, they were frequently attacked by raiding bands of enemy nomads, particularly Kazakhs, who were eager to exact revenge for the Kalmyks' own raids on their herds and tents. (There may have been as many as 1,000 Kazakh captives traveling with the Kalmyks, hostages who had been taken only a year earlier.[25])

In a final pitched battle on the border with China, Ubashi Khan led the Kalmyks to victory in a nighttime attack on Kazakh forces, opening the doorway to China and a return to the pasturelands of the past. Catherine protested vehemently to the Chinese authorities to hand over her Kalmyks, but the Qing emperor refused, insisting that they had come under his sovereignty of their own free will.[26] He soon organized them as frontier guards, with the nomads serving the same function in China that they had earlier served for the tsars. The Kalmyks who marched into the realm of the Qing emperor were greatly diminished, however. Two-thirds of those who originally set out perished during the eight months en route.[27] Those who survived, as one contemporary observer noted, "were reduced to the depths of misery."[28]

But not all the Kalmyks fled. In the 1790s, the Russian naturalist Peter Simon Pallas reported 8,229 tents, perhaps as many as 50,000 people, on the western bank of the Volga river, the area of the present-day Republic of Kalmykia inside Russia.[29] A few were to be found as far west as the Dnestr. These were the "Kalmoucks"—either real Kalmyks or perhaps misnamed Nogays—encountered by Ségur and Joseph II. Future travelers would continue to see the few genuine nomads who remained on the steppe as the epitome of picturesque restlessness, denizens of a wild landscape that was quickly becoming, for better or worse, domesticated. Ségur even picked up a peculiar souvenir, a young Kalmyk boy named Nagun—"the most original Chinese little figure that could be seen"—as a present from Prince Potemkin. He taught him to read and remained his guardian for some time, before giving him away, like an unwanted pet, when he returned to France.[30] Nagun was even more of a rarity than Ségur could have known. By the time the count arrived on the Black Sea steppe as part of Catherine's entourage, the long era of the steppe peoples had already passed.

A Season in Kherson

The gradual sedentarization of the peoples of the steppe, the rise of new towns, and the emergence of Russia as a Black Sea power were incentives for European merchants to establish trade ties with the newly acquired ports along the northern coast. Although European ships were still formally prohibited on the sea, they could evade the Ottomans' strictures by flying Russian flags of convenience. That was a beneficial arrangement not only for traders but for the Russian state as well: Crews and ships sailing under Russian flags could be impressed into military service in times of war, a boon for a navy that was still inadequately manned and provisioned.[31] From the late eighteenth century, the sea was slowly reintegrated into a pan-European—and for some goods, genuinely global—commercial network that had not been seen since the demise of the Italian trading colonies in the fifteenth century.

Under the direction of Potemkin, the Russians had begun to establish improved port facilities at Kherson on the Dnepr river, a new city that was to become the headquarters of the Russian Admiralty as well as a major economic center. Warehouses were constructed and European businessmen invited to sample the wealth of the newly conquered steppe, now increasingly tilled and sown with wheat. In 1780, the first Russian ship sailed from Kherson to Toulon, carrying a cargo of salted beef, and interest in the possibility of commerce was piqued.[32] In the early days, however, trade was a perilous business, not only because of the continuing political tensions between Russia and the Ottomans, but also because of the hazards of living and working in a place that could still seem frightfully close to the edge of the world. The formal annexation of Crimea and Catherine's ostentatious procession seemed to make a second war with the sultan inevitable, and the practical aspects of commerce—assembling ships and crews, transporting goods on an inhospitable sea, and negotiating with fickle Ottoman officials at the Straits—could be daunting.

One person who knew these perils intimately was Antoine-Ignace Anthoine de Saint-Joseph. Anthoine staked his good name and fortune on being the first businessman to establish regular contact with the Russian ports. His goal was to link them to the French Mediterranean, to create a system of economic ties that would enrich the state and place France in the position of sole commercial intercessor between the tsar and the rest of the world.

In the early 1780s, Anthoine was commissioned by the French government and the Russian minister in Istanbul to undertake a study of the feasibility of Franco-Russian commerce and, if possible, to outfit an expedition to sail from Marseilles and return with Russian goods. He was well-placed to do so. France was Russia's greatest ally in western Europe, and Anthoine's backers enjoyed the favor of the French court. Anthoine himself had worked for one of the greatest commercial concerns in Marseilles, the House of Seimandy, and had also served for a time as head of the French community in Istanbul.[33] He thus had the necessary experience in business and shipping, as well as the essential connections in several important cities.

In April 1781 Anthoine made an exploratory voyage from Marseilles to Kherson, visiting several other ports along the Black Sea's northern shore and finding many opportunities for commerce. With his Russian counterparts eager to do business, Anthoine secured a loan from the French government to buy warehouse space in Kherson. The government also granted a reduction on import duties and supplied ships and seamen, while Louis XVI gave his own royal imprimatur to Anthoine's commercial house.

By early 1784, Anthoine had assembled three ships in Marseilles. Hopeful of even further favors from Catherine, he christened the ships after three of her ministers (and probable lovers) and set off on a fair wind for Kherson, under a Russian flag. The sea journey was uneventful, and later in the summer, the ships returned to Marseilles laden with hemp and wheat, along with samples of wax, honey, pork bristles, and tea as possible commodities for future shipments.

Anthoine's enterprise was booming. The next year, twenty ships arrived at Marseilles from Kherson, and nearly that many set sail with French goods in the opposite direction. For his efforts to promote this new commerce, Anthoine was raised to the French hereditary nobility. Through his commercial connections with the Black Sea, he and his children entered the rarefied heights of French society, now introduced as the family of the baron Saint-Joseph.

Storm clouds soon began to gather, however. Kherson was a miserable place, and despite the best efforts of the Russian authorities to make it a thriving commercial port, it could not escape its geography. It was situated away from the coast, up the Dnepr where the river's many channels fingered their way toward the estuary. In July and August, the heat and stale air were unbearable, and summer floods produced pools of stagnant water that were breeding grounds for disease. In 1787 two of Anthoine's brothers, who had joined him in his business, fell ill and died. "Kherson resembled a vast hospital," Anthoine recalled. "All one could see were the dead and the dying."[34]

International politics also began to interfere. The Ottomans had formally opened the Black Sea to foreign commerce, but shippers still had to rely on the sultan's grace and favor for passage through the Bosphorus and Dardanelles. Officials would often determine that a ship exceeded the maximum allowable lading and then impound it in Istanbul. Then there were the British. What Anthoine called *la jalousie anglaise*—the desire of England to goad Russia into fighting the Ottomans, block French expansion in the sea, and conclude a preferential trade agreement with Istanbul—meant that the threat of war between the two Black Sea empires was ever present.

Conflict finally came in the summer of 1787. Seeking to take control of Crimea from the Russians, the Ottomans opened the second major war during Catherine's reign. Anthoine was caught in the middle. Some of his vessels were at sea when war was declared, and since they were flying Russian flags, they were promptly captured by Ottoman warships. Only a few made it back safely to Marseilles. When the war ended in 1792, Anthoine managed briefly to reestablish his trading house in Kherson, but things did not work in his favor. The disease-ridden port and the lackluster interest of European powers in establishing commercial houses there seemed to argue for transferring the center of Black Sea commerce elsewhere. (The Admiralty, in fact, was moved to Nikolaev in 1794.) In the end, the turmoil of the French revolutionary wars and the banning of French products from Russian ports in the early 1790s—Catherine's response to the unruly mobs now governing Paris—forced him to close shop. Anthoine returned to Marseilles where he eventually became mayor of the city and devoted his off hours to writing an account of his adventures in Russia.

Anthoine's *Historical Essay on the Commerce and Navigation of the Black Sea* is one of the best first-hand descriptions of the opening up of the sea to European shipping and the state of Russia's conquests under Catherine. It was widely known to travelers and diplomats of the period as a reliable guide to the northern coast and a practical primer on conducting business with the Russian empire via the Black Sea, especially when a vigorous trade with the Mediterranean began to pick up again in the early nineteenth century. But people read Anthoine's book less for his colorful anecdotes and descriptions of port facilities than for the magnificent maps bound with the text.

In planning his own voyage, Anthoine had difficulty acquiring accurate maps for his captains and had to rely on French charts from the 1770s, a time when the soundings and anchorages were still imperfectly known.[35] He commissioned Jean Denis Barbié de Bocage, a talented cartographer at the French ministry of foreign affairs, to draw custom charts. Barbié produced three extraordinarily detailed engravings of the Black Sea region, based on the latest reports of the Russian Admiralty. One showed the interior navigation of European Russia and Poland, a beautiful map of the waterways of the western empire and still awe-inspiring in its detail. Another showed the overland trading routes between the Black Sea and northern Europe. A third depicted the cataracts of the Dnepr river, the same series of rapids that traders had portaged around for a millennium or more, now clearly described and artistically presented.

It is not hard to see why Anthoine approached Barbié. The cartographer was already practiced in drawing the Black Sea. In the 1760s he had been commissioned by a Jesuit to draw a series of maps depicting a fantastic journey from southern Russia—"Scythia," as the Jesuit called it—to all the major sites of classical Greece.[36] Barbié, as it turns out, was the illustrator of the Abbé Barthélemy's bestseller about a barbarian named Anacharsis and his search for civilization beyond the shores of the Pontus Euxinus. On Barbié's drawing table, the old Scythia of Anacharsis literally overlapped with the new one of imperial Russia—a Scythia now almost denuded of its picturesque pastoral peoples but still tantalizingly wild to the many entrepreneurs, travelers, and soldiers who began to explore the sea and its environs.

Rear Admiral Dzhons

When Anthoine established his business in Kherson, the sea was open to Russian-flagged commercial vessels, but it was still technically closed to Russian warships. The victories in the war of 1768–74, as well as the appearance of merchantmen such as those outfitted by Anthoine, marked a major shift in the type of vessels seen on the Black Sea. The age of sail had dawned long before in the Mediterranean and the Atlantic, where ships-of-the-line—large vessels with multiple decks, masts, and courses of square sails—had been the mainstay of European fleets for half a century or more. They were still a rarity farther to the east. But the end of Catherine's first war against the Ottomans inaugurated a period of monumental change.

Full-rigged ships, rather than rowed galleys and small sailing vessels, were seen more and more frequently, not only among merchant fleets, but also among the navies of both the Ottomans and the Russians. The Russian fleet was, according to treaty, not allowed to stray beyond the mouth of the Dnepr and the harbor at Sevastopol, but when hostilities once again broke out in Catherine's second war with the Ottomans (1787–92), the change from earlier times was evident. One of the most detailed accounts of the beginnings of the age of sail comes from one of Anthoine's contemporaries, someone whom he may well have met, a rear admiral in the Russian imperial navy by the name of Dzhons.

Pavel Ivanovich Dzhons—or John Paul Jones (1747–92), as he is better known—was, of course, the captain of the famous *Bonhomme Richard*, hero of the American War of Independence, and father of the United States Navy. His ornate tomb in the chapel of the U.S. Naval Academy has been solemnly visited by generations of midshipmen. In 1788 Jones agreed to join the Russian side in Catherine's new war against the sultan, which had come about after an Ottoman ultimatum to quit Crimea and return it to its previous independent status. The inducement was that Jones would be given supreme command of the new Black Sea fleet, now wintering at Kherson and at Sevastopol. Jones was part of a long line of foreign officers in the employ of the Russian navy—going back to the Swiss Lefort in Peter's Azov fleet—and since the new United States had still not established a navy of its own, the opportunity for gaining a major command, even if under a foreign ensign, must have seemed an opportunity too good to miss.

Jones arrived in Kherson in the spring of 1788 to find the Russian force in disarray. Russia's southern navy consisted of the main fleet at Sevastopol, diminished after a storm at sea the previous autumn, and a small outfit now anchored at Kherson. Jones was placed in charge of the Kherson squadron, a dozen or so sailing vessels variously rigged, including his flagship, the *Vladimir*. All the other available ships, mainly light Cossack boats and cannon-fitted galleys—some of them simply recommissioned ceremonial galleys which had earlier floated Catherine down the Dnepr—were assembled in a flotilla designed by the British naval engineer Samuel Bentham (brother of the philosopher Jeremy) and commanded by another soldier of fortune, Prince Charles of Nassau-Siegen. Although Jones believed that he had been given command of the entire Black Sea fleet, his authority seemed to extend over only his squadron; Nassau took orders directly from the supreme commander of all land and sea forces, Potemkin, while the main fleet at Sevastopol was commanded by a Russian rear admiral, Voinovich.

The complexities of command and deployment were a particular problem for the Russians because, as Jones soon discovered, the Dnepr estuary, or *liman*, was to be the key to the entire war on the water. The two naval detachments were prevented from combining their forces by the strait which separated the estuary from the wider sea. Twin fortresses faced each other across the narrow strait. The one on the south side of the outlet, Kinburn, was held by the Russians, a prize that had been won in the Küçük Kaynarca treaty, but the fortress on the northern point, Ochakov, was commanded by the Ottomans. At the opening to the sea, the space between the fortresses was only about 3 km wide. The strategies of the two navies were thus determined by the conditions in which they were to fight. The Russians needed to open up the strait by suppressing or capturing Ochakov; the Ottomans needed to close it off to Russian egress while maintaining a supply line to the garrison on the northern point. The Ottomans were clearly in a superior position. Their naval force was united under a single commander, the talented admiral Gazi Hasan Paşa, a Georgian by birth. Even if the Russian forces had been concentrated, the Ottomans would probably have outnumbered them in both ships and guns, even though most of the Ottoman vessels were rowed galleys rather than sailing ships.[37]

The appearance of the Ottoman fleet at the end of May opened the fighting. Jones and Nassau moved their ships along the northern shore of the estuary, attempting to keep in line with the slow advance of the land forces under Prince Alexander Suvorov, one of Potemkin's ablest generals. There were a few small engagements, but it was not until a month later, in late June, that decisive action was joined. The Ottoman galleys made for the Russian lines, but the attack came to a standstill when the Ottoman flagship grounded in the estuary's shallow water. The Russians, waiting for a favorable wind, could not take advantage of the mishap, and it was already the next morning before they were able to advance against the Ottomans, by which time the flagship had come unstuck and the galleys turned around.

Nassau's flotilla, especially the deadly Cossack gunboats with which the Ottomans were intimately familiar, proved to be the most effective against the galleys. The flotilla was able to harass the Ottoman ships and set them alight, especially when the large galleys ran aground in the shallows. On the night of June 17–18, the Ottomans attempted a retreat out of the estuary, but the Russian battery at Kinburn opened up against the fleet, forcing the galleys close to the northern shore, where even more ran aground. In the early light of morning, Nassau's floating batteries and small boats set upon them and destroyed perhaps as many as fifteen vessels, including ten large ships. Ottoman losses were considerable: over 1,500 men taken prisoner and several hundred killed, versus fewer than a hundred Russian sailors killed or wounded.[38]

With the Ottoman fleet decimated, the land forces could at last turn to the task of taking Ochakov. In July, Russian forces under Potemkin laid siege while the navy prevented resupply, a strategy that would culminate in the early winter in the capture of the fortress and the wholesale destruction of the town and its inhabitants. Thousands of Ottoman bodies, including those of the wives and children of the garrison soldiers, were loaded onto carts and taken to the frozen estuary, where they lay stacked on the ice until the spring thaw.[39] Throughout the rest of the war, the other major Ottoman fortresses—Akkerman and Bender on the Dnestr river, Kilia and Ismail on the Danube—fell one by one as the army swept to the west and the Sevastapol fleet prevented the garrisons' receiving supplies and fresh troops by sea.

The estuary campaign was decidedly different from Jones's experience during the American War of Independence. In his most famous naval engagement, the battle with the British frigate *Serapis* off the Yorkshire coast in September 1779, Jones had bested the British captain by outmaneuvering him, coming quick around the bow and grappling to the side, then pounding the ship with heavy fire directed at the masts, until the enemy vessel was dead in the water. There was nothing of the gallantry of the duel between the *Bonhomme Richard* and the *Serapis* in the campaign of 1788. There, military victory depended largely on drawing the Ottoman galleys into shallow water, waiting for them to ground, and then attacking and sinking them with incendiary devices—"brandcougles," as Jones called them, a kind of grenade. As he later recounted, the results could be horrific to watch, as the Ottoman sailors, stuck fast on their immobile ships, "suffered themselves to be throttled like as many sheep."[40]

"In my whole life," Jones wrote, "I have never suffered so much vexation as in this one Campaign of the Liman, which was nearly the death of me."[41] A rift developed between Jones and Nassau, who emerged as the clear favorite of both Potemkin and Catherine. When Jones gave orders, they were often ignored by Nassau or countermanded by Potemkin. The illustrious command of the entire Black Sea fleet, which Jones felt he had been promised from the outset of his service, never materialized; already before the storming of Ochakov, he was relieved of his limited command and recalled to St. Petersburg. After his return to the capital, Jones saw his star fall even farther. He was accused of having raped a prepubescent girl (his defense centered not on the commission of the act but on the girl's alleged consent), and news of the scandal raced through Petersburg society. It was only because of the conflicting testimony of several ostensible witnesses that Jones was allowed to leave Russia without being court-martialed. He left the empire a laughing stock and died in Paris a few years later, in July 1792.

Although he could not have known it at the time, Jones was present at the end of an era. The battle of the Dnepr estuary was the last time that Russian warfare on the water would be restricted to the outer reaches of the Black Sea. The taking of Ochakov during the course of the war freed passage to the wider sea, and from then on contests between Russian, Ottoman, and other navies would take place on the open sea itself, not in its antechambers. It was also the last time that the rowed galley would be one of the major instruments of war. Nassau's floating batteries and small gunboats were probably the real source of the Russian victory in the estuary; Jones's sailing ships had been of marginal use in the shallows and narrows. But once action was extended to the open water, the full-rigged ship-of-the-line and, not much later, the armored steamer were to become the main vessels of both the Russian and Ottoman imperial navies.

The age of sail turned out to be rather brief, however. The early wars of the nineteenth century—1806–12 and 1828–9—were largely land campaigns, in which Russian forces rushed around the sea to attain the real prizes: access to the Danube and, were it not for the opposition of European powers, Istanbul and the Straits as well. Even later, during the Crimean war, the only major naval engagement, at Sinop in 1853, could hardly be counted as such; the Russians simply destroyed the Ottoman Black Sea fleet in port. Travelers throughout the late eighteenth and much of the nineteenth centuries commented on the parlous condition of both Russian and Ottoman sailing vessels. The ships were poorly outfitted and either under- or over-manned. It was not unusual for a new ship in either navy to rot in port before it had ever seen action.

Like Jones, many observers blamed the state of the two navies on the inherent inadequacies of Russians and Turks as mariners, the former given to pomposity and tyranny, the latter the victims of a congenital Oriental insouciance. The real reasons were rather simpler. After the estuary campaign of 1788, neither the Ottomans nor the Russians considered the other power to be a serious naval threat. The Russians maintained a slight superiority in naval technology, but the Ottomans knew that their friends, particularly the British, would step in to prop up their fleet if need be. And since no other power around the sea ever managed to develop much of a naval presence at all—the only worry to speak of were smugglers along the Caucasus coast and Laz pirates in the southeast—the two major empires had little reason to concern themselves with anything beyond coastal defense. One of the major goals of European diplomacy up to the First World War, and indeed to a degree even after, was to ensure that things stayed that way.

New Russia

In the treaty that ended Catherine's second war with the Ottomans, the Russian empire gained control of the entire northern littoral, all the way from the Dnestr to the Kuban river, as well as formal Ottoman recognition of the loss of Crimea. Those gains were consolidated and expanded in two wars fought by Catherine's successors. The lands between the Dnestr and Prut rivers (an area known as

Bessarabia) was absorbed into the empire, and then much of the Caucasus coast and portions of historic Armenia and Georgia also came under Russian suzerainty. Russia not only commanded the northern coast but also claimed a right to protect the Christians of the Danubian principalities and formally annexed most of the south Caucasus. Within a little more than a generation, from the Küçük Kaynarca treaty (1774) to the treaty of Adrianople (1829), Catherine and her successors had come close to realizing the goal of reaching across the sea to take Constantinople itself. The northern coast and hinterland, far from being a frontier, was now made into a Russian province, a region that tsarist administrators came to call, with all the unabashed optimism of empire-builders everywhere, New Russia (*Novorossiia*).

Catherine had a particular concern with reshaping the natural world according to her views of rationality and order, and as with many Enlightenment rulers, classical antiquity was seen as the epitome of both. For the new class of administrators across New Russia, rediscovering—or inventing—a connection with ancient Greece became an obsession. Settlements were stripped of their previous Tatar names and given labels derived from classical roots. The Crimean administrative center of Akmechet ("white mosque") became Simferopol ("the city of connections," as in roads).⁴² A flood-prone village on the Dnepr river was christened Kherson (after Chersonesus Taurica, the old Megarian colony in Crimea) and designated the center of Russian commerce and the seat of a major naval arsenal. The village of Akhtiar and its protected harbor, near the old Chersonesus, was renamed Sevastopol ("august city"), and made the headquarters of the Black Sea fleet. Of all the major towns in the south, only Bakhchisarai ("garden palace") retained its Tatar name, with the khan's palace and other buildings preserved as a museum of the Oriental splendor of a deposed sovereign. Crimea itself—the Tatar "Krym"—was rechristened Tavrida, the Russian version of its Greek name.

The growth of new cities along the coast altered the nature of shipping on the sea. Previously, the quadrangle of Caffa, Trabzon, Sinop, and Istanbul had been the natural link between the northern and southern coasts, an extension of the routes that led overland across the steppe to the north and east, and south across Anatolia to Persia. After the late eighteenth century, however, that water route fell into desuetude. The real center of commerce—and increasingly of urban life and culture—no longer lay in the middle of the sea, in the Crimean peninsula, but to the west, along the outlets of the Dnepr and Dnestr rivers, a return, in fact, to the important status of the northwest littoral during the age of Greek colonization.

The reasons for this shift lay in the imperatives of strategy and geography. Caffa and the other Crimean ports were really more a part of the southern coast than they were of the northern; they were separated from the Crimean interior by a chain of mountains and naturally looked out to the seaports of Anatolia, not to the flatlands of the north. That situation suited the Ottomans, of course, but it was a problem for the Russians, for whom the transport of goods over the mountains was time-consuming and expensive. Those ports were also far away from the other economic and strategic points of concern for Russian foreign policy in the eighteenth and nineteenth centuries—the Polish lands, the Danube, and the Balkans—and were easily exposed in the event of an Ottoman attack from the south.

The new center of gravity became Odessa, the greatest of modern Black Sea ports. For the past two centuries, Odessa has been synonymous with the idea of a Russian imperial city, and for good reason. It was the premier example of the new political and cultural optimism that pervaded Russia's acquisitions in the late eighteenth and early nineteenth centuries, the southern equivalent of the creation of St. Petersburg a hundred years earlier. The city's expanding population, drawn from across the empire, central Europe, and the Near East, became a microcosm of the multiethnic and multi-religious reality of the tsarist empire, more diverse and far less Russian than either of the twin imperial capitals, St. Petersburg and Moscow. Until the end of the empire, it remained the commercial, administrative, and cultural heart of the Russian Black Sea, the quintessential imperial seaport and the leading export center of the entire empire.

At the time of the Russian conquest, Odessa had little to recommend it. It was a dusty Tatar town named Hadji-bey, with no more than 2,000 inhabitants. Its harbor was unattractive because of its poor anchorage and exposure to easterly winds; in winter, ice could obstruct the bay for several weeks. Nevertheless, it was the most significant fortified town on the northwest coast (the small Ottoman fortress there had been captured by José de Ribas, John Paul Jones's former adjutant, in 1789) and held a commanding position between the Dnepr estuary and the Dnestr and Danube rivers; it was also a short race from the Russian fleet's base at Sevastopol. (Two other important sites, the forts at Ochakov on the Dnepr estuary and Akkerman on the Dnestr, both had serious disadvantages. The former had no natural harbor, and the latter could not host heavily laden vessels because of river silting.) In 1794 the town was rechristened Odessa, after the old Greek colony of Odessus. The feminization of the name was apparently the preference of the empress Catherine herself.

Credit for the development of the city belongs to two capable administrators whose collective tenure stretched over the better part of the early nineteenth century. Armand, duc de Richelieu, served as governor of the Odessa district from 1803 to 1814, latterly as governor-general of the entire New Russian territory. His statue now stands atop the famous granite steps that cascade from the upper city down to the modern port. Richelieu was a scion of the great family of French courtiers and statesmen, and like John Paul Jones and his other contemporaries, he sought adventure (and, in Richelieu's particular case, refuge from the revolutionary throngs of Paris) by joining the Russian army as a volunteer during the Russo-Turkish war. His service was repaid with a commission and, after the war, a post as administrator of the new city.

Richelieu's time in office was relatively short—only eleven years—after which he returned to France to serve as prime minister following the defeat of Napoleon; but the changes that he brought to the city and to the entire region were spectacular. Odessa's population grew to 35,000 inhabitants over the span of a decade. Richelieu founded banking facilities and a commercial court, laid out the modern street system, and encouraged the growth of printing, the theater, and the arts.[43] The romantic élan that he brought to raising a city up from the dust attracted the attention of many outside the empire; he may even have been a model for Byron's Don Juan.

Richelieu was succeeded by a compatriot, the comte de Langeron, whose short period of service normally goes unremarked, but it was under Langeron's successor, the long-serving governor-general Mikhail Vorontsov (in office 1823–45), that New Russia became fully a part of the growing empire, with Odessa as the jewel in the crown. A graduate of Cambridge, he laid the foundation for a university library and encouraged the growth of charitable societies. He also ordered the construction of the famous Odessa steps (criticized at the time as a costly folly) and planned the majestic buildings and boulevard that top the cliff overlooking the harbor.[44] Under his tenure, Odessa was also granted the status of a free port, exempt from tariffs. When he left office, the city's population had risen to some 78,000.[45]

Another of Vorontsov's achievements lay in Crimea. Odessa was the administrative hub of New Russia, but its military center lay at the naval arsenal of Sevastopol, on the southwest coast of the peninsula. The site was formerly a simple Tatar village, captured in 1783, but the location had powerful symbolic associations. It was located near the ancient colony of Chersonesus, the same place where St. Vladimir had converted to Christianity in the tenth century. Of even greater significance, however, were the natural advantages of the inlet that lay nearby. The deep harbor was entered by a very narrow passage, less than 1,000 yards wide, that could be easily closed off to intruders; the long inner harbor, surrounded by cliffs, had solid anchorage and a precipitous slope from the shore, which meant that ships could anchor close in without fear of running aground. It was unquestionably the finest natural site for a protected naval station on any coast, and with the addition of fortified roadsteads and gun emplacements in the 1820s, it became the focus of Russian naval might in the south.

Why had no other power realized the military advantages of Sevastopol? The short answer is that none had needed to. Neither Greeks nor Romans were much concerned with creating a naval station on the north coast, and for the Byzantines, relations with the city of Chersonesus—at times rebellious, at times congenial—depended on a delicate balance with the peoples of the interior, not on military strength. For the Ottomans, with their Tatar vassals in control of the entire Crimean peninsula, there was little reason to expend effort there, especially when the rivers—the Don, the Dnepr, the Dnestr, and the Danube—were far more threatening avenues for potential invaders (whence the attention given to holding the fortresses at Azov, Ochakov, Akkerman, and Kilia). It was only with the coming of a new, northern naval presence that having a fortified port in Crimea became imperative, and from the time of Catherine on, the city would become the most important naval outpost on the entire coast.

When the Russian naturalist Peter Simon Pallas traveled through New Russia in the 1790s, he found little to remark. Once great cities were in ruins, and even the promising port of Sevastopol was overrun by disease and the depredations of a wood-boring worm that wrought havoc on the hulls of Russian sailing vessels. The new Odessa was poor and choked with dust, and the port at Kherson had fallen into disuse because of the prevalence of infectious diseases, such as those that had taken Anthoine's brothers in the 1780s.[46]

Within only a few decades, however, the coast would have been nearly unrecognizable. The extension of Russian control to other littoral areas consolidated the security of the northern shore, and the Ottoman agreement to free passage of foreign-flagged commercial ships provided steady traffic to and from the Mediterranean. Once the sea was opened, the water provided a natural outlet for the province's products—and an outlet that was far cheaper and easier than traveling the poor roads that led off to the north. The railway did not arrive in Odessa until the 1860s, and travel through the interior was effected by caravans of ox-carts or, for passengers, by "posting," bumping along in a straw-lined cart drawn by horses that would be refreshed at regular post-stations along the road.[47] The new cities naturally looked out to the sea as their connection to the rest of the world.

The changes in the first decades of the nineteenth century were manifold. At Taganrog, on the Sea of Azov, a profitable trade in wine imports from the Aegean began. It was said that more wine was imported into the customs house there than in all other ports of the Russian empire combined.[48] Salt, scooped up from the coastal lakes in northern Crimea, was exported to the Caucasus, Poland, and even Istanbul.[49] Some of the towns that Pallas had found in ruins were beginning to revive. Caffa, which had been destroyed by the Russians in the last war, was now coming back. Its mainly Greek, Tatar, and Jewish population was again engaged in trade, spurred on by a regular sailing link with Istanbul, and foreign merchants soon reestablished the sailing routes to Sinop, Trabzon, and the Caucasus coast.[50] Kherson, once virtually abandoned, also had a new lease of life. The Dnepr river had been banked to prevent flooding, an engineering innovation which eliminated the pools of stagnant water that had accelerated the annual summer epidemics. The port was still largely inactive, due to the relocation of the Admiralty headquarters to Nikolaev, but rope-making factories and other sea-related industries were beginning to take off.[51] (Even the aging baron Anthoine managed to reestablish a small business there through an intermediary.[52]) "These ... towns," a British visitor noted already in 1802, "as well as the numerous villages which have suddenly reared their heads in a country formerly inhabited by lawless banditti, or traversed by roving hordes, are filled with Russians, with Tartars reclaimed from their wandering life, and with numerous colonists, particularly Greeks and Armenians, who migrated from the adjacent provinces of the Turkish empire."[53]

Among the new cities, Odessa clearly held pride of place. A mole was built to protect ships against northeasterly winds and to prevent the harbor's silting up from the currents produced by the mouth of the Dnepr; 150 sailing ships could be accommodated inside it. With the full opening of the sea to European commerce and the declaration of a tax-free regime in Odessa, Austrian and British flags dominated in the harbor. The city's population expanded and contracted over any given year, rising considerably in the summer when convoys from Poland and central Ukraine arrived in the city and petty traders crowded the marketplaces, but the number of permanent residents grew steadily. "Were it not for the swarms of Israelites, and the dreadful dust in the streets," commented a British sea captain in 1823, "the first impression of the town would be favourable."[54]

These "Israelites" and other diaspora peoples, however, were part of what drove the rapid development of the New Russian towns and seaports. The population of Slavic-speaking peasants and Cossacks had already begun to grow in the late eighteenth century and accelerated in the early nineteenth, the product of a state-sponsored program of resettlement to the borderlands.[55] But successive Russian governments also actively encouraged colonization from abroad—from central Europe, the Polish lands, and elsewhere. Tax concessions, exemption from military service, religious tolerance, loans, and grants of land were provided to groups that wished to populate the newly opened steppe.

Already under Catherine, German-speaking immigrants, especially Mennonites, had been given incentives to farm the steppeland and establish towns. Others, such as Greeks and Armenians, were resettled from Crimea or arrived from various parts of the Ottoman empire, drawn not only by the prospects of economic advantage but also by the hope of living in an empire governed by a beneficent Christian monarch. Jews, subjected to harsh restrictions in other parts of the empire, were given relative freedom of settlement and employment in the new border regions.

Foreign settlers were made subjects of the Russian empire, but their lives were largely separate from those of the Slavic peasants, Tatars, and Cossacks who surrounded them. Throughout the nineteenth century, the distinctiveness of these communities impressed outsiders, who saw the German towns in particular as islands of civilization on a frontier that was only recently integrated into a European empire. "The town is neatly laid out," wrote a British visitor about one major colony, "and beautifully supplied with clear water."

The church, the school, and a few of the most important buildings, are of stone, the rest of wood. Avenues of trees line the streets; and here, under the grateful shade, we can imagine the patriarchs of the community seated during the afternoon, enjoying tobacco of their own growing, moistening it with beer of their own brewing, and regarding the members of the happy little society as children of their own rearing.[56]

Life, of course, was hardly the idyll that some imagined, but the colonies did have a considerable impact on the economy of the region. Already by the end of Richelieu's tenure as governor-general, in 1814, the population of New Russia had increased by a million people, and land values had grown tenfold.[57] Agricultural surpluses grew rapidly and coincided with diminishing production in western Europe. Shipments of wheat from the New Russian colonies and from the large holdings of Russian nobles found their way to Livorno, Genoa, Marseilles, and other major ports. (Ease of shipment for cargoes of wheat had been specifically guaranteed in the treaty of Adrianople in 1829.) The repeal of the British corn laws in 1846, which eventually eliminated tariffs on foreign grain, opened up yet another major market. In only a decade, from the early 1840s to the early 1850s, the volume of annual wheat exports to France and Italy increased by about a quarter and to Britain by sevenfold. The total number of ships entering Russian ports more than tripled. By 1853 more than a third of all Russian exports passed through the Black Sea.[58] As more and more European businesses sprang up in the ports, however, the tsarist government became wary of delivering its commerce into the hands of British and French merchants, and a series of laws restricted brokerage activity to Russian subjects—a restriction that actually enhanced the position of the traditional "middlemen minorities" in the province such as Greeks, Jews, and Armenians.

By the middle of the century, New Russia was no longer simply a political and cultural periphery; it was on its way to becoming a well-integrated part of the Russian empire, governed by talented imperial administrators and populated by Russian and Ukrainian peasants, foreign colonists and businessmen, and Tatars both settled and, in diminishing numbers, semi-nomadic. Sailing ships could go from Crimea or Odessa to the Straits in three days, steamers in half that time, and from there to the major ports of southern Europe and the Atlantic.⁵⁹ There was, however, still an identifiable frontier in the region, and any traveler who arrived by ship, horse, or cart knew it intimately. Crossing it usually meant spending days or weeks in seclusion, deloused, examined, and left to cool one's heels in a quarantine house. The intersection of steppe and sea no longer represented a cultural frontier. It now marked an epidemiological one.

Fever, Ague, and Lazaretto

The plague—a catch-all term for several related bacterial diseases—had been known around the sea since at least the fourteenth century, and its effects were felt throughout the period of Russian expansion.⁶⁰ The great plague in Moscow in 1771 was probably the result of infected soldiers' returning from along the Dnestr river during the first war of Catherine's reign, and the wars of 1806–12 and 1828–9 were likewise marked by a raging epidemic throughout New Russia and the eastern Balkans. As new ports grew up in the nineteenth century, a major concern was preventing the spread of the disease from Anatolia and the Ottoman Balkans, where outbreaks were frequent and poorly contained, by ensuring that both goods and people were thoroughly inspected before being allowed into the towns.

From the plague's earliest appearance in western Europe, publicly funded systems were put in place to deal with its spread. Although physicians had little understanding of the exact causes of the disease or the mechanisms of transmission, they quickly discovered that isolating suspect patients—usually for the biblical period of forty days, whence the French word *quarantine*—allowed the disease to run its course. The infected patient died and the uninfected survived. The first quarantine hospital was founded in 1403 in Venice, and other Mediterranean port cities, such as Genoa and Marseilles, established their own not long after.

It was almost another four centuries before full quarantine systems were put in place around the Black Sea. The absence of large-scale foreign commerce coming to the seaports until the end of the eighteenth century meant that there was little concern about long-distance infection. It was only with the Russian acquisition of outlets on the northern coast and the revival of ties with the Mediterranean that transmission of the disease became an issue. (Previously, the major barrier lay on the Ottoman–Austrian land frontier, which ran along the border of modern Croatia and through central Romania.)[61] Even then, when there were outbreaks of the plague, the initial response was either to attempt to ameliorate the suffering of the sick—the famous British prison reformer John Howard died in Kherson in 1790 while ministering to an infected woman—or, in medieval fashion, to blame it on the Jews.[62] As it turned out, the early contacts between the Russian ports and Marseilles, pioneered by Anthoine, would eventually have an advantage beyond the purely commercial. Marseilles had the most sophisticated quarantine system in all of Europe in the eighteenth century, and the systems eventually put in place in the Russian ports were designed on the general lines of the Marseilles model.

The Marseilles system rested on five basic principles: isolation of all inbound ships for preliminary examination at a distance from the port; a determination of the health conditions in the port of embarkation; an assessment of the susceptibility of infection in the original port or en route; the strict segregation of newly arrived goods and passengers from the general population; and the further segregation of passengers already infected from those deemed to be in good health.[63] All ships coming from the Levant or other suspect ports were required to anchor in the gulf of Marseilles well outside the harbor. Through a speaking trumpet, a local official would solicit information on the port of departure, the name of the ship and its captain, the cargo, and the ship's health certificate. The certificate was a document issued by the French consul in the port of embarkation, attesting on pain of death to the condition of the ship upon departure: both ship and port free of plague (*patente nette*); ship appeared free but the port suspect (*patente touchée*); plague raging in the port and the ship suspect (*patente soupçonée*); or both port and ship known to be infected (*patente brute*). Ships with the first two types of certificate were directed to the outer harbor, where a further conversation at a distance would be conducted with the captain and a determination made about whether any period of quarantine should be imposed. Ships with certificates *soupçonée* and *brute* were directed immediately to the quarantine house, or lazaretto (a term derived from the biblical Lazarus).

The length of time in quarantine depended on several factors beyond the health certificate. Goods deemed particularly susceptible as plague carriers (such as wool, cotton, and other fibers, along with fur and skins) were enough to send a ship to quarantine. The port of embarkation also mattered. Ships coming from Morocco and Egypt were thought to have minimal probability of infection, but those from Istanbul and the Black Sea ports were required to complete forty days' quarantine plus three weeks of open airing of all cargo, regardless of the type of certificate or the nature of the goods on board.

Once ordered into quarantine, the ship would be anchored off the lazaretto, located on an island away from the main Marseilles harbor. Two guard boats prevented unauthorized communication with the shore. Food would be supplied to those on board by means of long poles, and the crew were required to report daily on any signs of illness. Passengers could choose to remain on the ship or be removed to the lazaretto, which was surrounded by a high fence and a moat. The passenger, with his luggage, would be fumigated, interrogated, and then directed either to the section for those infected or the one for those deemed healthy. The rooms were comfortable but spare, outfitted with iron bedsteads and fireplaces. Visitors were prohibited inside the buildings, but friends and relatives of those effecting the quarantine were allowed to yell across the moat. A person already infected with the plague was required to stay in confinement for twelve weeks, a period long enough for him to die. Afterwards, the body would be removed from the room with long iron hooks and buried in a lime-laced grave. The room would then be fumigated, whitewashed, and aired out for a month.

The authorities in Marseilles were well aware of the scope for corruption in this complex system, and they took great pains to guard against it. The super-intendent of the lazaretto was usually a wealthy merchant well-versed in trade with the Near East. He was to be unmarried or a widower and was paid a handsome salary, as were his lieutenants and the soldiers on duty—not only because of the personal danger associated with their jobs, but also to make less appealing the petty bribes that might be offered by captains or passengers to avoid the strictures of the system.

The Marseilles lazaretto was widely considered to be the finest in Europe. As it traveled east, however, the model underwent certain mutations. The British writer Edmund Spencer, traveling in 1836, gave an account of the quarantine at Galaţi, a Moldovan river port on the lower Danube, then under the control of the Russian empire:

My passport having been demanded—a regulation altogether novel in this govern-ment—was produced, and transferred to a pair of tongs several yards in length, the officer entertaining a deep and, it must be confessed, not unfounded horror of every-thing appertaining to a man who had just arrived from the city of the plague [Istanbul]. That important document being found perfectly correct, we were conducted under the escort of a general to the lazaretto, where any article of my luggage underwent a thorough fumigation; and when the medical officer had examined the state of our health, we were sentenced to fourteen days' quarantine, which I suppose was mitigated from twenty-one by the application to his conscience of a ducat.[64]

As Spencer discovered, the system did not always work as it was intended. Ships would be met in harbor by a sanitary officer, who would communicate with the passengers and crew by means of a long pole or tongs. But since there was no system for determining the situation in the port of embarkation (the Russians and Ottomans had separate quarantine systems and no consuls charged with issuing health certificates, as in the French system), the only document requested was a passport or other identification papers. Sometimes, indifferent officials would require no further evidence than a verbal oath—on a New Testament, an Old Testament or a Koran—that the traveler was free of the plague.[65] Ships from Ottoman ports were regularly subject to quarantine, but the period was in practice determined at the whim of the chief medical officer, not according to any preestablished regulations.

Once in the lazaretto, things were not nearly as Spartan as in Marseilles. Wealthy travelers could pay for suitable accommodation. In Odessa, there were cafes, restaurants, and even a billiard hall to relieve travelers of their boredom (and their cash), all staffed by workers who freely came in and out of the lazaretto each day.[66] Important travelers, such as diplomats or friends of local officials, would be taken out for cruises around the harbor.[67] For those willing to pay an extra "tax" to the officials, the quarantine could be reduced or effected somewhere besides the lazaretto. Visitors were even permitted inside the quarantine area. All of that, of course, undercut the rationale for the entire system.

Still, having the institution of a lazaretto was considered an advantage for any port. Without one, a port withered; with one, it could become a major business destination, the first stop for inbound ships required to perform quarantine before unloading or proceeding to lesser ports. In fact, the decline of Nikolaev and Kherson as trading centers in the early nineteenth century was due in part to the Russian government's decision to place a quarantine facility in Odessa.[68]

The presence of a quarantine house also provided substantial opportunities for personal enrichment. For many individuals, the fear of disease, especially one that tended to break out only every fifteen years or so, was far less powerful than the promise of profiting from the state-imposed system of regulation. In some instances, sanitary officers even had an incentive to produce an imaginary plague of their own. For example, one of the medical inspectors in Odessa was also the owner of a prominent theater. When ticket receipts were low, he would announce the discovery of a dire infectious disease among newly arrived passengers and order them quarantined, as usual, at their own cost. The mark-up on the expenses at the lazaretto would then be used to hire a major performer for the theater.[69] The severity of the "plague" was usually a good predictor of the quality of the upcoming opera season.

Despite the obvious occasions for graft, Edmund Spencer wrote, the sanitary officer was one of "the stars which herald in the dawn of European civilization" in the Russian ports.[70] The Russian quarantine system, combined with greater attention to the plague in the Ottoman ports, did lead to a decrease in outbreaks. By the middle of the nineteenth century, in fact, it had all but disappeared; the last major occurrences were in Bulgaria in 1840 and in central and eastern Anatolia in 1842, and from then on occasional outbreaks were mainly local and with diminished mortality.[71] Other major infectious diseases were still a concern—malarial fever along the swampy northern coast and cholera across the entire region—but, as for the plague, even an imperfect system turned out to be an improvement on no system at all.

A Consul in Trabzon

Most visitors to the northern and western coasts were impressed with the mere existence of quarantine facilities, inadequate as they might have been, for they represented at least a version of the European systems with which travelers were most familiar. Western Europeans who expected to find in New Russia "all sorts of Russo-Greco-Scythico-Tartaric churches and buildings," as a Scottish traveler wrote, instead encountered well-planned streets, stone buildings, and shops that reminded them of home.[72] Especially if a visitor arrived by sea rather than overland—where travel along rutted roads in bone-rattling wooden carts could be a trial—the scene that awaited him could be very pleasant: the sleepy Danube river ports, the bustling harbor of Odessa, the shipyards of Nikolaev, the ancient Crimean port towns, all connected by a string of well-maintained lighthouses said to rival those of Britain.[73] Even areas along the western coast and cities farther inland such as Bucharest and Iaşi, the capitals of the principalities of Wallachia and Moldova, were quickly changing. The British traveler James Henry Skene was surprised to find that one of his hosts, Prince Barbu Ştirbei of Wallachia, was able to serve up a meal that was surprisingly civilized:

truffles from Paris, oysters from Constantinople, and a pheasant from Vienna, all brought fresh by special couriers: and wines in perfection; hock of Prince Metternich's best vintage, claret warmed, and champagne not over iced; in short, everything was quite as it should be.[74]

The surroundings of the ports, river towns, and inland cities in the north and west were often so much "as they should be," in fact, that travelers were thrilled when they were actually able to find something genuinely Oriental. Anatole de Demidoff, a Russian geologist and one of the most famous travelers in south Russia in the early nineteenth century, recorded his impressions on entering the former Crimean khan's palace at Bakhchisarai:

We were now not in Vienna, the gay capital, nor Pesth [Budapest], the proud queen of young Hungary; nor on the Danube, with its inundated shores, its foaming eddies bearing down tranquil steam-boats: no, nor Bukharest or Yassy [Iaşi], cities discoloured by the pallid institutions of the east. We were in a perfect eastern Saraï [seraglio], a palace of the Arabian nights; we were on thoroughly Asiatic ground.[75]

Bakhchisarai was interesting precisely because it was so unusual, a museum of a way of life that had long since disappeared on the northern shore. Most of the urban centers of the north and west were new creations, cities such as Odessa that sprang up from the steppe, planned by foreign engineers, with streets that intersected at right angles and buildings that incorporated the latest architectural styles from central Europe. Even cities located near ancient sites, such as those in Crimea, had been thoroughly rebuilt, with new, planned suburbs located outside the former citadels. The contrast with the ports in the south and east was palpable. There, cities had grown up organically on top of ancient settlements, a jumble of streets and buildings of stone and wood pouring beyond the Byzantine-era battlements; the most modern buildings were often those that had been erected under the Genoese and Venetians. Communication systems in the northwest and southeast were also strikingly different. By the middle of the century, telegraph lines connected Varna on the Bulgarian coast with Balaklava and Sevastopol in Crimea; another line ran all the way from Simferopol around to Galaţi on the Danube, and spurs from both these lines led off to St. Petersburg, Paris, London, and Istanbul. Across the sea, however, not a single telegraph line connected Sinop and Trabzon with each other or with the Ottoman capital.[76]

The evident differences between the coasts were, in large part, the result of the contrasting visions and abilities of the Russian and Ottoman governments. The transformation of the northern littoral was the outcome of a strategic dream that had motivated Russian leaders from Peter the Great forward: to remove military threats on Russia's southern border, to gain access to the sea, perhaps eventually even to unseat the Ottomans and take control of the Straits. With the demand for grains and other products in western Europe, the New Russian lands found a ready market for exports and a business community eager to establish ties with the burgeoning cities. In the southeast, the picture was rather different. At the same time that the Russian state was expanding its imperial boundaries, the ability of the Ottoman central government to control local affairs in Anatolia was diminishing.

From the early eighteenth century until well into the nineteenth, much of Anatolia, including many of the major ports along the Black Sea coast, were under the control of hereditary, semi-feudal *derebeys* who managed their own affairs with little regard for one another or, least of all, for the sultan in Istanbul. Some were benevolent despots who looked after the interests of their own populations, but they had little incentive to improve port facilities or to explore trade relations beyond their restricted domains. Geography was also not in their favor. Like the Crimean ports, the cities in the south and east were naturally linked with the lands across the sea; travel overland into Anatolia was difficult, especially if it necessitated passing through the lands of an unfriendly *derebey*. With the reorientation of the northern ports after 1774—toward the coasting trade with one another and toward the export market of the Mediterranean and beyond—the Anatolian cities lost the natural cross-sea partnerships that had sustained them. There was also a simpler explanation for the insularity of the Anatolian ports: The Ottomans had agreed to open the sea to Russian ships under the Küçük Kaynarca treaty, but they were under no obligation to open their ports to them. It was not until 1829, in fact, that the sultan finally agreed to regular and unimpeded access of foreign ships to the Ottoman Black Sea ports themselves.

The changes in the northern reaches of the sea were initially greeted in western Europe as the advance of civilization against barbarism, the movement of a rising European empire into lands that had long suffered under the misrule of the Turk and his vassals. As the nineteenth century progressed, however, Russian ambitions came to be perceived rather differently, as the rapacity of an overzealous empire, grown confident from conquest and now threatening the interests of other European states.

Under Catherine, the acquisition of New Russia and Crimea had been cloaked in the language of enlightenment and the civilizing mission of a Christian sovereign; the downtrodden subjects of the sultan were to be freed from the yoke of Muslim despotism and introduced to the rationalizing policies of a European empire. That essential justification remained in place after Catherine, but the civilizing mission now took second place to the strategic aim of controlling the sea itself. Russia took the Christian kingdom of eastern Georgia under its protection in 1801. A little later, the empire assumed a protective right over Romanian-speaking Christians in the Danubian lands and soon began to exert a more powerful influence among Christian populations all over the Balkans and the Near East. The growth in Russian power directly affected the interests of the other major empire with strategic and commercial aims in the region: Britain.

Britain had long depended on a privileged relationship with the Ottoman sultan to secure trading rights in the Levant. Russian moves into the Black Sea zone were thus of some concern, not least because they coincided with Russian machinations even farther to the east, in central Asia and India, where British interests were manifold. A Russian war with Persia from 1826 to 1828 had ended with the tsar's gaining the right to exclusive navigation on the Caspian Sea. The fear in London was that a similar claim would be made on the Black Sea if Russia ever soundly defeated the Ottomans.[77] That would mean, of course, that the tsar could fully dictate the terms of trade with the ports in the north and west, where

Britain enjoyed a volume of commerce second only to that of the Austrians. But it would also mean that Russia could control access to the Ottoman ports as well, such as Odessa's counterpart almost directly across the sea along the southeast coast, the old port at Trabzon.

Trabzon had fallen on hard times after the decline of the cross-sea trade connection with Crimea. It could still be a visually impressive city; travelers commented on the picturesque Byzantine walls and the Greek-speaking communities in the valleys beyond the coast, who seemed a remnant of the lost empire of Trebizond. But apart from alum and copper brought in from mines in the mountainous interior and the agricultural produce of the lush valleys, Trabzon had little to recommend it. Like Odessa a few decades earlier, Trabzon was a point of interest to the Russians, British, and other European powers not because of any natural endowments, but because of where it was situated: at the head of the ancient overland route to Persia.

The Trabzon–Erzurum–Tabriz route had been active in the Middle Ages, but after the fifteenth century it was largely abandoned. The Ottoman closure of the sea to foreign commerce effectively ended the importance of Trabzon as a transit center; but the opening of the sea in 1774, and of all the Ottoman ports some time later, allowed for the possibility of a revival of the route to Persia, a trading partner eagerly courted by the British, French, and Russians alike. The transit trade with Persia via the Black Sea had been ongoing for some time before the 1820s, but the route was a circuitous one. Ships had to unload at Caucasus ports (either those controlled by Russia or by local notables), then pack the goods overland through Georgia to Tiflis and then on across Armenia to Tabriz.[78] The Trabzon route was much preferable. It was some 300 km shorter, which translated into ten days' difference in travel time.[79] Moreover, as political tensions between Britain and Russia began to rise—over economic relations with Persia and, most problematically, over central Asia—Britain had an incentive to find a route to the east that did not involve travel through the Russian-controlled Caucasus.

The future of Trabzon was thus of considerable concern to Britain. Having a say in the city's affairs and keeping open a regular and safe sailing route to Istanbul became the goal of British policy along the southeast coast. The British Foreign Office soon decided to open a permanent consulate in Trabzon to monitor local developments and shipping activity. In 1830 the British ambassador in Istanbul appointed a young diplomat, James Brant, as the first consul in the port. The ambassador's instructions to his new representative revealed the keen interest that Britain had begun to take in Russian actions around the sea. "The recent success of Russia and the extension of her domain in the quarter to which you are going," wrote the ambassador, Sir Robert Gordon, referring to the outcome of the 1826–9 wars with Persia and the Ottoman empire, "cannot have failed to produce a sensible effect upon the minds of the inhabitants, whether Christian or Mahomedan; and it is my wish that you should endeavour to ascertain the nature of that effect, and to acquaint me in how far it may be prejudiced to the interests of the Sultan."[80] In particular, the ambassador asked that Brant report on the various ethnic groups of the region (whether, for example, the local Armenian and Laz populations had any particular sympathy for Russia), as well as the political influence that Russian authorities might exercise in Trabzon and the extent of their commercial interests.

Brant reported regularly to the ambassador in Istanbul and compiled a series of annual reports that chronicled the changes taking place in the city. Already by the time Brant arrived, the sultan had begun to exercise more control over the city and the region around it; the old *derebeys* had been ousted in the centralizing reforms of Sultan Mahmut II (reigned 1808–39), and a provincial governor had been dispatched from Istanbul. As Brant discovered, that change meant that the sultan now had a direct hand in the affairs of the port and could command the tax revenue from the import and export businesses being carried on via foreign shipping companies. Given the influence that Britain enjoyed in both Istanbul and Tehran, British firms were well placed to profit from the full opening of the port to foreigners.

Brant found the roadsteads in inadequate condition and the local authorities not always cooperative. British shipping was miniscule compared to that of other countries; only two British ships entered Trabzon in 1831 as against fourteen Austrian and ten Russian.[81] Over the course of his tenure, things changed dramatically. The extension of Ottoman central control across Anatolia undercut the power of local notables and brought the empire back into a single administrative order. Better quarantine systems reduced the incidence of infectious diseases, which had at times brought the Persian transit trade to a complete halt. Regular steamship connections to the Anatolian ports cut down travel time to Istanbul and the Danube and ensured that goods could be delivered even in unfavorable weather. The first steamer to visit Trabzon was the British *Essex*, which called on the port in the summer of 1836, and later in the same year another British steamer opened a regular route to Istanbul. The Austrians, who exercised a virtual monopoly on steam transport on the Danube, soon launched their own route connecting Trabzon with Vienna.[82] In the mid-1840s the British P. & O. Company inaugurated a direct steam line running all the way from Trabzon to Southampton.[83] By 1835 Britain was in first place in the number of cargo ships visiting Trabzon annually.[84]

Brant left office in 1836, when he was transferred to the consulate in Erzurum. But the reports of his successors chronicled the steady growth of the Trabzon route and its vital importance in the British trade with Persia. Manufactured goods, especially cotton cloth from the mills of Manchester, as well as products from British colonial possessions, such as tea and sugar, were carried on British ships and then offloaded onto horse and camel caravans for the trip overland to Tabriz. On the return trip, ships carried Persian silks and other textiles, tobacco (mainly for sale in Istanbul), carpets, and dried fruits. Not insignificantly, the Trabzon road also became the central resupply route for British diplomats in Tabriz and Tehran. As some diplomats complained, when it was closed because of the plague, weather, or rebellious pashas, there was no sherry apéritif or postprandial port.[85]

For the first few decades after the opening of British trade with Trabzon, the port remained one of the key inlets for European commerce with the sizeable Persian market. Later in the century, it would ultimately fall victim to the opening of the Suez canal and the inauguration of Russian railway links with the Caucasus ports. In the 1830s and 1840s, though, it was still a key point of contention between Russia and Britain. The Russians, less favored by the sultan than the British, continually sought to redevelop the route to Persia via the Caucasus. That, however, depended on subduing the upland peoples of the Caucasus mountains, a persistent security problem for Russian towns along the coast as well as for persons traveling the overland "military highway" across the mountains to Tiflis. Russia's long-running frontier wars in the region sapped energy away from plans to create an alternative to the Trabzon route, and the Russian blockade of the Caucasus coastline—particularly the attempt to interdict the flow of weapons and, crucially, salt from the Ottomans to the Muslim highlanders—continually threatened to spark a major international incident. (In 1836 the Russian seizure of a British blockade runner, the *Vixen*, caused a diplomatic rift and provided fuel for political intrigues in London.) In the end, the fate of Trabzon, the Caucasus coast, and indeed the entire sea was wrapped up in a far larger contest between the British and Russian empires, the "Great Game" for mastery of central Asia; but it was a game that would reach its climax around the sea.

Crimea

The Crimean war was the only modern conflict fought largely on, and to a certain extent for, the Black Sea. Its origins lay in the growing rivalry between Britain and Russia across the Near East and central Asia, fueled by a mix of imperial ambition, commercial interests, and frontier politics, similar in some ways to that which had long complicated the relationship between Russia and the

Ottoman empire. The issue that stood at the center of that rivalry, however, was the future of the Ottoman state itself and, by extension, control of the Straits. Britain and Russia were united in their belief that the sultan's hold on his domains was tenuous and that some international agreement was necessary to delay the empire's collapse for as long as possible, to forestall a violent rush among European powers to gather up the pieces, and to make contingency plans for where the various bits should go once the empire disappeared. One part of that arrangement was the continued closure of the Black Sea to foreign warships in times of peace, an agreement that was affirmed in the Straits Convention of July 1841, signed by all the European great powers.

The irony is that a common understanding about the future of the Ottoman empire, backed up by an international treaty, should have led in just over a decade to a major war. But Britain's residual suspicions about Russia's aims in the east meant that, regardless of formal consultations and understandings, the tsar was never considered a fully reliable negotiating partner in London. Tsar Nicholas I had come to the throne in 1825 in the middle of an attempted military coup, the Decembrist rebellion, and the experience of it colored much of his long reign. Conservative, even reactionary in his politics and committed to preserving the territorial gains of his predecessors against threats real or perceived, Nicholas was particularly concerned that outsiders' efforts to profit from the demise of the Ottomans not lead to their profiting at Russia's expense as well.

That natural conservatism also showed itself in religious matters, in many ways the spark that produced the conflagration at mid-century. The trinity of Orthodoxy, autocracy, and nationality—the three components of the official state ideology developed during Nicholas's reign—affirmed the central place of the church in Russia's social life, the absolute power of the tsar as sovereign, and the romantic attachment to the Russian nation, even to a pan-Slavic brotherhood, as the embodiment of the ideals of the state. Those ideals soon found expression in Russian foreign policy. In 1850, when a local dispute erupted between Catholic and Orthodox hierarchs over the control of sacred sites in Jerusalem, Nicholas intervened. He pressured Ottoman authorities to recognize Orthodox demands against those of the Catholics, backed by France. When the sultan complained that Russia had no standing in the matter (the Orthodox communities, regardless of their connection to Russia, were still Ottoman subjects, after all), Nicholas occupied Moldova and Wallachia and made preparations for war.

Fighting broke out between Russia and the Ottomans along the Danube in October 1853, but there was little immediate naval action to accompany the land battles. The severity of the brewing winter weather, as well as the lack of intelligence about the disposition of forces, meant that ships often met only by chance and, even then, were often reluctant to engage. However, the decisive action in the war's first phase came only a month later. The Ottoman sailing fleet, commanded by Osman Paşa, was wintering in the harbor at Sinop, still training the crews that had been hastily assembled since the summer. The Russian fleet had quietly moved out of its base at Sevastopol and made the quick sail across the sea. On November 30, it appeared just outside Sinop harbor. In the dim light of early morning, with a cold winter rain falling, Admiral Pavel Nakhimov ordered his six ships-of-the-line to open fire.

As with the Dnepr estuary campaign almost seventy years earlier, there was little in the way of a real battle. The Russian ships were equipped with exploding shells, and they used them to devastating effect. In only about an hour, Osman Paşa's entire fleet was sunk. The batteries along the coast were destroyed and the town set on fire. More than 3,000 Ottoman seamen were killed, and Osman himself was taken captive. Only thirty-seven sailors were lost on the Russian ships.[86]

The attack on Sinop was stunning. It devastated the Ottoman fleet and illustrated the ability of Russian forces to rush across the sea to the south shore. As one British writer put it, Sinop was in fact a "second Gibraltar." If Russia were to seize it—as Nakhimov's fleet demonstrated it could do—the tsar would be able to squeeze the sea in half by commanding the finest natural harbors on the northern and southern coast, Sevastopol and Sinop. That would be the first step to taking the Bosphorus and then Istanbul itself.[87]

The attack convinced any doubters in London and Paris that the Russian empire intended not only to challenge the Ottomans, but to bury them. In the months that followed, European governments made plans to send their own ships to aid the demolished Ottoman fleet. In March 1854, the Allied powers—Britain, France, Austria, and, a short time later, Sardinia (which also had substantial interests in the Black Sea ports)—joined the fray on the side of the sultan.

The battle at Sinop had illustrated Russian superiority over the Ottomans, but it had also demonstrated the continued dependence of the Black Sea fleet on wooden sailing vessels, which were no match for the armored steamers that were increasingly dominant in west European navies. Over the course of the autumn, British and French ships patrolled the Anatolian coastline, protecting the southern harbors against a repeat attack from the north. Russian and Ottoman armies engaged on both sides of the sea, along the Danube and in the south Caucasus and eastern Anatolia, where the Russians delivered a dramatic blow by taking the fortress at Kars.

The real focus of fighting, especially once the Allied forces arrived in the autumn of 1854, was Crimea. Troop transports sailed through the Bosphorus and made straight for the peninsula. Allied ships blockaded the narrow entrance to

Sevastopol harbor, and with little ability to break the blockade, Russian admirals ordered much of the sailing fleet to be sunk to prevent the enemy from entering the inner harbor. In the meantime, Allied forces were landed at Balaklava and slowly made their way north to attack Sevastopol by land. The siege of the port wound on for eleven months, with constant shelling by Allied forces and terrible losses among Russian sailors, now a de facto land army engaged in a drawn-out, dug-in defense. (The hero of Sinop, Nakhimov, was among the victims.) Leo Tolstoy, then a young artillery officer in the city, described the scene on the Russian bastions in the last months of the siege:

[E]verything all around was falling in with a din. On the earth, torn up by a recent explosion, were lying, here and there, broken beams, crushed bodies of Russians and French, heavy cast-iron cannon overturned into the ditch by a terrible force, half buried in the ground and forever dumb, bomb-shells, balls, splinters of beams, ditches, bomb-proofs, and more corpses, in blue or in gray overcoats, which seemed to have been shaken by supreme convulsions, and which were lighted up now every instant by the red fire of the explosions which resounded in the air.[88]

In the end, a combination of superior Allied firepower, inadequate Russian supplies and communication, and most importantly rampant epidemics—typhus killed more men than did bombs and bullets—led to a Russian defeat. In September 1855, the Russians evacuated Sevastopol and scuttled all the remnants of the Black Sea fleet. Although the fighting was all but over, hostilities continued officially until the following spring. Alexander II, who had succeeded Tsar Nicholas during the course of the war, was forced to accept, in principle, the situation that the Allies had already created in fact: the elimination of his fleet and the dismantling of coastal fortifications and naval arsenals. Henceforth, all warships, even those of coastal powers, were prohibited from sailing on the sea.

The war and the treaty of Paris which ended it marked the close of an epoch on the Black Sea. In strategic terms, the war had demonstrated the willingness of western European powers to intervene on behalf of the Ottomans and to ensure that no single power, least of all the Russians, could take undue advantage of the empire's weakness. The status of the Danube and the Straits now became, more than ever before, a matter of international law, not simply a by-product of the balance of power between the two empires that faced each other from the northern and southern coasts. Control of the mouth of the Danube was returned formally to the Ottomans, but an international commission was created to secure freedom of navigation. The sea and the Straits were declared off limits to warships flying any flag, even the Russian and Ottoman ensigns, a provision that was to be guaranteed by the Allied powers. The war also featured the last major engagement between sailing ships in the region, the end-bracket to the period whose beginning John Paul Jones had witnessed in the 1780s. Sinop, however one-sided a battle, was the final encounter between ships-of-the-line, and both the Russians and the Ottomans left the war with a virtual blank slate in naval terms—a slate on which both would begin to draw the plans for an armored navy of steam-powered, propeller-driven ships by the 1870s.

The war guaranteed the freedom of foreign commerce—by securing unimpeded transport down the Danube and through the Straits—but it also literally opened up the Black Sea world to west Europeans. The exploits of Allied troops in Crimea were chronicled in a wave of popular writing. There were wide-eyed accounts for schoolboys and tales of selfless civilians such as Florence Nightingale. There was the gushing romance of Tennyson's "Charge of the Light Brigade" and other paeans to military valor (and foolhardiness). There were sober analyses of fortifications and troop movements recounted in the memoirs of former British and French officers. (Those analyses would be tested in less than a decade during the American Civil War.) A new breed of newspaper writer, the war correspondent, brought home the horror and heroism of the war in words, while sketch artists and photographers (another new profession) supplied the images.

All this sparked sufficient interest that the region experienced a virtual tourist boom in the decades that followed. It now became a legitimate destination for the foreign traveler, a point of interest to be taken in during trips to the Near East, a place still exotic enough to intrigue but sufficiently civilized to supply many of the accoutrements of home. Soon, Crimea in particular would be hit by yet another invasion, this time of writers, artists, and tourists who flocked to its congenial shores to stroll through the garden of the Russian empire.

NOTES

1. Denis Diderot, *Encyclopédie, ou Dictionnaire raisonné des sciences, des arts et des métiers* (1751–80; Stuttgart: Friedrich Fromman Verlag, 1966), "Pont-Euxin."

2. Michael Khodarkovsky, *Russia's Steppe Frontier: The Making of a Colonial Empire, 1500–1800* (Bloomington: Indiana University Press, 2002), p. 8.

3. Khodarkovsky, *Russia's Steppe Frontier*, p. 17.

4. Khodarkovsky, *Russia's Steppe Frontier*, p. 22.

5. Khodarkosvky, *Russia's Steppe Frontier*, p. 223.

6. R. C. Anderson, *Naval Wars in the Levant, 1559–1853* (Liverpool: Liverpool University Press, 1952), pp. 238–9.

7. Anderson, *Naval Wars*, pp. 240–2.

8. The standard account of the Volga–Don canal plan is John Perry, *The State of Russia Under the Present Czar* (London: Benjamin Tooke, 1716; reprint New York: Da Capo Press, 1968). Perry, a British Royal Navy captain, was the chief consultant on the project.

9. Louis-Philippe, comte de Ségur, *Memoirs and Recollections of Count Ségur, Ambassador from France to the Courts of Russia and Prussia*, 3 vols. (London: H. Colburn, 1825–7).

10. Ségur, *Memoirs and Recollections*, Vol. 3, pp. 2–3.

11. Ségur, *Memoirs and Recollections*, Vol. 3, pp. 18–19.

12. Ségur, *Memoirs and Recollections*, Vol. 3, pp. 91–2.

13. Ségur, *Memoirs and Recollections*, Vol. 3, p. 45.

14. Ségur, *Memoirs and Recollections*, Vol. 3, p. 104.

15. Ségur, *Memoirs and Recollections*, Vol. 3, p. 192.

16. Ségur, *Memoirs and Recollections*, Vol. 3, pp. 45, 230–1.

17. My account of the early Kalmyk migrations is based on Michael Khodarkovsky, *Where Two Worlds Met: The Russian State and the Kalmyk Nomads, 1600–1771* (Ithaca: Cornell University Press, 1992).

18. Khodarkovsky, *Where Two Worlds Met*, p. 225.

19. Peter Simon Pallas, *Travels Through the Southern Provinces of the Russian Empire, in the Years 1793 and 1794*, Vol. 1 (London: T. N. Longman and O. Rees et al., 1802–3), p. 117.

20. Henry A. S. Dearborn, *A Memoir of the Commerce and Navigation of the Black Sea, and the Trade and Maritime Geography of Turkey and Egypt*, Vol. 1 (Boston: Wells and Lilly, 1819), pp. 337–9.

21. Henry Augustus Zwick, *Calmuc Tartary; or a Journey from Sarepta to Several Calmuc Hordes of the Astracan Government; from May 26 to August 21, 1823* (London: Holdsworth and Ball, 1831), p. 87.

22. For a range of population estimates, see Khodarkovsky, *Where Two Worlds Met*, pp. 32–3, 232; "Kalmuk," *Encyclopaedia of Islam*; and Benjamin von Bergmann, *Voyage de Benjamin Bergmann chez les Kalmuks*, trans. M. Moris (Châtillon-sur-Seine: C. Cornillac, 1825), pp. 21, 336–7, 400.

23. This description is based on a later account of Kalmyks on the move in Zwick, *Calmuc Tartary*, pp. 95–7.

24. Thomas De Quincey, *Revolt of the Tartars* (New York: Longmans, Green, and Co., 1896), p. 3.

25. Khodarkovsky, *Where Two Worlds Met*, p. 233.

26. Le père Amiot, "Monument de la transmigration des Tourgouths, à Pe-king, le 8 novembre 1772," in *Mémoires concernant l'histoire, les sciences, les arts, les moeurs, les usages, etc., des Chinois, par les missionnaires de Pekin*, Vol. 1 (Paris: Chez Nyon, 1776), pp. 405–18.

27. Khodarkovsky, *Where Two Worlds Met*, p. 234.

28. Le père Amiot, "Extrait d'une lettre du P. Amiot, missionnaire en Chine, à M. Betin, Ministre et Secrétaire d'état, de Pe-king, le 15 octobre 1773," in *Mémoires concernant l'histoire, les sciences, les arts, les moeurs, les usages, etc., des Chinois, par les missionnaires de Pekin*, Vol. 1 (Paris: Chez Nyon, 1776), p. 422.

29. Pallas, *Travels*, Vol. 1, p. 115.

30. Ségur, *Memoirs and Recollections*, Vol. 3, pp. 166–7.

31. "Intelligence Relative to the Russian Naval Force in the Black Sea," (n.d.), Public Record Office, London (hereafter PRO) FO 95/8/9, ff. 485–6.

32. William Coxe, *Travels in Russia*, from his *Travels in the Northern Countries of Europe* (London, 1802), bound in John Pinkerton (ed.) *A General Collection of the Best and Most Interesting Voyages and Travels in All Parts of the World*, Vol. 6 (London: Longman, Hurst, Rees, and Orme, 1808–14), p. 890.

33. See Georges Dioque, *Un Haut-Alpin à Marseille: Le Baron Anthoine, 1749–1826, du grand négoce à la mairie* (Paris: Société d'Etudes des Hautes-Alpes, 1991).

34. Antoine-Ignace Anthoine de Saint-Joseph, *Essai historique sur le commerce et la navigation de la Mer-Noire*, 2nd edn. (Paris: L'Imprimerie de Mme. Veuve Agasse, 1820), pp. 30, 228–9.

35. See, for example, Bellin's "Carte réduite de la mer Noire" (1772) and Samuel Dunn's "First Part of Turkey in Europe" (1774). The Bellin map would certainly have been known to Anthoine; it still described the area around Kherson as "plaines desertes" and gave soundings only along the southeast coast of Crimea. The Dunn map left off Kherson altogether. The first accurate Russian map of the waterways of the empire, including the Dnepr cataracts, was not published until 1801.

36. Jean Denis Barbié de Bocage, *Recueil de cartes géographiques, plans, vues et médailles de l'ancienne Grèce, relatifs au voyage du jeune Anacharsis, précédé d'une analyse critique des cartes* (Paris: Imprimerie de Isidore Jacob, 1817).

37. Anderson, *Naval Wars*, p. 319.

38. Anderson, *Naval Wars*, p. 327.

39. Sebag Montefiore, *Prince of Princes: The Life of Potemkin* (New York: Thomas Dunne Books, 2001), p. 414.

40. John Paul Jones, *Life of Rear-Admiral John Paul Jones* (Philadelphia: Grigg and Elliot, 1846), pp. 274–5.

41. Quoted in Samuel Eliot Morison, *John Paul Jones: A Sailor's Biography*, new edn. (Annapolis: Naval Institute Press, 1989), p. 454.

42. Potemkin is alleged to have chosen Simferopol as the seat of the Crimean administration by asking his friends to vote between Akmechet and Bakhchisarai by casting rose petals as ballots. See Coxe, *Travels in Russia*, Vol. 6, p. 766.

43. Patricia Herlihy, *Odessa: A History, 1794–1914* (Cambridge, MA: Harvard Ukrainian Research Institute, 1986), pp. 37–44.

44. William Symonds, *Extracts from Journal in the Black Sea in 1841* (London: George Pierce, 1841), p. 19.

45. Herlihy, *Odessa*, pp. 120–1.

46. See Pallas, *Travels*. The seaworm remained a problem for several decades and was eventually defeated only by the addition of copper plating to the ships' hulls.

47. For a colorful description of traveling by "post" across the Black Sea steppe, see Laurence Oliphant, *The Russian Shores of the Black Sea in the Autumn of 1852*, 3rd edn. (London: Redfield, 1854; reprint Arno Press, 1970), pp. 104–9, 118–20.

48. George Matthew Jones, *Travels in Norway, Sweden, Finland, Russia, and Turkey; Also on the Coasts of the Sea of Azov and of the Black Sea*, Vol. 2 (London: John Murray, 1827), p. 142. The extreme shallowness of the Sea of Azov prevented Taganrog from becoming a major port. Vessels that drew more than 12 ft of water could not navigate it without fear of running aground, and when the winds were from the northeast, the depth could shrink to less than 3 ft in places.

49. Jean, Baron de Reuilly, *Travels in the Crimea, and Along the Shores of the Black Sea, Performed During the Year 1803* (London: Richard Phillips, 1807), bound in *A Collection of Modern and Contemporary Voyages and Travels*, Vol. 5 (London: Richard Phillips, 1807), p. 26.

50. Jones, *Travels*, Vol. 2, pp. 219, 223.

51. Jones, *Travels*, Vol. 2, pp. 295–300.

52. Dioque, *Un Haut-Alpin*, p. 185.

53. Coxe, *Travels in Russia*, Vol. 6, p. 889.

54. Jones, *Travels*, Vol. 2, p. 311.

55. See Willard Sunderland, "Peasants on the Move: State Peasant Resettlement in Imperial Russia, 1805–1830s," *Russian Review*, Vol. 52, No. 4 (October 1993):472–85.

56. Oliphant, *The Russian Shores*, p. 94. See also Anatole de Demidoff, *Travels in Southern Russia, and the Crimea; Through Hungary, Wallachia, and Moldavia, During the Year 1837*, Vol. 1 (London: John Mitchell, 1853), pp. 350–1; and Xavier Hommaire de Hell, *Travels in the Steppes of the Caspian Sea, the Crimea, the Caucasus, &c.* (London: Chapman and Hall, 1847), pp. 76–81.

57. Herlihy, *Odessa*, p. 34.

58. Mose Lofley Harvey, "The Development of Russian Commerce on the Black Sea and Its Significance" (PhD dissertation, University of California, Berkeley, 1938), pp. 100–1, 110, 124–6. Imports were very small compared with those arriving via the Baltic or overland routes. Figures are by value.

59. Reuilly, *Travels*, p. 72; Symonds, *Extracts from Journal*, pp. 13–14; Edmund Spencer, *Travels in Circassia, Krim-Tartary, &c.*, Vol. 1, 3rd edn. (London: Henry Colburn, 1839), p. 222.

60. For an original analysis of the differences among plague outbreaks in world history, see Samuel K. Cohn, Jr., "The Black Death: End of a Paradigm," *American Historical Review*, Vol. 107, No. 3 (June 2002) www.historycooperative.org/journals/ahr/107.3/aho302000703.html (May 27, 2003).

61. See Daniel Panzac, *Quarantaines et lazarets: L'Europe et la peste d'Orient (XVIIe-XXe siècles)* (Aix-en-Provence: Edisud, 1986).

62. Howard was buried near Kherson, but there is a monument in his honor in St. Paul's Cathedral, London. The duc de Richelieu, during an outbreak of the plague in Odessa, is said to have ordered the Jews expelled from the city. Adolphus Slade, *Records of Travels in Turkey, Greece, etc., and of a Cruise in the Black Sea, with the Capitan Pasha, in the Years 1829, 1830, and 1831*, Vol. 1 (Philadelphia: E. L. Carey and A. Hart, 1833), p. 252.

63. This description is based on Christian Augustus Fischer, *Travels to Hyères, in the South of France, Performed in the Spring of 1806* (London: Richard Phillips, 1806), bound in

A Collection of Modern and Contemporary Voyages and Travels, Vol. 5 (London: Richard Phillips, 1807), pp. 68–76.

64. Edmund Spencer, *Travels in the Western Caucasus*, Vol. 2 (London: Henry Colburn, 1838), p. 197. For a description of the system on the Russian–Persian border in the south Caucasus, see G. Poulett Cameron, *Personal Adventures and Excursions in Georgia, Circassia, and Russia*, Vol. 1 (London: Henry Colburn, 1845), pp. 4–8.

65. Demidoff, *Travels in Southern Russia*, Vol. 1, pp. 279–80.

66. Slade, *Records of Travels*, Vol. 1, p. 252.

67. For an account of the Odessa lazaretto in 1841, see Symonds, *Extracts from Journal*, pp. 15–16.

68. Conte Terristori, *A Geographical, Statistical, and Commercial Account of the Russian Ports of the Black Sea, the Sea of Asoph, and the Danube* (London: A. Schloss and P. Richardson, 1837), pp. 22–3; and Reuilly, *Travels in the Crimea*, Vol. 5, p. 83.

69. Oliphant, *Russian Shores*, p. 230.

70. Spencer, *Travels in the Western Caucasus*, Vol. 2, p. 197.

71. Daniel Panzac, *La peste dans l'Empire ottoman, 1700–1850* (Louvain: Editions Peeters, 1985), p. 507.

72. See Cameron, *Personal Adventures*, Vol. 2, p. 47, on Kharkov.

73. Slade, *Records of Travels*, Vol. 1, p. 251. The eleven lighthouses are beautifully illustrated on a map by T. Gonzalez, "Carta particular de la costa setentrional del Mar Negro, comprehendida entre la embocadura del Rio Dniester al O. y Kerson al E." (Madrid, 1821).

74. James Henry Skene, *The Frontier Lands of the Christian and the Turk; Comprising Travels in the Regions of the Lower Danube in 1850 and 1851*, Vol. 1, 2nd edn. (London: Richard Bentley, 1853), p. 276.

75. Demidoff, *Travels in Southern Russia*, Vol. 2, p. 16.

76. "Chart of the Black Sea and Surrounding Countries, Shewing the Telegraphic Lines Now Actually in Existence and Working and Those Contemplated" (February 20, 1856), PRO FO 925/3556.

77. Slade, *Records of Travels*, Vol. 1, p. 247n.

78. The Caucasus route actually ran all the way from Leipzig to Tabriz, via Odessa and Tiflis, and was largely controlled by Armenian merchants in the 1820s and 1830s. Hommaire de Hell, *Travels in the Steppes*, p. 17.

79. "Trebizond and the Persian Transit Route," PRO FO/195/2474, f. 2.

80. Sir Robert Gordon to Brant (August 5, 1830), James Brant Papers, British Library, Add. 42512, ff. 1–2 verso.

81. James Brant, "Report on the Trade at Trebizond" (February 15, 1832), PRO FO 195/101.

82. "Report on the Trade of Trebizond for the Year 1835" (December 31, 1835), PRO FO 195/101, n.p.

83. "Trebizond and the Persian Transit Route," PRO FO/195/2474, f. 2.

84. "Report on the Trade of Trebizond for the Year 1835" (December 31, 1835), PRO FO 195/101, n.p.

85. John McNeill to James Brant (November 1, 1837), James Brant Papers, British Library, Add. 42512, ff. 47–8.

86. Anderson, *Naval Wars*, p. 580.

87. Edmund Spencer, *Turkey, Russia, the Black Sea, and Circassia* (London: George Routledge, 1854), p. 233.

88. "Sebastopol in August 1855," in Leo Tolstoy, *Sebastopol* (Ann Arbor: University of Michigan Press, 1961), p. 226.

I wish Europe would let Russia annihilate Turkey a little—not much, but enough to make it difficult to find the place again without a divining-rod or a diving-bell.

Mark Twain, 1867

The passengers were a perfect babel, representing and speaking all the tongues of the East, with several Europeans mixed in, each wearing his own peculiar costume. There were Turks of all kinds and all classes and all ages wearing fezzes of red felt; there were Persians, wearing fezzes of black lamb's-wool; Albanians with fezzes of white felt, and Jews with turbans and long robes such as they used to wear in the days of the scriptures.... There were English, German, and French tourists and rug buyers on their way to Persia and Turkestan; a very fat Austrian woman who was going to visit her son, consul at Batoum, and several Russians who had been visiting Paris and the Riviera and were on their way back to their homes in the Caucasus.

William Eleroy Curtis, reporter for the Chicago Record–Herald, *on a ship off Trabzon, 1910*

In their luxurious and comfortable villas along the Black Sea coast, connected by highways illuminated as if by fairy dust, the capitalist money grubbers once lived it up at the expense of the workers.... For the region that it traverses, the Canal will have a revolutionary role. It will bring a new life, a life fundamentally different from the sorrows of the past.

Gheorghe Hossu, director of construction on the Danube–Black Sea canal, People's Republic of Romania, 1950

6
Black Sea, 1860–1990

Mark Twain saw Sevastopol in 1867, arriving by steamship from Istanbul during his jaunt through Europe and the Levant, the subject of his travelogue *The Innocents Abroad*. The Crimean war had ended just over a decade earlier, and the city had been the scene of some of the bloodiest fighting yet known in modern Europe. The population, around 43,000 at the beginning of the war, was now no more than 6,000. Few buildings had gone unscathed. Cannonballs lay lodged in walls. Visitors could stroll through the battlefields collecting broken ramrods and shell fragments as souvenirs. Any fortifications still left after the siege were destroyed by the Allies, and Russia was prevented by treaty from rebuilding them. "Ruined Pompeii is in good condition compared to Sebastopol," Twain wrote. "Here, you may look in whatsoever direction you please, and your eye encounters scarcely any thing but ruin, ruin, ruin!—fragments of houses, crumbled walls, torn and ragged hills, devastation every where! It is as if a mighty earthquake had spent all its terrible forces upon this one little spot."[1]

The conflict that had devastated Sevastopol also marked the endpoint of the sea's journey into Europe. After Crimea, the sea could no longer be called "Asian," as Diderot had labeled it in the 1750s. It was now a prize negotiated over and fought for by Europe's great powers. Commerce had been opened to international vessels, first under Russian flags of convenience and then under the ensigns of Austria, Britain, France, and other countries. In strategic terms, the major concern was no longer the threat posed by a single empire; Ottoman hegemony had been waning since the seventeenth century, and Russia's ability to dash across to the south, as had happened at Sinop, was now checked by the terms of the treaty of Paris, which prohibited warships larger than coastal cruisers. Russia would eventually repudiate the neutrality provision and, in the century's final Russo-Turkish war, attempt to encircle the Ottomans on both the western and eastern coasts. But that was the high-water mark of Russian aspirations. Making sure that no empire or state would ever wholly command the sea became the unwavering policy of European powers, and treaties and international institutions were put in place to buttress it.

The sea's new internationalization meant the reorganization of connections among the coasts. With the advent of direct Mediterranean shipping in the late eighteenth century, the local coasting trade and transshipping to the Aegean had begun to decline. The real outlet for goods produced on the northern shore was no longer Sinop and Trabzon but cities such as Vienna and Marseilles, soon serviced by regular steamer routes up the Danube or through the Straits. The opening of the Suez canal provided yet further markets for some products, but it also signaled the ebbing of the transit trade with Persia via ports such as Trabzon. Grain from southern Russia still dominated the export market, but new agricultural products, such as American sweet corn, began to displace older crops, bringing different patterns of commerce and even changing regional cuisine. New ports that had been little more than muddy villages before the Crimean war became centers for the export of the vanguard products of the industrial revolution: coal, iron, manganese, petroleum. Trains and steamships connected port cities with one another and with the rest of Europe. In the twentieth century, monumental changes in the physical environment—the damming of the Dnepr, the digging of a Volga–Don canal, the building of coastal highways—would complete the transformation of the region that began immediately after the Crimean war.

The sea's connections with Europe also provided a channel for the introduction of two ideas that would prove supremely powerful in remaking individual identities and recasting the boundaries of cultural and political communities: the concepts of the homogeneous nation and the hegemonic state. Both came rather late. Religion, especially in the Ottoman lands, mattered far more as a cultural marker than language or ethnicity; even then, the mutual influence of many traditions meant that situational and overlapping identities were common. Visitors from western Europe often reported that locals seemed confused about who they were—"Are you a Greek?" might be met with the reply "No, thank God, I am a Catholic"[2]—but any confusion was usually a product of the inappropriate categories used by the observer. Until well into the nineteenth century, for example, "Greek" (*Rum*) was the Ottoman administrative designation, and also often the self-designation, for any Orthodox Christian, people whom we would now call Greeks in an ethnic sense, but also many Romanians, Serbs, Bulgarians, Albanians, Arabs, Turks, and others. "To them religion is a nationality," wrote a British traveler disapprovingly in the 1870s,[3] and to many observers, this equation was evidence of precisely how backward the peoples around the sea remained.

Whether in the Ottoman empire or elsewhere, few people seemed to know who they really were. Outsiders often came to the Balkans, the Caucasus, and other remote areas expecting to find the residua of antique nations, pure Greeks, Scythians, Getae, Thracians, Colchians, and other peoples, now in the process of rediscovering their true heritage. In such "backwaters of life," wrote the Balkan traveler Edith Durham in 1909, one is "filled with vague memories of the cradle of his race, saying, 'This did I do some thousands of years ago;...so thought I and so acted I in the beginning of time'."[4] Geography, they hoped, might recapitulate phylogeny. But visitors were often disappointed. Until rather late—the twentieth century, in some instances—where they expected to find unsullied exemplars of one or another "race," they instead found individuals and communities for whom plural identities and mixed cultures were the norm. That situation was not to obtain for long, however. As the twentieth century progressed, it was the idea of the timelessly pure nation that eventually won out, often with tragic results.

Similar changes were at work in terms of state administration. The sea had long lain at the periphery of different imperial systems, and the major empires on the northern and southern coasts were content to rule some areas only indirectly, leaving local elites largely to their own devices. By the time of the Crimean war, that had already begun to change. Imperial modernization programs were under way in both Russia and the Ottoman empire. The old periphery was being absorbed into centralizing empires or allowed to go its own way as independent countries. By the end of the First World War, the imperial option was gone. Now, most of the sea was encircled by a new set of actors—modern states—that sought to appropriate the sea's wealth for their own political, economic, and strategic goals. No longer was the sea just an object of imperial desire. It was now part of competing state-building projects: first Romanian and Bulgarian, soon Soviet and Turkish, and by the end of the twentieth century, Georgian and Ukrainian as well. The coastline, the water, the land under it, and the fish in it were all claimed as the domain of new states—as well as the sacred patrimony of the historical nations that they represented. Poets and historians soon set about the task of discovering, or inventing, the nautical vocations of one or another national group.

In the latter half of the twentieth century, this proprietary vision of the sea was enhanced by the ideology of development, whether in the form of Soviet-style communism or state-building nationalism. The sea became a resource to be exploited using all the available technology of the state. Industrial concerns grew up along the coasts. Port cities expanded in both area and population. Commercial fishing fleets were dispatched to reap the harvest of the sea. Development transformed the coastline and brought genuinely "revolutionary change"—in the language of both communists and nationalists —to areas that were still among the poorest sections of the littoral countries, even after the Second World War. But there were also certain costs. In only a few decades, the grand plans for bringing modernity to the coasts and consuming the products of the sea had resulted in a body of water on the edge of environmental disaster. Never before had the shape of political boundaries, human identities, and ecological systems changed as rapidly as in the period from the 1860s to the 1990s, a time when politicians and planners labored to unmake the Black Sea as a region. By the end of the twentieth century, the health of the sea itself demanded that they work equally hard to reconstruct it.

Empires, States, and Treaties

Political relationships in the second half of the nineteenth century in many ways replicated those of the first. The Russian empire continued to pursue a strategy of positioning itself to take advantage of the end of the Ottoman empire, whose slow death had been a source of concern for more than a century. The Ottomans, having progressively lost control of much of the littoral, sought to maintain their meager hold on the ports of the southern coast; even that, as the debacle at Sinop had shown, could be tenuous in times of conflict. The great difference after the Crimean war was that the status of the sea—open or closed, neutral or otherwise—was no longer a derivative of peace treaties signed between these two empires. It was now the subject of a growing body of international law, put in place at international conferences and guarded by the commitment and vested interests of the European great powers.

Under the treaty of Paris, Russia was to give up the idea of a Black Sea fleet. Most Russian vessels already lay at the bottom of Sevastopol harbor, and with the empire's defeat, recreating a naval presence in the south was now formally abjured. Under the energetic minister of foreign affairs A. M. Gorchakov, the empire attempted repeatedly to alter the terms of the treaty, but for more than a decade after the war, Russia was allowed to maintain no more than six gunboats on the sea, for the purposes of police operations in coastal waters.[5] By the late 1860s, however, Gorchakov had begun to float the idea of a full repudiation of the Paris terms.

The timing was propitious. The previous decade had seen a revolution in naval technology. Major powers were rushing to scupper the remaining ships-of-the-line and build new iron-clad, coal-powered battleships, the ship design whose superiority had recently been proven in the American Civil War.

Russia had joined in the race by launching a major modernization program of the fleet in the Baltic Sea, the first line of defense for St. Petersburg. Moreover, the old Allied powers that had imposed the neutralization of the Black Sea were now preoccupied with other pressing diplomatic concerns. France and Prussia were quickly sliding toward war, and the need to keep Russia satisfied and out of the brewing conflict was increasingly felt in European capitals. In this atmosphere, in 1870 Gorchakov announced Russia's unilateral withdrawal from the neutrality provision of the Paris treaty; the change was formally recognized by the great powers the next year. Russia was now able to place warships on the sea and reconstruct its coastal defenses. The navy also put in place a construction plan designed not only to reinstate Russia's naval presence in the south but also to take advantage of new technologies: All new ships built for the Black Sea service were to be armored.[6]

The change in the neutrality provision was also to the advantage of the Ottomans, who could now begin their own building program. One of the ironies of the Paris treaty was that, even though the Ottomans had been a victor power, the sultan had actually given up as much as the tsar, perhaps more. The prohibition on warships and coastal arsenals applied to Ottoman vessels as much as to Russian ones. Ottoman ports were formally declared open to all merchant ships, with the only permissible restrictions being for customs, policing, and quarantine. A new Danube Commission, established to ensure free navigation on the river, included all riparian states plus the Allied powers; Ottoman representatives were, therefore, only one of a number of delegates, even though almost all the river's lower course lay within the empire. In exchange for these concessions, the Ottoman empire was at last recognized as a full player in the affairs of Europe, and its territorial integrity was guaranteed. (Even the latter provision came with an asterisk, however. The sultan agreed not to intervene militarily in the affairs of Moldova, Wallachia, and Serbia without the consent of the Allies.)

Russia's pressing for a change in the terms of the treaty thus also suited the interests of strategists in Istanbul. But whereas the Russians were able to capitalize relatively quickly on the chance to rebuild their naval forces, the Ottomans failed to do so. The process of naval modernization in the Ottoman empire had gone in fits and starts since the eighteenth century. Foreign advisers, mainly British, played a significant role, but the talents of these consultants were sometimes less than adequate. Finding seaworthy recruits was also a perennial problem. Sailors from the Aegean had long formed a significant component of Ottoman crews, but the independence of Greece in 1830 reduced that source. A series of stunning naval defeats not only destroyed parts of the Ottoman fleet in the Black Sea and the Mediterranean, but also delivered a huge psychological blow to the naval establishment. During the Greek war of independence, the Ottoman Mediterranean fleet was annihilated at the battle of Navarino in 1827; that was followed less than three decades later by Sinop. Steam technology came only gradually. Successive sultans remained unconvinced that steamships were anything more than toys for tooling up the Bosphorus. Even when the decision was at last taken, in the 1840s, to begin the large-scale construction and purchase of steam warships, the Ottomans faced yet another difficulty: The main source of fuel—the coal mines along the Anatolian Black Sea coast—was controlled by British companies.[7]

The two modernized navies at last had the chance to confront each other in the late 1870s, but the encounter was not much more memorable than it had been in the conflict of the 1820s, when there was virtually no engagement at all on the Black Sea.[8] The Russo-Turkish war of 1877–8 began with Russian concerns for Christian populations in the Ottoman empire—partly a reflection of Russia's view of itself as a guarantor of eastern Christendom, partly a convenient mask for imperial expansion. The Ottomans had ruthlessly suppressed an insurrection in Bulgaria, and European capitals were filled with news of the atrocities committed by Ottoman troops and irregulars. Serbia, still nominally an Ottoman vassal, joined in to support the Bulgarians, and in April 1877 the tsar declared war as well.

Conflict on the sea was limited. Despite the grand designs of the 1860s and early 1870s, the Russian Black Sea fleet was still unimpressive: only two new armored ships and several older corvettes.[9] Most of the Russian navy was located in the Baltic, and the British, again supporting the Ottomans, made it clear that any attempt to transfer Russian forces to the Mediterranean would be blocked. There was little reason for the Russians to challenge that state of affairs. The Ottoman naval presence in the Black Sea theater amounted to a squadron on the Danube and at Istanbul. The rest of the fleet sat out the war in the Mediterranean and the Red Sea.[10]

The major Russian strategy in the early stages of the fighting was to secure the Danube, and that demanded little in the way of naval strength. Russian troops simply mined the lower section of the river. This had a doubly unfortunate effect on the Ottomans. It prevented Ottoman warships from getting upriver to resupply troops and keep the Russian land forces from pushing to the south, and it kept Ottoman river craft from escaping to the open sea. Ottoman ships and gunboats were soon picked off from the shore by Russian artillery. By late June 1877, the Russian army had crossed the river and advanced to the south, where it met up with troops from Balkan states now in full revolt against the sultan.[11]

From that point, the war was an entirely land campaign, or two campaigns, in fact, one on either side of the sea. In the west, the Russian army and its Balkan allies pressed to the south, taking the key fortress at Plevna, one of the few decisive battles of the entire war, and marching across the Balkan mountains despite the onset of winter. Ottoman forces, widely dispersed and probably outnumbered by Russian, Romanian, Serbian, and Montenegrin troops, repeatedly failed in their efforts to retake lost ground. In the east, another Russian campaign pushed into Anatolia, taking the Ottoman fortress at Kars. In late January 1878, the Russian army controlled an offensive line all the way from the Black Sea to the Aegean and held several major fortresses in the south Caucasus and eastern Anatolia. The Ottomans sued for peace.

The treaty of San Stefano, which formally ended the war, created a massive Bulgarian principality, a state that was still formally a dependency of the Ottomans but was, in practice, influenced by Russia. It also granted Russia possession of Kars and other fortresses in the east, including the important port at Batumi. As had happened earlier in the century, however, the European powers grew concerned about Russia's rising influence in the Near East and held an international conference to revise the terms. The resulting treaty of Berlin whittled down the Bulgarian principality, but many of the other provisions of San Stefano remained in place. Some of the Ottomans' strategic assets in the east, including Kars and Batumi, were again ceded to Russia. Serbia and Montenegro became independent, governed by their own royal houses. Romania, a state that had been formed from the voluntary union of Moldova and Wallachia already in 1859, was likewise recognized as sovereign; a German prince ruled as king. Russia's holdings along the littoral now stretched all the way from the Danube delta, around the northern shore, to the last major port on the Caucasus coast, Batumi. Several significant territorial changes would come in the twentieth century—not least the creation of a larger independent Bulgaria early in the century and an independent Russia, Ukraine, and Georgia at the end—but for the most part the political shape of the modern Black Sea coast was created in 1878. Very quickly after that, Russians and others set about the task of fully integrating the littoral into the states and empires among which it was now divided.

Steam, Wheat, Rail, and Oil

If quarantine facilities were one of the chief determinants of a port's success in the late eighteenth and early nineteenth centuries, the coming of the railway was the equivalent from the mid-nineteenth century forward. Laying new rail was part of a broad project to modernize many of the coastal areas, in both the Russian and Ottoman lands.

For Russia, the defeat in Crimea had been due in part to the inferior communication between the empire's central regions and the coast, and a plan to improve both the ports and their connection to the hinterland was launched shortly after the war. Rail spurs and direct lines were built to inland cities, while new steamship lines, subsidized by the government, linked the ports with one another. The Ottomans, although on the winning side in Crimea, quickly came to understand that military victory was no guarantee of lasting power. Russian influence on the sea had been temporarily squelched, but Odessa and other northern cities remained centers of international commerce, in marked contrast to the generally underdeveloped Ottoman ports. Even Trabzon, revitalized by the overland trade with Persia in the early part of the century, was quickly falling behind the cities of southern Russia.

The modernizing policies inaugurated by Sultan Abdülmecit I (reigned 1839–61)—which began the so-called *Tanzimat* (Reform) period in Ottoman history—were meant to change that situation. A new administrative province, or *vilayet*, was created along the Danube and the western coast in the 1860s. A talented reformist administrator, Midhat Paşa (1822–84)—the equivalent of Richelieu and Vorontsov in New Russia—was appointed governor of the province and charged with building roads, bridges, and railways. The Tuna (Danube) *vilayet* soon became a model of Ottoman modernity, and its major port cities, Köstence and Varna, were meant to rival Odessa as international outlets for agricultural products from the western coast.[12]

Between the 1860s and the turn of the century, railways expanded rapidly. In Russia, lines were built first in the west, to Odessa, Nikolaev, and Kherson; connections in the east followed soon after. The Transcaucasus railway opened in 1885, linking Batumi with Baku on the Caspian Sea. By the early twentieth century, there was hardly a productive piece of territory in southern Russia that was more than 80 km from a railway.[13] The Ottoman coasts were less well-endowed, but in the Tuna province, lines were laid from Köstence and Varna to towns on the Danube. (After 1878, with the emergence of independent Romania—which included part of the old Tuna *vilayet*—new foreign concessions were granted to expand the rail system pioneered by Midhat Paşa.)

The coming of the railroad meant that port cities that had been backwaters before the Crimean war rapidly rose to prominence. Rostov, up the Don river from the site of the ancient Tanais, was no more than a village before the war, but it soon became an emporium for products from the steppe. Dredging allowed the navigation of large ships, and new loading facilities and quays made the city attractive to foreign businesses. Immigrants from other parts of Russia and from abroad flocked to the city. The seaport of Novorossiisk had been founded already in the 1830s as a minor entrepôt for trade from the Kuban river region north of the Caucasus; but the completion of a railway line and harbor improvements in the 1880s allowed the city to take off. By the end of the century, it was one of the leading export centers in the entire Russian south.

Beyond the Caucasus mountains, the small port at Poti was designated the center of Russian trade along the borders with the Ottoman empire and Persia. In 1872 a rail line was completed between Poti and Tiflis, the seat of the Russian imperial viceroy in the Caucasus. Poti grew quickly, but it was soon outstripped by its neighbor just down the coast, Batumi. The building of a rail spur to the main Poti–Tiflis line allowed the city to become the most important port in the Russian Caucasus. What had been a small Ottoman town with little more than a few inns, coffee-houses, and a colorful bazaar before 1878 rapidly eclipsed Poti—and soon even Trabzon—as the major city on the southeastern sea. Even older towns that had long been dormant, such as Nikolaev and Kherson, were revived with the advent of rail. The growth in population in all the Russian ports, both old and new, was phenomenal. In the second half of the nineteenth century, Nikolaev's population grew threefold, Odessa's sixfold, Rostov's tenfold.[14]

On the water, the development of steam transport, especially screw-driven ships that had begun to displace sailing vessels even before the Crimean war, meant that getting from one coastal city to another was easier than ever. Riverboats of the Austrian Steam Navigation Company ran down the Danube from Vienna, and ships of the Austrian Lloyd Company sailed from Trieste. By the early twentieth century, Italian, French, and German steam lines had established their own long-distance routes. In four weeks, one could travel from London to Odessa, with stops in Malta, Alexandria, Istanbul, and other Mediterranean ports.[15] The Russian Steam Navigation Company, established with Tsar Alexander II's imprimatur in 1857, ran routes that crisscrossed the sea. Regular circle lines took goods and passengers from Odessa as far east as Batumi, with calls at all the Crimean and Caucasus ports; river lines ran up the Dnepr. Once every two weeks, Russian ships docked at Trabzon and the other Ottoman ports.[16]

The chief advantage of many of the Russian ports was their proximity to the fertile black-earth region, the heartland of the empire's grain production. Already by the middle of the century, the Black Sea ports accounted for nearly two-thirds of Russia's grain trade, including almost 90 percent of wheat exports.[17] From the 1880s to the First World War, Russia's total output in cereals probably doubled, and the Black Sea ports became busy centers of commerce with Britain, France, Germany, and even farther afield.[18] The opening of the Suez canal extended the Russian grain trade to the Far East—just as it undercut the importance of Trabzon as an overland route to Persia. In fact, given the ease of travel by sea and through the canal, the Black Sea ports also became Russia's primary means of communicating with its own possessions in eastern Siberia and the Pacific littoral.

Grain—barley, rye, and especially wheat—remained the mainstay of Russian business; Russian wheat accounted for up to a third of world wheat exports before the First World War. New products also began to compete for the attention of foreign shippers and investors. Extractive industries such as coal and manganese, an ore used in steel production, were developed in the Caucasus by British, German, and other European concerns. But in the decades after the Crimean war, it was one industry in particular that began to spark the interest of Russian, European, and even American businessmen.

Petroleum deposits around the Black Sea and the Caspian had been known since antiquity. Strabo noted oil seepages along the Caspian coast, and the Byzantines used crude petroleum from around the Sea of Azov as the basis for their secret weapon, sea-fire. The commercial potential of the substance was only realized in the mid-nineteenth century. Refining crude oil into kerosene for lighting and as an industrial lubricant was developed principally by John D. Rockefeller's Standard Oil Company, which had cornered the market on production and distribution from the fields of western Pennsylvania. Soon, foreign companies sought to break Standard's stranglehold on the international exploitation and transport of oil by focusing on two important sources in the Caspian and Black Sea regions.

One was Baku, a city perched on a peninsula jutting out into the Caspian, which had been taken under Russian control only in the early 1800s. Petroleum was at first collected from hand-dug pits, but after the middle of the century, drilling rigs were erected on the model of those used in the Pennsylvania fields. The elimination of the tsar's official monopoly on oil exploration and transport in the early 1870s opened the door to foreign industrialists, among them the Swedish Nobel brothers and the Rothschilds. Within only a couple of decades, the area around Baku became a forest of black derricks cut by rivers of oily mud.

The other major petroleum source lay across the Black Sea. Oil pits in the region around Ploieşti, in south-central Romania, had been in operation since the middle of the century, and drilled wells were sunk in the 1860s and 1870s. After independence in 1878, the country developed its own refining industry, and international investors, principally Germans, were soon clamoring to have a stake in the Romanian oil business.

The problem with both the Baku and Ploieşti fields was their relative inaccessibility. They lay rather far from major sea-ways—Baku was on the land-locked Caspian, Ploieşti was inland from both the Danube and the Black Sea—and neither was served by major rail links. Late into the nineteenth century, getting oil from well to market was still accomplished in the same way as in the earliest Pennsylvania fields: pumping crude oil into wooden barrels and then hauling it in wagons over impassable roads.

The opening of the rail spur from Batumi to Poti and, in the 1880s, the completion of the Transcaucasian railway made Batumi the chief conduit for the export of Russian oil. After arriving at the port in tanker cars, the crude oil could be pumped into newly designed ocean-going tankers and sent across the sea to the Mediterranean and beyond. Pipelines soon replaced railcars as the primary means of moving oil from field to port.

In the west, construction on a rail link with Köstence had been under way much earlier, since the late 1850s, and it would soon become one of the premier transport projects undertaken by Midhat Paşa. The original impetus was the grain trade. Köstence (the ancient Tomis) was one of the finest natural harbors on the western coast, but the lack of easy access to the interior—muddy roads across the Dobrudja steppe, plus the difficulty of crossing the Danube—was a brake on its development. The plan was to build a railway from the port to the Danube, where it would link up with a further rail line to Bucharest. The Köstence line was to provide an alternative to transport up the Danube and a direct link to roadways and rail connections across the Danube plain and into central Europe. The sultan engaged a group of foreign engineers to plan the route and to begin laying the track. Work was frequently halted, especially during the wars of the 1850s and 1870s; at the end of the last Russo-Turkish war, the port and the Dobrudja region passed from the Ottoman empire to independent Romania. It was not until 1895 that the rail line was finally completed with much fanfare by the Romanian state—which renamed the port Constanţa. Soon, oil from the Ploieşti fields was flowing from Constanţa just as the Caspian fields had found an outlet at Batumi.

These and other modernized ports became the natural conduits for the raw materials and products of the industrial revolution, into and out of the western Caucasus and the eastern Balkans. They were part of a growing network of rail links around the sea from Bulgaria to Georgia. Under the power of steam, goods could be taken all across Europe by rail, then across the sea itself by steamship to the other shore. Varna, which had been linked by rail with the Danube already in the 1860s, had a population of nearly 40,000 by the early twentieth century; it later became the major port of the new kingdom of Bulgaria. Constanţa remained smaller in population, but the active petroleum trade made it a vital commercial center for the Romanian kingdom. Batumi was likewise far less populous than many other ports, but it was unrivaled as an export center. The value of Batumi's exports increased by well over 300 percent from the 1870s to the 1910s.[19] Visitors frequently compared even the lesser Russian and Balkan ports, with their right-angle streets and industrial warehouses, to those on the southern coast, which had been largely bypassed by the changes of the late nineteenth century. "It was pleasant to escape the musty smells which are attached to every Turkish town," wrote an American traveler to Batumi in 1910, "and to see healthy, clean dogs that could be touched without contamination."[20]

"An Ignoble Army of Scribbling Visitors"

The successive troubles across the Near East after the 1850s brought the Black Sea world literally into the drawing rooms of west Europeans. Many families in Britain and France now had personal ties to the region, through fathers, sons, and uncles who had fought in Crimea, or sisters and aunts who cared for the sick and wounded. Vicarious connections were also forged by the many news reports and engravings that chronicled a series of international crises. Beautifully produced war albums on the conflict of 1877–8 could be purchased at local booksellers. Newspapers carried vivid stories of the persecution of Christian populations in the Ottoman empire, many based on actual episodes of horrific communal violence: the Bulgarian atrocities of the 1870s, the Armenian massacres of the 1890s, the mutual bloodletting of Christians and Muslims during the Balkan wars of 1912 and 1913. Pulp fiction writers seized upon the themes of the exotic Orient, the mysterious seraglio, the barbarous Turk, and the tempestuous sea to thrill audiences in London, Paris, and New York.

The growing familiarity with the region among outsiders also produced a desire to travel there, perhaps to visit the resting place of a relative from the Crimean conflict or simply to see a world that seemed to breed turmoil. Steam travel made the journey by sea far easier than in the past, and rail connections to major cities in the Balkans and Istanbul meant that part of the journey could be completed overland in the comfort of a first-class carriage. Guidebooks instructed intrepid travelers on the most propitious routes and most interesting sites. The London publisher John Murray printed its first guide to "the East," including the Anatolian coast, already in 1840; revised and expanded editions were issued during the Crimean war and periodically thereafter.[21] The German firm of Karl Baedeker joined the industry later in the century, producing its first guide to Russia in 1883.

Baedeker recommended a tour of eight weeks across the Russian empire, from Warsaw to St. Petersburg, then south to Kiev, Odessa, and Crimea, and finally across the sea to Batumi and the Caucasus. The first English-language edition, published in 1914, warned tourists that some of the things they might encounter would be unexpectedly civilized. "Odessa ... is a modern town," the guide reported, "and offers little of interest to the tourist." Nevertheless, for travelers sailing on to the Caucasus, especially if they intended to go off the beaten path, Baedeker advised procuring the following items in Odessa or, in a pinch, in Tiflis:

rugs
a lantern
an air-cushion
rubber overshoes
an alarm clock
pins and needles
thread
string
straps
preserved meats
condensed milk
bread ("seldom obtainable in the mountains and never good") or biscuits
tea
sugar
quinine
opiates
Vaseline
carbolic acid
bandages
soap
matches
candles
insect powder
wrapping paper
writing materials[22]

If one had difficulty acquiring these goods, or met with an intransigent official, one could always apply to a local consular agent—British, French, Austrian, even American—who could be found in ports from the Danube to the Caucasus.

One still needed a penchant for adventure to travel the sea. Quarantine restrictions delayed passage, venal customs officers required their pound of flesh, and as Baedeker put it, "hotels in the European sense" were sometimes hard to find, especially in areas not serviced by rail or steamer. Yet that, according to some writers, was the chief appeal of a journey across the Near East. "Some travellers may make Kustendjie [Köstence/Constanţa] the point of departure for Constantinople," wrote the British travel writer Thomas Forester.

[A] few be tempted to cross the Black Sea to the once imperial Trebizond, whence they may easily make excursions to the sources of the Tigris and Euphrates, or, in a journey not longer than that from London to Marseilles or Milan ... visit Erzeroum,—or Kars (a place for ever famous),—Erivan, and even Tehran.... All this may be accomplished with ease in the course of a long autumnal vacation; .... And now that all the old continental routes are "used up," may not some part of the perennial stream of travel be turned into fresh fields offering many attractions, and, considering the distance from point to point, unequalled facilities of access?[23]

As time passed, visitors who hoped to find something of the untamed steppe or the intriguing Orient along their journey were increasingly disappointed. Already in 1867, Mark Twain was surprised at Odessa's broad streets and new houses. "I have not felt so much at home for a long time as I did when I 'raised the hill' and stood in Odessa for the first time," he wrote. "There was not one thing to remind us that we were in Russia."[24] Twain's experiences were not unusual in the cities of the northern shore, and the glut of wide-eyed foreigners, including Americans, often frustrated later arrivals. A British traveler in Crimea complained about the traces left behind by his American predecessors. "The United States appears to have sent an ignoble army of scribbling visitors as her contingent to the Crimea, and the soft stone of the country has been delightful to their pocket knives. ... [It] is carved and cut by nobodies, anxious to inform the world that they were 'raised' in New York or Philadelphia."[25]

The expanding transport industry supported not only foreign visitors but also growing numbers of well-heeled locals. Russian nobles and imperial administrators built impressive chateaux along the temperate Crimean coast. Mikhail Vorontsov, governor of New Russia and later viceroy in the Caucasus, was responsible for the most famous of these, his summer palace at Alupka; it was completed in the 1840s and, with its mixed architectural styles and elaborate gardens, remains the premier example of Victorian-era pastiche in Russia—not surprising, since it was designed by the builder of Buckingham Palace. These summer houses and gardens provided the nucleus for new public resorts. Crimea had been hailed by poets and tsarist propagandists as the "garden of the empire," and as the century progressed, the garden burst into full bloom.

During the bathing season, which ran from mid-August to mid-October, resorts at Yalta, Alupka, and Alushta housed visitors from across the Russian empire and abroad. Elaborate villas, casinos, and bathing establishments grew up along the coast. Modern quays and embankments were crowded with fashionable nobles stepping off the steamer from Odessa and drinking in the salubrious air of the Russian Riviera. Vasilii Sidorov, an amateur botanist and travel writer, described the scene that awaited a visitor to Yalta in the 1890s:

"Yalta the Pure"—with its miniature public gardens; with its tourist shops where everything is sold for three times more than in other cities of Russia; where the same unnecessary tchotchkes bearing the phrase "Souvenir de Jalta" are flogged in every store window; with its dachas, bathing areas, post office and telegraph, club and library, the well-dressed walkers on the boulevard . . . . Yalta lives for visitors; here everything is made for visitors: music in the garden, beautiful carriages, Tatar cicerones in their colorful costumes waiting for you on the embankment, saddle horses, rowboats for taking a turn on the sea.[26]

Other travelers embarked from Odessa or the Crimean ports for a holiday in Istanbul or, for the more pious, a longer journey to the Holy Land. Russian steamers made the quick journey across the sea very pleasant. Tourists crowded the decks to be the first to spot the opening to the Bosphorus, while delightful meals were offered to those with first-class accommodation. As another Russian traveler wrote in 1898:

Finally the table was set for evening tea—just like at home: Biscuits and pretzels, fresh from the oven, gave off a delicious odor. Candles in bell-glasses threw a flickering light on the white tablecloth as gentle shadows danced on the inclined faces of the passengers, who were conscientiously engaged in studying their Baedekers.[27]

The expansion of travel and tourism meant that more and more people were beginning to experience their own seacoasts for the first time. Popular Russian, Romanian, and other writers began to record their journeys across the sea, and publishing houses in Moscow, Kiev, Bucharest, and Sofia produced a steady stream of travel books for the growing literate populations farther inland. Some were simple diaries filled with tales of ingratiating Tatar baggage handlers, jolly Greek steamer captains, and salacious Turkish officials. Others were more contemplative works about life on the frontier; the coastline, although now integrated into modernizing states and empires, still represented the romantic ideal of the unspoiled borderland—but one that could be conveniently transgressed and observed, rather than feared.

Most authors focused on the strange habits of their foreign neighbors. To Russian writers, the Romanian of Bessarabia was a gypsy ready to steal one's purse. To the Romanian, the Bulgarian of Dobrudja was a clownish peasant unsure of his real identity. To them all, the Turk was a natural outsider whose time on the European continent was thankfully drawing to a close. If they could afford it, travelers could even take back a graphic representation of the sea as a turbulent meeting place of civilizations. Artists such as Ivan Aivazovsky

(1817–1900), a native of Feodosiia and the nineteenth century's nonpareil painter of Pontic seascapes, captured the essence of the tempestuous sea and its coastline, the waves battering against the ancient cliffs of Crimea, the wild water lapping against primeval shores that were at last on their way to becoming civilized. A region that had been traversed and described by British and French travel writers for more than a century was now discovered anew by observers from the emerging urban centers of the hinterlands.

Many travelers were surprised to find how little they knew about their own homelands. They encountered people who spoke languages different from their own, with mores that reminded them of the decadent Orient, not the refined Christian countries that now ringed most of the coast. Visitors from Moscow and St. Petersburg, for example, usually returned home with the news that, beyond the tourist resorts of Crimea, their seacoast was in fact another country. Russian writers decried the influence of Mammon in their ports, especially Odessa, where the "endless supply of Jews" created a city with a dead spirit, consumed by commerce.[28] The port cities, swelled by the booming trade in grain, petroleum, and other products, had attracted a bewildering collection of peoples, each with their own language and style of life. As some complained, the Russian character of these cities, the empire's very antechamber, had been perilously diluted. "Unfortunately, Novorossiisk is a city that is far from being completely Russian," a popular Russian guidebook noted in 1891. "Both in the [urban] population and in the population of neighboring villages, foreign elements—Greeks, Germans, Armenians, Czech-Catholics, usually foreign subjects—are very strong, as are local foreigners."[29]

All around the sea, these "local foreigners"—Jewish innkeepers, Greek and Armenian merchants, Muslim highlanders—would become of increasing concern to governments in the national capitals. The visions of timelessly pure nations now being taught in the schools and universities farther inland, the struggle for national liberation being celebrated during public holidays, and the theories of ethnic purity and religious piety being expounded by poets and historians were, as many visitors were discovering, sorely at odds with the multifarious reality of the coast.

Trouble on the Köstence Line

One of the earliest European observers of the rapid changes in transport, commerce, and travel after the Crimean war was a young British civil engineer named Henry Barkley. In the late 1850s Barkley was invited by his elder brother, a prominent businessman with connections to the Ottoman state, to help design and build railways in the coastal region of Dobrudja, soon to become the Tuna *vilayet*.

The Barkley firm was the prime mover in the growth of railways along the western Black Sea. It won the concession to lay rail lines from Varna and Köstence to river stations on the Danube, and the firm would later complete the project by building the first major railroads in independent Romania. Just as the Russians would embark on the Transcaucasian railway project as a way of undercutting the importance of British interests in Trabzon, so the Ottomans reckoned that rail links to Varna and Köstence would help these ports compete with Odessa—especially since, at the time the Ottomans began the project, wheat was still being brought to Odessa in ox-carts, not railcars.

Barkley arrived in Varna by steamer, seasick after a particularly wave-tossed journey from Istanbul; an equally bumpy wagon ride brought him to Köstence. He spent the next several weeks cooling his heels in the port and taking frequent hunting trips into the marshy plain, returning with great quantities of hare, partridge, and bustard. At last the home office in London sent word that construction work could commence. That was when the real adventure began.

Barkley was put in charge of some 500 workmen tasked with leveling the track for the rail line. They were drawn from across the Dobrudja province—Christian and Muslim, Moldovan, Wallachian, Bulgarian, and Turk, in various combinations—and were overseen by a cudgel-wielding foreman from Durham, whose lazy eye spooked some of the natives.

It was an inhospitable place to work. Insects rose in clouds from the marshes, and malarial fever was a frequent problem. The popular way of warding off mosquitoes—by burning heaps of manure—was scarcely more bearable. The work itself was also hard going. The earth on the plain was packed hard in summer, and in digging it up the workmen frequently encountered carved stones and barrow graves which were a nuisance to remove or dig through. Barkley usually ordered the antiquities to be broken up and scattered, but some he sent back to the university museum in Oxford.

The rail line from Köstence to the village of Karasu on the Danube was finally completed in 1860. But as the first engines began to make the short trip across the steppe, further problems arose. The local peasants did not understand that trains could not be easily stopped, and they would drive their sheep across the rails just as an engine approached. The results could be stomach-turning. "I shall never forget the awful appearance the engine presented...," Barkley later wrote, describing a train's encounter with a flock of seventy sheep. "From the rails to the top of the funnel it was one mass of gore, and though I bobbed behind the firebox I was not much better, and it made me feel sick to feel the hot blood bespattering my face and hands."[30]

Over the next few decades, however, rail became the driver of Dobrudja's progress. The completion of a bridge over the Danube in 1895 allowed the rail link to be extended to Bucharest, where it joined the main trunk line that led on to central Europe. Just as Köstence/Constanţa became Romania's primary seaport after 1878, so Varna became the outlet for the Bulgarian principality also created by the Berlin treaty. Both seaports became regular stops on the route from the Danube to Istanbul.

Barkley knew that he was participating in a project that would make a major contribution to commerce along the western shore. But of all the things he witnessed during his several years in Dobrudja, there was one event in particular that stood out in his mind, and one on which he dwelt at some length in his memoirs.

For much of the period Barkley spent in the region, Crimean Tatars had been streaming into Dobrudja by land and sea. Many were fearful of reprisals by the tsarist government, which blamed the entire Tatar people for the actions of a few Allied collaborators during the Crimean war. Others sought farmland that was being promised by the Ottoman state as a way of increasing the Muslim population in a largely Christian province. Barkley saw ships literally overflowing with Crimean Tatar immigrants as they sailed into Köstence harbor.

Steamers and sailing vessels, all without food or water, carried hundreds of passengers packed tightly together. Any remaining space was taken up with their belongings, including farm implements, carts, and even camels and other livestock. Many Tatars suffered from seasickness or, even worse, infectious diseases such as smallpox, typhus, and measles, which jumped from the ships to the ports and then across the entire province. Those who died at sea were simply thrown overboard, even if the ship was already in port, and the beaches from Köstence to Varna were littered with the bodies of the dead.

On Barkley's direction, the new rail line was soon put to use. The Tatar immigrants were loaded onto rail cars and taken to the Danube. They were then to be transferred to river transports and moved upstream to resettlement areas designated by the Ottoman state. Once they arrived at the river, however, there were often too few boats waiting. Thousands of people had to sleep rough on the river banks until one arrived. The spectacle was horrific. "Many of them were so ill they were quite unfit to be moved, but they were equally unfit to remain exposed on the beach, so all were carried away," Barkley recalled. "Many died in the waggons and were thrown out as the train moved along by their friends, now apparently rendered callous by extreme misery. Others were left where they died in the waggons, and were trodden on and crushed by their living comrades."[31]

Barkley was witness to the first in a long line of large-scale population movements that would utterly reshape the character of the Black Sea littoral. In the 1850s and early 1860s, hundreds of thousands of Crimean Tatars moved out of the

Russian empire and into Ottoman lands, some to Anatolia but most to Bulgaria, Serbia, and Thrace. They were soon followed by other, even larger waves: the forced migrations of Circassians and other Muslim highlanders in the wake of Russia's wars of conquest in the north Caucasus; the massacre of Armenians and other Christians in eastern Anatolia in the 1890s; the flight of refugees, both Christian and Muslim, in the Balkan wars and then during the First World War; and the organized killing and deportation of Armenians, Greeks, and others in the Ottoman empire from 1915 through the early 1920s. Modern technologies of transport brought easier methods of getting goods such as wheat and petroleum across the sea, but they also now provided a new and efficient way of getting rid of "local foreigners."

The Unpeopling

The forced movement of people, as refugees from armed conflict or as settlers uprooted by governments and planted again in new territories, is nothing new around the Black Sea—nor, indeed, in any other part of Europe. In antiquity, the port cities were places of exile for impious poets and political dissenters. In the Ottoman period, the exile of entire villages, a practice known as *sürgün*, was used either as punishment for unruly locals or as a form of colonization to populate low-density areas. Similar policies were adopted as the Russian empire expanded south in the eighteenth and nineteenth centuries. Tatars, Greeks, and Armenians were moved out of Crimea, and Slavic peasants were moved south to help settle the New Russian steppe. The line between exile as punishment and exile as demographic policy was always fluid, of course, but rarely did forced population movements rest on the notion of the collective guilt of a distinct cultural group. Empires engaged in demographic engineering because doing so was the prerogative of the sovereign, whether caesar, sultan or tsar.

From the middle of the nineteenth century, organized population transfers both accelerated and changed in nature. Moving people could be accomplished more easily than in the past; railroads and steamships made mass transport far simpler than in the age of ox-cart and sail. There was a new philosophical impetus as well. The rise of nationalism, first as a cultural movement among European-educated intellectuals and then as a state policy that linked political legitimacy with the historical destinies of culturally defined nations, provided an additional reason for moving people from one place to another.

Subtle shifts in the central organizing ideas of the states around the sea were clear. Both the Ottoman and Russian empires had experienced periods of substantial reform in the middle of the century. During the *Tanzimat* period, the Ottomans aimed to catch up with the technological superiority of Europe and to recast the Ottoman imperial identity—which, though tolerant of other religions, had placed Islam at the center—as multiconfessional. Russia had likewise embarked on a series of reforms, spurred on by the defeat in the Crimean war, which led to the ending of serfdom. Both periods were shortlived, however. The *Tanzimat* experiment effectively came to an end with Sultan Abdülhamit II (reigned 1876–1909), a reactionary who worked to put back in place the most conservative visions of the empire as an Islamic state. Tsars Alexander III and Nicholas II likewise instituted counter-reforms and again promoted the triune ideology of Orthodoxy, autocracy, and nationality as the basis for state power. Within and around these empires, smaller but no less exclusive visions of the nation were also in evidence. Romania had been granted independence in 1878 and soon set about creating a state by and for an ethnic Romanian nation, to the exclusion of Jews and other religious and ethnic minorities that lived on the same territory. The consequence of all these ideas—of cultural purity, of national territory, and of the alien within—would be a vast reengineering of settlement and identity on a mammoth scale.

In the nineteenth century's earliest instances of forced population movements, compulsory immigration was a concomitant of border warfare, a strategy of frontier pacification not unknown in many other parts of the world. When a restive indigenous population refused to recognize the suzerainty of an expanding power, the government simply moved the people somewhere else. The expansion of Russia into the Caucasus highlands was accompanied by the cutting back of forests, destruction of villages, and movement of civilians to new locations—a policy pioneered by the imperial viceroy, Vorontsov, who had earlier served as governor of New Russia. After the military defeat of the remaining highland opposition groups in the early 1860s, the Russian government organized the systematic emptying of Caucasus villages and the expulsion of hundreds of thousands of highland Muslims—Circassians, Chechens, and others—to the Ottoman empire. Ships were dispatched from the Caucasus ports to Sinop, Trabzon, and Varna, where the highlanders were simply offloaded on the docks. So great was the level of death from disease, dehydration, and starvation that observers labeled the ships "floating graveyards."[32] There was, however, a reverse side to the policy of expulsion. Just as the Russians had hoped to rid the frontier of rebellious Muslims and resettle it with Slavic peasants and Cossacks, the Ottomans dispatched the highlanders to resettlement areas on their own restive frontiers in the Balkans, eastern Anatolia, and the Arab lands.

The movement of Tatars, Caucasus highlanders, and other Muslims out of the Russian empire in the latter half of the nineteenth century was spectacular—in round figures, perhaps 1.5 million migrants from Crimea and the Caucasus, many of whom died en route or shortly after arrival at their final destinations. According to one calculation, as a direct result of Muslim flight, the population of Crimea may have dropped by as much as a quarter and the population of the Caucasus uplands by a little more.[33] The 1877–8 war prompted the exodus of still further communities, particularly Tatars and other Muslims (including people whom we would now call Turks) from Serbia and Romania; more left in the turmoil of the Balkan wars of 1912 and 1913. In all, at least 2.5 million Muslim civilians, probably far more, died as a direct result of war and official policies of ethnic cleansing in Russia and the Balkans in the century leading up to the First World War.[34]

On the other side of the sea, along the southeast coast, similar developments were taking place among Christian communities in the Ottoman port cities and deep into the Anatolian hinterland. The long history of commerce in cities such as Trabzon, Samsun, and Rize had attracted Greek and Armenian merchants and other Christian communities from Anatolia, the Aegean, and elsewhere, communities that now formed significant portions of the population. The Armenians in particular, with their strong social and family ties across the Near East, were at the core of the international trading network that stretched all the way from the bazaars of Tabriz to the markets of Leipzig. For the most part, religious communities lived in relative peace, with each exercising some degree of control over their own communal institutions and affairs, the basis of the Ottoman *millet* system of confessional self-governance. But the influx of Caucasus Muslims into the ports and their resettlement inland led to numerous disputes over land rights and periodic raiding by the highlanders. New settlers felt exploited by the older communities, while Armenians and other Christians felt overwhelmed by the tide of Muslim deportees.

The Russo-Turkish war and the peace settlement afterward gave a political tenor to these communal tensions. Encouraged by the success of Balkan Christians in throwing off Ottoman control and establishing new states, Armenian leaders, especially those living in western Europe and Russia, increasingly militated for the creation of an autonomous or independent Armenia. Revolutionary societies were formed for achieving that goal, if necessary by force. The tsar, seeing a potential lever against the Ottomans, stoked those aspirations. The experiences of the 1870s set the stage for growing conflict between Armenian communities and the Ottoman state. In the ports, support for the most radical Armenian groups was probably limited, but there was dissatisfaction with the Ottoman tax system. Raiding by Kurds and other Muslims in the interior, including the Caucasus refugees, were also sources of discontent.

In the summer of 1894 a tax revolt by Armenians in Sason, in eastern Anatolia, was the tocsin for the revolutionary associations, who hoped to enkindle a full-scale rebellion against the empire. Their efforts failed, but the hint of revolution was a convenient cover for Abdülhamit II, who had come to question the loyalty of Armenians to the Ottoman state. From 1894 to 1896, Ottoman irregular troops were dispatched to quell a string of supposed insurrections, and large-scale attacks on Armenian communities followed. As many as 80,000—some estimates go as high as 300,000—Armenians and others were killed in a mêlée of officially sanctioned punishment, chaotic brigandage, land disputes, and communal revenge.[35]

The Hamidian massacres were not aimed at the wholesale extermination or expulsion of the Armenians, but they did mark an important change from the flight of the Tatars and Circassians three decades earlier. Russian tactics in the Caucasus campaigns had been abominable, with villages scorched and men, women, and children rounded up for movement to new locales. Yet the motive was not who the Muslims were but where they were—in the path of Russian imperial expansion, in the unconquered highlands that were seen as a security threat by the Russian state. In the Armenian case, however, communities were targeted because of their identity. Armenian civilians in the port cities along the coast and in the major cities and villages all across eastern Anatolia presented little immediate danger to the Ottoman government; revolutionary activity was limited to bands of guerrilla fighters who were mainly based abroad—and usually at odds with Armenian elites within the Ottoman empire. As it turned out, the Hamidian massacres were only the opening act in a long drama of human suffering, in which individuals all around the sea would be labeled as inherent threats to states and empires, uprooted from their homes, and killed or forced to migrate. The ideas of "local foreigners" and enemy peoples would reach their apotheosis a short time later, in a great unmixing of the multiethnic and multiconfessional communities along the coast from 1915 to 1923.

The First World War came slowly to the Black Sea, and naval operations were strategically inconsequential compared with the movement of troops along other stretches of the eastern front. Russia and Turkey formally entered the war on opposite sides in November 1914, but it was not until the next year that Bulgaria joined on the side of the Central Powers. Almost another year passed before Romania was persuaded to break its neutrality and throw in its lot with Britain and France. Early on, the Allies worked to capture the greatest strategic asset in the region—the entryway to Istanbul and the sea at the Dardanelles—but their ill-fated assault at Gallipoli dragged on through most of 1915.

On the sea, Russian and Ottoman navies clashed infrequently. Both entered the war in imperfect condition. The Russian fleet was poorly furnished in terms of both men and equipment; the dire living conditions on board Russian ships had been the cause, in the summer of 1905, of the famous incident on board the cruiser *Potemkin*, when a mutinous crew seized the ship and sailed it to Constanța. The Ottomans were in no better shape. Spending on the navy was insignificant; the state's massive public debt meant that further borrowing was impossible. In any case, the Ottomans by this stage were far more concerned about internal rebellion than projecting their power at sea. Before the war, expenditure on the gendarmerie—one of the instruments of the violence of the 1890s—exceeded the entire naval budget.[36] Still, the sultan had made the strategically important move of trading in the longstanding connection with the British navy for a closer relationship with Germany, a relationship that eventually led to the transfer of armored warships, along with their German crews, to the Ottoman service.

The Ottomans made preemptive attacks on Russian bases even before the tsar's declaration of war. Ottoman ships bombarded Sevastopol, Novorossiisk, and Odessa, but Russian losses were inconsiderable. Russia quickly responded with a massive mine-laying effort along the Anatolian coast and disruption of coal transport, a strategy that destroyed virtually all the Ottoman navy's collier ships by mid-1915. (The navy resorted to using Bosphorus passenger ferries and small sailing ships to transport coal.) The only major battle was a brief fog-bound encounter off the Crimean coast between the German dreadnought *Goeben*, now Ottoman-flagged, and Russian battleships, which led to no more than a dozen casualties. On land, the Russians pushed from the south Caucasus into eastern Anatolia, taking Erzurum and Trabzon by the spring of 1916. The collapse of the Russian armies in the revolutions of 1917 allowed the Ottoman forces to retake the southeast coast, but by that stage, the Black Sea was already a secondary front. The real fate of the Ottomans lay to the southwest, in clashes with British forces in the Levant, and Ottoman successes across the Near and Middle East were progressively reversed over the course of the next year.

The war spawned a series of massive population movements that dwarfed the multiple exoduses of the late nineteenth century. In eastern Anatolia, an uprising of Armenian revolutionaries had accompanied the Russian successes on the Caucasus front. An Ottoman counteroffensive against the Russians included reprisals against Armenian civilians. These massacres and deportations, now sanctioned by a government that had rejected the tolerant Ottoman ideals of the past for a new form of ethnic Turkish nationalism, culminated in an organized genocide in 1915. The Italian consul-general in Trabzon later recalled his experience in the port:

The passing of the gangs of Armenian exiles beneath the windows and before the door of the Consulate; their prayers for help, when neither I nor any other could do anything to answer them; the city in a state of siege, guarded at every point by 15,000 troops in complete war equipment, by thousands of police agents, by bands of volunteers ...; the hundreds of corpses found every day along the exile road; the young women converted by force to Islam or exiled like the rest; the children torn way from their families or from the Christian schools, and handed over by force to Moslem families, or else placed by hundreds on board ship in nothing but their shirts, and then capsized and drowned in the Black Sea and the River Deyirmen Deré [Değirmendere]—these are my last ineffaceable memories of Trebizond....[37]

Throughout the Ottoman empire, but especially in the eastern provinces of Anatolia, somewhere between 800,000 and 1.5 million Armenians and other Anatolian Christians were killed or died in forced marches to resettlement areas away from sensitive border regions.

In the Balkans, the advance of Allied armies led to the flight of local Muslims, and all across the collapsing Ottoman and Russian empires, refugees of all religions fled to the seaports to escape violence and starvation. Civilians crowded the harbors, waiting for Russian, British or American ships to ferry them to safety. European and American relief workers arrived to organize distribution of food and clothing, while thousands of orphaned children were sent to new lives abroad.

The armistice produced a formal cessation of hostilities on the western front, but north of the sea, the continuing violence of the Russian civil war meant further refugee outflows and mass starvation on the steppes of Ukraine. Soon, a major relief program was established to deal with the consequences. In early 1919, the U.S. Congress appropriated $100 million for relief assistance to Russia, as well as to Armenians, Greek Orthodox, and other Christian and Jewish populations in Asia Minor. A new American Relief Administration, headed by Herbert Hoover, was set up to organize the disbursement of assistance, and hundreds of agents were dispatched to the Balkans, Russia, Turkey, and the Caucasus to oversee the programs. Operations continued in Russia, even under the Bolshevik government, until the autumn of 1922. U.S. and other Allied ships patrolled the Black Sea harbors, provided security in the ports, and assisted in the evacuation of Russian refugees to Greece and other countries. Soon, however, the European powers would actively assist not only in moving people to safe locations but in actually sanctioning their permanent deportation—an instance of ethnic cleansing by international treaty.

When the First World War ended, much of the Ottoman Black Sea coast was controlled by Allied powers. The Straits had been taken soon after the Ottomans signed the armistice in October 1918. Later, British forces quickly seized Batumi and the Transcaucasian railroad all the way to Baku. Other Allies took control of the northern Black Sea ports, now filled with refugees fleeing the brewing civil war across the former Russian empire. The ports then became channels not only for civilian relief, but also for Allied assistance to anti-Bolshevik armies fighting in Ukraine and southern Russia. The Allied High Commission, headquartered in Istanbul, became the effective government of the Ottoman empire and much of the Black Sea coast, overseeing assistance to the starving and displaced, not only in Anatolia but in southern Russia as well.

The Ottoman state had been defeated and occupied, but a Turkish nationalist force was massing in central Anatolia. Mini-states—including a Greek "Republic of the Pontus"—had been declared by local powers. The difficult question of what to do with the remnants of the empire was formally resolved with the signing of the treaty of Sèvres by the Ottoman government and the Allies in 1920. The treaty provided for the creation of a rump and virtually demilitarized Turkish state, surrounded by areas carved off into Greek and Italian protectorates, and an independent Armenia and Kurdistan. The outer reaches of the empire were placed under British and French mandates. An international commission was appointed to govern the Straits, now declared open to all vessels in both peace and war. The Ottoman navy was to be almost completely disbanded.

Sèvres satisfied few. To the remnants of the Ottoman army, which now exercised de facto control over much of Anatolia, the treaty was the last capitulation of a defunct empire. To some Allies, particularly Greece, the treaty did not go far enough, since it did not allow the recreation of a "Greek empire" with its center in Istanbul. In the end, renewed war was the tool for resolving these differences. Greek forces, which had been given the task of occupying the Aegean coast, began to push across central Anatolia. Bedraggled elements of the Ottoman army regrouped under the command of one of the heroes of Gallipoli, Mustafa Kemal, and began to organize a counterattack. A new Greek–Turkish war raged until the signing of an armistice in October 1922.

At the end of the conflict, negotiations were undertaken to replace the treaty of Sèvres with a new agreement that would recognize the realities created by the Greek–Turkish conflict. The war had devastated Anatolia, moving populations around and virtually leveling vital cities such as Smyrna, which had been torched as the Greek army fled in the face of the advancing Kemalists. The retreat of the Greek expeditionary force had been accompanied by even further refugee flows and Turkish attacks on any group—Greek, Armenian or other—thought to be sympathetic to the old terms of the Sèvres treaty. The Ottoman empire was at a definitive end; the sultanate had been abolished and a new republic, now avowedly Turkish and national rather than Ottoman and imperial, was declared. Kemal, soon recast as Atatürk, headed a party that won elections for a new parliament.

The outcome of the new round of negotiations was the organized movement of people on a staggering scale, an exchange sanctioned by the treaty of Lausanne, signed by Turkey and the Allies in July 1923.[38] In an effort to homogenize the ethnic populations of both Greece and Turkey and protect minorities from reprisals by either government, the treaty authorized the compulsory transfer to Greece of up to 1.5 million Orthodox Christians from Anatolia, including the Black Sea coastal cities, as well as the movement of some 350,000 Muslims from Greece, especially Aegean Macedonia. (Greek Orthodox in Istanbul and Muslims in western Thrace were declared exempt from expulsion.) In addition to the psychological trauma of deportation—this time approved by the major European powers—the physical toll on the deportees was dramatic. Makeshift camps housed families before their transfer to crowded ships. Bandits and venal administrators liberated their possessions before they stepped on board and as soon as they stepped off. Provisions for their integration into the new host societies were often inadequate. Moreover, the very identities of the deportees often made integration difficult. The Lausanne treaty had been written as if distinguishing between "Greeks" (the term used for Orthodox Christians) and Muslims was an easy thing—and as if both communities should have felt some affinity for Greece and the new Turkish Republic as their natural homelands. But in many communities, the lines were indistinct. A person of Orthodox religious affiliation—the only criterion, according to the treaty, for being "Greek"—might speak only Turkish or a variety of Greek unintelligible to a Greek-speaker from the Aegean. A Muslim from Greece likewise might be most comfortable in Greek or a Balkan Slavic language, not Turkish.

Nevertheless, communities were marked for wholesale removal based on their presumed ethnic traits. Disputes over whether a person or family was, in fact, "exchangeable"—subject to compulsory deportation—were adjudicated by a special intergovernmental committee established under Lausanne. By the middle of the 1920s, Trabzon, Samsun, and Sinop had been virtually emptied of Christians. Even the Greek-speaking communities of the Pontic uplands, the Matzouka region where the last remnants of Byzantium had lingered on in monasteries and villages for centuries, came to an end. People who still called themselves Romans—*Romaioi* or *Rumlar*—suddenly became "Hellenes," just as people who had once been simply Muslims now became "Turks." And both found themselves in new, national homelands to which they had never owed allegiance. It was "a thoroughly bad and vicious solution," declared Lord Curzon, one of the framers of the Lausanne treaty, "for which the world would pay a heavy penalty a hundred years to come."[39]

Were these forced migrations and the deaths they produced instances of genocide? Most of the population movements differed on two key criteria usually used to distinguish genocide from other forms of organized violence: the degree to which there is an intent to eliminate a people as such, rather than simply remove them from a piece of territory, and the existence or otherwise of a clear ideology—of racial superiority, say—to justify killing. Only rarely, such as the Armenian case in 1915, did there seem to be an eliminationist impetus to the actions of governments; rarer still was a coherent ideology to rationalize it. Yet the easy conceptual distinctions between genocide, ethnic cleansing, and forced migration are normally lost on the targets of state-organized violence. For most of the victims and their descendants, the deportations and killings are now treated as discrete historical events, turning points in the collective consciousness of the groups involved. Like all such events, they have names: the *Ch'art* to Armenians, the *Katastrophe* to Pontic Greeks, the *Mübadele* to Turks.

The demographic changes on the seacoasts from the 1860s to the 1920s were the direct result of government policies and were unprecedented in scope and in their tragic consequences for the victims. The Crimean Tatar population, diminishing since the eighteenth century, was cut still further by the out-migration to Bulgaria and other Ottoman lands. The western Caucasus uplands were virtually depopulated, with Circassians and other highlanders scattered across the Balkans and the Middle East. The Armenian communities in Trabzon, Samsun, and other ports along the southern and southeastern coasts began to disappear in the massacres of the 1890s and were then wiped out in the organized killing of 1915. Less than a decade later, Orthodox Christians—Greeks, of a sort, but usually with little sense of connection to the Greek nation-state—were removed from the littoral areas and "returned" to Greece.

The rest of the twentieth century would see still further diminution of the cultural heterogeneity that had long defined the coast, most spectacularly with the mass killing of Jews and further deportations of Crimean Tatars and Caucasus peoples during the Second World War. In tandem with this rapid cultural homogenization of the coastline, historians, writers, and other nationalist intellectuals were engaged in a similar pursuit in their own domains: an effort to purify the historical record and to uncover—or, in most cases, construct—an ancient and unassailable link between the nations of the hinterland and the sea itself.

"The Division of the Waters"

The emergence of new states around the coastline in the late nineteenth and early twentieth centuries raised the issue of state control over the sea and its resources. Already in 1878, the question of "the division of the waters" of the Danube— that is, the delimitation of control over fisheries and the demarcation of state boundaries in the shifting channels of the delta—had been taken up in the treaty of Berlin. Over the coming decades, determining which state owned which bits of the sea would assume increasing importance as a subject of diplomacy among the coastal powers.

The idea of "territorial waters" is an obvious oxymoron, the result of the extension of concepts derived from control of land to the sea. It was a concept still imperfectly enshrined in international law well into the twentieth century. Its development depended on a host of factors: the emergence of international legal institutions, scientific advances in measurement of latitude and longitude, and improvements in naval technology which allowed states to patrol waters that they claimed as theirs. On the Black Sea, the clarification of interstate boundary lines lagged behind other parts of the world. Even today, there is no international agreement concerning the distance from shore that Black Sea littoral states may assert as their exclusive domain, and disputes over fishing rights have been problems. In 2000 a Ukrainian coastguard ship fired on and sank a Turkish trawler that had strayed into waters claimed by Ukraine.

However, between the world wars, two important conventions were worked out to govern international relations on the sea and in the Straits. The same Lausanne treaty that had approved the Greek–Turkish population exchange also regulated passage between the Aegean and the Black Sea. The treaty affirmed the complete freedom of navigation through the Straits in times of peace, for both merchant ships and vessels of war; but the maximum military force to be sent into the Black Sea was never to be greater than that of the most powerful fleet maintained by one of the littoral countries: the kingdoms of Bulgaria and Romania, the Soviet Union, and Turkey. The shores of the Bosphorus and Dardanelles were to be demilitarized, with Turkey giving up the right to station troops and equipment within 15 km of the coasts. Dissatisfaction with that provision prompted Turkey to call for a revision of the Lausanne treaty a decade later. A new international document, the 1936 Montreux convention, returned full Turkish sovereignty over the coastal reaches of the Straits and reaffirmed the principle of free passage in peacetime. When at war, Turkey reserved the right to govern passage through the Straits at its own discretion. The convention also set limits on the size and number of naval vessels that foreign powers could send into the Black Sea and the length of time they were allowed to remain there. With the exception of a few safety regulations instituted unilaterally by Turkey in the 1990s, the Montreux convention is the international instrument that has governed access to the sea to this day.

Yet there was a deeper sense in which states began to exercise greater interest in what happened on the water. The sea and its territorial waters became not only the purview of the states around the shore; both were also celebrated as the patrimony of the historical nations which those states were held to represent. Historians searched back through history to find evidence of a seafaring inclination among the Getae and Daci, the Thracians, and other ancient peoples. The link with the sea was lauded as the essence of national greatness, a vital connection to the wider world. Already at the christening of the first Romanian steam-powered gunboat in the late nineteenth century, the minister of war argued that its major tasks would be not only "to instruct the sons of the people in the art of navigation" but also "to encourage them to regain the lost dominion" on the water.[40] In late imperial Russia, the preeminent historian N. S. Solov'ev was clear on the ways in which the sea connected the Rhos of the ninth century—now recast as proto-Russians— to the rest of Europe, and the tragic invasions of nomadic peoples that eventually severed this economic and cultural tie:

Southern Rus' proper was a borderland, the European fringe of the steppe. It was a low fringe, unprotected in any way by nature, therefore open to frequent overflow of nomadic hordes.... Not only did the nomads attack Rus', they cut it off from the Black Sea coast, making communication with Byzantium difficult.... Barbarian Asia strove to deny Rus' all routes and ways by which it communicated with educated Europe.[41]

Solov'ev's multivolume history of Russia ended in the mid-1770s, when Russia's reestablishment of connections with both northern and southern Europe— through the partition of Poland and the opening of the Black Sea—had at last undone the alienation created by the barbarian invasions centuries earlier. Both the empire and the Russian nation had at last, according to Solov'ev, reestablished their place among the leading European peoples, with access to the world's oceans.

The ancient inhabitants of the seaboard were brought into these emerging narratives of nations and their rightful connection to the water. The new science of ethno-history sought the origins of modern states and peoples in the murky past. The Rhos became Russians or, for later historians in Ukraine and its diaspora, Ukrainians. Getae and Daci, Latinized after Trajan's conquest of the lands north of the Danube, were treated as inchoate Romanians. Thracians became Bulgarians. In the rare instances when living versions of these antique forebears could be found, states developed policies to cultivate connections with them. For example, in the southern Balkans, the Romanian kingdom worked to foster ties with the Vlachs, upland shepherds who still spoke a latinate language similar to Romanian. Before the First World War, Romania sponsored schools and scholarships for Vlach children and, in the 1920s, embarked on a state-subsidized "colonization" program that brought thousands of Vlach families from Albania, Greece, and Macedonia to Dobrudja. From the state's point of view, colonization was doubly appealing: It brought an unredeemed component of the Romanian nation back to their putative motherland, and it also helped tip the demographic balance in favor of Romanian-speakers in a part of the country that was largely Bulgarian, Turkish, and Tatar.

The effort to rediscover the ancient peoples of the coast could sometimes lead in bizarre directions. Just before the First World War, stories began to surface about a population of "Negroes" living around the port of Batumi. They were said to be the descendants of former African slaves once taken into Ottoman service or, in the most fantastic speculations, one of the lost tribes of Israel or even remnants of the curly-haired Colchians (who, according to Herodotus, were descended from the Egyptians). Russian ethnographers rushed to study the strange people, but they usually found little more than a few individuals with dark complexions, hardly the "tribe" that they had expected. Nevertheless, tales of the Black Sea Negroes popped up periodically throughout the century. Soviet propagandists between the world wars used them as examples of the "friendship of peoples" and cultural tolerance promoted within the Soviet state, while some black American activists pointed to this "tribe" as evidence of the racial harmony that communism could engender.[42]

The appropriation of the sea and its lost peoples did lead to certain contradictions, of course, because the heritage claimed by one group was also claimed by at least one other. Romanian and Bulgarian historians clashed over the ancient indigenous population of Dobrudja—proto-Romanian for some, proto-Bulgarian for others. Russians and Romanians debated the history of the medieval Moldovan and Wallachian principalities north of the Danube—representatives of a Slavic culture for some or of a latinate culture for others. Bulgarians and Tatars both claimed the legacy of the ancient Bulgar khanates, which originated along the Volga river. Ukrainians and Russians both looked back to the Rhos as the progenitors of their respective nations, as well as the earliest example of a Slavic state north of the sea.

For many historians in the countries that now touched the littoral, demonstrating the essential connection between the nation and the water was crucial to justifying the existence of an independent state and blocking the natural imperial ambitions of the Russians. The sea, declared the great Romanian historian Nicolae Iorga in 1938, "lives in our poetry and in our conscience...[It has been] linked throughout our history to the totality of our way of thinking and of feeling."[43] His contemporary, the Ukrainian historian Mykhailo Hrushevs'kyi, was similarly categorical about the place of the sea in the history of his own nation. "While the historical circumstances of life have oriented Ukraine toward the west," Hrushevs'kyi wrote in a famous passage on the "Black Sea orientation" of the Ukrainian people, "geography has oriented her toward the south, toward the Black Sea—'that sea of the Rus', as the Kievan chronicle of the twelfth century has it, or in modern terminology, the Ukrainian sea."[44]

Debates on the true ownership of the sea and the coasts were carried on in the pages of learned journals and books. During peace conferences at the ends of major wars, they were published in pamphlet form and expedited to Europe's great powers to convince diplomats of the justice of one or another position. The outcome of these arguments had real political consequences. The work of historians was used to justify a particular territorial settlement, and claims about the historical right to territory remained the basis for irredentist movements in peacetime and often the starting point for another war. At one time or another over the course of the late nineteenth and twentieth centuries, the status of virtually every littoral area—Dobrudja, Bessarabia, Crimea, Abkhazia, the Pontic coast, and other disputed enclaves—would turn in part on the ability of states to field the most convincing arguments about their respective nations' historical rights to a piece of real estate and, by extension, access to the water.

But just as historians, ethnographers, and other intellectuals were appropriating the sea for their distinct national programs, others were beginning to understand the Black Sea as a discrete unit. Rather than dividing it among nations and states, new generations of scientists were uncovering the ways in which what happened in one part of the sea was intimately linked with the fate of every other.

Knowing the Sea

The modern science of ecology begins with the idea that no organism is an island. Living creatures are connected to one another in a complex system of interdependence, and changes to one part of that system inevitably affect the ability of any of the other constituents to stay alive and reproduce. Philosophers and scientists from Aristotle forward had intimations of these essential connections, but the systematic study of the natural environment—that is, its study as a system—is a young science. The earliest appearance of the word "oecology" dates only from the 1870s, and it did not come into general use until many decades later.

Seeing oceans and seas as ecosystems was a particularly late development. Large bodies of water are startlingly complex; understanding them requires the input of a variety of otherwise unrelated fields, from fluid mechanics to microbiology. Oceanography, as a catch-all name for the many scientific fields involved in the study of marine environments, requires both an intimate knowledge of the peculiar physical interactions of water, land, and weather, and an understanding of the way in which all of them affect the animal and plant species that live throughout the biological column, from surface dwellers to the inhabitants of the dark depths.

The oceanographic study of the Black Sea has a long pedigree as speculative philosophy but a rather short one as science.[45] Aristotle and Leonardo da Vinci had theories to account for some of the sea's obvious peculiarities, such as why a body of water that takes in so many rivers manages not to overflow. But it was not until the late seventeenth century that the first experimental model was devised to explain one of the sea's most important characteristics, the exchange of water with the Mediterranean.

In 1679 a young Italian count, Luigi Fernando Marsigli, traveled to Istanbul and became intrigued by stories about the double current in the Bosphorus, a top one flowing from the Black Sea to the Mediterranean and an undercurrent flowing in the opposite direction. Marsigli confirmed the existence of the two currents by lowering a rope, to which he had affixed pieces of white cork, into the strait. As he predicted, the corks near the surface floated toward the Mediterranean while those farther down on the rope began to arc in the opposite direction, toward the Black Sea. That was not news; any fisherman who cast a net into the strait knew of the same phenomenon. What was novel was Marsigli's explanation.

Previous speculations about the cause of these currents had rested on the nature of the strait itself or on the weather. Perhaps the underwater geography was somehow responsible, or maybe winds from the north pushed water from the sea into the Mediterranean. Marsigli proposed that the twin currents had nothing to do with the supposed slope of the sea floor or the prevailing winds, but rather with the nature of the water itself.

He began with the observation that the upper and lower layers of water in the strait exhibited different properties. Even Aristotle had known that the Mediterranean, and therefore the bottom current, was saltier than the Black Sea; with so much fresh water entering the Black Sea through its river system, its salinity was far less than the world's oceans. Marsigli argued that the differential salinity also represented a substantial difference in density, and he simply measured the specific gravity of water samples from the top and bottom of the strait to prove his point. The cause of the double current, he reckoned, lay in this basic observation: The differential densities produced a pressure gradient that in turn created motion in opposite directions, a standard hypothesis of fluid mechanics. Marsigli gathered his observations in a famous letter to the queen of Sweden, a document that would become the first genuinely scientific study of the physical peculiarities of the Black Sea.[46]

Marsigli was a typical example of the Enlightenment naturalist, a European aristocrat who engaged in scientific research as an adjunct to other pursuits, in this case adventure travel in the Orient. Others followed his example in the eighteenth and early nineteenth centuries, but they usually confined their work to the coastline. Peter Simon Pallas, a German geologist in Russian service, conducted important research on the paleogeography of the northern coast in the 1790s. He was followed by another Prussian, the Baron von Haxthausen, who conducted geological and botanical studies on the steppe and in the Caucasus in the early nineteenth century.[47] It was not until some time later, though, that Marsigli's real successors would appear.

The development of oceanography on the wider sea depended on two things: relative peace between the Ottoman and Russian empires and the growth of state-sponsored, professional institutions that could engage in long-term scientific study. Both finally began to emerge after the 1820s. The establishment of a permanent Russian naval presence in Sevastopol and the creation of a southern Admiralty at Kherson and, later, Nikolaev provided the institutional support for the growth of a science of the sea. There was also, of course, a strategic rationale: Russian and foreign captains needed a better understanding of the currents and anchorages. There had been limited work in these directions—the Barbié maps in Anthoine's memoirs were based on reports from the Russian Admiralty—but for more than half a century after the opening of the sea to European vessels, there were still no reliable maps of major sections of the coastline, not to mention studies of the water and its characteristics.

That soon began to change. In 1832 the first preliminary hydrographic atlas of the Black Sea appeared in St. Petersburg. Published by the general directorate for roads and communications, a division of the Russian interior ministry, the atlas contained nearly sixty plates that mapped in detail the coastal areas from the Danube to the Caucasus. The atlas not only showed the physical features of the coastline and ports but also indicated soundings based on the latest Admiralty data. A decade later an even more elaborate atlas, drawn by the cartographer Egor Manganari, was issued by the newly created Black Sea Hydrographical Office in Nikolaev. Manganari's work deserves to be counted among the greatest contributions to the cartography of the sea.[48] His *Atlas of the Black Sea*, published in 1841, was dedicated to Tsar Nicholas I, and the tsar's own large presentation copy was bound in green leather with rich gilt lettering. The intricate maps of the coastline were based on more than a decade of research. The atlas also featured remarkable drawings of each of the major ports, including those on the Ottoman coasts, and even showed the placement of individual buildings. Soundings were given for all the Russian-controlled coastline and the entire northwestern shelf of the sea, farther out into the depths than had ever been recorded. The atlas featured beautifully drawn elevations, a prominent feature of nineteenth-century coastal cartography in general, which gave the viewer a sense of what the coastline would look like from a ship at sea.

The Manganari atlas marked the beginning of serious attempts to chart the physical features of the sea as a whole, not simply the parts controlled by one or another power. There were holes, of course. The Russians had little intelligence about the urban landscape of the Ottoman ports, which is why some of the overhead views of cities such as Sinop and Trebizond have blank spots where fortifications, batteries, and other sensitive structures were located. But in its day, the Manganari atlas was an extraordinary achievement. For the first time someone sitting well beyond the sea had an intimation of two things that would only really become available in the late twentieth century: something approximating a modern satellite image of port facilities and the ability to take a "virtual" sail along the coastline by examining in sequence the striking coastal views.

Over the rest of the nineteenth century, Russian cartographic efforts followed in the Manganari tradition. Expeditions were launched farther into the sea to take soundings and record the currents. More intelligence was gathered on the nature of the Ottoman ports and anchorages. But as the century progressed, scientists around the sea took a greater interest in subjects beyond the sea's physical features. They also began to analyze sea life and the ways in which the different parts of the sea—the northwest shelf, the shallow Sea of Azov, the depths along the southern coast—were linked together in a single ecological web. The growth of specialized scientific bodies that could sponsor research (and could pressure the military to provide ships and other assistance) facilitated serious study of the sea's geology, chemistry, and biology. There was also now a political imperative: the growing desire by governments to understand precisely what kinds of riches lay in the sea and how they could best be exploited.

In 1890 the pioneering Russian geologist Nikolai Andrusov conducted the first systematic study of the Black Sea depths. Using a steamer on loan from the Russian navy, Andrusov logged over 3,000 km in only eighteen days, taking depth measurements, recording temperature and salinity at various points, charting the currents, and recovering dredgings from the sea floor. Andrusov's chief discovery was the sea's anoxic layer, a phenomenon that he correctly surmised was enhanced by the decay of organic matter. Just as the Manganari atlas had been a quantum leap in the accurate representation of the sea's physical geography, Andrusov's work contributed a great deal to understanding the sea's chemistry and its relationship to natural biological processes.

One of Andrusov's contemporaries was the Romanian zoologist Grigore Antipa. Like many in his generation, he received his training abroad, in Germany and Italy, and returned to Romania in the 1890s to begin a career in state service. He was tasked with completing a study of Romanian fisheries—how they might apply the latest scientific techniques to increase productivity—and creating a museum of zoology that would highlight the natural wealth included inside the country's new borders, redrawn by the treaty of Berlin. A comprehensive study was necessary, for knowledge about the coast and the sea was sparse in Romania. (The first Romanian map of the country's Black Sea coastline would not be produced until 1900; the Romanian navy was still using it in the 1950s.)[49] Over the course of his career, Antipa became Romania's leading expert on the Black Sea and one of the country's foremost authorities on fisheries and water resources. He was arguably the father of modern biological research in his country, and the museum of natural history in Bucharest, an institution which he directed, was later named in his honor.

Manganari, Andrusov, and Antipa represented a new type of scientist around the sea. They were young, all under thirty at the time of their most important early work. They were part of the first generation of local scientists in their respective fields—cartography, marine geology, biology—and had been trained in central and western Europe. They taught in the new universities that sprang up in national capitals and provincial cities and used their knowledge in the service of the state. They were part of a growing international community of scientists and scholars who shared their findings in learned papers and at international conferences—and sometimes shared even more: Andrusov was married to the daughter of the archaeologist Heinrich Schliemann, discoverer of Troy.

The work of these and other researchers pushed the scientific knowledge of the sea to a level that had never before been attained. They founded new scientific sub-disciplines and were among the first to treat the Black Sea as a unit of study, a complex system that had to be understood as a whole through an analysis of its geography, geology, chemistry, and biology. But the goal of their research was not simply disinterested science. Throughout his career, Antipa in particular was clear about the extra-scientific nature of his work. Understanding the sea was valuable on its own, of course, but that knowledge was linked in Antipa's mind with the greater project of using the sea's riches to fulfill the historical destinies of the nations around it. In his magisterial work *The Black Sea* (1941), a summation of his entire career of scientific research, Antipa emphasized the link between science and the national goals that it was meant to further:

We should recognize that today we…have the necessary geographic base to carry out an important maritime activity which…our location at the mouth of the Danube and our very territory obliges us to carry out. …Therefore, today, when we are laying the basis for the development and organization of our…state, it is of utmost necessity that we clearly affirm and forcibly protect the vital national interests…that we have along the seacoast, which opens to us a wide route for…trade in the produce of our country and of the work of our people.[50]

The chief task, Antipa argued, was to prevent neighboring states from taking undue advantage of the sea's wealth. The Black Sea should never become "an internal Russian lake," he wrote, and the other states around the rim—Romania, Bulgaria, Turkey—should cooperate to prevent any encroachments by the Soviet imperialists of the north.

Even the science of the sea could not escape the lure of the national idea. Where it had once been celebrated as the patrimony of nations newly freed from the Ottoman yoke, the sea was now touted as a treasure to be guarded against the rapacity of the expansionist Soviet Union. Antipa was not alone in viewing things in this light. There were political leaders, too, who had a vision for building a bulwark against the country that now controlled the majority of the shoreline, from the Danube to the south Caucasus.

The Prometheans

After the First World War, all four states around the Black Sea were, in different ways, young countries. All were built on the ruins of older states or empires, but each had either new borders or, in the case of republican Turkey and the Soviet Union, radically new bases for social order. All faced problems of integrating new territories, rebuilding after the devastation of war, and defending sovereignty and independence against a range of threats.

For three of these states, the central strategic conundrum was how to deal with the existence of the fourth. The ideology embraced by Romania, Bulgaria, and Turkey—nationalism—was powerful but self-limiting. Each state had territorial disputes with at least one of its neighbors, but these disputes did not go beyond arguments about rectification of borders. The Soviet Union, by contrast, espoused an ideology that proclaimed its own universality: the liberation of all toiling masses from the triple perils of imperialism, capitalism, and nationalism. The international relations of the Black Sea region thus necessarily concerned how to build a system of alliances to ward off the Bolshevik threat, while consolidating the independence and borders of the new states that had emerged from the peace treaties.

As in the rest of Europe, the war had brought profound geopolitical change to the region. Romania emerged from the postwar treaties with the former Hungarian region of Transylvania, Russian Bessarabia, Austrian Bukovina, and part of Bulgarian Dobrudja now inside its borders; these changes doubled the country's territory and population. Bulgaria, although losing some of its seacoast to Romania, was nevertheless confirmed in its independence, which had only been fully won from the Ottomans in 1908. In the turmoil of the Bolshevik revolution and the ensuing civil war, the Crimean Tatars had declared their own country, as had Georgia, Armenia, and Azerbaijan; several different states had emerged, although hardly consolidated, on the territory of Ukraine. The Ottoman empire had been transformed into the Turkish Republic, fighting for its own independence against an invading army of Greeks and Allied occupiers.

By the mid-1920s, this complicated milieu had become rather clearer, often with tragic results. Ukraine, with Crimea, was absorbed into the new Soviet state, after the desperate flight of White Russian soldiers and ordinary civilians from Novorossiisk, Odessa, and other ports aboard British and American warships. Georgia, Armenia, and Azerbaijan were conquered by the Bolshevik army, their national governments exiled and their briefly independent countries erased from history. Romania, Bulgaria, and Turkey fared rather better, but even in these new states, Soviet agents were active in the capitals and the borderlands, attempting to foment revolution or to dislodge peripheral regions under the guise of liberation for national minorities.

In this environment, several of the leading political figures in each of the anti-Bolshevik states banded together to form a movement which represented the first modern attempt to think about the Black Sea as a distinct political unit. Their aim was to create a community of small states across the Near East, a community that would ensure stable borders and real independence against any attempt to exert complete control on or around the sea.

The Promethean project—or *Prométhée*, as it was known, after the journal around which it centered—has largely been forgotten by historians, but in its time, the 1920s and 1930s, it was a carefully crafted plan for creating an alliance of Black Sea states. Consisting originally of a group of émigrés from the former Russian empire, settled in Paris, the Prometheans were dedicated not only to the liberation of the captive peoples of the Soviet Union, but also to their cooperation against the Soviets as a regional hegemon. There was no shortage of such groups in the interwar years, of course; politicians dissatisfied by the postwar peace treaties, romantic nationalists, and many others worked either to break apart the countries that had been constructed at Versailles or to resurrect the lost empires on whose rubble they had been built. But the uniqueness of the Promethean project lay in the array of countries and peoples among whom it originated, and their conception of the importance of the sea in the international relations of the wider southeast Europe.

Many people would later lay claim to the Promethean idea, in particular Polish patriots who saw it as an emanation of the anti-Soviet foreign policy conducted by the interwar Polish leader, Józef Piłsudski. The Polish government clearly played a major role, contributing money to propaganda campaigns and recruiting non-Russian émigrés from the Soviet Union into the Polish military and intelligence services.[51] The expectation among Poles was that an alliance of small states on the Soviet periphery would hem in Russian expansionism and, in the end, strengthen Poland's own defenses against its eastern neighbor. But the Prometheans were an eclectic group. They included the most illustrious names in anti-Bolshevik circles from Ukraine, the Caucasus, and beyond, now in exile in western Europe or Turkey, as well as their supporters in the Balkans and elsewhere: Mehmet Emin Resulzade and Noe Zhordania, the former premiers of the briefly independent Azerbaijan and Georgia; Cafer Seydahmet, foreign minister of the fleeting Republic of Crimea; Ayaz İshaki, one of the leaders of the Tatars of the Volga region, who had also proclaimed independence when the Russian empire collapsed; as well as a bevy of leading west European politicians, professors, and writers on east European affairs. All were united in their goal of seeing the liberation of the small nations of eastern Europe and their defense against the revisionism of both Germans and Russians.[52]

The first issue of *Prométhée* appeared in Paris in November 1926, edited by the Georgian expatriate Georges Gvazawa and subtitled "the organ for the national defense of the peoples of the Caucasus and Ukraine." "We are animated," wrote Gvazawa in the first issue, "by the sole desire to serve peace and international justice" and to strengthen the Caucasus and Ukraine as "avant-postes" against the Bolshevik conquest of the rest of the Near East.[53] By the late 1930s, *Prométhée* had broadened its mandate to include not only the Caucasus and Ukraine, but all the subjugated peoples of the Soviet Union.[54] Through their journal, the Prometheans lobbied foreign governments and attempted to expose the injustice of the absorption of Ukraine and the Caucasus states into the new Soviet Union. The editors sponsored lectures and symposia, initiated letter-writing campaigns to heads of state, held artistic festivals centered around the cultures of the "captive peoples," and organized other public events to highlight their cause. They were, somewhat before their time, a think-tank of former politicians and diplomats, biding their time before an eventual return to office in countries that now no longer appeared on any map.

The Black Sea lay at the center of the Prometheans' attention. From the earliest issues of *Prométhée*, contributing writers had argued that free commerce on the sea—one of the mainstays of European policy since the 1770s—would be impossible without an equal European commitment to free states around it.[55] That goal, they argued, would only be reached with the break-up of the Soviet state and the reemergence of the small republics that had burst into being with the collapse of the Russian empire. By the 1930s, some Prometheans had even begun to call for the creation of a political and economic alliance of Black Sea states, including Turkey, Romania, and Bulgaria, as well as a future independent Ukraine and Georgia. For one Ukrainian contributor to the journal, the strategic value of such an alliance was clear: "With its left wing touching on Poland, passing by the friendly lands of the Cossacks of the Don, Kuban, and Urals, and with its right wing reaching out to the oppressed peoples of Asia, Turkestan, and other areas, this bloc of states will stop once and for all the imperialist tendencies of Russia, whether of the Red or White variety...."[56] The Black Sea question, for the Private Prometheans, was the essence of the Eastern Question as a whole.

The Promethean project ultimately failed, of course, at least for the better part of the twentieth century. The Caucasus republics remained firmly inside the Soviet Union. Romania's borders were changed by force, to the advantage of the Soviets, during the Second World War. After the war, Turkey became a member of NATO and lost its links with the states of the Balkans, now communist. Yet the Promethean idea remained alive within émigré communities in London, Paris, and elsewhere. In 1949 former Promethean activists living in western Europe organized a conference in Munich with the goal of reigniting the movement. At the conference, members resolved to restart their activities and to move the headquarters to the United States, now the leader of the global struggle against the Soviet Union. The leadership was given to Roman Smal-Stocky, a history professor living in Milwaukee, Wisconsin.[57] In 1951 Edmund Charaszkiewicz, an old Polish Promethean, sent out a general letter to the former leaders, urging them to revive the organization and again take up the banner of liberating the sea and its coasts from the communists. But as he complained nearly twenty years later, "life and new circumstances" conspired to hinder the initiative.[58] After that, the idea of a Black Sea community would become little more than a quixotic project of émigré cold warriors—but one that would receive a new lease on life once the cold war came to an end.

Development and Decline

The new circumstances that frustrated Charaszkiewicz and his associates were the changed strategic relationships around the sea created by the Second World War. In June 1941 Romania joined Nazi Germany in the attack on the Soviet Union. The previous summer, Stalin had ordered the seizure of the eastern Romanian province of Bessarabia, an event that automatically gave the Romanian government and populace a reason for welcoming the Nazi invasion—and an event that also accelerated the emergence of Romania's homegrown fascist government. Bulgaria's relations with Germany had long been cordial. The country fought with the Central Powers in the First World War and shared in the defeat as a result; the promise of regaining lost lands, perhaps even of creating the greater Bulgaria that had been promised in the San Stefano treaty many decades earlier, proved too powerful to resist. In the early stages of the war, Bulgaria was even able to regain the territory of southern Dobrudja at the expense of its neighbor, and now ally, Romania. Turkey remained formally neutral for almost the entire war, joining on the Allied side in the final days and thereby ensuring its status as a victor power.

As during the First World War, naval operations on the Black Sea were only a complement to the far more important land operations on the eastern front, a rapid push to the east by German, Romanian, and other Axis forces that would eventually be reversed at Stalingrad. Rather early in the war, the Soviet Union lost the use of the major ports to the German army and Axis navies. Odessa, Novorossiisk, Nikolaev, and Sevastopol fell in succession, the last one leveled by bombardment, as it had been almost a century before, and finally succumbing after a siege that lasted the better part of a year. But from the lesser ports such as Poti and Batumi, the Soviet navy was able to run interference operations on the high sea. German ships spent much of the war immobilized in the Romanian and Bulgarian ports, fearful of venturing out because of Soviet destroyers and British vessels on patrol. Soviet naval aviators also launched repeated raids on Constanţa, Novorossiisk, Galaţi, and other cities held by the Germans and their allies. After Stalingrad, the ports were quickly retaken by the revived Soviet army. German and Romanian forces were driven from Novorossiisk in September 1943; Nikolaev fell the following March and Odessa in April. It was only a matter of time before the Soviet fleet was able to reestablish supremacy and secure one port after another along the western and eastern coasts.

During the war, policies of ethnic cleansing and genocide were energetically pursued by both the Axis and the Soviets. While German and Romanian forces occupied the northwest littoral, including the city of Odessa, hundreds of thousands of Jews were removed from Romania, parts of occupied Ukraine, and Odessa to the region east of the Dnestr river, the notorious killing fields of Transnistria. Some Jews managed to escape by chartering ships from the Black Sea ports and heading for Palestine. Even then, however, the restrictive immigration policies of the British mandate government often kept them out. On the water ships packed with refugees had to steer clear of both Allied and Axis war vessels, which would sometimes target the civilian ships as belligerents. The Soviet navy eventually adopted a policy of firing on even neutral ships, as a way of cutting off supplies to Axis forces. In the most infamous incident, the passenger ship *Struma*, carrying nearly 800 Jewish refugees from Constanţa en route to Palestine, was sunk by a Soviet submarine off the entrance to the Bosphorus in the winter of 1942. Turkish fishermen pulled only a single survivor from the icy water.[59]

Other groups suffered from the same policy of deportation experienced on the southern coast decades earlier. Toward the end of the war, the Crimean Tatars were accused by the Soviet government of supporting the Nazi invasion force. (Some Tatar elites had no doubt welcomed German troops as liberators, perhaps as the first step toward realizing the Promethean goal of a Crimean republic—even though Nazi planners had concocted a project to turn Crimea into the province of "Gothia," to be colonized by Germans from South Tyrol.) In May 1944, some 189,000 Tatars were loaded onto sealed boxcars and deported to central Asia; perhaps 45 percent of those deported died along the way or shortly after arriving at their destinations in the east. Other groups in Crimea and along the eastern coast—15,000 Greeks, 13,000 Bulgarians, 10,000 Armenians—were also removed by the Soviets as "enemy nations," now defined solely in terms of the collective guilt as "collaborators" which they were held to bear.[60] Earlier in the year, a similar calamity had already been visited upon other punished peoples—over half a million Chechens and Ingush in the northeast Caucasus, Turkic-speakers such as the Balkars, Karachai, and Kumyks of the north Caucasus, ethnic Germans along the Volga river—all of whom were likewise sent to central Asia in inhuman conditions. Many of these groups were officially rehabilitated after the death of Stalin, and some were even allowed to return to their ancestral lands. Large-scale returns of Tatars to Crimea would not begin until the 1990s, however.

The turmoil of war gave way to an uneasy peace, one that in many ways replicated the strategic contest between the northern and southern coasts that had lasted for more than two centuries. It was perhaps fitting that a body of water that had long been considered vital by Europe's great powers would host the conference that determined the postwar fate of all of eastern Europe. At the resort of Yalta in February 1945, Churchill, Roosevelt, and Stalin made plans for reorganizing the political map of the region, carving out what would soon become spheres of influence for the Soviet Union and the West.

The result around the sea was the integration of politics, culture, and economics from the Balkans to the Caucasus on a scale that had never before been seen. Romania and Bulgaria became "people's democracies" and were soon linked with the Soviet Union in a defensive military alliance and common economic bloc. Trade, agriculture, and industry were carried on within the confines of state-regulated plans, which were in turn coordinated with the production targets and needs of the Soviet Union. The southern coast remained outside this scheme, of course. Turkey was taken under the defensive umbrella of the West, joining NATO in 1951, and for most of the second half of the twentieth century, the cold war produced a period of peace, of sorts, on the sea. The vanguard of the capitalist West looked out at a horseshoe coastline of the communist East—or, from the Turkish perspective, the communist North. The Soviets repeatedly attempted to revise the terms of the old Montreux convention, with the aim of restricting passage through the Straits only to the ships of littoral states, a change that in practice would have made the sea very nearly a Soviet lake. But throughout the cold war, Turkey and the United States insisted on maintaining the sea's status as an international waterway open to both commercial and naval vessels, a point underscored by the routine dispatch of U.S. warships through the Straits under the terms of Montreux.[61]

For all the differences between the two social systems that now encircled the Black Sea—Soviet-style communism and the state-led nationalism of the Turkish Republic—both shared an ideology of revolutionary change that targeted the sea and its coastline. The half century after the end of the Second World War saw the development of the coastal regions at an unprecedented pace. The riches of the sea, particularly its fish stocks, were no longer simply the purview of individual coastal communities, nor were they items to be guarded or taxed by emperors at a distance. They were now the property of four states, each firmly committed to rapid development—three of them driven by the desire to challenge the capitalist model of economic success, the fourth conscious of the economic backwardness that had doomed its imperial predecessor. All were engaged in a contest to catch up with the rest of Europe and break through to modernity, and all would soon suffer the unintended consequences which that contest produced.

Serious environmental change around the Black Sea is not new. The grasslands in the north and west began to disappear in the late eighteenth century, broken by ox-drawn plows. Wooded northern riverbanks were clear-cut at the same time, as were dense forests in the upland Caucasus. The forests of the Balkan foothills disappeared even earlier. Yet, in the latter half of the twentieth century, the combination of mechanized agriculture, industrialization, urban growth, and new energy technologies accelerated change along the coastline. The appearance of tractors, combines, and other agricultural machines made what was left of the steppe into some of the world's most fertile farmland. The black-earth region had already produced a boom in grain production in the middle of the nineteenth century, a boom fed by the introduction of more efficient tilling techniques, improved wheat varieties, and the expansion of rail transport; but the agricultural revolution of the 1960s, including the introduction of chemical fertilizers, made the fields of Ukraine and southern Russia the pride of the Soviet Union.

Industrial concerns expanded right to the water's edge. The foundation for the petroleum extraction and refining industries had already been put in place in the very late nineteenth century, but in Romania and the Soviet Union, these industries grew rapidly after the Second World War. Pipelines carried oil from Baku and other Caspian oilfields to Novorossiisk; tankers took it through the Bosphorus to the rest of the world. Oil refineries sprouted up along the Romanian coast, with state planners often placing them right next to pristine beaches—the pride of communist industry easily visible from the workers' resorts that now punctuated the coast.

Changes to the physical environment accompanied industrialization. The Dnepr rapids, a natural obstacle to fishermen and traders for millennia, vanished in 1932. The Dneprostroi hydroelectric power station on the lower river, considered one of the finest industrial achievements of the Stalin era, raised the water level to cover them. Although destroyed by the withdrawing German army during the Second World War, the dam was rebuilt in the late 1940s; the new facility raised the river level some 40 m and once again buried the famous Dnepr cataracts. Farther to the east, a Volga–Don canal was completed by the Soviets in 1952, the realization of a vision for connecting the Caspian and Black Seas that both an Ottoman sultan and Peter the Great had abandoned as unworkable. What had once required overland portage between the two rivers could now be accomplished on the water. Another canal that linked the Danube to the seacoast—bypassing the delta, which had always been a problem for shipping because of silting and shifting channels—was finished in Romania in 1984. With the opening of the German Main–Danube canal in the early 1990s, a ship could go all the way from the North Sea to the Caspian—nothing novel, of course, to the Norse traders of the Middle Ages, but now a route that could be completed by large seagoing vessels. All along the coast, new highways and rail links allowed goods and people to be transported as easily by land as by sea, while air travel connected international hubs with one another and provincial cities with national capitals.

Each of these projects had its costs, of course, both human and environmental. Forced labor was used on many of the major building projects completed in the communist lands. The Danube–Black Sea canal was popularly known in Romania as the "Canal of Death," because of the high mortality among the political prisoners who were used in the first stages of construction in the early 1950s. But the projects also had a major impact on the health of the sea. The sea's natural state, a relatively thin layer of livable water above a mass of hydrogen sulfide, was naturally precarious. The irony was that just as Turkey and its communist neighbors were fully realizing the developmental advantages of their position as littoral countries, the sea was beginning to die.

Part of the sea's sickness was the direct result of the growth of industry and urban centers around the coasts, particularly in the north and west. Ports such as Novorossiisk, Odessa, Constanţa, and Varna continued to expand after the Second World War, becoming major regional centers with sprawling suburbs, dockyards, and industrial concerns. Industrial effluents, including oil and chemical pollutants from terminals and processing facilities, ran into the sea. Hydroelectric power stations built on the northern rivers raised the temperature of the water in the estuaries and led to the demise of sensitive fish species. Farther inland, industrialized agriculture, using chemical pesticides and fertilizers, created run-off that bled into the water. All these problems, however, were experienced by many other bodies of water in the twentieth century. But in the case of the Black Sea, two specific processes were at work, and each contributed substantially to the sea's problems. One was a result of the sea's own idiosyncrasies, the other the fault of an American interloper.

In inland seas, life depends on a steady supply of organic nutrients brought in by rivers. But there can be too much of a good thing. Excessive organic matter, in the form of run-off from farm land or the waste produced by cities upriver, is a particular danger in the Black Sea. The process of natural organic decay uses up oxygen, which in turn further depletes the thin oxygen-rich layer at the top of the sea. More importantly, excessive nutrients allow the flourishing of plant life, particularly forms of plankton that also absorb the scarce oxygen, a process known as eutrophication; these plankton upsurges can have a devastating effect on fish stocks. Periodic increases in hypoxia (low oxygen levels in the life-supporting layer of the sea) are the result of these processes. From 1973 to 1990 the area affected by hypoxia increased from 3,500 sq. km to some 40,000 sq. km, particularly in some of the shallowest reaches of the sea, the northwestern shelf along the coasts of Romania and Ukraine.[62]

The marked increase in agricultural run-off and urban waste in the last three or four decades of the twentieth century was only one worry. The other was a newcomer to the ecosystem, which began to appear only in the early 1980s. Hiding in the bilge water of ships arriving from the Mediterranean was a species of large invertebrate known to scientists as *Mnemiopsis leidyi*, an animal similar to a jelly-fish. *Mnemiopsis* is native to the temperate zones of the Atlantic, but it found the Black Sea an agreeable home. The plankton increase, which coincided with the jelly's appearance, provided huge amounts of fodder, which in turn allowed the creature to reproduce at a startling rate. Today, *Mnemiopsis* and its jelly-fish cousins are readily visible to anyone strolling along the Bosphorus, where the jellies bob in a seething mass in the back-channels along the shore, hundreds and thousands of them, some as big as basketballs. By the late 1990s, the estimated mass of *Mnemiopsis*, about 900 million tons, was greater than the annual fish harvest of the entire planet.[63] The jellies gorged themselves on plankton, fish larvae or food usually eaten by small fish, and their appetite led directly to the decline of several fish species. That, in turn, meant a food shortage for other commercially important fish higher up the food chain.

The advent of *Mnemiopsis* coincided with another important development in the health of the sea: the knock-on effects of large-scale commercial fishing. The rise of industrial fishing after the Second World War led to a huge increase in fish takes. New technologies, especially dredge nets that could reach deep into the sea, even scraping the bottom and yielding huge catches, produced abundant fish hauls in the middle of the century. But the price of increasing yields was a progressive fall-off in fish stocks as time passed. Catches fell by perhaps a third from 1986 to 2001. In the 1960s, some twenty-six species were fished commercially, but by the 1990s only six were available in sufficient quantities to allow large-scale harvesting.

According to Laurence Mee, a British oceanographer and one of the world's leading experts on the sea's ecology, the sum of all these developments was, by the end of the century, "an environmental catastrophe."[64] Some species, especially some types of plankton essential for higher forms of sea life, were virtually eliminated, gobbled up by the hungry jellies. Fish species that were of significant commercial value—as they had been for millennia, in fact—were found in such small numbers that they were simply no longer worth trying to catch. Some species known to ancient authors for their annual migrations around the seacoast were difficult to find. The anchovy, long a dietary staple along the southern coast, was wiped out in some parts of the sea.

The human consequences of these changes were predictable but devastating. Fishing fleets were laid up. Fish processing centers were closed and their workers fired. A major source of protein began to disappear from regional diets. Migration from the coasts to urban centers inland increased. Tourist facilities, troubled by coastal erosion and polluted beaches, were boarded up. Coastal communities now faced perhaps the greatest environmental, economic, and social crisis in their entire history. For more than two millennia, empires, states, and nations had staked out their claims, both political and historical, to the waters of the Black Sea. By the end of the twentieth century, it was no longer clear that the sea was a prize worth having.

NOTES

1. Mark Twain, *The Innocents Abroad*, in *The Complete Travel Books of Mark Twain*, Vol. 1 (Garden City, NY: Doubleday, 1966–7), p. 253.

2. Adolphus Slade, *Records of Travels in Turkey, Greece, etc., and of a Cruise in the Black Sea, with the Capitan Pasha, in the Years 1829, 1830, and 1831*, Vol. 2 (Philadelphia: E. L. Carey and A. Hart, 1833), p. 155.

3. Henry C. Barkley, *A Ride Through Asia Minor and Armenia: Giving a Sketch of the Characters, Manners, and Customs of Both the Mussulman and Christian Inhabitants* (London: John Murray, 1891), p. 146. Barkley was speaking specifically of Armenians.

4. Edith Durham, *High Albania*, reprint edn. (London: Phoenix Press, 2000), p. 1.

5. F. N. Gromov et al., *Tri veka rossiiskogo flota*, Vol. 1 (St. Petersburg: Logos, 1996), p. 210.

6. Gromov et al., *Tri veka rossiiskogo flota*, Vol. 1, p. 218.

7. Bernd Langensiepen and Ahmet Güleryüz, *The Ottoman Steam Navy, 1828–1923*, trans. James Cooper (Annapolis: Naval Institute Press, 1995), p. 3.

8. See Slade, *Records of Travels*. Slade was the British naval adviser to the Ottomans and witnessed the full extent of naval engagements on the Black Sea during the 1828–9 war.

9. Gromov et al., *Tri veka rossiiskogo flota*, Vol. 1, p. 242.

10. Gromov et al., *Tri veka rossiiskogo flota*, Vol. 1, p. 242.

11. Langensiepen and Güleryüz, *The Ottoman Steam Navy*, p. 6.

12. Midhat Paşa would later be twice named grand vizier, before being banished to Arabia for treason under Sultan Abdülhamit II. He was strangled while in prison. On Dobrudja under Midhat Paşa, see the standard biography by his son, Ali Haydar Midhat, *The Life of Midhat Pasha* (London: John Murray, 1903; reprint New York: Arno Press, 1973), and Georgi Pletn'ov, *Midkhat Pasha i upravlenieto na Dunavskiia vilaet* (Veliko Turnovo: Vital, 1994).

13. Mose Lofley Harvey, "The Development of Russian Commerce on the Black Sea and Its Significance" (Ph.D. dissertation, University of California, Berkeley, 1938), p. 130.

14. Harvey, "The Development of Russian Commerce," pp. 158, 163, 171.

15. Karl Baedeker, *Russia, with Teheran, Port Arthur, and Peking*, 1st English edn. (London: T. Fisher Unwin, 1914), p. xviii.

16. Nikolai Nikolaevich Reikhel't, *Po Chernomu moriu* (St. Petersburg: A. S. Suvorin, 1891), pp. 230–1.

17. Harvey, "The Development of Russian Commerce," p. 104.

18. Harvey, "The Development of Russian Commerce," p. 147.

19. Harvey, "The Development of Russian Commerce," p. 181.

20. William Eleroy Curtis, *Around the Black Sea: Asia Minor, Armenia, Caucasus, Circassia, Daghestan, the Crimea, Roumania* (New York: Hodder and Stoughton, 1911), p. 57.

21. *A Hand-Book for Travellers in the Ionian Islands, Greece, Turkey, Asia Minor, and Constantinople, Including a Description of Malta; With Maxims and Hints for Travellers in the East* (London: John Murray, 1840); *A Handbook for Travellers in Turkey*, 3rd rev. edn. (London: John Murray, 1854).

22. Baedeker, *Russia, with Teheran*, pp. xvi, 445.

23. Thomas Forester, *The Danube and the Black Sea; Memoir on their Junction by a Railway Between Tchernavoda and a Free Port at Kustendjie* (London: Edward Stanford, 1857), pp. 210–11.

24. Twain, *The Innocents Abroad*, pp. 255–6.

25. R. Arthur Arnold, *From the Levant, the Black Sea, and the Danube*, Vol. 2 (London: Chapman and Hall, 1868), pp. 193–4.

26. Vasilii Sidorov, *Okol'noi dorogoi: Putevyia zametki i vpechatleniia* (St. Petersburg: Tipografiia A. Katanskago, 1891), p. 259.

27. N. Begicheva, *Ot Odessy do Ierusalima: Putevyia pis'ma* (St. Petersburg: Tipografiia Glavnago upravleniia udelov, 1898), p. 10.

28. Sidorov, *Okol'noi dorogoi*, p. 79.

29. Reikhel't, *Po Chernomu moriu*, p. 59.

30. Henry C. Barkley, *Between the Danube and the Black Sea, or Five Years in Bulgaria* (London: John Murray, 1876), p. 263.

31. Barkley, *Between the Danube and the Black Sea*, pp. 228–9.

32. Mark Pinson, "Ottoman Colonization of the Circassians in Rumili After the Crimean War," *Etudes balkaniques*, Vol. 8, No. 3 (1972):76.

33. Alan W. Fisher, "Emigration of Muslims from the Russian Empire in the Years after the Crimean War," *Jahrbücher für Geschichte Osteuropas*, Vol. 35, No. 3 (1987):356.

34. Justin McCarthy, *Death and Exile: The Ethnic Cleansing of Ottoman Muslims, 1821–1922* (Princeton: Darwin Press, 1995), p. 339.

35. Mark Levene, "Creating a Modern 'Zone of Genocide': The Impact of Nation- and State-Formation on Eastern Anatolia, 1878–1923," *Holocaust and Genocide Studies*, Vol. 12, No. 3 (Winter 1998):396; Ronald Grigor Suny, *Looking Toward Ararat: Armenia in Modern History* (Bloomington: Indiana University Press, 1993), p. 99.

36. Kaori Komatsu, "Financial Problems of the Navy During the Reign of Abdülhamid II," *Oriente Moderno*, Vol. 20, No. 1 (2001):218.

37. "Trebizond: Extracts from an Interview with Comm. G. Gorrini, Late Italian Consul-General at Trebizond, Published in the Journal 'Il Messaggero,' of Rome, 25th August 1915," in Arnold J. Toynbee (ed.) *The Treatment of Armenians in the Ottoman Empire, 1915–1916* (London: HMSO, 1916), pp. 291–2.

38. Technically, the treaty merely sanctioned a separate convention concluded between Turkey and Greece the previous January.

39. Quoted in Stephen P. Ladas, *The Exchange of Minorities: Bulgaria, Greece and Turkey* (New York: Macmillan, 1932), p. 341.

40. Quoted in Nicolae Bîrdeanu and Dan Nicolaescu, *Contribuţii la istoria marinei române*, Vol. 1 (Bucharest: Editura ştiinţifică şi enciclopedică, 1979), p. 164.

41. S. M. Solov'ev, *History of Russia*, Vol. 3 (Gulf Breeze, FL: Academic International Press, 1976–2002), p. 164.

42. V. P. Vradii, *Negry Batumskoi oblasti* (Batumi: G. Tavartkiladze, 1914). See also Allison Blakely, *Russia and the Negro: Blacks in Russian History and Thought* (Washington: Howard University Press, 1986), chapter 1.

43. Nicolae Iorga, "Poporul românesc şi marea," *Revista istorică: Dări de samă, documente şi notiţe*, Vol. 24, Nos. 4–6 (April–June 1938):100.

44. Mykhailo Hrushevs'kyi, *Na porozi Novoï Ukraïny* (Kyiv: Naukova dumka, 1991), p. 16.

45. Parts of this section rely on Adam Tolnay, "From the Water System to the Ecosystem: The Black Sea in the Development of Oceanography," unpublished manuscript (Georgetown University, 2002).

46. On Marsigli, see Margaret Deacon, *Scientists and the Sea, 1650–1900* (Ashgate: Aldershot, 1997), pp. 148–9.

47. Peter Simon Pallas, *Travels Through the Southern Provinces of the Russian Empire, in the Years 1793 and 1794*, 2 vols. (London: T. N. Longman and O. Rees et al., 1802–3); August von Haxthausen, *Transcaucasia: Sketches of the Nations and Races Between the Black Sea and the Caspian* (London: Chapman and Hall, 1854).

48. Egor Manganari, *Atlas Chernago moria* (Nikolaev: Gidrograficheskii chernomorskoi depo, 1841). The copy located in the Library of Congress belonged to Tsar Nicholas II.

49. Bîrdeanu and Nicolaescu, *Contribuţii la istoria marinei române*, Vol. 1, p. 228.

50. Grigore Antipa, *Marea Neagră* (Bucharest: Academia Română, 1941), Vol. 1, pp. 16–17.

51. Charles Warren Hostler, *Turkism and the Soviets* (London: George Allen and Unwin, 1957), pp. 157–8. See also Etienne Copeaux, "Le mouvement 'prométhéen'," *Cahiers d'études sur la Mediterranée orientale et le monde turco-iranien*, No. 16 (July–December 1993):9–45.

52. On the activities of these groups inside Turkey, see Lowell Bezanis, "Soviet Muslim Emigrés in the Republic of Turkey," *Central Asian Survey*, Vol. 13, No. 1 (1994):59–180.

53. Untitled editor's note, *Prométhée*, Vol. 1, No. 1 (November 1926):1–2.

54. T. Schätzl, "Polish Group 'Prometheus' in London," MS dated March 19, 1951, Archives of the Piłsudski Institute of America, New York (hereafter "APIA"), Apolinary Kiełczyński Papers, II/2/A-B, Teka I/2, File "Materiały balkanskie," p. 2.

55. "La Mer Noire," *Prométhée*, No. 24 (November 1928):1–3.

56. Dmytro Boug, "La Mer Noire," *Prométhée*, No. 73 (December 1932):22.

57. "Kommunikat Prometeiskoi Ligi Atlanticheskoi Khartii," March 1949, APIA, Jerzy Ponikiewski Papers, Sz.D/4, T. 1, file "Prometeusz," pp. 3–6.

58. Letter from Edmund Charaszkiewicz to Ali Akish, November 4, 1969, APIA, Charaszkiewicz Papers, II/3/D, T. 1, file "Sprawy ogólno-prometejskie," p. 65.

59. The story of the *Struma* is recounted in Douglas Frantz and Catherine Collins, *Death on the Black Sea: The Untold Story of the Struma and World War II's Holocaust at Sea* (New York: Ecco, 2003).

60. Norman M. Naimark, *Fires of Hatred: Ethnic Cleansing in Twentieth-Century Europe* (Cambridge, MA: Harvard University Press, 2001), pp. 101–4.

61. On the Black Sea in cold war strategy, see Harry N. Howard, *Turkey, the Straits, and U.S. Policy* (Baltimore: Johns Hopkins University Press, 1974).

62. Yu. Zaitsev and V. Mamaev, *Marine Biological Diversity in the Black Sea: A Study of Change and Decline* (New York: United Nations Development Program, 1997), p. 15.

63. "Bleak Story of the Black Sea Highlighted in Global Assessment of World's Waters," United Nations Environment Programme Press Release, October 12, 2001.

64. Laurence David Mee, "Protecting the Black Sea Environment: A Challenge for Co-operation and Sustainable Development in Europe," Centre for European Policy Studies (Brussels) and International Centre for Black Sea Studies (Athens), 2002, p. 4. From 1993 to 1998, Mee coordinated the Black Sea Environmental Program in Istanbul.

The majority of the most important wars of the century have been Frontier wars. Wars of religion, of alliances, of rebellion, of aggrandisement, of dynastic intrigue or ambition—wars in which the personal element was often the predominant factor—tend to be replaced by Frontier wars, i.e., wars arising out of the expansion of states and kingdoms, carried to a point, as the habitable globe shrinks, at which the interests or ambitions of one state come into sharp and irreconcilable collision with those of another.

Lord Curzon, 1907

Sharing the common vision of their regional cooperation as a part of the integration process in Europe, based on human rights and fundamental freedoms, prosperity through economic liberty, social justice, and equal security and stability . . .

Charter of the Organization of Black Sea Economic Cooperation, Yalta, 1998

Try something national! It's good to try something national!

Woman selling Tatar pastries, Chufutkale, Crimea, 2000

7
Facing the Water

All ports, Fernand Braudel wrote, face both ways—out toward the sea and the multiple influences that come drifting in on the water, in toward the hinterland and the terrestrial cultures that anchor them to a particular place. From the mid-nineteenth century forward, many actors around the Black Sea worked systematically to turn both faces landward, to excise the multifarious identities that characterized life along the shore, and to claim the littoral regions as the patrimony of young nations and the property of even younger states. During the cold war, the sea became a barrier between rival countries and social systems. Each sought to differentiate itself from its antithesis across the water, even as their ideologies made the coasts and the sea itself into objects of state-led development.

Similar processes have continued even after the end of communism and the collapse of the Soviet Union. New states appeared on the littoral—an independent Ukraine, Russia, and Georgia in 1991—but the habit of setting oneself apart from near neighbors has been perpetuated by the contest to join such institutions as NATO and the European Union. The portrayal of one's own country as more attractive to foreign investors, more politically stable, even more civilized than those just down the coast has remained the normal mode of discourse. Today, there are few places in the world where political elites and average citizens know less about their neighbors than around the Black Sea. But this is a willful ignorance, furthered by versions of history that take the nation as timeless, the state as predestined, and the region as ephemeral. In the not very distant past, having a close connection with a fisherman, a trader, a port official, or even a relative on the other side of the water would have been unremarkable. It is testimony to the triumph of a particular way of understanding history, politics, and social relations that such connections seem less easy to imagine now.

Today, environmental degradation, migration, economic development, and other policy areas all demand that exclusionary definitions of the nation and hegemonic visions of the state both be transcended. The problems that the Black Sea region faces require two things that seem inherently at odds: on the one hand, strong and capable states, and on the other, states that are willing to cooperate with their neighbors by surrendering up some of their sovereignty. But as the 1990s confirmed, simultaneously building and unbuilding the state is no easy enterprise.

Just after the exchange of populations between Greece and Turkey in the 1920s, Arnold Toynbee wrote that the "fundamental and identical interest of all the Near Eastern peoples lies in peace, in aloofness from the intrigues and ambitions of the great powers, and in the moral and economic support of some international organization."[1] That was the recipe that generations of European diplomats had recommended: Internationalize the status of the sea and its outlets—the Danube and the Straits—in order to prevent any regional power from monopolizing them, especially by using the slogan of national liberation to do so.

In one sense, the Toynbee strategy has proved eminently successful. Despite the many territorial disputes and the mutual distrust inherited from the pre-communist and communist pasts, armed conflict among the states of the Black Sea zone is now virtually unthinkable. In only one instance—the Armenia–Azerbaijan conflict over the enclave of Nagorno-Karabakh, which ended in a ceasefire in 1994—did a territorial dispute between two states lead to war. The only other major instance of potential international strife concerned the status of the old Soviet Black Sea fleet, whose ships and personnel were claimed by both independent Ukraine and the Russian Federation. But the stand-off was settled amicably in 1997, when the two governments agreed to divide the naval assets, with the majority of ships going to Russia. Ukraine further agreed to lease port facilities to the Russian navy, and both countries now share dock space in the fleet's traditional home, Sevastopol. Of course, none of this is much comfort to victims of the Karabakh violence and to the hundreds of thousands of displaced persons that have yet to return to their homes in Azerbaijan or, indeed, to the many people affected by the several other civil wars in the region. But in a part of the world which, in Toynbee's day, still appeared the powder keg that it had been for much of the previous century, the near absence of international conflict is remarkable.

In the early 2000s, it is not the power of states that threatens the peace and stability of this zone, but rather their weakness. In many areas, poverty is endemic, not simply the result of the "transition" from communist central planning but a long-term, structural feature of local economies. Government institutions, where they function at all, sometimes do so only because they represent sources of revenue for office holders, in the form of petty bribes and large-scale kickbacks. The inadequacy of social services makes daily survival a self-help game, and the reliance on old social networks—of family, clan, and ethnic group—in turn discourages individuals from thinking of themselves as equal citizens of a modern state. More ominously, the lack of effective policing means that trans-state criminal networks, trafficking in everything from arms to drugs to humans, can operate with virtual impunity. Environmental degradation and potential ecological disasters, some left over from communism and others the product of ill-conceived industrial and agricultural policy under the successor governments, are hazards to present and future generations. Transit migrants and asylum-seekers increasingly regard Turkey and the postcommunist states as accessible waiting rooms for eventual migration, whether legal or illegal, into the European Union. Refugees from armed conflicts in the Balkans and the Caucasus have put further burdens on states that have difficulty providing for their own citizens, much less those of neighboring countries. It is no exaggeration to say that the population movements of the 1990s and the early 2000s—the flow of economic migrants, asylum-seekers, transit migrants, and refugees—may yet transform the demographic structure of the region in at least as profound a way as the great unpeopling from the 1860s to the 1920s.

The particular problems of weak states are most striking in the outcome of the region's separatist movements and civil wars. In the early 1990s, several small wars and insurgencies raged across the wider southeast Europe, but by the middle of the decade, most had decrescendoed into relative stability. In the Balkan and post-Soviet conflicts, full-scale peace agreements or temporary ceasefires were signed; in some instances, international reconstruction efforts were put in place and foreign peacekeepers deployed. Turkey's capture of the Kurdish leader Abdullah Öcalan in 1999 largely deflated the rebel movement in the southeastern part of the country. In four important instances, however, the end of all-out war did not produce a real solution to the conflicts. Instead, unrecognized but functional states grew up in the former conflict zones, de facto countries that have done an exceptional job of surreptitiously acquiring the accoutrements of sovereignty.

South Ossetia, Abkhazia, Nagorno-Karabakh, and Transnistria are little known to the wider world, but they have spent more than a decade as really-existing entities in the Black Sea zone. The internationally recognized governments that play host to them—Georgia, Azerbaijan, and Moldova—have continually called for outside help in settling the disputes, and representatives of the United Nations and other international mediators have been on the ground to do just that. Negotiations, in one form or another, have dragged on for years without a final settlement. Yet, in this limbo between war and peace, Eurasia's unrecognized states have created real institutions that function, in some cases, about as well as those of the countries of which they are still supposedly constituents. All have the basic structures of governance and the symbols of sovereignty. All have military forces and poor but working economies. All have held elections, however undemocratic, for political offices. All have set up currency structures, border regimes, and educational systems separate from those of the recognized states. These four entities even cooperate with each other, sending representatives to regular summits and ministerial meetings. Most maps show only six states around the Black Sea, but if a baseline test of a "state" is simply the ability to exercise control over a defined piece of territory, then there are in fact rather more—depending on who is doing the counting.

It was, in part, to deal with the problems of state weakness and to ensure that internal disputes would not erupt into international war that the littoral states and their neighbors launched a program of regional cooperation in the early 1990s. A new forum, Black Sea Economic Cooperation, or BSEC, was established on the initiative of the Turkish government. The forum was an outgrowth of Turkey's new-found vocation as a regional leader after the end of the cold war; but it was also a way of enhancing the sovereignty of the region's many new states, some of which were experiencing real independence for the first time.

In June 1992, the heads of state of all the Black Sea littoral countries and other regional neighbors met in Istanbul to proclaim the emergence of a broad cooperation program, a set of initiatives that would eventually include policy areas such as the environment, crime and corruption, investment, taxation, and education. Six years later, the eleven member states—Russia, Ukraine, Turkey, Georgia, Romania, Bulgaria, Albania, Armenia, Azerbaijan, Moldova, and Greece—signed a charter that upgraded BSEC to the status of an international organization and created a permanent secretariat, now located in an impressive villa just up the Bosphorus from central Istanbul. A Black Sea parliamentary assembly, an investment bank, a multinational naval unit, a summer university, and a policy research center were also established. For the first time ever, the coasts of the Black Sea were to be brought together not by conquest or the informal networks of commerce, but rather by the purposeful effort of political leaders to craft a secure and cooperative region with the sea at its center.

Clearly the most pressing area of concern was the environmental degradation of the sea itself, and this is the area in which BSEC has concentrated its attention. Already in April 1992, the six coastal states signed the Bucharest Convention on environmental protection; a year later, at a meeting in Odessa, they agreed to establish conservation zones in the coastal areas of each country, coordinate anti-pollution policies in the river systems that feed into the sea, and share vital scientific information on pollution and biodiversity. In 1996, under the aegis of BSEC, the first multi-country analysis of the causes of Black Sea pollution was completed, with assistance from the United Nations and other international organizations. Now, every five years, scientists in all coastal countries work together to issue a "state-of-the-sea" report, a diagnostic venture that is a truly gargantuan step away from the mutual suspicion that prevented such efforts during the cold war.

There are already some signs of hope. Nutrient enrichment declined over the course of the 1990s, and that in turn produced a slow-down in the plankton and algae blooms that had depleted oxygen and nurtured the fecund jellies. Industrial pollution also eased somewhat, and overfishing was scaled back. Some of these developments, though, are only serendipitous. The parlous state of agriculture in the former communist states—including a universal fall-off in production and, therefore, a decline in the use of chemical fertilizers—has had the beneficial effect of reducing nutrient run-off into the sea. The sharp decline in the fishing fleets of the littoral states was a result of overfishing after the 1960s and the economic crisis in the communist states from the late 1980s forward; but the scaling back of industrial fishing may now allow fish stocks to recuperate. (Because of the laying up of boats in the former communist countries, some 90 percent of the annual catch is now hauled in by Turkish vessels alone. If one needs convincing, just try to order a fish dinner at a restaurant on the Romanian coast.) Industrial pollution, still acute in some areas, has become less of a problem on the sea as a whole, simply because of the shutdown of large industrialized centers from Bulgaria to Georgia. As the economies of littoral states begin to recover, however, the most serious environmental problems will no doubt return. Without proper care, what may be good in the short term for the people along the coast—a return to the relative economic stability of the past—may well do further long-term harm to the sea.

In areas other than the environment, BSEC has not lived up to its original grand vision. In fact, on just about any thumbnail indicator, the Black Sea region, as a political or economic entity, is today hard to see. On average, the BSEC member states conduct only about 12 percent of their trade with other members. National airlines are far more likely to connect their capitals with European and North American hubs than they are with nearby states. One of the few places where the region shows up clearly is at the beach: When tourists from Black Sea states go abroad on holiday, they are most likely to visit one of their neighbors—Turkey.[2] Heads of state meet at summits, ministers travel to conferences, non-governmental organizations occasionally work out action plans on an issue of common concern. But the emergence of a genuinely vibrant and cooperative region stretching from Greece to Azerbaijan is still a long way away.

The reasons for BSEC's difficulties are not hard to gauge. A regional organization that includes Russia, Turkey, and Greece—three mid-size powers with divergent interests and goals—was bound to run into problems. Each of these anchor states has its own vision of a foreign policy role in the region, but none is sufficiently wealthy to finance the kinds of programs that would make those visions a reality. Moreover, BSEC's emergence was less the result of any genuine commitment to regional cooperation than the product of a peculiar concatenation of geopolitical interests. In the early 1990s, Turkey sought a new regional role, perhaps to demonstrate to the European Union its potential as a force for stability; the newly independent states of Eurasia were eager to join any international organization that would have them; and Greece and Russia were not about to let Turkey define a new "Black Sea region" without them. Build it and they will come, the Turkish president Turgut Özal, the original cheerleader for BSEC, might have thought in 1992. And come they did—to multiple summits, working group sessions, special conferences, and other forums for discussions about the future of the sea. The far trickier issue, however, has been to figure out what exactly this new club is supposed to do, now that the membership list has been assembled.

No politician around the sea today believes that BSEC should be a substitute for the kinds of regionalism that really matter: membership in NATO and the European Union. Romania and Bulgaria were invited to join the former in 2002, and they are engaged in ongoing negotiations for accession to the latter, perhaps by 2007. Turkey has been a NATO member almost since the organization's inception, but EU membership has remained elusive; still, European states have declared their willingness to consider Turkish membership in the future. While presidents and prime ministers repeatedly affirm their commitment to building a Black Sea region, in practice there is little incentive to cooperate with countries whose prospects for membership in the truly important organizations are even slimmer than one's own. For all the energetic summitry that has defined BSEC, it is the policies of NATO and the European Union that are today the driving forces behind the international politics of the Black Sea zone.

As the century progresses, the politics of energy will also bring together the countries and peoples of BSEC in new ways and will remain a source of rivalry in others. In the early 1990s, the promise of oil and gas from the fields around the Caspian Sea, one of the largest sources of marketable hydrocarbons outside the Middle East, sparked a contest among individual states and multinational corporations. For much of the decade, the various channels that Caspian oil might take were the subject of wide-ranging debate. Some companies and governments advocated traditional routes to ports on the eastern coast of the Black Sea and then via tanker to the Mediterranean. The Turkish government objected that the resulting increase in traffic though the Bosphorus would surely lead to an environmental catastrophe, such as an oil spill along the heavily populated coasts, in the heart of Istanbul. Others argued for a new pipeline that would avoid the Black Sea region altogether and head south through Iran, a proposition rejected as politically unpalatable by the United States.

The politics of pipelines finally ended with an agreement to construct an underground transit system from the south Caucasus to the eastern Mediterranean. In early 2003 construction began on a new pipeline, built by an international consortium headed by BP (the former British Petroleum), that runs from Baku, via Tbilisi, to the Turkish port of Ceyhan on the Mediterranean. The pipeline bypasses the Black Sea ports and will undercut the need for increased tanker traffic through the Bosphorus to handle Caspian output. By 2009 the line is expected to carry a million barrels of oil per day. In the 1880s the completion of the Transcaucasian railway reshaped the regional economy of the southeastern coast and, indeed, the international commerce of the entire sea; the Baku–Tbilisi–Ceyhan line has been hailed as its equal in the early twenty-first century. However, since the terminus lies far away from the Black Sea, in southern Turkey, it is unclear what impact the much-vaunted pipeline will really have on the sea as a whole. It may well make the port cities even more marginal than they were before.

Thinking of the Black Sea only in terms of high-level politics is too narrow a view of the region, however. The sea still binds, but sometimes in unexpected ways. Shuttle traders—the successors to the coastal merchants of centuries past, but now with airline tickets instead of permits of passage from a Byzantine or Ottoman official—carry Turkish manufactured goods for resale in Odessa, Kyiv, and Moscow. Manual laborers from the north work on construction projects in the south, while Turkish construction companies design and build houses and commercial buildings across the former Soviet Union. Immigrant sex workers (the "Natashas" of Turkish argot) find customers in Istanbul and Ankara, a movement of women born of the same mix of force, tragic necessity, and misplaced optimism that drove Circassians to the seraglio. These kinds of regional linkages are, of course, hostage to the vicissitudes of the macroeconomy. The collapse of the Russian ruble in the late 1990s probably slowed down the active "suitcase trade" with Istanbul, and the movement of sex workers from the former Soviet republics also seems have declined. But the connections are still there. One need only stroll through the Laleli district of Istanbul—the center of the informal trade between the city and the former Soviet north—or walk into a hotel lobby in Trabzon to see evidence of the low-level bonds that reemerged at the end of the twentieth century.

There is also some evidence of a growing appreciation for the old multicultural identities of the seacoast. Archaeological investigations, often in cooperation with west European and American partners, uncover ancient sites and reveal patterns of mutual influence in antiquity. Regional museums in Constanţa, Varna, and Simferopol embrace the multiple cultures of the coasts, in ways that are often at odds with the images found in "national" museums in the capital cities. In Turkey, one can now purchase books on the Hemşin, Laz, and other peoples of the Pontic coast, something that was unthinkable only a few years ago, when literature on ethnic minorities was practically nonexistent. None of this means that any of the littoral areas is likely to experience a renaissance soon, however. Out-migration from almost every part of the coast remains high. Local economies are stagnant. The reassertion of cultural identities has also sometimes led to conflict. The return of Tatars to Crimea has sparked disputes over land rights and problems of social integration, while the region's several quasi-states, from Transnistria to Karabakh, exist in an uneasy truce with internationally recognized governments. Holiday-makers can now enjoy spectacular beaches and resorts in Bulgaria, but many other parts of the sea remain decidedly unwelcoming.

In his magisterial account of the aftermath of the First World War *The Western Question in Greece and Turkey*, Arnold Toynbee identified three false antitheses inscribed on the minds of most Westerners who looked at the eastern Mediterranean and the Black Sea.[3] The first was the antithesis between Christianity and Islam, the second between Europe and Asia, the third between civilization and barbarism. The boundaries between these opposing categories might look clear enough from a distance, Toynbee said, but as soon as one stepped off a ship or alighted from a train in Istanbul or Odessa or Batumi, they began to look simply laughable.

As the Black Sea becomes the eastern frontier of NATO and the European Union, bisected by distinct immigration policies, trade restrictions, and security doctrines, one wonders whether the boundaries between Toynbee's antitheses may harden—boundaries that will be different from those erected by tsars and sultans or by the social systems that defined the cold war, but nevertheless real to anyone who tries to transgress them. The visa officer and the customs agent may become the twenty-first century's equivalent of the quarantine doctor of the nineteenth. Yet their efforts, as with those of their counterparts in centuries past, will no doubt be frustrated by the activities of expert boundary-crossers, people who, by their very desire for movement, have long bound the Black Sea world together, in defiance of the best-laid plans of empires and states. Along the coasts, however, this new frontier may well be populated by fewer and fewer people, as young men and women seek better lives in urban areas inland or, for a select few, even farther afield in London, Berlin, and New York. In the present century, the old

Black Sea may live on, like many lost civilizations across Europe's east, mainly in the hearts of people from the region but no longer in it.

But regions also have legs. Vibrant Black Sea communities can be found far removed from the sea itself: among the descendants of Pontic Greeks in Athens and Thessaloniki; among Turkish and Laz bakers, construction workers, and entrepreneurs in New York; among Jews, Romanians, Russians, Ukrainians, Armenians, Georgians—and virtually any combination of these categories—in Paris, Los Angeles, and Tel Aviv. Even well beyond the sea, the tug of regional affiliations can still be felt. When they move abroad, immigrants from the Anatolian coast are more likely to resettle in multiethnic environments, among the same diverse communities that they knew in their home towns and villages, rather than among their ethnic kin.[4] Especially for first-generation migrants, one's regional neighbor (*hemşeri*, in Turkish), someone from the same village, mountainside or stretch of coastline, can still be a far closer associate than a member of the imagined communities of nation or religion. In spite of the homogenizing categories used by outsiders—civilized and barbarian, native and foreigner, pure and adulterated—facing the water and embracing its multiplicities can still be a respectable way of living one's life.

NOTES

1. Arnold J. Toynbee, "The East After Lausanne," *Foreign Affairs*, Vol. 2, No. 1 (September 1923):86.
2. These data are incomplete and only suggestive of general trends. I thank Adam Tolnay for compiling them.
3. Arnold J. Toynbee, *The Western Question in Greece and Turkey*, 2nd edn. (New York: Howard Fertig, 1970 [1923]), p. 328.
4. Lisa DiCarlo, "Migration and Identity Among Black Sea Turks" (Ph.D. dissertation, Brown University, 2001), p. 23.

Sources for Introductory Quotations

Tournefort   Joseph Pitton de Tournefort, *A Voyage into the Levant*, trans. John Ozell, Vol. 2, (London: D. Browne, A. Bell, J. Darby et al., 1718), p. 124.

Byron   Byron, *Don Juan*, Canto 5, v.

Auden   W. H. Auden, "Archaeology," ed. *Selected Poems: New Edition*, Edward Mendelson (New York: Vintage International, 1979), p. 302.

Herodotus   Herodotus, *The Histories*, 4.46.

Xenophon   Xenophon, *Anabasis*, 4.7.

Ovid   Ovid, *Tristia*, 3.3.1–14, in Ovid, *Poems of Exile*, trans. Peter Green (New York: Penguin, 1994).

Procopius   Procopius, *History of the Wars*, 3.1.10-11.

Rubruck   *The Journal of Friar William of Rubruck*, *Contemporaries of Marco Polo*, ed. Manuel Komroff (New York: Dorset Press, 1989), pp. 58–9.

Peyssonnel   Claude Charles de Peyssonnel, *Observations historiques et géographiques sur les peoples barbares qui ont habité les bords du Danube et du Pont-Euxin* (Paris: N. M. Tilliard, 1765), p. 7.

Pirî   Pirî Reis, *Kitab-ı bahriye*, trans. Robert Bragner, Vol. 1, (Istanbul: Historical Research Foundation, 1988), p. 57.

Gilles   Pierre Gilles, ed. *The Antiquities of Constantinople*, Ronald G. Musto, trans. John Bell, 2nd edn. (New York: Italica Press, 1988), p. xxxviii.

Evliya   Evliya Çelebi, *Narrative of Travels in Europe, Asia, and Africa, in the Seventeenth Century*, trans. Joseph von Hammer, Vol. 2, (London: Oriental Translation Fund of Great Britain and Ireland, 1834), pp. 67, 74.

Johnson   Samuel Johnson, *The History of Rasselas, Prince of Abissinia* (Oxford: Oxford University Press, 1988), p. 123.

Ségur   Louis-Philippe, comte de Ségur, *Memoirs and Recollections of Count Ségur, Ambassador from France to the Courts of Russia and Prussia*, Vol. 3, (London: H. Colburn, 1825–7), p. 84.

Melville   Herman Melville, *Journal of a Visit to Europe and the Levant, October 11, 1856–May 6, 1857* ed. Howard C. Horsford (Princeton: Princeton University Press, 1955), p. 94.

Twain   Mark Twain, *The Innocents Abroad*, in *The Complete Travel Books of Mark Twain*, Vol. 1 (Garden City, NY: Doubleday, 1966–7), pp. 291–2.

Curtis   William Eleroy Curtis, *Around the Black Sea: Asia Minor, Armenia, Caucasus, Circassia, Daghestan, the Crimea, Roumania* (New York: Hodder and Stoughton, 1911), pp. 3–4.

Hossu   Gheorghe Hossu, *Importanţa canalului Dunăre–Marea Neagră în construirea socialismului în R. P. R.* (Bucharest: Editura de Stat, 1950), p. 3.

Curzon   Lord Curzon of Kedleston, *Frontiers: The Romanes Lecture, 1907* (Oxford: Clarendon Press, 1907), p. 5.

Bibliography and Further Reading

A work on the history, society, and politics of the Black Sea necessarily crosses several boundaries: the disciplinary ones between history and the social sciences, and the regional ones between central and eastern Europe, the Russian empire/former Soviet Union, and the Ottoman empire/Turkey. The purpose of this section is to offer the reader a sense of the sources I have used in several of these fields and to provide a few signposts for anyone interested in journeying deeper into the Black Sea world. More detailed references, including those in languages other than English, can be found in the notes to each chapter.

GENERAL WORKS

Any book on seas, frontiers, and regions trails along behind two giants, Owen Lattimore and Fernand Braudel. Lattimore's *Inner Asian Frontiers of China* (New York, 1951) and Braudel's *The Mediterranean and the Mediterranean World in the Age of Philip II* (London, 1972) are fundamental works. An influential study that follows in (and responds to) the Lattimore tradition is William McNeill's book on southeastern Europe on the eve of modernity, *Europe's Steppe Frontier, 1500–1800* (Chicago, 1964). On the meaning of regions, there is still no more thoughtful primer than Oscar Halecki's *The Limits and Divisions of European History* (London, 1950). On the mutability of regional labels in Europe, two excellent guides are Larry Wolff, *Inventing Eastern Europe* (Stanford, 1996) and Maria Todorova, *Imagining the Balkans* (Oxford, 1997).

The history of seas, although it does not yet have a name as a scholarly field (pelagic history? benthology?), is a boom area. Martin Lewis and Kären E. Wigen make the case for paying more attention to bodies of water in *The Myth of Continents* (Berkeley, 1997). Sea-centered works that I have found useful are, on the Mediterranean, Peregrine Horden and Nicholas Purcell's *The Corrupting Sea* (Oxford, 2000); on the Indian Ocean, K. N. Chaudhuri's classic *Trade and Civilisation in the Indian Ocean* (Cambridge, 1985) and Richard Hall's brilliantly readable *Empires of the Monsoon* (London, 1996); on the Pacific, O. H. K. Spate's sweeping three-volume *The Pacific Since Magellan* (Minneapolis, 1979, 1983, 1988) and Walter A. McDougall's engaging but at times plain wacky *Let the Sea Make a Noise* (New York, 1993); and on the Atlantic, Barry Cunliffe's beautiful *Facing the Ocean* (Oxford, 2001).

On the Black Sea in particular, two books that served as inspirations for my own are Gheorghe Ioan Brătianu, *La Mer Noire: Des origines à la conquête ottomane* (Munich, 1969) and Neil Ascherson, *Black Sea* (London, 1995). The former is a magisterial work of interpretive history by a major Romanian historian; the anticipated second volume was preempted by the author's death in a communist prison. The latter is part travelogue and part historical essay, a beautifully written meditation on the meanings of civilization and barbarism. An older synthesis, which liberally plagiarizes other published works, is Henry A. S. Dearborn, *A Memoir of the Commerce and Navigation of the Black Sea, and the Trade and Maritime Geography of Turkey and Egypt* (Boston, 1819). Anthony Bryer and David Winfield's two-volume *The Byzantine Monuments and Topography of the Pontos* (Washington, 1985) is a stunning analysis of the geography, archaeology, architecture, and history of the southeastern littoral. It will never be surpassed, if for no other reason than that some of the sites that the authors catalogued have since been destroyed by town planners and highway engineers.

The past of the lands and peoples around the sea is divided among a number of disparate history-writing traditions. Mark Mazower's extended essay *The Balkans: A Short History* (New York, 2000) is the best two hundred pages written on that region; the best thousand is perhaps L. S. Stavrianos's *The Balkans Since 1453* (New York, 2000). Much Ukrainian history-writing is marred by an uncritical nationalism, but a good balance is to read Orest Subtelny's *Ukraine: A History*, 2nd edn. (Toronto, 1994) and then Andrew Wilson's *The Ukrainians* (New Haven, 2000). There is simply too much to read on Russia, the steppe, and the sea, but the best place to start is with two important works: Michael Khodarkovsky, *Russia's Steppe Frontier* (Bloomington, 2002), the title of which doffs a hat to McNeill (above), and Willard Sunderland, *Taming the Wild Field* (Ithaca, 2004).

The Caucasus is unfortunately still understudied compared to Russia or the Balkans, but Yo'av Karny's *Highlanders* (New York, 2000) is an astute journalistic treatment of the region and its history. For a more scholarly analysis, the older *Caucasian Battlefields* (Cambridge, 1953), by W. E. D. Allen and Paul Muratoff, is a good point of entry. On the Ottoman empire and modern Turkey, the works of Halil İnalcık, Suraiya Faroqhi, Bernard Lewis, and Stanford Shaw have set the standard. Erik J. Zürcher's *Turkey: A Modern History*, rev. edn. (New York, 1998) is a very useful synthesis. On Bulgaria and Romania, the basic works are Richard Crampton, *A Concise History of Bulgaria* (Cambridge, 1997) and Keith Hitchins's two volumes, *The Romanians: 1774–1866* (Oxford, 1996) and *Rumania: 1866–1947* (Oxford, 1994).

The Studies of Nationalities book series, published by Hoover Institution Press at Stanford University, is the best source for focused works on several of the peoples around the sea: on the Georgians and Armenians, Ronald Grigor Suny's

The Making of the Georgian Nation (1988) and *Looking Toward Ararat* (1993); Alan Fisher's *The Crimean Tatars* (1978); and my own *The Moldovans* (2000). Two other series, one published by Macmillan–Palgrave and the other by Curzon Press, offer overviews of peoples such as the Abkhaz, Circassians, Laz, and others.

Beyond these general studies, I have used archives, primary accounts of travelers from antiquity to the present, and a vast secondary literature in specialized fields. Some of the major sources are discussed below.

ARCHIVES AND PRIVATE PAPERS

Writing a history of the Black Sea based on archival sources would consume several careers, since it would demand a detailed investigation of collections in many countries and many languages, some of which are even now not easily accessible. I have sampled only some of them.

The Hoover Institution Archives at Stanford University hold the papers of the American Relief Administration, an extremely valuable collection on humanitarian efforts in southern Russia during and after the First World War. I also made use of the S. N. Paleologue Papers, on the evacuation of Russians to the Balkans during the war, along with the private papers of Mikhail N. Girs (Russian minister in Constantinople) and Frank A. Golder (a member of the American Relief Administration). The records of the U.S. Military Mission to Armenia in 1919 provide a remarkable portrait of human suffering in eastern Anatolia after the end of the war.

At the Library of Congress, the Roger Fenton Crimean War Photograph Collection (now available online) is a priceless photographic chronicle of the war. The library's Geography and Map Reading Room houses a useful array of historic Black Sea maps, including the extremely important atlas of Egor Manganari from 1841.

At the archives of the Piłsudski Institute of America in New York, I consulted the papers of Edmund Charaszkiewicz, Jerzy Ponikiewski, and Apolinary Kiełczyński. These personal papers, along with the journal *Prométhée* (published in the 1920s and 1930s in Paris), are some of the basic sources for the history of the Promethean movement.

The Public Record Office in London contains valuable information on Black Sea commerce in the nineteenth century in the annual reports of the British consular offices around the sea, all in the Foreign Office files. The Admiralty and War Office files are less rich but still provide revealing documents, especially about the Second World War.

The first British consul in Trabzon, James Brant, was a keen observer of the sea in the 1830s; his private papers are available at the British Library. At the library,

I also consulted the papers of Henry Ellis and A. H. Layard, which contain correspondence related to Brant's career.

In Romania, I studied the history of the Vlach colonization program in Dobrudja through the files of the Ministry of Education, the National Office of Colonization, and the Society for Macedo-Romanian Culture, among others, located at the Central Historical Archive, National Archives of Romania, Bucharest. Little of this research actually made it into the final version of this book, but for an intrepid Ph.D. student, there is a fascinating story to be told about finding lost brothers and the problems of bringing them to the homeland.

TRAVELERS' ACCOUNTS AND OTHER PRIMARY TEXTS

Meticulous bibliographies of travelers in the Black Sea region from various periods can be found in the journal *Archeion Pontou*, Vol. 32 (1973–4) and Vol. 33 (1975–6), and in Bryer and Winfield (above).

For antiquity, the basic texts are well known: Herodotus, not always a sober guide; the military adventurer Xenophon; the careful geographer Strabo; and the whinging Ovid, one of our earliest postcard writers. Apollonius's *Argonautica*, from the third century BC, is the chief source for the Jason legend. The "Borysthenitic Discourse" of Dio Chrysostom is a fascinating but tainted account of a major Black Sea colony in the first century AD. The important *periplus* of Arrian from the second century reveals a great deal about the Roman military on the southern and eastern coasts. Ammianus Marcellinus, the historian of the late Roman empire, discusses the Black Sea in some detail, but his highly eccentric version of the truth owes much to Herodotus and Pliny the Elder, both of whom had their own vices as writers. Occasional references to the sea and intriguing tidbits about the peoples around it can be found in many other ancient writers, but most of what they have to say is derivative of earlier accounts.

From the Byzantine period, two major writers stand out. Procopius, the historian of the reign of the emperor Justinian, offers various views of the difficult frontier beyond the coast. The emperor Constantine Porphyrogenitus wrote an instructional guide to empire management (*De administrando imperio*), part of which focuses on relations with barbarians on the northern shore. In the later Byzantine period, a number of travelers left accounts of the sea, particularly of the Genoese and Venetian trading colonies. One collection is Manuel Komroff (ed.) *Contemporaries of Marco Polo* (New York, 1989). Other important records are those of Josafa Barbaro and Ambrogio Contarini (*Travels to Tana and Persia* [London, 1873]), Pero Tafur (*Travels and Adventures, 1435–1439* [New York, 1926]), Ibn Battuta (*Travels in Asia and Africa, 1325–1354* [New York, 1929]), and Ruy González de Clavijo (*Embassy to Tamerlane, 1403–1406* [London, 1928]). Francesco

Balducci Pegolotti's fourteenth-century guidebook for Italian merchants in the East is available as *La pratica della mercatura*, Allen Evans (ed.) (Cambridge, MA, 1936). To track down Slavic/Russian accounts of the Black Sea, from the Middle Ages forward, the best guide is Theofanis G. Stavrou and Peter R. Weisensel, *Russian Travelers to the Christian East from the Twelfth to the Twentieth Century* (Columbus, 1985).

Among Ottoman travelers there is no one to rival the seventeenth-century writer Evliya Çelebi, who suffered a shipwreck off the Crimean coast and witnessed an unsuccessful Ottoman assault on the fortress of Azov. A condensed version of his *Seyahatname* is *Narrative of Travels in Europe, Asia, and Africa, in the Seventeenth Century* (London, 1834). On the encounters between Ottomans and Cossacks on the sea, the major source is Guillaume Le Vasseur, sieur de Beauplan, *A Description of Ukraine* (Cambridge, MA, 1993).

There is a wealth of travelers' accounts, some more informative and reliable than others, from the late eighteenth century forward, when the sea was reopened to foreign commercial vessels. Louis-Philippe, comte de Ségur, accompanied Catherine the Great on her journey to Crimea in 1787 and left an entertaining record in his *Memoirs and Recollections of Count Ségur* (London, 1825–7). There is no better first-hand account of the difficulties of trade in the late eighteenth century than Antoine-Ignace Anthoine de Saint-Joseph's *Essai historique sur le commerce et la navigation de la Mer-Noire*, 2nd edn. (Paris, 1820). Another Frenchman, E. Taitbout de Marigny, tried his hand at trade with the Caucasus coast in the early nineteenth century and recorded his travails in *Three Voyages in the Black Sea to the Coast of Circassia* (London, 1837). The most accurate Western description of Ottoman social life and of Istanbul in the nineteenth century is Charles White, *Three Years in Constantinople; or, Domestic Manners of the Turks in 1844* (London, 1845). On the Ottoman navy, there is the account of a British adviser, Adolphus Slade, published as *Records of Travels in Turkey, Greece, etc., and of a Cruise in the Black Sea, with the Capitan Pasha, in the Years 1829, 1830, and 1831* (Philadelphia, 1833). J. A. Longworth was an observant and patriotic traveler in the north Caucasus and recorded his journey in *A Year Among the Circassians* (London, 1840).

The preeminent descriptions of the southern Russian empire in the eighteenth and nineteenth centuries are Peter Simon Pallas, *Travels Through the Southern Provinces of the Russian Empire* (London, 1802–3) and Anatole de Demidoff, *Travels in Southern Russia, and the Crimea* (London, 1853). The equivalents for the Anatolian and Caucasus coasts are William Hamilton, *Researches in Asia Minor, Pontus, and Armenia* (London, 1842) and August von Haxthausen, *Transcaucasia: Sketches of the Nations and Races Between the Black Sea and the Caspian* (London, 1854). Edmund Spencer was one of the most prolific and perceptive writers about the sea in the mid-nineteenth century, even if his accounts are strongly biased against anything

Russian. See his *Travels in the Western Caucasus* (London, 1838) and *Turkey, Russia, the Black Sea, and Circassia* (London, 1854).

There is a fine collection of travel writing by women, especially concerning Crimea. See Elizabeth, Lady Craven, *A Journey Through the Crimea to Constantinople* (Dublin, 1789); Marie Guthrie, *A Tour, Performed in the Years 1795–6, Through the Taurida, or Crimea* (London, 1802); and Mary Holderness, *New Russia: Journey from Riga to the Crimea, by Way of Kiev* (London, 1823).

Henry Barkley recorded his experiences as a railway engineer on the western coast in *Between the Danube and the Black Sea, or Five Years in Bulgaria* (London, 1876). Barkley witnessed the flight of Tatars from Crimea to Bulgaria, and many years later saw resettled Tatars, Circassians, and other Muslim refugees eking out a living in Anatolia, which he recounted in his *A Ride Through Asia Minor and Armenia* (London, 1891).

The demise of the grand tour meant that the market for wide-eyed accounts of the exoticisms of the East diminished (although, unfortunately, it was revived in the 1990s by the books of Robert Kaplan and others). But there are still several twentieth-century travel books worth reading. James Colquhoun was a British businessman whose copper mine in the Caucasus fell victim to the Bolsheviks. He tells his story in *Adventures in Red Russia* (London, 1926). William Eleroy Curtis, a Chicago reporter, recorded his own journey *Around the Black Sea* (New York, 1911). Stanley Washburn, another Chicago journalist, sailed back and forth across the sea in the middle of the 1905 Russian revolution; his account is *The Cable Game* (Boston, 1912). A touching memoir of the mutual cultural influences along the Pontic coast and the deportations of the 1920s is Thea Halo, *Not Even My Name* (New York, 2001).

OTHER SECONDARY SOURCES

Environment and Ecology

As an introduction to the physical features of the sea, there is nothing to beat the *Black Sea Pilot*, in multiple editions, published by the British Admiralty. The flood thesis on the sea's origins is presented in popular form in William Ryan and Walter Pitman, *Noah's Flood* (New York, 1998). The general idea of a dramatic drowning of the coastlands is debated in the scientific journal literature. In the "pro" camp is Robert D. Ballard et al., "Further Evidence of Abrupt Holocene Drowning of the Black Sea Shelf, " *Marine Geology*, Vol. 170 (2000):253–61. In the "con" camp is Naci Görür et al., "Is the Abrupt Drowning of the Black Sea Shelf at 7150 yr BP a Myth?" *Marine Geology*, Vol. 176 (2001):65–73. A report on the exciting possibilities of marine archaeology is Robert D. Ballard et al., "Deepwater Archaeology of the Black Sea: The 2000 Season at Sinop, Turkey," *American*

Journal of Archaeology, Vol. 105 (2001):607–23. A good survey of the sea's ecology is Yu. Zaitsev and V. Mamaev, *Marine Biological Diversity in the Black Sea* (New York, 1997).

History

700BC–AD500

The Black Sea has been a poor cousin to the study of areas closer to the centers of the Greco-Roman world—at least for scholars writing in Western languages—but since the late 1990s an upsurge in research on Greek encounters with the sea has promised to change things. Two books edited by Gocha Tsetskhladze, *The Greek Colonisation of the Black Sea Area* (Stuttgart, 1998) and *North Pontic Archaeology* (Leiden, 2001), give overviews of the state of the field. The "Colloquia Pontica" book series, published by Brill in the Netherlands, presents the most important monographs on the new archaeology of the region. The Black Sea Trade Project, based at the University of Pennsylvania and headed by Fredrik Hiebert, has been a major forum for discussion about the sea as a distinct space of interaction. The project's website is at www.museum.upenn.edu/Sinop/SinopIntro.htm. The British Academy has also launched a Black Sea research program. Its website, at www.biaa.ac.uk/babsi, is the best portal for locating scholars around the world, particularly archaeologists, classicists, and Byzantine specialists, with Black Sea interests.

The best introduction to Greek colonization in general is John Boardman, *The Greeks Overseas* (London, 1980). Jonathan Hall explores the meaning of "Greekness" in the ancient world in his *Hellenicity* (Chicago, 2002). Renata Rolle's *The World of the Scythians* (Berkeley, 1989) is an attempt to understand the ancient nomads of the northern steppe. Two older works—Ellis Minns, *Scythians and Greeks* (Cambridge, 1913) and Mikhail Rostovtzeff, *Iranians and Greeks in South Russia* (New York, 1969)—are mines of information on the material culture of the pastoral peoples. The equivalent for the western shore is Vasile Pârvan's *Getica* (Bucharest, 1926). David Braund's *Georgia in Antiquity* (Oxford, 1994) is a magnificent interpretation of the eastern Black Sea during the first millennium of vigorous exchange with the Mediterranean world. On the general subject of Romans and barbarians, I found particularly enlightening Peter Wells, *The Barbarians Speak* (Princeton, 1999). On the elusive Mithridates, the foremost study is B. C. McGing, *The Foreign Policy of Mithridates VI Eupator, King of Pontus* (Leiden, 1986).

Most of what I know of the technical aspects of ancient seafaring comes from two studies: Lionel Casson's *Ships and Seamanship in the Ancient World*, rev. edn. (Baltimore, 1995) and Jamie Morton's *The Role of the Physical Environment in Ancient Greek Seafaring* (Leiden, 2001), whose modest title belies the brilliant and wide-ranging essays within. On the Goths and the Khazars, the place to start is still with the classics: A. A. Vasiliev, *The Goths in the Crimea* (Cambridge, MA, 1936) and D. M. Dunlop, *The History of the Jewish Khazars* (New York, 1967). There are several recent and beautifully illustrated works on Scythian and Sarmatian art which have accompanied museum exhibitions, for example, Joan Aruz et al. (eds.) *The Golden Deer of Eurasia* (New York and New Haven, 2000).

500–1500

The most readable general work on the Byzantines, although at times not the most dispassionate, is John Julius Norwich, *A Short History of Byzantium* (New York, 1997). Its more sober counterpart is Warren Treadgold, *A History of the Byzantine State and Society* (Stanford, 1997). A major multivolume analysis of the Byzantine economy, including Black Sea commerce, is *The Economic History of Byzantium: From the Seventh Through the Fifteenth Century* (Washington, 2002), edited by Angeliki Laiou.

The classic political history of the empire of Trebizond is William Miller, *Trebizond: The Last Greek Empire of the Byzantine Era, 1204–1461*, new edn. (Chicago, 1969). The foremost living historian of Trebizond and the eastern sea is Anthony Bryer, whose many essays have been collected in several volumes of reprints. On the Genoese colonies, the essential text is Michel Balard, *La Romanie génoise (XIIe–début du XVe siècle)* (Rome, 1978), which has the rare quality of being frighteningly detailed and lucidly written. On the Byzantine navy, Hélène Ahrweiler, *Byzance et la mer* (Paris, 1966) has not been surpassed. The standard text on the transitional period between Byzantium and the Ottomans is Speros Vryonis, Jr., *The Decline of Medieval Hellenism in Asia Minor and the Process of Islamization from the Eleventh Through the Fifteenth Century* (Berkeley, 1971). There is as yet no comprehensive history of the Byzantine Black Sea.

1500–1700

The Ottoman Black Sea also awaits its historian, but surely the leading candidate is Victor Ostapchuk. His extended article on the sea in the seventeenth century (in the journal *Oriente Moderno*, Vol. 20, No. 1 [2001]) anticipates a major work to come. Two provocative books which challenge many of the older models of the origins of the Ottomans (and fine companions to the Vryonis above) are Rudi Paul Lindner, *Nomads and Ottomans in Medieval Anatolia* (Bloomington, 1983) and Cemal Kafadar, *Between Two Worlds* (Berkeley, 1995).

On Ottomans and the water, see Palmira Brummett, *Ottoman Sea Power and Levantine Diplomacy in the Age of Discovery* (Albany, 1994). An analysis of the sea's role in the Ottoman economy can be found in the first volume of Halil İnalcık and Donald Quataert (eds.) *An Economic and Social History of the Ottoman Empire* (Cambridge, 1994). Insightful analyses of Ottoman slaveholding include Ehud

R. Toledano, *The Ottoman Slave Trade and Its Suppression, 1840–1890* (Princeton, 1982) and Y. Hakan Erdem, *Slavery in the Ottoman Empire and Its Demise, 1800–1909* (New York, 1996).

1700–1860

Khodarkovsky and Sunderland (both above) were very influential on my thinking about the relationship between Russia and the steppe, as was McNeill (also above). On the naval history of the sea, the best source is R. C. Anderson's old but still lively *Naval Wars in the Levant, 1559–1853* (Liverpool, 1952). The major work on Peter the Great's Azov fleet is Edward J. Phillips, *The Founding of Russia's Navy* (Westport, CT, 1995). On diplomacy, M. S. Anderson's *The Eastern Question, 1774–1923* (London, 1966) is still a good guide. For a comparison of the Ottoman and Russian imperial systems, Dominic Lieven's *Empire* (New Haven, 2001) is compelling reading. The best introductions to Catherine's adventures in the south are Isabel de Madariaga's much-read *Russia in the Age of Catherine the Great* (New Haven, 1981) and Sebag Montefiore's biography of Potemkin, *Prince of Princes* (New York, 2001). On the Kalmyks, the essential text is Michael Khodarkovsky, *Where Two Worlds Met* (Ithaca, 1992).

Patricia Herlihy's *Odessa: A History, 1794–1914* (Cambridge, MA, 1986) is a model of urban/port history; there is unfortunately nothing of equal quality for the other major ports, such as Trabzon or Constanța. For the rise of the southern Russian cities, the basic source is a Ph.D. dissertation from long ago, Mose Lofley Harvey's "The Development of Russian Commerce on the Black Sea and Its Significance" (University of California, Berkeley, 1938). For Russian-speakers, a useful narrative history of the Russian navy is the three-volume *Tri veka rossiiskogo flota* (St. Petersburg, 1996), edited by F. N. Gromov et al., although it suffers from the professional deformations of most military histories.

1860–Present

A very helpful introduction to Ottoman naval history is Bernd Langensiepen and Ahmet Güleryüz, *The Ottoman Steam Navy, 1828–1923* (Annapolis, 1995). On the removal of Muslims from the Caucasus and the Balkans, a much understudied subject, a good overview is Justin McCarthy, *Death and Exile* (Princeton, 1995). Norman Naimark's *Fires of Hatred* (Cambridge, MA, 2001) surveys the history of ethnic cleansing in the twentieth century. The work of the American Relief Administration is recounted in Bertrand Patenaude, *The Big Show in Bololand* (Stanford, 2002).

There is a great deal of poor-quality work on the Armenian genocide and the Greek–Turkish population exchanges, but two exceptional books are Stephen Ladas's classic *The Exchange of Minorities* (New York, 1932) and Renée Hirschon's collection of essays *Crossing the Aegean* (New York, 2003). My thinking on the intellectual appropriation of the sea and the coastline was influenced by Victor A. Shnirelman, *Who Gets the Past?* (Washington, 1996). The story of the sinking of the *Struma* is retold in vivid detail in Douglas Frantz and Catherine Collins, *Death on the Black Sea* (New York, 2003).

Beginning in the 1990s, there was much talk of interstate cooperation around the sea, and a flood of reports and analyses followed. There is relatively little, however, that can be recommended. The best sources on the international politics of the zone are two collections of essays: Tunç Aybak (ed.) *Politics of the Black Sea* (London, 2001) and Renata Dwan and Oleksandr Pavliuk (eds.) *Building Security in the New States of Eurasia* (Armonk, NY, 2000).

The literature on each of the countries in the wider Black Sea region is rather better, but that illustrates the degree to which the nation-state remains a powerful lens of analysis. On Ukraine, Andrew Wilson's *Ukrainian Nationalism in the 1990s* (New Haven, 1997) is the best starting point. There are many things to read on Russia, but little about Russia's specifically regional foreign policy around the sea. On the Caucasus, Svante Cornell's *Small Nations and Great Powers* (London, 2001) is the best analytical survey. On Turkey there is a great deal, but one of the better popular treatments is Nicole and Hugh Pope, *Turkey Unveiled* (New York, 2000). On Turkish foreign policy, see Philip Robbins, *Suits and Uniforms* (London, 2003). There are unfortunately no up-to-date general books on the politics and society of either Bulgaria or Romania that can be recommended without qualification. However, Vladimir Tismaneanu's *Stalinism for All Seasons* (Berkeley, 2003) is the definitive work on the communist period in Romania and its echoes in the present.

One field that has produced truly exciting research is anthropology. There is a growing literature on social relations along the southeast coast, the work of a small but dedicated group of ethnographers and cultural anthropologists. See, for example, Ildiko Beller-Hann and Chris Hann, *Turkish Region* (Santa Fe, 2000) and Michael Meeker, *A Nation of Empire* (Berkeley, 2002).

TRAVEL GUIDES AND LITERATURE

There is no travel guide to the Black Sea as a whole, but there are several first-rate books that treat parts of it. John Freely's *The Black Sea Coast of Turkey* (Istanbul, 1996) is an excellent companion from the Bosphorus to the Georgian border. The indispensable scholarly work, though too bulky to carry in a backpack, is the Bryer and Winfield (above). For the rest of the coast, the relevant sections of the *Blue Guides*, including Freely's on Istanbul, are generally good, as is the Lonely Planet series.

The Black Sea has not been a major literary subject. There are plenty of references here and there, but little that focuses on the sea itself. Here is my idiosyncratic list of things worth taking along on a trip:

Rose Macauley's *The Towers of Trebizond* is a picaresque story of an English matron's search for that lost empire. Mark Twain met the Russian tsar in Crimea and recorded the event in *The Innocents Abroad*, along with his droll impressions of Istanbul and Odessa. Russian writers had plenty to say about the northern coast and the Caucasus but not much about the sea. Pushkin's "The Bakhchisarai Fountain" should be read while touring Crimea. Lermontov's *A Hero of Our Time* and Tolstoy's novella *Hadji Murat* and his short story "A Prisoner of the Caucasus" will either entice one to visit the Caucasus or guarantee that one does not. As a portrait of a Black Sea port, nothing is better than Isaac Babel's *Odessa Stories*. John Steinbeck fell in love with Georgia and told his readers so in *A Russian Journal*. Kurban Said's novel *Ali and Nino* is on the list of most travelers to the Caucasus, which is unfortunate, for it wallows in all the standard stereotypes of the region.

As for contemporary authors, one cannot go wrong with Ascherson (above), a model of literary nonfiction, and the novels of the Turkish writer Orhan Pamuk (especially *The White Castle* and *The Black Book*) and the Albanian writer Ismail Kadare (particularly *The File on H*, which is not about the Black Sea but is about mutual misunderstandings between East and West—and about the search for the elusive ancient Greeks). Victor Pelevin's *The Life of Insects* is about an unusual group of visitors to Crimea.

Index